MW01202095

LIBRARY OF HEBREW BIBLE/ OLD TESTAMENT STUDIES

576

Formerly Journal for the Study of the Old Testament Supplement Series

CONSTRUCTIONS OF SPACE V

Place, Space and Identity
in the Ancient Mediterranean World

edited by

Gert T. M. Prinsloo

and

Christl M. Maier

B L O O M S B U R Y

LONDON · NEW DELHI · NEW YORK · SYDNEY

Bloomsbury T&T Clark

An imprint of Bloomsbury Publishing Plc

50 Bedford Square   1385 Broadway
London   New York
WC1B 3DP   NY 10018
UK   USA

www.bloomsbury.com

Bloomsbury is a registered trade mark of Bloomsbury Publishing Plc

First published in 2013
Paperback edition first published 2014

British Library Cataloguing-in-Publication Data
A catalogue record for this book is available from the British Library.

ISBN: HB: 978-0-567-25563-1
PB: 978-0-567-65687-2

Library of Congress Cataloging-in-Publication Data
A catalog record for this book is available from the Library of Congress.

Typeset by Forthcoming Publications Ltd (www.forthpub.com)

CONTENTS

Part III
PLACE, SPACE, IDENTITY:
THEORY AND PRACTICE

ABBREVIATIONS

AB	Anchor Bible
ABD	*The Anchor Bible Dictionary.* Edited by David Noel Freedman. 6 vols. New York, 1992
AJA	*American Journal of Archaeology*
AJSR	*Association for Jewish Studies Review*
AOAT	Alter Orient und Altes Testament
BA	*Biblical Archaeologist*
BARev	*Biblical Archaeology Review*
BBR	*Bulletin for Biblical Research*
BE	Biblische Enzyklopädie
Bib	*Biblica*
BibInt	*Biblical Interpretation: A Journal of Contemporary Approaches*
BIS	Biblical Interpretation Series
BKAT	Biblischer Kommentar: Altes Testament
BN NF	*Biblische Notizen. Neue Folge*
BOT	De Boeken van het Oude Testament
BR	*Bible Review*
BTAT	Beiträge zur Theologie des Alten Testaments
BTB	*Biblical Theology Bulletin*
BZAW	Beihefte zur Zeitschrift für die alttestamentliche Wissenschaft
CAD	*The Assyrian Dictionary of the Oriental Institute of the University of Chicago.* Chicago, 1956–
CBQ	*Catholic Biblical Quarterly*
CBQMS	Catholic Biblical Quarterly, Monograph Series
CEJL	Commentaries on Early Jewish Literature
CRBS	*Currents in Research: Biblical Studies*
FAT	Forschungen zum Alten Testament
FRLANT	Forschungen zur Religion und Literatur des Alten und Neuen Testaments
Greg	*Gregorianum*
HAR	*Hebrew Annual Review*
HBS	Herders Biblische Studien
HKAT	Handkommentar zum Alten Testament
HR	*History of Religions*
HTR	*Harvard Theological Review*
HTS	*Hervormde Teologiese Studies*
HTSSup	Hervormde Teologiese Studies Supplementum
IBC	Interpretation: A Bible Commentary for Teaching and Preaching
ITC	International Theological Commentary
JANESCU	*Journal of the Ancient Near Eastern Society of Columbia University*

JAOS	*Journal of the American Oriental Society*
JBL	*Journal of Biblical Literature*
JBQ	*Jewish Bible Quarterly*
JNSL	*Journal of Northwest Semitic Languages*
JQR	*Jewish Quarterly Review*
JSHRZ	Jüdische Schriften aus hellenistisch-römischer Zeit
JSNT	*Journal of the Study of the New Testament*
JSOT	*Journal for the Study of the Old Testament*
JSOTSup	*Journal for the Study of the Old Testament*, Supplement Series
JSP	*Journal for the Study of the Pseudepigrapha*
LHBOTS	Library of the Hebrew Bible/Old Testament Studies
NCB	New Century Bible
NEchtB	Neue Echter Bibel
NICOT	New International Commentary on the Old Testament
OBO	Orbis Biblicus et Orientalis
OLB	Orte und Landschaften der Bibel
OTE	*Old Testament Essays*
OTG	Old Testament Guides
OTL	Old Testament Library
OTS	Oudtestamentische Studiën
POut	De Prediking van het Oude Testament
Proof	*Prooftexts: A Journal of Jewish Literary History*
PzB	*Protokolle zur Bibel*
QD	Quaestiones disputatae
ResQ	*Restoration Quarterly*
SBAB	Stuttgarter biblische Aufsatzbände
SBLDS	SBL Dissertation Series
SBLMS	SBL Monograph Series
SBLSP	Society of Biblical Literature Seminar Papers
SBLSympS	SBL Symposium Series
SBS	Stuttgarter Bibelstudien
SK	*Skrif en Kerk*
SOTSMS	Society for Old Testament Study Monograph Series
STAR	Studies in Theology and Religion
ThWAT	*Theologisches Wörterbuch zum Alten Testament.* Edited by G. J. Botterweck and H. Ringgren. Stuttgart, 1970–95
TSAJ	Texts and Studies in Ancient Judaism
TynBul	*Tyndale Bulletin*
VT	*Vetus Testamentum*
VTSup	Supplements to Vetus Testamentum
WBC	Word Biblical Commentary
WiBiLex	*Das wissenschaftliche Bibellexikon im Internet* (www.wibilex.de)
WMANT	Wissenschaftliche Monographien zum Alten und Neuen Testament
WUNT	Wissenschaftliche Untersuchungen zum Neuen Testament
ZAW	*Zeitschrift für die alttestamentliche Wissenschaft*
ZDPV	*Zeitschrift des deutschen Palästina-Vereins*
ZTK	*Zeitschrift für Theologie und Kirche*

LIST OF CONTRIBUTORS

Gerda (G. G.) de Villiers. Editor of www.teo.co.za and part-time lecturer in Ancient Myths and Ancient Religions. Department of Old Testament, University of Pretoria, Pretoria, South Africa

Michaela Geiger. Lecturer of Old Testament. Department of Protestant Theology, Philipps-University Marburg, Marburg, Germany

Maria Häusl. Professor of Biblical Studies. Faculty of Arts, Humanities and Social Science, Technische Universität Dresden, Dresden, Germany

Christl M. Maier. Professor of Old Testament. Department of Protestant Theology, Philipps-University Marburg, Marburg, Germany

Johnny Miles. Adjunct Instructor. Department of Religion, Texas Christian University, Fort Worth, Texas, USA

Mary Mills. Adjunct Professor of Biblical Studies. Department of Theology, Philosophy and Religious Studies, Liverpool Hope University, Liverpool, United Kingdom

Gert T. M. Prinsloo. Professor of Ancient Near Eastern Languages and Cultures. Department of Ancient Languages, University of Pretoria, Pretoria, South Africa

Reineth (C.E.) Prinsloo. Senior Lecturer in Family Development and Guidance. Department of Social Work and Criminology, University of Pretoria, Pretoria, South Africa

Johanna Rautenberg. Research assistant in the Collaborative Research Centre (SFB) 804 "Transzendenz und Gemeinsinn." Technische Universität Dresden, Dresden, Germany

Jo-Marí Schäder. Lecturer in Ancient Near Eastern Languages and Cultures. Department of Ancient Languages, University of Pretoria, Pretoria, South Africa

Matthew Sleeman. Lecturer in New Testament and Greek. Oak Hill Theological College, Southgate London, United Kingdom

Carla Sulzbach. Independent Researcher and Research Fellow in Ancient Textual Studies. Montreal, Canada and North-West University, Potchefstroom, South Africa

Ronald van der Bergh. Lecturer in Biblical Greek and Classic Culture. Department of Ancient Languages, University of Pretoria, Pretoria, South Africa

INTRODUCTION:
PLACE, SPACE AND IDENTITY
IN THE ANCIENT MEDITERRANEAN WORLD

Christl M. Maier and Gert T. M. Prinsloo

From 2009–2011 the "Place, Space, and Identity in the Ancient Mediterranean World Program Unit" organized sessions at the Society of Biblical Literature International Meetings in Rome (2009), Tartu (2010) and London (2011). The aim of the program unit was to investigate the inherent *spatiality* of human existence and how it affects human behavior, ideology, identity, and orientation. The unit also aimed at enhancing both attentiveness to and research on spatial readings of ancient texts and contexts among scholars on an international scale. Participants in the unit's sessions were encouraged to apply various approaches to spatiality to the spectrum of ancient Mediterranean cultures in order to enhance our understanding of these cultures in their lived historical and social realities.

In Rome (2009) one session was dedicated to the question of how "space" in text and culture could be assessed hermeneutically and methodologically. Papers of a second session addressed perceptions of space in the Ancient Mediterranean world. In Tartu (2010) papers focused on the role of sacred space in the formation of identity as well as on space and gender in ancient texts and cultures. In London (2011) two sessions were allocated to the interrelation between space and identity.

The current volume, the fifth to be published in the *Constructions of Space* sub-series of the Library of the Hebrew Bible/Old Testament Studies, contains selected, peer-reviewed contributions from the three meetings of the program unit. Some participants of our sessions provided new essays related to their ongoing studies in critical spatiality. The contributions are representative of the themes discussed over the period of three years and the division within this volume approximately reflects the subsequent main topics.

Part I, Prospectives, Perspectives and Methods, looks at various theoretical approaches to spatiality that can be applied to the ancient

Mediterranean contexts. In "Place, Space and Identity in the Ancient Mediterranean World: Theory and Practice with Reference to the Book of Jonah" Gert Prinsloo (University of Pretoria) argues for a comprehensive approach to spatial analysis that includes ancient Near Eastern concepts of space. He illustrates his comprehensive methodological approach with reference to the book of Jonah.

Michaela Geiger (Philipps-University, Marburg) applies Wolfgang Iser's theory on fiction and the imaginary besides Martina Löw's sociology of space to indicate the book of Deuteronomy's intentional fictional character. Her essay, "Fiction and Space in Deuteronomy," demonstrates how a fictional space like Horeb shapes ideas about spaces for human-divine encounters among readers of the narrative.

In "Critical Spatial Theory 2.0" Matthew Sleeman (Oak Hill Theological College, London) provides an assessment of the development of critical spatiality within biblical studies. He argues that the spatialization of biblical studies is an irreversible and ongoing process that heralds a radical conception of scripture, of *spatial* scriptures while at the same time inviting more transdisciplinary research and a wider range of scholarly contexts.

In Part II, Sacred Space and the Formation of Identity, attention shifts to the important role of sacred space in ancient Mediterranean societies' sense of belonging and identity. In "The Implied Transcendence of Physical and Ideological Borders and Boundaries in Psalm 47" Jo-Marí Schäder (University of Pretoria) argues that YHWH is depicted in Psalm 47 as a universal deity that knows no boundaries. Consequently, physical and ideological boundaries are crossed and the nations are no longer depicted as an entirely separate entity to Israel.

In "Jerusalem, the Holy City: The Meaning of the City of Jerusalem in the Books of Ezra–Nehemiah," Maria Häusl (Technische Universität Dresden) indicates that the designation of Jerusalem as Holy City characterizes the city as a public place of meeting with God. Since the idea of holiness is expanded beyond a specific cultic meaning, Jerusalem serves as an important theological topos for the construction of post-exilic Israel's identity.

In "Whose Mother? Whose Space? Jerusalem in Third Isaiah" Christl Maier (Philipps-University, Marburg) interprets different portraits of Zion/Jerusalem in Third Isaiah with the help of Henri Lefebvre's three perspectives on space and Paula Cooey's evaluation of the personified female body as an ambiguous medium that conveys both sentience and agency to the readers of these texts. Maier argues that collected passages in Isaiah 56–66 successively comment on Second Isaiah's oracles of salvation and simultaneously adjust their grandiose outlook to a later situation.

Johanna Rautenberg (Technische Universität Dresden) discusses "The Meaning of the City of Jerusalem in the Book of Tobit: An Analysis of the Jerusalem Hymn in Tobit 13:8–18." In her view, the book of Tobit emphasizes not the city's geographical dimension, but her significant role as a relational entity. Jerusalem is depicted as mother and as a "social" space constituted in the loving care of God toward the people as well as the people toward Jerusalem.

Part III, Place, Space, Identity: Theory and Practice, gathers a variety of both ancient Mediterranean contexts and applications of spatial theory to texts from these contexts. In her essay "From the Walls of Uruk: Reflections on Space in the Gilgamesh Epic" Gerda de Villiers (University of Pretoria) argues that the spatial theories of Edward Soja and Nicholas Wyatt have a heuristic function with regard to the Gilgamesh Epic. Uruk serves as a Secondspace narrative construct from where wisdom and insight into life issues are reflected. Moreover, this city is also a central point for Gilgamesh in terms of his self-orientation.

Reineth and Gert Prinsloo (University of Pretoria) read Genesis 34 from a general systems theory and spatial perspective in "Family as Lived Space: An Interdisciplinary and Intertextual Reading of Genesis 34." They argue that the "Dinah Affair" sets in motion a series of incidents with far-reaching consequences. Read against the background of the post-exilic identity building project, the narrative implies that neither Dinah's crossing of social borders to the Canaanites, nor her brothers' violent defense of these borders, nor Jacob's silence can ensure a life "at-center." In contrast, taking YHWH upon his word and acknowledging his promises ensures contact with the divine sphere and a sustainable future.

In "(Re-)Siting Space and Identity of Gibeonites and Japanese Americans," Johnny Miles (Texas Christian University) explores the confluence of space and identity in Gibeonite and Japanese American colonization utilizing the postcolonial spatial constructs of Edward Soja and Arjun Appadurai. Sociological insights identified high boundedness and exhaustiveness as factors present in the narrative *ethnoscape* of Gibeonites and Japanese Americans. It delimits their social space and fixes their identity at the *ideoscape* site. Their ostracism to a culturally hybrid status as "other," Miles argues, additionally opens up a site of resistance from which to reconfigure identity from a non-essentialist stance utilizing cultural traditions.

Exploring "Narrative Space and the Construction of Meaning in the Book of Joel" Mary Mills (Liverpool Hope University) uses the concept of religious geography as a lens through which to analyze the book of Joel. In her view, Joel visibly links land, city, and shrine and thus deals with sacred space as the means of controlling events in the natural and human worlds. The study explores the manner in which the imaginative universe of a literary text creates an ordered response to chaotic events through its deployment of religious geography.

In "Unfocused Narrative Space in Tobit 1:1–2:14" Ronald van der Bergh (University of Pretoria) uses the concept of "unfocused space" and the so-called model-reader in his spatial analysis of the first two chapters of the book of Tobit. He argues that these chapters reveal a gradual movement from freedom to confinement. The use of unfocused space, when read from the perspective of a model-reader, masterfully attributes to the build-up of tension in the narrative.

Finally, Carla Sulzbach (Research Fellow, North-West University, Potchefstroom) engages in a spatial reading of two cities often juxta-posed in biblical and early Jewish writings, namely Jerusalem and Babylon, in "From Urban Nightmares to Dream Cities: Revealing the Apocalyptic Cityscape." At the high end of the apocalyptic spectrum, John's New Jerusalem, like that of Ezekiel, becomes a New Babylon. In contrast, Ezekiel's plan for the renewed city, at the low end of the same spectrum, is grounded and down-to-earth and describes a case of urban planning. According to Sulzbach, the underlying motivation for the metaphor in Revelation differs radically from the same image in Jewish apocalyptic writings. In the latter the metaphor is used in response to the destruction of the Temple, whereas in Revelation it signals a departure from the need to have a physical sanctuary.

The editors wish to thank all participants in the "Place, Space, and Identity in the Ancient Mediterranean World Program Unit" for their contributions over the period of three years, especially those who contri-buted to this volume. We hope that the publication of a representative sample of the work done in the program unit will stimulate a deeper and broader understanding of the inherent *spatiality* of human existence and how it affects human behavior, ideology, identity, and orientation. We also would like to thank Dr. Beatrice Martin who did the language editing for this volume, Jo-Marí Schäder and Josephine Haas for their assistance in editing the manuscript, Claudia Camp for her willingness to accept this volume in the Constructions of Space sub-series, Bloomsbury T&T Clark for publishing our work, and our copy-editor, Duncan Burns, for preparing the volume for publication.

Marburg and Pretoria, July 2012

Part I

PROSPECTIVES, PERSPECTIVES AND METHODS

Place, Space and Identity in the Ancient Mediterranean World: Theory and Practice with Reference to the Book of Jonah

Gert T. M. Prinsloo

ויאמר אליהם עברי אנכי	*He answered them: "A Hebrew I am!*
ואת־יהוה אלהי השמים אני ירא	*And YHWH, the God of the heavens, I worship,*
אשר־עשה את־הים ואת־היבשה:	*he who made the sea and the dry ground."* (Jonah 1:9)

I am an African.
I owe my being to the hills and the valleys, the mountains and the glades, the rivers, the deserts, the trees, the flowers, the seas and the ever-changing seasons that define the face of our native land...
A human presence among all these, a feature on the face of our native land thus defined, I know that none dare challenge me when I say: I am an African![1]

1. Introduction

The quotations above suggest an intimate relationship between identity, a sense of belonging, and place. Place is more than geographical location, it is the space where people exist as human beings. Our "sense of both personal and cultural identity is intimately bound up with place identity."[2] Special feelings, with a sense of identification or alienation, are attached to environments that become "panels of the set on the natural

---

1. Statement by T. M. Mbeki at the adoption of "The Republic of South Africa Constitution Bill 1996," Cape Town, May 8, 1996. Available online: http://www. anc.org.za/show.php?id=4322 (accessed 09 April 2012).

2. A. Buttimer, "Home, Reach, and the Sense of Place," in *The Human Experience of Space and Place* (ed. A. Buttimer and D. Seamon; London: Croom Helm, 1980), 166–87 (167).

stage on which we act out the foolish deeds of the theatre of our day."[3]
Space, often regarded as a "contingent," not a "constitutive" element of
existence,[4] has grown in stature since the early 1970s and is recognized
as "a vital…category of discourse."[5] In what has become known as the
"spatial turn,"[6] "human" geography resisted positivistic, empirical ten-
dencies by emphasizing the human aspect of geography, giving rise to
critical spatial studies.[7]

The Bible is "obsessed with space."[8] The Christian Bible commences
and concludes with creation and recreation (Gen 1–3; Rev 21–22).
Between creation and recreation, human beings act out their foolish
deeds "at a place and in a space of some kind";[9] the "spatial turn" is
reflected in biblical studies, especially with emphasis upon critical-
spatial analyses of biblical texts.[10]

The present study recognizes the importance of critical spatiality, but
is a plea for going beyond critical spatiality in reconstructing the spatial
world of biblical texts. A combination of perspectives from *narrative*

---

3. Quoted from Mbeki's statement (cf. n. 1). The quotation hints at the insepa-
rable link between time and space. Its consequences have not yet been addressed
adequately in biblical scholarship.

4. P. J. Nel, "The Symbolism and Function of Epic Space in Jonah," *JNSL* 25
(1999): 215–24 (215); G. Genette, *Narrative Discourse* (trans. J. E. Levin; Oxford:
Blackwell, 1980), 164–69; G. Zoran, "Towards a Theory of Space in Narrative,"
Poetics Today 5 (1984): 309–35 (310).

5. J. L. Berquist, "Critical Spatiality and the Construction of the Ancient World,"
in *"Imagining" Biblical Worlds: Studies in Spatial, Social and Historical Constructs
in Honor of James W. Flanagan* (ed. D. M. Gunn and P. M. McNutt; JSOTSup 359;
Sheffield: Sheffield Academic, 2002), 14–29 (14).

6. Cf. the contribution by M. Sleeman in the present volume.

7. Critical spatiality "self-consciously attempts to move beyond modernist,
mechanistic, essentialist understandings of space" and "understands all aspects of
space to be human constructions that are socially contested" (Berquist, "Construction," 15). Cf. also J. L. Berquist, "Introduction: Critical Spatiality and the Uses of
Theory," in *Constructions of Space I: Theory, Geography, and Narrative* (ed. J. L.
Berquist and C. V. Camp; LHBOTS 481; New York/London: T&T Clark International, 2007), 1–12, and, in the same volume, M. K. George, "Space and History:
Siting Critical Space for Biblical Studies," 15–31.

8. Berquist, "Construction," 25.

9. G. T. M. Prinsloo, "The Role of Space in the שירי המעלות (Psalms 120–134),"
Bib 86 (2005): 457–77 (458).

10. Cf. Gunn and McNutt, eds., *"Imagining" Biblical Worlds*; Berquist and
Camp, eds., *Constructions of Space I*, and *Constructions of Space II: The Biblical
City and Other Imagined Spaces* (LHBOTS 490; New York/London: T&T Clark
International, 2008).

theory[11] and *critical spatiality*,[12] contextualized within *ancient Near Eastern views of the cosmos and spatial orientation*, can "provide a window into the ancient world."[13] The study has a threefold purpose: to propose a comprehensive theoretical spatial approach; to apply the theory to the book of Jonah; to illustrate that spatial analysis can be an indispensable tool in the interpretation of biblical texts.

2. *"Literary" Space: Theoretical Considerations*

The three spatial approaches proposed above share one characteristic: space is constructed, produced or represented by means of words.[14]

a. *Narrative Space*

The roots of *narrative theory* lie in French/Russian *structuralism/formalism*.[15] Events, characters, time and space are the constitutive elements of narratives.[16] Three dimensions interact in a narrative: story (*histoire/fabula*: narrated events reconstructed in chronological order); text (*récit/sjuzet*: the actual spoken/written discourse); narrating (*narration*: the process of production, involving both the real/implied narrator and the reader).[17]

11. D. Darby, "Form and Context: An Essay in the History of Narratology," *Poetics Today* 22 (2001): 829–52; E. van Eck, *Galilee and Jerusalem in Mark's Story of Jesus: A Narratological and Social Scientific Reading* (HTSSup 7; Pretoria: Promedia, 1995), 125–41.

12. J. W. Flanagan, "Ancient Perceptions of Space/Perceptions of Ancient Space," *Semeia* 87 (1999): 15–43.

13. P. M. Venter, "Spatiality in Psalm 29," in *Psalms and Liturgy* (ed. D. J. Human and C. J. Vos; JSOTSup 410; London: T&T Clark International, 2004), 235–50 (235). The proposed methodology does not include all spatial perspectives. For a cognitive-linguistic approach, focusing mainly on the perception of physical space, cf. J. Brinkman, *The Perception of Space in the Old Testament: An Exploration of the Methodological Problems of Its Investigation Exemplified by a Study of Exodus 25 to 31* (Kampen: Kok Pharos, 1992). P. Hubbard et al., eds., *Key Thinkers on Space and Place* (London: Sage, 2004), discuss no fewer than 52 "key thinkers" on space and place.

14. Berquist, "Construction," 14–15.

15. J. Sturrock, *Structuralism: With a New Introduction by Jean-Michel Rabaté* (2d ed.; London: Blackwell, 2003); Cf. S. Rimmon-Kenan, *Narrative Fiction: Contemporary Poetics* (2d ed.; London: Routledge, 2002), 136–40; Van Eck, *Galilee and Jerusalem*, 137.

16. Van Eck, *Galilee and Jerusalem*, 129.

17. Genette, *Narrative Discourse*, 25–27; Rimmon-Kenan, *Narrative Fiction*, 3 (the French/Russian terms in brackets are taken from Genette's work).

The role of space in narratives is controversial. A narrow view regards space as an aspect of the text only, arguing that space cannot, like time, be "doubled" on the level of story (narrated time) and text (narrative time). Text space has two dimensions. It is objective (a neutral setting where events take place) or subjective (space that determines a character).[18] Some argue that space is an aspect of narration only, applying it to the narrator's place of production, perspective, or focalization when producing the narrative.[19]

According to a broader view, space functions on the levels of both story and text. Story-space refers to the space where events occur. The reader creates or imagines it by listening to or reading the narrative. Discourse-space is space seen through the eyes of the narrator who assigns symbolic value to space.[20] Some argue that space functions on all three narrative dimensions.[21] References to physical place function on the level of the story; place becomes space on the level of the text, where place is seen through the eyes of the narrator or characters in the narrative; focalization, or the point of view of the real/implied narrator, functions on the level of narration.[22]

Narratology aids interpreters in identifying the spatial contours of a text and emphasizes the complicated process in the production of literary space, involving the narrator with his/her point of view, the text he/she produces, and the construction of space by the reader during the process of reading. It can be argued that "three worlds interact in the interpretation of any work: the social-historical milieu from which the work arose, the world of the reader or hearer, and the world created in the work itself."[23]

As the textual level is "the only one directly available to textual analysis,"[24] I propose the following approach:[25] *narrative space* is the

18. H. Vandermoere, *The Structure of the Novel* (2d ed.; Leuven: Acco, 1982), 125; R. Ronen, "Space in Fiction," *Poetics Today* 7 (1986): 421–38 (421–25).

19. Genette, *Narrative Discourse*, 161–62; Rimmon-Kenan, *Narrative Fiction*, 78–79.

20. S. B. Chatman, *Story and Discourse: Narrative Structure in Fiction and Film* (London: Cornell University Press, 1978), 9, 104, 143.

21. M. Bal, *De Theorie van Vertellen en Verhalen: Inleiding in de Narratologie* (4th ed.; Muiderberg: Dick Coutinho, 1986); A. P. Brink, *Vertelkunde: 'n Inleiding tot die Lees van Verhalende Tekste* (Pretoria: Academica, 1987).

22. Bal, *Theorie van Vertellen*, 52–54, 101–7, 108–21.

23. L. L. Thompson, *Introducing Biblical Literature: A More Fantastic Country* (Englewood Cliffs, N.J.: Prentice–Hall, 1978), 4.

24. Genette, *Narrative Discourse*, 27.

25. Brink, *Vertelkunde*, 109–12; Nel, "Epic Space," 216; Prinsloo, "Role of Space," 459 n. 13.

point of departure. It refers to the space created by the narrative, the world of words produced by the text. It can be a description of a physical location (setting), or a representational space intended to affect the reader (focal space).[26] The *narrator's space* contextualizes narrative space. It refers to the narrator's point of view/focus/spatial perspective, revealing his/her ideological stance. Simultaneous reading of narrative and narrator's space produces *narrated space*, the space constructed by the reader with reference to clues in the narrative text and the effect it has upon the reader.[27]

b. *Social Space*
Social-scientific criticism is embedded in postmodernist critique against "the stability, certainty, absolutism, and hegemony" of modernism.[28] *Critical spatiality* elucidates the importance of notions of spatiality for understanding human behavior. Michel Foucault provided the stimulus for the development of critical spatiality in his 1967 lecture "Of Other Spaces."[29] He argues that we live in "heterogeneous" spaces that are clearly delineated and not super-imposable on one another (e.g. sites of rest or sites of labor). Two sites neutralize or invert the set of relations reflected by heterogeneous spaces: "utopias" are sites with no real place, where the relation to real space is inverted; "heterotopias" are counter-sites on the fringes of society, like cemeteries.[30]

The French Marxist philosopher Henri Lefebvre did seminal work in the field of *critical spatiality*. He proposes a trialectic approach towards space: "first, the *physical*—nature, the Cosmos; secondly, the *mental*, including logical and formal abstractions; and, thirdly, the *social*."[31] He distinguishes between perceived space (the spatial practice of society); conceived space (representations of space, conceptualized space, the dominant space in any society); and lived space (spaces of representation,

26. Van Eck, *Galilee and Jerusalem*, 137–39.
27. Applications of narrative theory to biblical texts do not reflect this complex process; cf. R. Alter, *The Art of Biblical Narrative* (New York: Basic Books, 1981); S. Bar-Efrat, *Narrative Art in the Bible* (JSOTSup 70; Sheffield: Almond, 1989), 184–95; J. P. Fokkelman, *Reading Biblical Narrative: An Introductory Guide* (trans. I. Smit; Louisville, Ky.: Westminster John Knox, 1999), 97–111.
28. Flanagan, "Ancient Perceptions," 16.
29. M. Foucault, "Of Other Spaces," *Diacritics* 16 (1986): 22–27. Cf. Berquist, "Construction," 18.
30. Foucault, "Of Other Spaces," 23–24.
31. H. Lefebvre, *The Production of Space* (trans. D. Nicholson-Smith; Oxford: Blackwell, 1991), 11. Cf. Berquist, "Construction," 19.

space as experienced through images and symbols, space "which the imagination seeks to change and appropriate").[32]

The American geographer Edward Soja modified Lefebvre's theories.[33] He also proposes a trialectic of spaces:[34] Firstspace (physical/concrete/perceived space), that is, the description of a place or an environment; Secondspace (imagined/conceived/abstract space), "space produced by language, metaphor, and ideology";[35] Thirdspace (lived space), the confrontation between various social groups and their space(s). Thirdspace is "the terrain for the generation of 'counterspaces,' spaces of resistance to the dominant order arising precisely from their subordinate, peripheral or marginalized positioning."[36] Thirdspace is "Thirding-as-Othering," because it "produces what may best be called a cumulative *trialectics* that is radically open to additional otherness, to a continuing expansion of spatial knowledge."[37] Soja emphasizes that these are three dimensions of space, not three separate spaces. He regards *"lived space as a strategic location* from which to encompass, understand, and potentially transform all spaces simultaneously."[38]

Theoretical considerations of the relevance of critical spatiality for biblical studies and critical-spatial readings of biblical texts have become increasingly popular.[39] Biblical scholars warn against an over-simplified application of critical spatiality when working with ancient texts reflecting customs and ideologies very different from our (Western) epistemological point(s) of departure.[40]

---

32. Lefebvre, *Production*, 38–39.

33. E. W. Soja, *Thirdspace: Journeys to Los Angeles and Other Real-and-Imagined Places* (Oxford: Blackwell, 1996). Cf. Berquist, "Construction," 20.

34. Soja, *Thirdspace*, 66–67.

35. C. M. Maier, "Daughter Zion as Gendered Space in the Book of Isaiah," in Berquist and Camp, eds., *Constructions of Space II*, 102–18 (103).

36. Soja, *Thirdspace*, 68.

37. Ibid., 60–61.

38. Ibid., 68 (italics original).

39. Cf. Berquist, "Construction"; Flanagan, "Ancient Perceptions," 15–43; C. M. Maier, "Daughter Zion as Gendered Space," 103–5; V. H. Matthews, "Physical Space, Imagined Space, and 'Lived Space' in Ancient Israel," *BTB* 33 (2003): 12–20; P. M. McNutt, "'Fathers of the Empty Spaces' and 'Strangers Forever': Social Marginality and the Construction of Space," in Gunn and McNutt, eds., *"Imagining" Biblical Worlds*, 30–50 (32–37). For comprehensive spatial interpretations, cf. C. M. Maier, *Daughter Zion, Mother Zion: Gender, Space, and the Sacred in Ancient Israel* (Minneapolis: Fortress, 2008); M. K. George, *Israel's Tabernacle as Social Space* (SBL Ancient Israel and Its Literature 2; Atlanta: SBL, 2009).

40. According to C. V. Camp, "Storied Space, or, Ben Sira 'Tells' a Temple," in Gunn and McNutt, eds., *"Imagining" Biblical Worlds*, 64–80 (66–69), "biblical"

c. *Ancient Near Eastern Spatial Orientation*

Narrative theory and critical spatiality are rooted in (post)modern literary theory and philosophy. Interpretative approaches to ancient texts should be contextualized in the framework of pre-scientific, pre-modern worldview(s).[41] Reconstructing these views is difficult, as ancient Near Eastern literature contains no systematic description of the cosmos.[42] One should guard against reconstructions of a closed, systematic system that represents "the" ancient Near Eastern worldview. Various worldviews co-existed.[43] The discussion below is a reconstruction of views of the cosmos based upon a variety of sources, focusing on spatial orientation.

Spatial orientation can be plotted along two axes.[44] Horizontally, primary orientation is to the east, hence "in front" is east, "behind" is west, "right" is south, "left" is north.[45] "Far" and "near" are key concepts. Far is negative, near is positive. East–west orientation represents the temporal dimension. "In front" is the past, "behind" is the future. One moves backwards towards the future, with the past receding in front of him/her. As the past becomes remote, it becomes the realm of myth.[46] Connotations with the rising and setting sun imply that east symbolizes life and new beginning and west death and the end. South–north orientation represents the moral dimension. Right (south) is good, and left (north) implies danger. "Proximity to the self as 'centre' implies reality…expressed as holiness… Temples…are places of 'reality' and therefore of sacredness. Distance from the self means a progressive approach to the 'end of the world,' where reality breaks down."[47]

---

spaces are mainly reconstructed via written sources. Soja regards written material as products of Secondspace (Soja, *Thirdspace*, 67). Camp argues that the categorization of ancient spaces cannot be decided by the question of whether is it written.

41. G. T. M. Prinsloo, "Šᵉ'ôl → Yerûšālayim ← Šāmayim: Spatial Orientation in the Egyptian Hallel (Psalms 113–118)," *OTE* 19 (2006): 739–60.

42. B. Janowski, "Das biblische Weltbild: Eine methodologische Skizze," in *Das biblische Weltbild und seine altorientalischen Kontexte* (ed. B. Janowski and B. Ego; FAT 32; Tübingen: Mohr Siebeck, 2001), 3–26; A. Berlejung, "Weltbild/Kosmologie," in *Handbuch theologischer Grundbegriffe zum Alten und Neuen Testament* (ed. A. Berlejung and C. Frevel; Darmstadt: Wissenschaftliche Buchgesellschaft, 2006), 65–72.

43. C. Houtman, *Der Himmel im Alten Testament* (OTS 30; Leiden: Brill, 1993), 283–317; Janowski, "Das biblische Weltbild," 13.

44. Prinsloo, "Šᵉ'ôl," 741–44.

45. N. Wyatt, *Space and Time in the Religious Life of the Near East* (Sheffield: Sheffield Academic, 2001), 35–37. "Orientation" implies to turn one's face to the rising sun (Latin *oriens*).

46. Ibid., 39.

47. Ibid.

The vertical axis "points to the transcendent and infernal dimensions,"[48] and is imagined as consisting of various building blocks—
usually heaven, earth and netherworld.[49] Heaven is the realm of the gods,
earth the realm of humans, the netherworld is an entirely negative space,
the realm of the dead. Earth is imagined "as a flat plate...at the centre of
a great sphere. Outside this sphere...lies the 'cosmic ocean'."[50] It is a
symbol of the primeval waters of chaos, thus an extension of the netherworld. On this plane, "up" and "down" are key concepts. Ascending is
good, entering the realm of the gods; descending is bad, entering the
realm of the netherworld, cutting off any possibility of contact with the
divine sphere.[51]

The cosmic center of the universe lies at the intersection of the
horizontal and vertical axes. It is thought of as a mountain where the
temple of the high god stands,[52] the most sacred space, the meeting point
of the divine and human spheres.[53] The temple in Jerusalem was Israel's
spatial center. Ascending to the temple mountain is positive and is
associated with YHWH and deliverance. Descending is negative, to leave
YHWH's saving presence, to sink into the depths of Šᵉʾôl.[54] To be in
Jerusalem is to be in the center, to experience peace and life; to be far
from Jerusalem is to be on the periphery, in the realm of chaos and
death.[55] The contrast between "far/near" and "ascend/descend" leads to

---

48. Ibid., 40.

49. W. Horowitz, *Mesopotamian Cosmic Geography* (Mesopotamian Civilizations 8; Winona Lake: Eisenbrauns, 1998), xii; A. Krüger, "Himmel—Erde—Unterwelt: Kosmologische Entwürfe in der poetischen Literatur Israels," in Janowski and
Ego, eds., *Das biblische Weltbild*, 65–83. Sometimes only two elements are present
(heaven–earth), cf. O. Keel, *Die Welt der altorientalischen Bildsymbolik und das
Alte Testament am Beispiel der Psalmen* (Neukirchen–Vluyn: Neukirchener, 1972),
21–29.

50. Wyatt, *Space and Time*, 55.

51. Ibid., 40.

52. Ibid., 147; B. Janowski, "Die heilige Wohnung des Höchsten: Kosmolo-
gische Implikationen der Jerusalemer Tempeltheologie," in *Gottesstadt und
Gottesgarten: Zu Geschichte und Theologie des Jerusalemer Tempels* (ed. O. Keel
and E. Zenger; QD 191; Freiburg: Herder, 2002), 24–68 (32–37); M. Haran,
"Temple and Community in Ancient Israel," in *Temple in Society* (ed. M. V. Fox;
Winona Lake: Eisenbrauns, 1988), 17–26.

53. M. Eliade, *The Sacred and the Profane: The Nature of Religion* (trans. W. R.
Trask; New York: Harcourt, Brace & World, 1959), 20–65; Wyatt, *Space and Time*,
147.

54. Thompson, *Introducing Biblical Literature*, 59–60.

55. Janowski, "Heilige Wohnung," 42–46.

the idea of "boundaries." The city is a safe space, the steppe outside an unsafe area. The temple in the heart of the city is holy, the world outside unholy. Approaching the temple, one traverses increasingly holy ground. An unclean person cannot enter the holy space before partaking in cleansing rituals.[56]

Within this framework of horizontal and vertical orientation points, humankind is depicted from one of two perspectives: "man at-center properly orientated to his world, or man off-center in chaos and dis-orientation."[57] The world imagined by the authors of the Hebrew Bible is peculiar in the sense that it "realistically represents the life of man with all his limitations while it brings that representation into dialogue with a construct of the religious imagination that passes beyond those limits."[58]

d. *A Synthesis of Spatial Approaches*
An appreciation of the Bible's inherent spatiality will be enhanced if a comprehensive spatial approach taking cognizance of different spatial perspectives is applied. Space can be plotted according to the following matrix:

Figure 1. *A Matrix for Spatial Analysis*

		SOCIAL SPACE				
		Firstspace	*Secondspace*	*Thirdspace*		
NARRATIVE SPACE	*Narrative*				Up	ANE VERTICAL (Ascend-descend)
					Down	
	Narrator				Up	
					Down	
	Narrated				Up	
					Down	
		Near | Far	Near | Far	Near | Far		
		ANE HORIZONTAL (Near-far)				

My intention with the matrix is not to impose an "objective" blueprint upon spatial analysis. It rather serves as a reminder that any spatial approach should take cognizance of the complicated processes involved in producing space. *Narrative space, social space* and *spatial orientation* on the *horizontal* and *vertical* levels interact in the production of literary space. Any given space can function on a number of levels at the same time. On the narrative level Jonah's Nineveh, for example, is depicted as

56. Berlejung, "Weltbild/Kosmologie," 66–67.
57. Thompson, *Introducing Biblical Literature*, 13.
58. Ibid.

a Firstspace location far away (1:2; 3:2); as a Secondspace location it is classified as "wicked" (3:2); as a Thirdspace location it is horizontally and vertically off-center. However, it becomes a place of repentance and forgiveness where YHWH is present (3:3–10). The reader is compelled to "read Nineveh" through the eyes of YHWH, the God of all creation, including Nineveh.

3. *A Spatial Reading of the Book of Jonah*

In the following paragraphs I focus entirely upon *narrative space* in the book of Jonah, departing from the hypothesis that a spatial reading will enhance our understanding of the narrator's intent.[59] Prominent characteristics of the book[60] and its interpretational problems[61] will receive little attention. I read the book against a late Persian/early Hellenistic background (fifth–third centuries B.C.E.). The book engages particularistic theological trends in the post-exilic community.[62] A spatial reading reveals the author's intent to portray YHWH as the universal God with compassion for everyone who turns "from his evil way" (3:8).[63]

a. *Four Focal Spaces*[64]
Jonah has a parallel structure (A: 1:1–2:11 // B: 3:1–4:11).[65] Two introductions with parallel commands to Jonah (1:1–2; 3:1–2) and his reactions (1:3; 3:3) hint at this pattern. Each section can be subdivided

---

59. Verses are numbered according to the Masoretic text, not the Septuagint: MT 2:1 = LXX 1:17; MT 2:11 = LXX 2:10.

60. I. Willi-Plein, "Jona als Beispiel narrativer Diskussionskultur," in *Prophetie und Psalmen: Festschrift für Klaus Seybold zum 65. Geburtstag* (ed. B. Huwyler et al.; AOAT 280; Münster: Ugarit-Verlag, 2001), 217–29.

61. R. B. Salters, *Jonah and Lamentations* (OTG; Sheffield: JSOT, 1994), 13–62; K. M. Craig, "Jonah in Recent Research," *CRBS* 7 (1999): 97–118; J. Magonet, "Jonah, Book of," *ABD* 3:936–42.

62. H.-W. Wolff, *Obadiah and Jonah* (trans. M. Kohl; Minneapolis: Augsburg, 1986), 76–78; J. M. Sasson, *Jonah* (AB 24B; New York: Doubleday, 1990), 20–28; Salters, *Jonah*, 23–27.

63. Salters, *Jonah*, 51–62; Wolff, *Jonah*, 85–88; A. S. van der Woude, *Jona, Nahum* (POut; Nijkerk: Callenbach, 1978), 10; J. Limburg, *Jonah* (OTL; London: SCM, 1993), 33–36.

64. In essence, this section contains a summary of narrative space in Jonah. In the next section specific attention will be paid to the key verses Jonah 1:1, 9, 14; 3:9–10; 4:2.

65. S. Goodhart, "Prophecy, Sacrifice and Repentance in the Story of Jonah," *Semeia* 33 (1985): 43–63 (45–47).

into two spatial scenes: on a ship in stormy seas (A1: 1:4–16) and in the belly of a big fish (A2: 2:1–11); in Nineveh (B1: 4:3–10) and outside Nineveh (B2: 4:1–11). The pairs of scenes are parallel (A1//B1; A2//B2).[66]

These four locations are focal spaces inspiring change in (some) characters. All four locations can be plotted on the horizontal and vertical axes of orientation. Geographical positioning in terms of Jonah's perceived location at-center is a key to understanding the book on the horizontal axis, while proximity to and contact with YHWH is a key to understanding the book on the vertical axis. Vertical orientation determines identity and the ability to live in close contact with YHWH *as* the center of the universe.

Jonah 1:1–3 and 3:1–3 provide the setting for everything that transpires in the four focal spaces. Spatial orientation is mainly horizontal, westward in 1:1–3 and eastward in 3:1–3. YHWH commands Jonah to go to "Nineveh the great city."[67] Although not explicitly mentioned, Jonah is at his perceived at-center location in Palestine. YHWH's command requires Jonah to leave his country, exit sacred space, depart from YHWH's presence, go to the eastern extremities of the world, and deliver a message to heathens.[68] The reference to "Nineveh, the great city" is of utmost importance.[69] *Narrative time* (1:1) suggests that the character Jonah lived during the time of the New Assyrian Empire when Nineveh

---

66. J. H. Potgieter, *'n Narratologiese Ondersoek van die Boek Jona* (HTSSup 3; Pretoria: Perskor, 1991), 9–16 and 88–94; Sasson, *Jonah*, 16–19. Cf. J. Jeremias, "Die Sicht der Völker im Jonabuch (Jona 1 und Jona 3)," in *Gott und Mensch im Dialog: Festschrift für Otto Kaiser zum 80. Geburtstag* (ed. M. Witte; 2 vols.; Berlin: W. de Gruyter, 2004), 1:555–67 (557–59), for an overview of similarities and dissimilarities between the parallel sections in the book.

67. קום לך אל־נינוה העיר הגדולה (1:2; 3:2). In 1:2 a message is proclaimed "over" the city (וקרא עליה כי־עלתה רעתם לפני) with emphasis upon Nineveh's wickedness (Wolff, *Jonah*, 100; Sasson, *Jonah*, 75). In 3:2, however, the reader is aware that Jonah is not the average obedient prophet. Now the emphasis falls upon Jonah's obligation to proclaim YHWH's message "to" the city (וקרא אליה את־הקריאה אשר אנכי דבר אליך; see Wolff, *Jonah*, 139; Sasson, *Jonah*, 226).

68. D. Stuart, *Hosea–Jonah* (WBC 31; Waco: Word Books, 1987), 445; Nel, "Epic Space," 217.

69. Cf. Gen 10:11–12. Nineveh is העיר הגדולה in 1:1; 3:1; 4:11. In 3:3 the size of the city is described in superlative terms: Nineveh was great "even to God" (ונינוה היתה עיר־גדולה לאלהים). גדול also qualifies the nouns "wind" (1:4); "storm" (1:4, 12); "fear" (1:10, 16); "fish" (2:1); "evil" (4:1); and "joy" (4:6). For a spatial reading of Nineveh from the perspective of moral geography, cf. M. M. Mills, "Urban Morality and the Great City in the Book of Jonah," *Political Theology* 11 (2010): 453–65.

was a Firstspace location.[70] The book's real readers, however, live at a time when Nineveh had long since been destroyed. Yet Nineveh remains in their imaginations the ultimate Secondspace symbol of evil, violence, and oppression. YHWH expects an Israelite prophet to do the unimaginable—to preach to the ultimate representative of Israel's most feared enemies.[71]

In Section A (1:4–2:11) spatial orientation is mainly vertical and downwards. Jonah's reaction to YHWH's command is "to flee to Tarshish away from YHWH" (1:3).[72] As Firstspace locations, Nineveh and Tarshish lie at opposite ends of the horizontal axis—Tarshish west and Nineveh east.[73] In Jonah 4:2 the reader discovers that Jonah suspected YHWH might just be present at the eastern extremity of the world and reveal his compassionate character there.[74] Rather than going east (a symbol of life and new beginning), Jonah chooses to go west (a symbol of death and the end). Jonah deliberately leaves his perceived center to go off-center. His decision to go west is a choice for death, as it implies constant descending—to Joppa (1:3), a ship (1:3), the innermost part of the ship (1:5), finally to the "roots of the mountains" (2:7).[75] Jonah chooses death rather than obedience.

In the first scene (A1: 1:4–16) YHWH surprises the recalcitrant prophet by throwing "a great wind on the sea," threatening to break the ship into pieces (1:4).[76] הים, "the sea," is more than a (Firstspatial) body of water. It symbolizes the (Thirdspatial) monster of chaos. The ship becomes a focal space in the confrontation between Jonah and heathen sailors.[77]

---

70. For Nineveh as Firstspace location, especially as capital of the New Assyrian Empire during the reign of Sennacherib (705–681 B.C.E.), cf. Limburg, *Jonah*, 40; Sasson, *Jonah*, 70–72.

71. Wolff, *Jonah*, 99–100. Jonah shares a special interest in Nineveh with Nahum (cf. Nah 3:1–7) and Zephaniah (cf. Zeph 2:13–15). In Jonah the negative portrayal of Nineveh becomes positive; cf. Limburg, *Jonah*, 40–42.

72. תרשיש occurs three times in 1:3 (cf. 4:2), מלפני יהוה occurs twice (cf. 1:10). Jonah makes a frantic attempt to escape YHWH. The location of Tarshish is uncertain; cf. Wolff, *Jonah*, 100–102.

73. Limburg, *Jonah*, 43, remarks: "…the function of Tarshish in the story is clear: Jonah is planning to set out toward the farthest point in the opposite direction from Nineveh."

74. Stuart, *Jonah*, 452; Limburg, *Jonah*, 42.

75. Potgieter, *Narratologiese Ondersoek*, 60–61 (contra Stuart, *Jonah*, 451, who negates any symbolic meaning of ירד). For ירד, cf. 1:3 (×2), 5; 2:7. For לקצבי הרים, "to the roots of the mountains," cf. Wolff, *Jonah*, 136.

76. For הים, cf. 1:4 (×2), 5, 9, 11 (×2), 12 (×2), 13, 15 (×2).

77. According to Jeremias, "Sicht der Völker," 564, the sailors "in ihrer bunten Mischung der Herkunftsländer spiegeln die Vielfalt der Völkerwelt wider."

Initially, Jonah experiences the ship as a positive space, allowing him to escape YHWH's presence, descend into the innermost part of the ship, lie down and fall into a deep sleep (1:5).[78] For the sailors, the ship is a place of grave danger, forcing them to seek help from the divine sphere (1:5). The captain confronts Jonah with his apathy,[79] and urges him to pray to his god, "maybe[80] this god[81] will take notice of us and we will not perish" (1:6). When Jonah is singled out as the one responsible for the storm (1:7), the sailors confront Jonah with a barrage of questions about occupation, country and people (1:8).[82] Jonah identifies himself with reference to ethnicity ("a Hebrew I am") and worship ("and YHWH, the God of heavens, who made the sea and the dry ground, I worship," 1:9). The significance of this identification will be considered in the next section. For the moment, it should be noted that, by Jonah's own confession, YHWH is the God who rules all three tiers of the universe, including הים.[83]

The mention of YHWH causes a dramatic change. The ship becomes an unsafe place for Jonah, but a place of worship for the sailors. Jonah confesses that he is fleeing from his universal God (1:10) and advises the sailors to throw him into the sea (1:11–12). The sailors, afraid to apply Jonah's advice, try to reach dry ground while the sea becomes even rougher (1:13). Then the sailors pray to YHWH. They acknowledge

---

78. For שכב as metaphor for death, cf. Ezek 32:21, 27–30; Ps 88:4–5. Nel, "Epic Space," 218, notes that sleep "is a deliberate…withdrawal from reality," thus וירדם symbolizes death (cf. Wolff, *Jonah*, 112).

79. מה־לך נרדם (1:6) is reminiscent of the question asked to Elijah during his flight to Horeb (מה־לך פה אליהו, 1 Kgs 19:9) in a context where a prophet flees (1 Kgs 19:3; Jonah 1:2–3), prays to die (1 Kgs 19:4; Jonah 4:3; cf. 4:8) and falls asleep (1 Kgs 19:5; Jonah 1:5).

80. The captain and the king of Nineveh express hope that Jonah's God might just be the heathens' only hope: "*maybe* (אולי) this god will take notice of us, and *we will not perish* (ולא נאבד)" (1:6); "*who knows* (מי־יודע)—this God may turn around and show compassion…and *we will not perish* (ולא נאבד)" (3:9); cf. Jeremias, "Sicht der Völker," 562.

81. In Jonah 1 the term אלהים becomes increasingly significant. Of the sailors it is said that each calls upon "his god" (אל־אלהיו, 1:5). The captain admonishes Jonah—"call upon your god" (קרא אל־אלהיך)—and adds: "maybe this god (האלהים) will take notice of us and we will not perish" (1:6). In 1:9 "this god" is identified as "YHWH, the God of heaven (יהוה אלהי השמים)…who made the sea and the dry ground." Now the sailors no longer call upon their gods, but upon YHWH (ויקראו אל־יהוה in 1:14), they revere him (1:15).

82. Stuart, *Jonah*, 460.

83. Jonah's confession is at the same time a condemnation of himself (Van der Woude, *Jona*, 25).

YHWH as the universal God who does as he pleases (1:14). When Jonah goes overboard, the sea becomes calm (1:15). While Jonah—at his own request—descends into the realm of Šᵉʾôl, the ship becomes a meeting place between heaven and earth. The sailors revere YHWH and make vows (1:16). The ship is a focal place where, ironically, Jonah's lived experience changes and safety becomes danger, but *he* does not change—he still chooses death. The sailors' lived space also changes and terror becomes awe in the presence of the divine, while *they* change too—they pray and sacrifice and make vows to YHWH.

Irony dominates the second scene (A2: 2:1–11) in the belly of a big fish. At face value, the scene describes Jonah's salvation. YHWH, after all, supplies "a big fish" to swallow Jonah (2:1) and after "three days and three nights" (2:1)[84] commands the fish to vomit Jonah upon dry ground (2:11), presumably back on Jonah's home soil. The prophet returns (from Šᵉʾôl, no less!) to his perceived space at-center. Jonah's prayer (2:2–10)[85] contains a large number of expressions associated with the sea as metaphor for the netherworld, and develops in two phases.[86] In 2:2–7 Jonah gradually descends into the netherworld, until "the earth—her bars (were) behind me forever" (2:7). In 2:7–10 a miraculous change occurs. The prophet proclaims: "but you, YHWH my God, brought up from the pit my life" (2:7). Jonah's prayer becomes a pre-emptory song of thanksgiving for miraculous divine intervention (2:8–10). However, on a spatial level there is a catch: in both the descending and ascending phase, Jonah expects to meet YHWH בהיכל קדשך, "in your holy temple" (2:5, 8), where he will sacrifice to YHWH and make vows (2:10). Jonah repeats the religious actions of the sailors (1:16), but for him salvation is exclusively connected with the temple. YHWH is present there, acts there, only there Jonah can be at-center. The temple is Jonah's ultimate destination. The sailors (and the reader) know better—they have already met YHWH

---

84. The expression occurs only here and in 1 Sam 30:12. The exact implication of the temporal indication is not clear (Limburg, *Jonah*, 62), but probably links up with a popular belief in ancient times that the journey to Šᵉʾôl takes three days (Stuart, *Jonah*, 474–75). If this is true, there might be an ironic play between 2:1 and 3:3–4. Jonah experiences the full period of journey time to Šᵉʾôl, prays fervently, and is brought back to life. He does not, however, grant Nineveh the same privilege. In Nineveh he does not travel for three days, but just for one, and then delivers his short oracle of doom.

85. For a discussion of the origin of Jonah's prayer, cf. Wolff, *Jonah*, 128–30. For Jonah's prayer as an anthology of other texts, cf. ibid., 133–39; Limburg, *Jonah*, 63–64.

86. For a discussion of the poem's structure, cf. M. L. Barré, "Jonah 2,9 and the Structure of Jonah's Prayer," *Bib* 72 (1991): 237–48.

in the modest surroundings of a storm-battered ship. The message is clear: the center of the universe is where YHWH is—and that is where human beings worship him. Jonah's perceived salvation is not salvation at all. In the focal space of the fish's belly, even when the gates of Šᵉʾôl close behind him, Jonah remains convinced that the temple is the only place where YHWH can (and should!) be present.[87]

Reservations about Jonah's "salvation" are confirmed in the second part of the book (B: 3:1–4:11). In this section Nineveh becomes a most surprising focal space. It is mentioned eight times and becomes a space larger than life, a legendary place, a big city "even to God, a journey of three days" (3:3).[88] As legendary capital of the powerful New Assyrian kingdom, it is a symbol of wickedness, abuse, ungodliness—a place that should be razed to the ground. Nevertheless, it becomes the ultimate meeting point between the divine and human spheres.

YHWH's second command to Jonah to go to Nineveh (3:2) and Jonah's journey eastward (3:3) introduce the third scene (B1: 3:4–11), a second confrontation between Jonah and a group of heathens. For Jonah, spatial orientation is mainly horizontal. His Thirdspatial experience of the city remains constant. He dislikes the place and wishes destruction on it. Hence his short penetration into the city (one day) and very short sermon:[89] עוד ארבעים יום ונינוה נהפכת, "Another forty days[90] and Nineveh

---

87. A. Brenner, "Jonah's Poem Out of and Within Its Context," in *Among the Prophets: Language, Image, and Structure in the Prophetic Writings* (ed. P. R. Davies and D. J. A. Clines; JSOTSup 144; Sheffield: Sheffield Academic, 1993), 183–92 (184). Willi-Plein, "Jona als Beispiel," 227, indicates that Jonah's prayer also discloses why he does not want to go to Nineveh: "Er war ihm lästig, da er die Entfernung aus der Nähe des Tempels bedeutete."

88. Cf. נינוה (3:3, 4, 5, 6, 7); נינוה העיר הגדולה (3:2; 4:11). In 3:3 the size of the city is (over)emphasized: ונינוה היתה עיר־גדולה לאלהים מהלך שלשת ימים (for the superlative, cf. Limburg, *Jonah*, 78). Four times Nineveh is simply referred to as העיר (3:4, 5 [×3]). In Josh 10:2 and Jer 22:8, respectively, Gibeon and Jerusalem are also called "great cities," both in contexts where the cities are condemned. According to Wolff, *Jonah*, 148, Nineveh is portrayed as "an antitype to Jerusalem," the ultimate place where YHWH is not to be found, yet in Jonah it becomes the place where the divine and the human spheres meet. It is possible that גדולה לאלהים is a *double entendre* implying "important to God" (Stuart, *Jonah*, 487).

89. R. W. L. Moberly, "Preaching for a Response? Jonah's Message to the Ninevites Reconsidered," *VT* 53 (2003): 156–68.

90. For ארבעים יום, cf. Gen 7:4, 12, 17 (the flood); Exod 24:18; 34:28; Deut 9:9, 11, 18, 25 (Moses on Mount Sinai); Num 13:25; 14:34 (the spies in the Promised Land); 1 Sam 17:16 (Goliath taunting the Israelites); 1 Kgs 19:8 (Elijah's journey to Horeb). Limburg, *Jonah*, 79, remarks: "Jonah's short speech has a biblical ring!" (cf. Sasson, *Jonah*, 233–34).

will be destroyed!"[91] (3:4). Jonah exits the scene to be heard of again only in Jonah 4.[92] In the city great turmoil erupts. Now orientation is mainly vertical and upwards. The Ninevites' Secondspatial perception of their city as the ultimate symbol of power, security, prosperity, comfort and protection is shattered.[93] Jonah's sermon changes their lived experience dramatically. The inhabitants "believed in God, declared a fast and put on sackcloth" (3:5). When the news reaches the king of Nineveh, there follows an exaggerated penitence ritual that includes the king and his nobles, the inhabitants and even their domestic animals (3:6–8).[94] Nineveh becomes the ultimate example of focal space, a place of safety and a positive encounter with God. Jonah 1 already prepared the reader (but not Jonah!) for the unimaginable: YHWH is present on a ship at sea and in wicked Nineveh. Nineveh can also be located at the center of the universe (3:10). Heathens discover YHWH at-center, while YHWH's prophet remains off-center.

The last scene (B2: 4:1–11) occurs mainly outside Nineveh. Spatial orientation is horizontal and directed to the west (4:5) and vertical and directed downwards (4:3, 9). The chapter contains the only direct confrontation between YHWH and Jonah. In 4:5 it becomes clear that Jonah departed from the city, erected a shelter east of the city and "sat under it in the shade until he could see what would happen to the city." Presumably, the initial dialogue between YHWH and Jonah (4:1–4) took place after Jonah delivered his short sermon and while the conversion of the city commenced. Jonah traversed Nineveh from west to east until he found himself outside the city. The dialogue in 4:1–4 is most surprising.

---

91. הפך "change, destroy" is ambiguous (Stuart, *Jonah*, 489; Sasson, *Jonah*, 234–37). In some contexts (e.g. Gen 19:28) it has negative connotations and suggests total annihilation (cf. Deut 29:23; Isa 13:19; Jer 20:16; 49:18; 50:40; Lam 4:6; Amos 4:11; cf. Limburg, *Jonah*, 79). That is how Jonah intended his speech. In other contexts (e.g. Exod 14:5; 1 Sam 10:6, 9; Jer 31:13; Hos 11:8; Neh 13:2) it has positive connotations and indicates a change in disposition (cf. Wolff, *Jonah*, 149). That is what happens in Nineveh. Jonah is proclaiming a message "over" Nineveh (cf. 1:1), while YHWH is speaking "to" the city (cf. 3:1). In that sense Jonah is, as in Jonah 1, not fulfilling YHWH's command (cf. n. 67; contra Stuart, *Jonah*, 489, who is of the opinion that Jonah proclaims "exactly what Yahweh told him to say").

92. Stuart, *Jonah*, 486.

93. According to Jeremias, "Sicht der Völker," 564, the Ninevites represent "speziell…die Gewalt einer bedrückenden Fremdmacht."

94. Wolff, *Jonah*, 151–53; Limburg, *Jonah*, 81–83. The "king of Nineveh" becomes an antitype of the Judean king Jehoiakim (Jer 36) who hears a message similar to the words expressed by the "king of Nineveh" (Jer 36:3), but acts in exactly the opposite way by destroying the scroll with the message (Jer 36:23); cf. Jeremias, "Sicht der Völker," 561–62.

It opens with the statement that "Jonah was greatly displeased" (4:1) and closes with YHWH's question directed to Jonah: "Is it right for you to be angry?" (4:4). Framed by anger, a prayer appears (as in Jonah 2). Here, however, there is no sign of thanksgiving for the salvation of Nineveh. On the contrary, Jonah now reveals why he fled to Tarshish in the first place (4:2). He did it precisely because he suspected that Israel's confession about the nature of YHWH as a gracious and compassionate God, uttered since the time of the Exodus (cf. Exod 34:6–7), was in actual fact true. Jonah's reaction upon YHWH's compassion for Nineveh is not thanksgiving, but the wish to die (4:3). When Jonah was confronted by Šᵉʾôl, he prayed for salvation. Now he is confronted by salvation and prays for death. Jonah does not change—his spatial orientation remains vertical and downwards.[95]

In 4:5–11 the scene shifts to Jonah's shelter outside the city. He initially experiences the place as desolate, without God, an off-center location where he is dependent upon his own devices to stay alive while he watches the final outcome of his journey to Nineveh (4:5). Then, however, YHWH, the God who brought Jonah up from the pit (2:7), surprises the prophet. The desolate location outside the city becomes an at-center haven when YHWH supplies a plant "to grow up over Jonah… to deliver him from his misery." Such is the nature of the compassionate God, and Jonah is "exceedingly happy" (4:6). Then disaster strikes. God supplies a worm to destroy the vine (4:7) and, as the sun rose, also "a scorching east wind" resulting in Jonah becoming faint. Once again, Jonah wishes to die (4:8) and YHWH asks a second time: "Is it right for you to be angry about the vine?" Jonah reacts: "It is right for me to be angry unto death!" (4:9). The book concludes with an open-ended speech by YHWH. YHWH points out to Jonah the unfairness of his anger. Jonah is angry about a mere plant, nothing but a symbol of YHWH's unexpected compassionate acts towards Jonah (4:10).[96] Yet YHWH should not be concerned about Nineveh, its many inhabitants and its domestic animals (4:11).[97] The speech emphasizes that YHWH is God of all of creation. He can show compassion to whomever he chooses. At-center is where YHWH is. To remain off-center is Jonah's deliberate choice and it results in death.

95. Stuart, *Jonah*, 479–80.
96. Ibid., 506.
97. Sasson, *Jonah*, 308–15. The inhabitants are "a hundred and twenty thousand people who cannot tell their right hand from their left" (4:11). Sasson (ibid., 310) remarks that the "accent…is on multitudes and crowds." From a spatial perspective the Ninevites' inability to "tell their right hand from their left" implies moral inability—they do not know right from wrong (cf. Van der Woude, *Jona*, 61).

b. *Space, Identity, and Spatial Focal Points*

YHWH and Jonah, the two main characters in the narrative, are introduced in 1:1.[98] Both are characterized in various ways. Jonah is characterized twice: by the author/narrator (1:1), and by Jonah himself (1:9). In 1:1 Jonah is introduced as יונה בן־אמתי, "Jonah, son of Amittai." The name also appears in 2 Kgs 14:25, a short report on the reign of Jeroboam II of Israel (2 Kgs 14:23–29). In spite of the negative judgment of his reign (2 Kgs 14:24), Jeroboam reigned for forty years and "restored the boundaries of Israel…in accordance with the word of YHWH, the God of Israel, spoken through his servant Jonah son of Amittai" (2 Kgs 14:25). YHWH saved the suffering Israelites through Jeroboam because "he had not said he would blot out the name of Israel from under heaven" (2 Kgs 14:26–27). The wicked Jeroboam's success is ascribed to YHWH, explicitly called יהוה אלהי ישראל, "YHWH, God of Israel," the national deity. The intertextual play between Jonah 1:1 and 2 Kgs 14:25 suggests that the narrative will bode well for Israel and will be concerned with Israel's success in the realm given to them by their God. The specific command to go to Nineveh and preach "against" (עליה) the mighty and wicked empire of Jeroboam's time (Jonah 1:2) strikes a positive note when read in conjunction with 2 Kgs 14. Nevertheless, a surprise awaits.

Jonah's self-characterization in 1:9 is revealing and carries explicit spatial connotations. Jonah's response to the sailors' barrage of questions is a curt עברי אנכי, "a Hebrew I am" (1:9), that answers all of them.[99] עברי has important intertextual connections. It occurs 35 times in the Hebrew Bible, often with the connotation of demarcating a "Hebrew" among foreigners.[100] "Hebrew" is closely associated with YHWH's power of salvation and his special bond with his people. Jonah defines himself narrowly in terms of a specific group occupying a specific territory, allotted to them by none other than YHWH according to tradition and

---

98.   Stuart, *Jonah*, 445. Jonah is mentioned 18 times; YHWH 26 times. אלהים appears nine times, האלהים five times and אל once. YHWH is thus mentioned 41 times in 48 verses. For the significance of these references, cf. Salters, *Jonah*, 37–38; Limburg, *Jonah*, 45–46.

99.   H. Angel, "I Am a Hebrew: Jonah's Conflict with God's Mercy Toward Even the Most Worthy of Pagans," *JBQ* 34 (2006): 3–11 (4–6).

100.   It demarcates Joseph as a "Hebrew" among Egyptians (Gen 39:14, 17; 40:15; 41:12; 43:32) and the Israelites from Egyptians (Exod 1:15, 16, 19; 2:6, 7, 13). The Pharaoh explicitly calls the Israelite God אלהי העברים, "the God of the Hebrews" (Exod 3:18; 5:3; 7:16; 9:1, 13; 10:3; cf. also 1 Sam 4:7–9). The term carries definitive ethnological connotations and emphasizes the distance between Jonah and the sailors (cf. Van der Woude, *Jona*, 24–25; Limburg, *Jonah*, 53; Sasson, *Jonah*, 115–17).

popular belief. This is implied in the second part of Jonah's self-identi-fication, unsolicited information implied when he says "and YHWH, the God of heavens, I worship."[101]

YHWH is explicitly characterized four times: twice by Jonah (1:9; 4:2) and twice by non-Israelites (1:14; 3:9–10). In each case, Jonah "mis-interprets" the character of YHWH, while the non-Israelites understand his true nature. Jonah's identification of YHWH in 1:9 has explicit spatial connotations. He is "YHWH, the God of the heavens…who made the sea and the dry ground."[102] This identification hints at the traditional three-tiered universe, implying that YHWH is a universal God. In contrast to Jonah's narrow self-identification, he identifies YHWH as a universal God who has dominion over the cosmos. How ironic, then, that Jonah attempts to flee from this God.[103] YHWH's characterization by the sailors in 1:14 also hints at his universal dominion. When they are on the brink of throwing Jonah overboard, they pray: "O YHWH, please do not let us perish on account of the life of this man. Do not hold against us innocent blood, because you are YHWH, as you please you do."[104] They understand that YHWH controls the fate of everyone and everything, but Jonah is blind to YHWH's universal power.

In Jonah 3:9–10, YHWH is characterized by the king and inhabitants of Nineveh as a potentially compassionate God. The king calls upon his subjects to repent and remarks: "Who knows—this God may turn around and show compassion, he might relent from his fierce anger so that we will not perish."[105] YHWH promptly illustrates his compassion in 3:10 by

101.   Wolff, *Jonah*, 115.

102.   For אלהי השמים, cf. Gen 24:3, 7; 2 Chr 2:11; 36:23; Ezra 1:2; Neh 1:4, 5; Ps 136:26. For the Aramaic אלה שמיא, cf. Dan 2:18, 37, 44; Ezra 5:11; 7:12, 21, 23. The Aramaic phrase also occurs in the Elephantine papyri (cf. Wolff, *Jonah*, 115; Sasson, *Jonah*, 118). The phrase is typical of the Persian period and expresses that YHWH "is not a local or national deity" (Wolff, *Jonah*, 115; cf. also Stuart, *Jonah*, 461).

103.   For YHWH's dominion over sea and dry ground, cf. Exod 10:13–19; 14–15; Num 11:31; Isa 50:2; Jer 49:32–36; Amos 4:13; Pss 95:5; 135:7; Job 26:12 (Stuart, *Jonah*, 461).

104.   Sasson, *Jonah*, 131, calls this prayer "the heart of Jonah's first chapter, for it catches the moment in which illumination finally strikes the sailors." Cf. Potgieter, *Narratologiese Ondersoek*, 43–45.

105.   Three key terms with important intertextual connections appear in 3:8–9 (רעה, "evil"; שוב, "to turn around"; נחם, "to show compassion"; cf. Sasson, *Jonah*, 260–64). In Exod 32:12–14 Moses intercedes for the people because YHWH wanted to do evil (רעה) to them and pleads that YHWH should turn around (שוב) and repent (נחם) from this evil. YHWH then changes his mind (נחם) about the evil (רעה). In Jer 18:7–8 (cf. also 26:3, 13, 19; 36:3, 7) the possibility is left open that YHWH will

refraining from acting against the inhabitants of Nineveh. Thus is the nature of this universal God who can do what he wants. To Jonah the "Hebrew" it is unacceptable (4:1). He expresses anger in spatial terms when he characterizes YHWH in 4:2–3: "O YHWH, is this not what I said when I was in my land, therefore I was quick to flee to Tarshish. I indeed know that you are a gracious and compassionate God, slow to anger and abounding in love, and who relents from evil."[106] The "Hebrew" deliberately turns his back upon compassion.

Thus, the two main characters have diametrically opposing focal points. Jonah's focal point is narrow, restricted to his own country and his own God. When called upon by YHWH to broaden his scope, he deliberately chooses to get away from YHWH as far as possible, first in geographical terms by departing for Tarshish, secondly in cosmic terms by deliberately choosing to descend into Šeʾôl, a spatial location traditionally "outside" the sphere of divine influence. Ironically, when he indeed descends to the "roots of the mountains" (2:7), he recalls YHWH's great acts of salvation (2:7–8) and gives thanks for being restored to "your holy temple" (2:5, 8). Jonah's spatial focal point is restricted to YHWH in his holy temple.

YHWH's focal point is universal, including the entire cosmos and all its inhabitants.[107] YHWH's universal rule is confirmed by the fact that he causes a "great storm" to rise upon the sea (1:4) and calms the sea again when Jonah is thrown overboard (1:15). YHWH controls a "big fish" (2:1, 11), a "plant" (4:6, 7, 9), a "worm" (4:7) and a "scorching east wind"

---

show compassion (נחם) if the people turn away (שוב) from their evil (רעה). The theme is taken to be Deuteronomistic; cf. Judg 2:18; 2 Sam 12:22; 24:16 (Wolff, *Jonah*, 153–55). The phrase מי־יודע ישוב ונחם occurs only in Joel 2:14 and Jonah 3:9 (cf. 2 Sam 12:22). In Joel, Israel is called to repentance, but in Jonah it is the heathen king who expresses a glimmer of hope, causing Jonah to become angry (4:1), because YHWH is true to his character (cf. ibid., 153). Wolff (ibid., 155) indicates that Jonah's application of Exod 34:12–14, Jer 18:7–8 (also Jer 26 and 36), and Joel 2:14 to the Ninevites "must have sounded like bitter mockery" because "through this fulfillment Israel's last privilege loses its force."

106. T. B. Dozeman, "Inner-biblical Interpretation of Yahweh's Gracious and Compassionate Character," *JBL* 108 (1989): 207–23. Joel and Jonah contain a unique version of the so-called *Gnadenformel* (Joel 2:13; Jonah 4:2; cf. Exod 34:6–7; Pss 86:15; 116:5; 145:8; Neh 9:17) with the concluding phrase ונחם על־הרעה, "who relents from evil." It is generally accepted that Jonah is dependent upon Joel; cf. Wolff, *Jonah*, 77, 166–68.

107. T. Forti, "Of Ships and Seas, and Fish and Beasts: Viewing the Concept of Universal Providence in the Book of Jonah through the Prism of Psalms," *JSOT* 35 (2011): 359–74.

(4:8). YHWH's spatial focal point is apparent in his concern for Nineveh (1:2; 3:2, 3; 4:11) and all its inhabitants, human and animal (4:11). Jonah has an obsession to get away from YHWH at all costs. YHWH is motivated by compassion for his creation. Even Nineveh, the ultimate Thirdspatial symbol of power, abuse and wickedness, associated with war, destruction and exile for anyone from Israel/Judah, can become the center of the universe when its people turn to YHWH (3:6–10).

c. *Journeys to Nowhere...*

In each section of the book Jonah undertakes a spatial journey. The nature of the journey, and consequently the destination, differs dramatically. Jonah 1–2 describes Jonah's journey mainly in vertical terms. While the customary orientation for ancient Near Eastern people is eastwards and upwards, Jonah goes the opposite way. He travels west when he should have gone east (1:1–3) and gradually descends into the depths of Š^{e}'ôl (2:2–6). When he finally prays, his destination, seen from his perspective, is YHWH's holy temple (2:5, 8). In his prayer he arrives at the destination, but in reality he only reaches "dry ground" and receives the command to continue his journey.

The journey has two phases. In the first phase (Jonah 1), Jonah is confronted by heathen sailors who act in a most surprising manner. They pray, they take the initiative to discover who causes their impending calamity, they resist Jonah's initial command to throw him into the sea, they pray for mercy, they sacrifice to YHWH and make vows when the storm subsides. In the second phase (Jonah 2), Jonah is confronted by his God. The confrontation is, however, a monologue directed to YHWH as a pre-emptory song of thanksgiving for deliverance yet to come. Jonah twice expresses the longing to be restored to YHWH in his holy temple. In that, he is disillusioned and merely ended up on dry ground. It is striking that Jonah's journey takes him from his perceived center (a Hebrew, at-center in his country) to Š^{e}'ôl and back to his illusionary center (YHWH's holy temple), but he actually never reaches his destination.

Jonah 3–4 describes Jonah's journey mainly in horizontal terms. Jonah traverses the face of the earth from west to east. As instructed by YHWH, his destination is "Nineveh, the great city" (3:1). The size of the city is (over)emphasized (3:3) and Jonah barely enters Nineveh (3:4) when he delivers a very short, one-sided sermon about Nineveh's destruction (3:4). The message brings about a huge upheaval in Nineveh (3:5–9), but meanwhile Jonah continues his journey, supposedly walking through the city from west to east. He ends his journey outside the city (4:5), sitting down "east of the city" (4:5), thus again facing west (as in Jonah 1). Jonah constantly and deliberately defies facing in the right direction.

This journey also continues in two phases. In the first phase (Jonah 3), Jonah is confronted by the inhabitants of Nineveh and their king who act in a most surprising manner. They believe Jonah's message and promptly declare a day of fast for all (3:5). The king and his nobles even officially proclaim this fast for people and animals, hoping that God might change his mind and show compassion (3:6–9). As can be expected, YHWH does exactly that (3:10). In the second phase (Jonah 4), a direct confrontation between YHWH and Jonah follows. Jonah explains that it was exactly because of YHWH's gracious and compassionate nature that he fled his country to go to Tarshish in the first place (4:2). He sits east of the city, facing west, awaiting developments under the shelter that he made, turning away from the past, unwilling to see the true nature of his God. YHWH acts, and as in Jonah 2, he "supplies" (מנה in 4:6, 7, 8) a plant, a worm, and a scorching east wind to teach the prophet a lesson in compassion—all to no avail. YHWH's final remark (4:10–11) makes it clear that Jonah, in spite of two eventful journeys, remains the particularistic Hebrew who does not understand the heart of his compassionate, universal God. The surprising aspect of the second part of the book is that Nineveh, not the temple in Jerusalem, becomes the center of the universe. In YHWH's presence people encounter the gracious and compassionate God. One's perceived space can be at-center ("your holy temple," 2:5, 8) without ever arriving at-center—and that is where "YHWH, the God of heaven who made the sea and the dry ground" (1:9) shows compassion to penitent evildoers, even in Nineveh (3:9–10).

4. *A Note on the Narrator's and Narrated Space*

If the spatial reading of Jonah has merit and my assumption that Jonah's author/narrator and his audience are inhabitants of Yehud during the late Persian/early Hellenistic period is correct, it has important implications for the interpretation of the book. A section of the Yehudite community became increasingly particularistic, focusing inward, adhering to the belief that YHWH can only be found at the temple in Jerusalem. These sentiments echo strongly in the books of Ezra and Nehemiah[108] and find expression in the Psalter, especially in so-called pilgrimage songs such as Pss 113–118[109] and 120–134.[110] The author/narrator of Jonah criticizes the fixation upon a place rather than upon YHWH. He deliberately chooses a character and a location from the distant past to illustrate

---

108.   Cf. the contribution by M. Häusl in the present volume.
109.   Prinsloo, "Šᵉʾôl," 755–57.
110.   Prinsloo, "Role of Space," 472–77.

his point. Both character and location have symbolic (Second- and Thirdspace) value. Jonah is the nationalistic prophet from the time of Jeroboam II, when YHWH aided Israel in spite of their king's wickedness. Nineveh symbolizes everything that is wicked and violent. Space in the book of Jonah ultimately is "focal" space intended to confront the listener/reader with his/her perceptions, presuppositions and ideologies.[111] The narrator's intention is clear. He warns against a narrow interpretation of YHWH's compassion, emphasizing that YHWH is indeed the "God of heaven who created the sea and the dry ground" (1:9). Moreover, he adds the indispensable element of a relationship with YHWH and repentance to his final statement in the book: "However, I should not be concerned about Nineveh, the great city, that has more than a hundred and twenty thousand people that do not know right from left, and many cattle" (4:11).

5. *Conclusion*

This study focused on the concepts of space/spatiality in narrative texts. I have argued that insights from the fields of narratology and critical spatiality can aid modern interpreters in reconstructing the ancient Mediterranean world and provide an interpretative window into the texts of the time. Both theoretical approaches emphasize that space in ancient narratives is "constructed" by means of words. As such, a careful spatial reading will aid the interpreter in reconstructing the author/narrator's point of view. No reconstruction of ancient spatial concepts can be complete without contextualizing it according to the ancient Near Eastern worldview. Here the concepts of being "off-center" or "at-center" on both the horizontal and vertical planes play an important role. By applying these principles to the book of Jonah, the book's surprising message could be elucidated. YHWH, the universal God of heaven, determines whether one is off- or at-center. A relationship with him turns even the most unlikely locations, a storm-battered ship or a violence-ridden city, into meeting places, points of contact between the divine and human spheres. The book of Jonah warns the people of Yehud living under Persian/Greek hegemony, seeking identity in Jerusalem and the temple and the cult, rather to find their identity in a relationship with YHWH, who, as universal Creator-God, is free to show compassion to anyone.

---

111. Van Eck, *Galilee and Jerusalem*, 137–39.

Fiction and Space in Deuteronomy

Michaela Geiger

As a "wheel within a wheel," to echo Ezekiel's vision (Ezek. 1:16), Deuteronomy is an act of communication within an act of communication. Moses' oral "words" unfold as the written "words" of the framing book—Deuteronomy. Or, the other way around, Deuteronomy is an act of communication about an act of communication. The book's narrator starts the narration, but almost immediately hands it over to its dramatis persona, whose direct speech gives the work its distinctive ring.[1]

This characterization of the book of Deuteronomy is the starting point of Jean-Pierre Sonnet's study on Deuteronomy, which analyzes the course of growth and the formation of the book. Sonnet understands Deuteronomy as a "historiographical narration."[2] Following the historian Hayden White, the fictional dimension of historiography has been analyzed,[3] so that the ratio of fictional and factual narration may respectively be determined.[4] Biblical texts contain a "mixture of both, in which

---

1. J. P. Sonnet, *The Book Within the Book: Writing in Deuteronomy* (BIS 14; Leiden: Brill, 1997), 1.
2. Ibid., 9–12. As to Deuteronomy's narrative character, cf. also K. Finsterbusch, *Weisung für Israel: Studien zu religiösem Lehren und Lernen im Deuteronomium und seinem Umfeld* (FAT 44; Tübingen: Mohr Siebeck, 2005); J. Taschner, *Die Mosereden im Deuteronomium: Eine kanonorientierte Untersuchung* (FAT 59; Tübingen: Mohr Siebeck, 2008); M. Geiger, *Gottesräume: Die literarische und theologische Konzeption von Raum im Deuteronomium* (Stuttgart: Kohlhammer, 2010) as well as a number of articles by Norbert Lohfink; cf. N. Lohfink, *Studien zum Deuteronomium und zur deuteronomistischen Literatur I–V* (SBAB; Stuttgart: Katholisches Bibelwerk, 1990–2005).
3. The main works of H. V. White are *Metahistory: The Historical Imagination in 19th Century Europe* (Baltimore: The Johns Hopkins University Press, 1973), and *Tropics of Discourse: Essays in Cultural Criticism* (Baltimore: The Johns Hopkins University Press, 1978).
4. C. Klein and M. Martínez, "Wirklichkeitserzählungen: Felder, Formen und Funktionen nicht-literarischen Erzählens," in *Wirklichkeitserzählungen: Felder, Formen und Funktionen nicht-literarischen Erzählens* (ed. C. Klein and M. Martínez;

fictional and factual modes of representation merge."[5] This essay will not emphasize the ratio of fictional and factual elements in Deuteronomy, but will focus on a remarkable feature of the book, namely, that of disclosing its own fictional character and thus creating a specific effect. Moreover, the fictionality of Deuteronomy is tied to the book's spatial conception: the spatial construct serves as a signpost of fictionality, allowing the reader to orient him/herself between fictive and real world. Thus, Deuteronomy's theology may be characterized as "space within a space within a space," to adapt Sonnet freely. The readers of Deuteronomy find themselves in a series of spaces: Moses, who passes on YHWH's words from *Horeb*, addresses them as the people in *Moab* and reminds them of their way out of *Egypt* and through the *wilderness*, thereby obliging them to adhere to these words within the *Promised Land*.[6] The pragmatics of Deuteronomy is therefore based on the merging of fictional communication and the spatial dimension of the book.

In this essay, the combination of fiction and space will be analyzed—based on (1) Wolfgang Iser's theory of fictionality and (2) Martina Löw's sociology of space. The intentional intertwining of fiction and space will be demonstrated (3) in a discussion of the introduction of the book (Deut 1:1–5). Any fictional narration unfolds its effect by the

---

Stuttgart: Metzler, 2009), 1–13 (4–5), distinguish between "factual narrations presented in a fictionalizing mode of telling," "factual narrations with fictive contents," "fictional narrations with factual contents" and "fictional narrations presented in a factual mode of speaking."

5. I. Müllner, "Fiktion," *WiBiLex* (September 2008), www.wibilex.de (accessed May 15, 2012) (author's translation). Cf. also M. Kutzer, *In Wahrheit erfunden: Dichtung als Ort theologischer Erkenntnis* (ratio fidei 30; Regensburg: Friedrich Pustet, 2006), 203–4: "In their focus upon the present, historical narrations should also be considered as poetic texts. They are poetic in the sense that they present a textual world which is construed as one's own past, in the light of which the present may also be interpreted" (author's translation).

6. The Deuteronomic conception of space is based on nouns: on toponyms, names of buildings or landscapes and parts of the body, which are not described but frequently repeated in the Deuteronomic formulaic speech. To underline the conceptual character, I will put these spatial terms in italics. For a more detailed spatial and narrative analysis of Deuteronomy, cf. Geiger, *Gottesräume*, as well as "Creating Space Through Imagination and Action: Space and the Body in Deuteronomy 6:4–9," in *Constructions of Space IV: Further Developments in Examining Social Space in Ancient Israel* (ed. M. K. George; LHBOTS 569; New York/London: T&T Clark International, forthcoming), and "Raum," *WiBiLex* (January 2012), www.wibilex.de (accessed September 14, 2012). The thoughts expounded in the present study about merging of space and fictionality in Deuteronomy, however, lead beyond my earlier studies.

possibilities of identification granted to the reader. In Deuteronomy, the text pragmatics (4) is intensified by linguistically identifying the readers with the persons addressed in the text. For orientation between the different levels of the text, spaces again are crucial. This strategy of identification aims not only at placing the readers under an obligation of fulfilling the commandments, but also of finding an adequate interpretation of the commandments in the readers' respective contexts. The contradiction between the spatial conception of the commandments in Deut 12–26, compared to the narrated situation in *Moab*, necessitates (5) a creative actualization of the text. As I will demonstrate, (6) the interpretation of the commandments is theologically founded by the presence of God at *Horeb*; this is considered (7) as a generative matrix of Moses' speeches and thus for the creation of spaces in the *Promised Land* according to the commandments. The conjunction of *Horeb* as a place and the text of Deuteronomy is reflected metafictionally (8) by making the writing itself a subject in Deuteronomy.

1. *Wolfgang Iser: Reality–Fiction–Imagination*

Wolfgang Iser develops a triad in order to describe the functionality of fiction. He aims at overcoming the over-simplified binary opposition of reality and fiction, which states that something is either true or invented. "The fictionalizing act" emphasizes the fact that fiction is not an ontological factor but an "intentional act."[7] The fictionalizing act correlates with three factors: the "real," the "fictive" and the "imaginary." For Iser "real" refers to the "empirical world," being part of "thought systems, social systems, and world views as well as other texts."[8] Elements of reality are singled out by an act of *selection*[9] and then arranged in a different *combination* in the fictive text.[10] Finally the *self-disclosure* is

7. W. Iser, *The Fictive and the Imaginary: Charting Literary Anthropology* (Baltimore: The Johns Hopkins University Press, 1993), 305 n. 3.
8. Ibid., 305 n. 2. Iser's interest does not lie on the level of differentiating the "real" from the fictional and he therefore does not attempt to deconstruct "reality." With regard to many of Iser's formulations, Mirja Kutzer (*Wahrheit*, 146) assumes a "naive comprehension of reality beyond a mere linguistically communicated perspective" (author's translation). This critique does not cause a problem for my approach since the openness of Iser's definition allows, as far as biblical texts are concerned, for the transmission of different perspectives on reality, where the emphasis is on the merging of the fictive with space and not on the reference to possible realities.
9. Iser, *The Fictive*, 4–7.
10. Cf. ibid., 7–8.

constitutive for the "fictive."[11] By textual signals of fictionality "the incorporated 'real' world is, so to speak, placed in brackets to indicate that it is not something given, but is merely to be understood *as if* it were given. In the self-disclosure of its fictionality, an important feature of the fictional text comes to the fore: it turns the whole of the world organized in the text into an 'as-if' construction."[12] Iser describes two acts of transcending boundaries between the "real" and the "fictive": one transforms elements of the "real" into the "fictive," the other one comes from the other end of the triad—the "imaginary." Since the imaginary itself is rather hazy, shapeless, unfixed and without reference to an object,[13] the fictionalizing act "aims at something that in turn endows the imaginary with an articulate gestalt—a gestalt that differs from the fantasies, projections, daydreams, and other reveries that ordinarily give the imaginary expression in our day-to-day experience."[14] Through the fictionalizing act the imaginary "assumes an appearance of reality in the way it intrudes into and acts upon the given world."[15] Iser's theory of fiction may be adapted well to the specific conditions of the formation of biblical texts, which can be demonstrated by exploring the textual formation of Deuteronomy. Frank Crüsemann, for instance, assumes that Deuteronomy's "fictive clothing in a speech of the far past"[16] was constitutive for the first, pre-exilic version of the book:[17]

> Only in the name of an authority that is not only superior to the king enthroned on Mount Zion by God, but also to all others who are speaking in the name of God in the present, Deuteronomy is able to formulate the liberal self-conception of the Deuteronomic movement based on the constitutional provisions by creatively interpreting old traditions like the

11. Cf. ibid., 11–12.
12. Ibid., 12–13.
13. Cf. ibid., 3.
14. Ibid.
15. Ibid.
16. F. Crüsemann, *Die Tora: Theologie und Sozialgeschichte des alttestamentlichen Gesetzes* (2d ed.; Gütersloh: Gütersloher Verlagshaus, 1997), 273 (author's translation).
17. Crüsemann considers Deut 5–28* as pre-exilic, albeit with later supplements. Among scholars the pre-exilic form of Deuteronomy is highly controversial—see the latest outline of the most important theses by Finsterbusch, *Deuteronomium*, 17–27. However, a possible pre-exilic version of Deuteronomy might have existed without clothing it in a fictional speech of Moses. G. Braulik, "Das Buch Deuteronomium," in *Einleitung in das Alte Testament* (ed. E. Zenger et al.; 7th ed.; Studienbücher Theologie 1/1; Stuttgart: Kohlhammer, 2008), 278–88 (144), characterizes the "Josianic document of the covenant" as follows: "It was a law, without narrative embedding" (author's translation).

Exodus. This interpretation is achieved by the historicised clothing as Moses' speech, thus reshaping an old legitimizing tradition of the Court of Jerusalem (Ex 18).[18]

By fictionalizing Deuteronomy as a speech of Moses, the direct reference of the commandments to the daily life of the addressed persons is already broken up in the primary layer without writing off Deuteronomy's claim of shaping society. The validity of the commandments has to be proven over and over again by adapting them to the context of the respective persons addressed.[19] The legal fiction of Deuteronomy singles out elements of the real world, that is, the given legal practice and legal texts like the book of covenant (*selection*), and recombines them (*combination*). Exilic and post-exilic layers of the book include elements of Israel's changed experience (during the Babylonian exile and the Persian Empire) into the fiction. Furthermore, the textual base of selection broadens: redactors choose elements from the Pentateuch narrative or the Deuteronomistic History respectively and newly combine them with their text at hand. In its final version, the book of Deuteronomy creates a Moses figure (aside from the characterization of Exodus–Numbers) that presents to the readers a potential perspective on their past and transfers God's commandments into their present. The exact scope of the successive layers of Deuteronomy and their respective reference to reality can only be assumed.

This essay is limited to the Deuteronomic fiction as included in the final version of the Hebrew Bible. From a theological point of view, Iser's third element of the triad, the imaginary, is fascinating. According to Mirja Kutzer, biblical texts are based on the conviction "that God in fact acted in history, that he actually approaches people by means of texts and that he personally guarantees a proposition to interpret their world."[20] At the same time, the texts themselves vouch for this conviction by narrating God's actions in the fictive world and thus making them "real." The assumption that God is the "original point of reference"

18. Crüsemann, *Tora*, 315 (author's translation).

19. According to Crüsemann, clothing Deuteronomy as a speech of Moses aims at refounding the three institutions of the constitution (the kingdom, the central court and the "prophet like Moses") in a way that guarantees maximum freedom for the Judaean עם הארץ. Crüsemann does not consider the consequences of fictionalization for the execution of the commandments—rather, he emphasizes the exact matching of the commandments as far as the pre-exilic society during the time of Josiah is concerned (cf. Crüsemann, *Tora*, 242–51).

20. M. Kutzer, "Die Gegenwelt des Erfundenen: Fiktionale Texte als Medium biblischer Verheißung," *PzB* 15 (2006): 44–45 (author's translation).

of the biblical texts, who "coordinates the texts and withdraws from them at the same time,"[21] originates in the imaginary. This assumption is hoped for, dreamed of, believed in or feared and thus motivates the narration of the biblical fiction that creates a world where the presence of God is real. Iser therefore interprets the imaginary as "generative matrix of the text."[22] Meir Sternberg emphasized the particular position of the biblical narrator "between God and humankind":[23] this narrator is omniscient, yet aims at "showing emphatically God's omnipotence to the biblical audience."[24]

In the book of Deuteronomy, the imaginary is expressed in different ways: the Deuteronomic construct of history describes how God guides Israel's fate: from the liberation from *Egypt* via the march through the *wilderness* into the *Promised Land* (6:20–25) into the exile and back (4:25–38). The Deuteronomic commandments provide patterns of behavior for the readers, patterns which enable them to refer to the presence of God and experience it in the world in which they live (12:5–12). Finally, the whole Deuteronomic narration presents itself as a transmission of God's words at the theophany at Horeb (1:6; 5:1–31).

The fictionality of Deuteronomy provides the readers with "vicarious experiences…enabling them to know how it feels to be in particular situations and thus to acquire dispositions to act and feel in certain ways."[25] On the fictive level, it is possible to believe in the presence of God in the history of Israel even though this contradicts one's own real experience. This counter-experience can motivate to "examine the given facts."[26] Especially the Deuteronomic commandments remind of the possibility that one's own reality may be changed. This change is permitted by the theological foundation of the commandments by the liberation from *Egypt* (5:6).

Without the self-disclosure of fictionality, Deuteronomy could be considered as totalitarian for idealizing the exclusive submission of a people to God and his commandments (14:2), according to which misbehavior will lead to immediate exclusion or death (cf. 13:7–12; 21:18–21). The disclosure of the fictional character of this social vision

21. Ibid., 46 (author's translation).
22. Iser, *The Fictive*, 21.
23. M. Sternberg, "Ideologie des Erzählens und erzählte Ideologie," in *Bibel als Literatur* (ed. H. P. Schmidt; Paderborn: Fink, 2008), 59–80 (76, author's translation).
24. Ibid., 75 (author's translation).
25. J. Culler, *Literary Theory: A Very Short Introduction* (Oxford: Oxford University Press, 2000), 108.
26. Kutzer, *Wahrheit*, 317 (author's translation).

challenges the readers to interpret the text in a creative way, so that fundamental convictions and individual elements may be translated into their own reality.

2. *Martina Löw: Spacing and Synthesis*

The theological conception of space in Deuteronomy can be explained effectively by Martina Löw's sociology of space. Löw defines space as a "relational arrangement of living beings and social goods at places."[27] This formulation discerns two processes. On the one hand, space is created by people arranging things, that is, by such actions as erecting, building or positioning. Löw addresses this process as "spacing."[28] On the other hand, a spatial arrangement has to be recognized or perceived as such, in the sense that people or objects can be connected to a mental representation of space. This process of conception is called "synthesis."[29] Both processes—"spacing" and "synthesis"—are determined by social conventions: human beings reproduce spaces they are familiar with and recognize spaces because they know them.[30] Spaces can be called "institutions" when they evoke habitualized patterns of behavior. Such patterns of behavior are practiced by routines and repetitive acting.[31] A space may be considered as an institution when its existence "remains effective beyond one's action and entails standardized syntheses and spacing."[32]

Being a sociologist, Löw deals with the constitution of social spaces; this theory does not explicitly apply to texts. Nevertheless, Löw explains her theory of space by means of a literary, non-fictive text, which may be considered as a "descriptive narration of reality."[33] From a theological point of view, this specific text is remarkable. A passage of the autobiography of the Israeli pianist and composer Josef Tal describes how the spatial concept of the Western Wall was changed by the destruction of the historic alleys of the Arabic part of town after 1968:

27. M. Löw, *Raumsoziologie* (Frankfurt a.M.: Suhrkamp, 2001), 271 (author's translation).

28. Cf. ibid., 158.

29. Cf. ibid., 159. In this study, I refer to this thought by talking about the "space concept" of the place to be chosen by God (Deut 12:5), which is created by actions and imaginations.

30. Cf. ibid., 161.

31. Löw adopts the term "routines" from Anthony Giddens; cf. ibid., 161–64 and 36–44.

32. Ibid., 164 (author's translation).

33. Klein and Martínez, *Wirklichkeitserzählungen*, 6.

[Before the Six-Day-War] you walked through a closely meshed labyrinth of narrow alleys and suddenly reached a steep wall made of enormous blocks of stone. Only a narrow strip of blue sky remained high on the upper end between the walls of the alley... Nowadays you approach the wall by crossing a large terrain, providing room for thousands of visitors to pray and celebrate religious feasts. Of course, the blocks of stone remained the same but their message has been changed by the new surroundings. The open space separating them from the narrow alleys spreads their wailing echo widely and not only upward, thus giving another sense to the prayer.[34]

When Löw analyzes the representations of space and actions creating space within the text, both of these are related to the location "Western Wall" outside the text. It is remarkable that Deuteronomy already deals with the spatial constitution of the very same place: in Deut 12–26 all space-related commandments are centralized in the "place that YHWH will choose to put his name there" (16:2; this set phrase appears 21 times in different versions in Deuteronomy). The spatial concept of this *place* will be created by the spatial practice of the addressed persons: "You shall eat there before YHWH your God, and you shall rejoice, you and your house(hold)" (14:26). Such repetitive actions are performed in reference to the imaginary choice of the *place* by YHWH and the resulting presence of God ("before YHWH") at this place; in this way, synthesis allows practice, a practice that in return shapes and memorizes synthesis. Similarly, further places, which will be part of the *Promised Land* in future, will be shaped by spacing and synthesis, especially the *house* (cf. 6:7–9) and the *gates* (cf. 12:18; 14:28–29; cf. also section 6 of this essay). Imagination and action also constitute the spaces that are "past" in relation to the story time, like *Egypt*, *wilderness* or *Horeb*. The concept *Egypt* is constituted by Israel's experience during slavery (5:15) and by the action of YHWH, who "brought you out of the land of Egypt, out of the house of slavery" (5:6). As far as the addressed persons in *Moab* are concerned, both processes—former spacing and synthesis—establish a new synthesis, which will determine their imagination and action in the present and the future; if they will act accordingly, YHWH will not bring them back to *Egypt*, back to slavery again (cf. 17:16; 28:68). Thus, spacing and synthesis are essential elements of both the text pragmatics of Deuteronomy and of constructing the Deuteronomic fiction. This connection can now be illustrated as follows with the introduction of Deuteronomy as an example.

---

34. J. Tal, *Der Sohn des Rabbiners: Ein Weg von Berlin nach Jerusalem* (Munich: Deutscher Taschenbuch Verlag, 1987), 87, quoted from Löw, *Raumsoziologie*, 152 (author's translation).

3. *Deuteronomy 1:1–5 as Introduction to the Deuteronomic Fiction*

[1] These are the words that Moses spoke to all Israel beyond the Jordan, in the wilderness, on the plain opposite Suph, between Paran and Tophel and Laban and Hazeroth, and Di-zahab. [2] It is eleven days from Horeb by the Mount Seir road to Kadesh-Barnea.
[3] It was in the fortieth year, in the eleventh month, on the first of the month, that Moses spoke to the Israelites in accordance with all that YHWH had given him as commandment for them. [4] After he had defeated Sihon king of the Amorites, who lived in Heshbon, and Og king of Bashan, who lived at Ashtaroth in Edrei. [5] Beyond the Jordan in the land of Moab, Moses began to explain this Torah saying…

Already in the introduction (Deut 1:1–5), the fictional character of Deuteronomy is denoted by a number of characteristics. Although, to a certain extent, such signals of the self-disclosure of fictionality may be generalized,[35] they will always, however, be tied to the context:

> For these signals can become significant only through particular, historically varying conventions shared by author and public. Thus the signals do not invoke fictionality as such, but rather conventions, which form the basis of a kind of contract between author and reader, the terms of which identify the text not as discourse but as "enacted discourse."[36]

The introduction of Deuteronomy does not attempt to conceal its fictionality—in fact, the self-disclosure is actually a condition for the desired effect of the text.

The beginning with the nominal phrase אלה הדברים (1:1) focuses on the speech level of the narrative and (over)emphasizes its authenticity as a speech of Moses. The fact that "these words" are addressed to "all Israel" reveals that the fictional narration claims validity for all readers belonging to Israel. Fictionalizing a farewell speech of Moses provides the possibility of including the commandments into the existing narration of the Pentateuch. The allocation within the Pentateuch is effected by spatial means that may be transferred into temporal ones in line with the Deuteronomic conception of a journey. The geographical localization of

---

35. Cf. G. Moers, *Fingierte Welten in der ägyptischen Literatur des 2. Jahrtausends v. Chr.: Grenzüberschreitung, Reisemotiv und Fiktionalität* (Probleme der Ägyptologie 19; Leiden: Brill, 2001), 79–105; the survey of A. Nünning, "Fiktionssignale," in *Metzlers Lexikon Literatur- und Kulturtheorie* (ed. A. Nünning; 3d ed.; Stuttgart: Metzler, 2004), 182–83, and the summary of H. Liss, "Kanon und Fiktion: Zur literarischen Funktion biblischer Rechtstexte," *BN* NF 121 (2004): 17–19.
36. Iser, *The Fictive*, 11–12.

Moses' speech is articulated by three aspects: the toponyms for places in the story, a fictive specification of the place of Moses' speech, and the connection to the narration of the Pentateuch. All terms frequently used for places/spaces in Deuteronomy do not only serve as geographical points of reference, but are also combined with a theological concept of space.

The expressions "beyond the *Jordan*" (1:1, 5; cf. 4:41–46, 47) and "in the land of *Moab*" (1:5; cf. 28:69; 34:1, 5, 6, 8) are characteristic for Deuteronomy's story place. They serve to lead the readers back to the present location of Moses' speech, after the narrations about past (1:6–3:29) and future spaces (12:1–26:19). Yet, the exact place cannot be identified by these vague descriptions. Besides their geographical reference, both expressions offer emblematic concepts of the respective spaces: with the deictic denotation "beyond the Jordan" the narrator points out that he/she looks from "this side of Jordan," that is, west of *Jordan* within the *Promised Land* to the Eastern border of the *Jordan* River. This location alludes to a central topic of the first speech of Moses (1:6–4:40): the "narrated" Israel is still located outside of the *Promised Land*, yet according to 2:1–3:29 starts taking possession of the land "beyond the Jordan." At the same time, Moses finally finds out that he will never set a foot on the land, which from his perspective is located "beyond," that is, west of the *Jordan River* (3:20, 25). While the location "beyond the *Jordan*" remains vague, an intentional confusion concerning *Moab* takes place. In spite of the conquest of the land east of *Jordan*, Moses' location is still allocated to the foreign land *Moab*. However, according to Deut 2:18, the "region of the Moabites" is located further south, between the rivers Sered and Arnon. According to the narration, Israel is passing this region during the speech of God (Deut 2:18–23), so that the presence of Israel in the "region of the Moabites" is not explicitly stated anywhere. These contradictions are signals of fictionality which demonstrate that the narrator does not signify a precise place, but aims at incorporating Deuteronomy into the preceding Pentateuch narration, which ended in the "plains of Moab" (Num 36:13), as Deuteronomy itself records (34:8). Moreover, *Moab* signals the allocation of the story place to the "foreign land" (cf. 3:25–27). The narrative about Moses' death (Deut 34) emphasizes that while he may see the *Promised Land* (34:2–4), he will die and be buried in the foreign land (34:5, 6, 8). Therefore, the implications of the spaces "beyond the *Jordan*" and "land of *Moab*" for the spatial conception of Deuteronomy's narration may be considered as signals of fictionality.

In Deut 1:1, there is also a second kind of location for the place of Moses' speech, which at first glance seems to be more precise. The descriptive "in the wilderness, on the plain opposite Suph, between Paran and Tophel and Laban and Hazeroth, and Di-zahab" characterizes the narrator as well informed, yet without providing informed readers with a reliable orientation: "The numerous toponyms stated in 1:1–5 are confusing and may only be understood as a faked historical and geo-graphical closeness to the reported incidents."[37] Lothar Perlitt interprets the variety of toponyms as a deception of the readers instead of recog-nizing their significance for fictionality: according to Harald Weinrich, such intentional omission of certain circumstances concerning story place or time belongs to the *"Orientierungssignale"*[38] of fictionality. The toponyms in Deut 1:1–5 remind of locations in the *wilderness*: Suf (סוף) and the Sea of Reeds (ים־סוף), Paran (פארן, Num 12:16; 13:3), Laban (לבן, cf. לבנה, Num 33:20–21) and Hazerot (חצרות, Num 11:35; 12:16; 33:17–18), whereas there is no other biblical reference to Tofel (תפל) and Di-Sahab (די זהב).[39] There is no clear pattern for the order of the toponyms. By means of these allusions Deuteronomy presents the story place as a space in-between: it is located "in the desert"[40] between stations of the *wilderness* and at the same time in the cultivated land of the Arabah—another contradiction, indicating that the quality of the story place as space in-between is more important than its precise localization. Moreover Israel is located "across from the (Sea of) Reeds," the beginning of the wilderness and at the same time across from the "Sea of the End" (from סוף, "end"). The emblematic use of the name Suph along with the spatial vagueness may be considered as another signpost of fictionality.

Finally, there is a third kind of spatial allocation in vv. 2 and 4, one which simultaneously introduces Deut 1–3 and incorporates the story place into the narration of the Pentateuch. Verse 2 refers to the way from

---

37. L. Perlitt, *Deuteronomium* (BKAT V/1–4; Neukirchen–Vluyn: Neukirchener, 1990–2006), 4 (author's translation).

38. Cf. W. Schmid, *Elemente der Narratologie* (2d ed.; Berlin: W. de Gruyter, 2008), 33.

39. Nünning, "Fiktionssignale," 182, interprets "data about place, time and figures without reference" as signals of fiction.

40. Besides *Jordan* and *Moab*, the *wilderness* is a further central Deuteronomic concept of space, which is unfolded in Deut 8:2–4, 15–16 in particular. The "great and awesome wilderness" is the place of extreme dependency on YHWH's care, and thus becomes translucent for the "great and awesome God" (compare Deut 8:15 with Deut 7:21).

Horeb to *Kadesh-Barnea*, the starting point of the conquest of the *Promised Land* (Num 13:26), which should only have taken eleven days.[41] After Num 13–14, the following speech of Moses (1:6–46) explains for a second time what happened to make it take forty years (v. 3). Mention of the Jordanian kingdoms in v. 4 records that Moses' farewell speech is held after the conquest of the land east of the Jordan River (Num 21:21–35).

The localization of the story place in Deut 1:1–5 does not claim to be factual, but serves as an introduction into the spatial structure of the book, which is simultaneously a temporal structure: in the narrated present "beyond the *Jordan*," "in the land of *Moab*" (vv. 1 and 5) Moses speaks to the people of Israel and reminds them of the (narrated) past in the wilderness (v. 1), at *Horeb*, in the mountains of Seir, in *Kadesh-Barnea* (v. 2) and during the conquests of the land east of the *Jordan River* (v. 4). The third level of time—the future of the narrated time, for which Moses proclaims commandments in Deut 12–26, is only implicitly mentioned in this introductory passage. The repeated specification "beyond the Jordan" (vv. 1 and 5) allows the imagining of a future, when Israel will look back from the land on "this side of the *Jordan River*" to their past stay "beyond the Jordan." Mention of the conquests in the land east of the Jordan River makes it clear that the capture of the *Promised Land* has already started. The locations mentioned in Deuteronomy may therefore be translated into time data, allowing the readers an orientation between the analepses and prolepses in Deuteronomy. Moreover, the crucial concepts of space bear theological significance: each of them implies a specific quality of Israel's relationship to God.

The introduction "Moses began to explain this Torah saying" (v. 5), may finally be classified as a signal of metafictionality claiming that the following text will be simultaneously Torah and an explanation of Torah. Similar signals of metafictionality may be found in other introductions of Moses' Deuteronomic speeches, qualifying them as "Torah," as "testimonies, statutes, and judgments" (4:44–46; cf. 5:1; 6:1; 12:1). Thereby the space of narration is expanded to a "space of reflection"[42] which challenges the readers ("all Israel," v. 1) to explore the text's claim on their own lives (also cf. v. 8).

---

41. As to the delocalization of Horeb as a signal of fictionality, cf. section 7.

42. Cf. W. Wolf, "Metafiktion," in Nünning, ed., *Metzlers Lexikon Literatur- und Kulturtheorie*, 447–48 (448).

4. Identification of the Implied Readers
with the People of Moab

The description of the narrative spaces in Deut 1:1–5 will introduce the readers to the book's fictional world. The claim that Moses' speech addresses "all Israel" (v. 1), as well as the fact that it is metafictionally identified as "Torah" (v. 5), points out that Deuteronomy is not only a fictional narration, but aims at involving the implied readers in the narration in more than one way. Sonnet therefore calls Deuteronomy an "act of communication about an act of communication."[43] In Deuteronomy, acts of communication take place on two levels: first, as in any other fictional narration, the narrator addresses him/herself to the implied readers—supposedly "all Israel." Secondly, the narrator presents to the readers a world in which Moses is speaking to the assembled people in *Moab*. Since not only the implied readers but also the textual addressees of Moses are part of "Israel," the narrative communication becomes diffuse: the implied readers, together with the people in Moab, are addressed with the words "Hear, O Israel" (Deut 4:1; 6:4; 9:1), as well as by the almost continuous speech that uses second person singular or plural forms. For the implied readers this effect is intensified the less the people in Moab are present on the textual level. The direct speech to the readers becomes most intense during the course of Deut 12–26, where Moses refers to the narrative context only by introductory comments such as "when you come into the land…" (19:9). In Deut 12–26, Moses as character and his audience in Moab take back seats.

The text pragmatics of identifying the readers with the people "beyond the *Jordan*" is amplified by the spatial dimension. The readers find themselves in the fictive place *Moab* as part of the people that Moses addresses. Since this place is hardly described, but only delineated by toponyms,[44] the readers can create it in their own imagination (synthesis) and thus get involved with the story and Moses' commands. On the other hand, the distance between implied readers and the textual addressees is crucial for the text pragmatics of Deuteronomy. The narrator's remarks repeatedly refer to the fictive context of Moses' speech, which, however, does not accord with the context of the readers. Besides the introductions to the speeches, Deuteronomy additionally uses the metafictional stylistic

---

43. Sonnet, *The Book Within the Book*, 1.

44. According to Deut 1:1 the place is located on the plain (בערבה) and is delimitated by the River Jordan. According to Deut 34:1, Mount Nebo is rising from the "plains of *Moab*" (בערבה מואב cf. 34:8).

device of "frame-breaks,"[45] that is, unexpected comments of the narrator (2:10–12, 20–23; 3:9, 11, 13, 14; 10:6–9) that remind the readers of the text's fictionality: they are distracted from Moses' speech and confronted with their own time and situation (עד היום הזה, "to this day," 3:14). Such distancing between the narrated world and the readers creates a space of reflection and allows the readers to conceptualize references between the two worlds. Through the abrupt change between identification and distance in the book's beginning chapters, the readers become accustomed to a reading strategy that simultaneously immerses them into the fictional world and urges them to relate this world to their own.

5. *The Deuteronomic Commandments as a Fictive Speech of Moses*

For the readers of Deuteronomy it must be evident that the commandments proclaimed in Deut 12–26 target a spatial structure other than the narrated space of *Moab*. They assume that the addressees do have *houses* (22:8), subsist on mixed farming (14:22–23; 15:19–23) in fortified places with *gates* (14:23–24), that they do have a court of the elders (25:7–10) and celebrate their feasts at a central *place* (16:1–17). This tension is not resolved, but is merely explained by the construct that Moses has already received from God at *Horeb* the final commandments, which are applicable for the future life in the *Promised Land* (5:27–31), and that he now passes them on to "all Israel" before they enter the *land* (6:1–3; cf. section 7). The text of the commandments rarely reflects this future perspective, except in introductions like "when you come into the land that YHWH, your God is giving you…" (18:9), or when talking about the "place that YHWH will choose" (12:5). Nonetheless, the formulation of the commandments assumes that they would be fulfilled immediately.

In Deut 12–26, the commandments themselves do not have a fictional character. A series of requests (second person singular or plural) is combined with paraenetic elements to motivate the readers to fulfill them (cf. 15:15, 18). The inclusion of the commandments into a fictional narration leads to a fundamental change in their function: "A legislative text becomes a fictional text—the legislative text turns into literature and

---

45. With regard to Deuteronomy, R. Polzin, *Moses and the Deuteronomist: A Literary Study of the Deuteronomistic History: Part 1. Deuteronomy, Joshua, Judges* (New York: Seabury, 1980), 31, receives this definition from the sociologist Erving Goffman: "…frame-breaks of this kind are a frequent device by which an author/editor, even of an ancient work, may involve his readers more in his message."

is thus exempt from the juridical context."[46] Thus the commandments do not claim to be directly applicable for the readers, since in the first place they are relevant in the context of the fictional narration. The relevance of the commandments for the situation of the readers can only be determined through a creative act of reading.

The process of reading starts by first taking into consideration the difference between the space that the commandments presuppose and the spatial setting of the assembly in Moab and then the difference between the respective contexts of the individual readers in comparison to the situation assumed in the commandments. According to Crüsemann, these differences may have been relatively unimportant as far as the pre-exilic Deuteronomy is concerned,[47] but the "draft constitution"[48] was probably not that congruent to reality. As to the exilic Deuteronomy, the contextual differences must have played a major role: in exile, there did not exist a central place attributed to God's presence, nor constitutional institutions like a king, a central court and a "prophet like Moses."[49] The identification with the people in Moab would therefore be more likely, since the exilic readers, too, lived outside the land, without a governmental structure, but organized in families (cf. the elders in 5:23; 27:1; 29:9). In sum, the fictional structure of the final Deuteronomic text provides links to different reading contexts.[50]

The process of reading is challenged, however, by two opposing signals of the text: on the one hand, the readers are requested to fulfill the commandments by identifying themselves with the people of *Moab*; on the other hand, the difference of context prohibits the immediate application of the commandments. The fictionalizing act creates a "doubling

---

46. So states Liss, "Kanon," 30, in relation to the inclusion of legislative texts into the priestly work (author's translation).

47. Cf. Crüsemann, *Tora*, 242–51.

48. Ibid., 273.

49. Nevertheless, these three positions were filled. Jehoiachin lived at the Babylonian court and was accepted as king; cf. R. Albertz, *Die Exilszeit: 6. Jahrhundert v. Chr.* (BE 7; Stuttgart: Kohlhammer, 2001), 90; the independent court organization was replaced by the limited function of the elders (ibid., 114) and prophets, too, appeared in exile—but with contradictory messages, however, and not fulfilling the function of "a prophet like Moses" (cf. the prophets Ahab son of Kolaiah and Zedekiah son of Maaseiah in Jer 29:21–22, Ezekiel, and the group of Second Isaiah).

50. In exile the empathy with Moses is an essential reading strategy, see R. Lux, "Der Tod des Mose als 'besprochene und erzählte Welt': Überlegungen zu einer literaturwissenschaftlichen und theologischen Interpretation von Deuteronomium 32,48–52 und 34," *ZTK* 84 (1987): 395–425, and Geiger, *Gottesräume*, 75–81.

structure," a conscious coexistence of the narrated world and the world of the readers: "The doubling structure of these fictionalizing acts creates the area of play by holding on to everything that has been overstepped, thus making it a partner in the game of countermoves."[51] A space of reflection is created, which provides the opportunity of finding inventive possibilities of fulfilling the commandments. The fulfillment of the commandments requires more than mere execution and becomes a creative act performed repeatedly by the readers in their individual contexts. The fictionalizing act is almost a condition for the timeless validity of the commandments, as stated by Mirja Kutzer concerning prophetic texts: "The original function of reference, resulting from a concrete situation, is exempted, so that the once proclaimed word of the prophet will remain important and valid. The fictionalizing act is almost the presupposition to endow significance to the text over all time and to make the word of the prophet universal."[52] The fictionality of the Deuteronomic commandments in the narration of *Moab* entails an infinite process of interpretation, which consistently aims at actualizing these commandments. The Deuteronomic fiction combines the absolute claim of validity with the liberty of situational realization without canceling each other.

6. *Imaginary Spaces for the Creation of Concrete Spaces*

The Deuteronomic commandments offer instructions to shape the spaces in the *Promised Land*, which belong to the future of the narrated time. The spacing (Martina Löw) intended in the commandments revolves around the *gates* and the *place* to be chosen. All Deuteronomic feasts will be celebrated in common at the place "that YHWH, your God, will choose to put his name there" (14:24 etc.). The presence of YHWH there (synthesis) is only put into effect by the actions of people (spacing) performed with reference to the presence of God (לפני יהוה): "you shall eat there before YHWH your God, and you shall rejoice, you and your house(hold)!" (14:26 etc.). The common feast constitutes the synthesis conceptualizing all families as "you" (second person singular or plural), as counterpart of YHWH, including foreigners, widows and orphans (16:11 etc.). The repeated change of focus in Deut 12, the beginning of the Deuteronomic law, establishes the connection between the *place* to be chosen (מקום, 12:5, 11, 13, 18, 21, 27) and the gates (שערים, 12:12, 15, 17, 18, 22), the Deuteronomic expression for settlements. The focus

---

51. Iser, *The Fictive*, 229.
52. Kutzer, *Wahrheit*, 196 (author's translation).

on "your gates" (12:12 singular; 12:15 plural) originates from the perspective of the central sanctuary, so that all *gates* in the *land* are
allocated to the addressed community of Israel.[53] From this perspective
oriented towards community, the Levites, foreigners, orphans and
widows (14:29) are all part of the *gate* community, who will provide
them at least triennially with the tithe. In Deuteronomy, the spatial
concept of the *gates* always implies the synthesis of the gate community
as a space of responsibility. The commandments thus create the fiction
or—according to Martina Löw—the synthesis of a world where all
spacing is performed in reference to the presence of God (cf. Deut 6:4–9)
so that YHWH's presence will be spread all over the land and will lead to
social justice for the whole community. The synthesis will be interpreted
as realization of the fundamental spacing act of YHWH who liberated
Israel from *Egypt*, from the *house* of slavery (5:6; 15:15).The social
order of Deuteronomy has repeatedly been characterized as "utopian."
Gustav Hölscher was the first to call the Deuteronomic laws "ideal
demands" which were "impracticable."[54] The concept of utopia assumes
that there is an ideal place or time where the text of the commandments
and the context will come together and the discrepancy between the two
will be offset. In contrast, the emphasis of fictionality aims at using the
discrepancy as a starting point for new contextual interpretations. The
difference between the two concepts is not fundamental, however, since
according to the understanding of the Old Testament a utopia may open
up new vistas "in which direction the concrete praxis has to go in *hic et
nunc*, since hope guides the action."[55] A fictional understanding of the
Deuteronomic commandments emphasizes that it is not desirable to form
a society by literally applying the law. In fact, the adaptation of the commandments to one's own reality is sought after: the imaginary, shaped in
these commandments, may activate new forms of realization. This is
specific for fictionality, since it "constitutes a possible world and enables
an understanding of reality based on its possibilities."[56] According to the
Deuteronomic spatial conception, this effect is generated by the presence
of God at *Horeb*, which guarantees the validity of these commandments.

---

53. Cf. E. Otto, "שער," *ThWAT* 8 (1995): 358–403 (376): "The continuous pl.
š°āréká voices the perspective of an observer who looks from a central perspective
over the variety of settlements in the land" (author's translation).

54. G. Hölscher, "Komposition und Ursprung des Deuteronomiums," *ZAW* 40
(1922): 161–255 (227).

55. K. Koenen, "Eschatologie (AT)," *WiBiLex* (January 2007), www.wibilex.de,
section 3.3 (accessed May 15, 2012) (author's translation).

56. Kutzer, *Wahrheit*, 214 (author's translation).

7. Horeb *as "Generative Matrix" (Iser)* *of the Deuteronomic Fiction*

Deuteronomy's conception of space originates in the presence of God at *Horeb*.[57] During his farewell speech, Moses reminds the assembled people three times of the sojourn at *Horeb* (4:10–14; 5:2–31; 9:7–10:11), where YHWH proclaimed the Deuteronomic commandments to Moses. According to Deuteronomic fiction, the mediation via Moses is made by the people's own demand, for they were afraid of the presence of God (5:5, 23–27) and appointed Moses as mediator (with God's approval 5:28–31). The presence of God at *Horeb* has no beginning—unlike Exod 19:18, 20; 34:5, God descending to the mountain (ירד) is not mentioned[58]—and there is no end to the presence of God as in Exod 19–34. Each time Moses reminds his addressees of *Horeb*, the mountain is characterized as "burning in fire" (ההר בער באש, 4:11; 5:23; 9:15). There is no further description of the space than the fire "to the heart of heaven" (4:11) and "darkness, cloud, and obscurity" (4:11; 5:22, 23). The spacing of the protagonists creates the spatial concept *Horeb*. The people remain "at the foot of the mountain" (4:11; 5:5; 9:16, 17) while Moses respectively ascends (עלה, 9:9; 10:3) and descends (ירד, 9:15; 10:5) three times in order to prostrate himself before YHWH (ואתנפל לפני יהוה, 9:18, with reference to the first sojourn, as well as 9:25). These spacing acts amplify the particularity of the place, to which only Moses, but not the people, may accede. The synthesis of this space includes the presence of God, which causes Moses to prostrate himself and the people to react with awe and fear (5:5, 25, 26, 29).[59]

Since the generation of adults present at Horeb had to die in the wilderness (1:35–40; 2:14–15), the people assembled in *Moab* cannot remember the incident at *Horeb*. Moses nevertheless narrates the incidents at *Horeb* in the second person plural, so that the addressees are identified with the generation at *Horeb*: "Face to face YHWH spoke with you at the mountain out of the midst of the fire" (5:4); "When you heard the voice out of the midst of the darkness, while the mountain was burning with fire, you came near to me, all the heads of your tribes and

---

57. For the spatial concept *Horeb*, cf. Geiger, *Gottesräume*, 295–98, 215–23.

58. Cf. also Exod 24:16 (שכן); Exod 33:19, 22 (עבר) for the beginning of the presence of God.

59. I. Wilson, *Out of the Midst of the Fire: Divine Presence in Deuteronomy* (SBLDS 151; Atlanta: Scholars Press, 1995), 58, states: "...the emphasis is on the people as those who have experienced the divine communication 'out of the midst of the fire'."

your elders…" (5:23). In spite of the logical contradiction, this construction works on the level of fiction, since by the mediation of Moses' speech his audience in *Moab* is flashed back into the presence of God at *Horeb* and will therefore be able to remember it later. This identification is continued on a second level: since the Deuteronomic construction identifies the readers of the book with the people in *Moab*, the readers, too, are taken back to *Horeb*. This creates a hermeneutic circle: in *Moab* Moses communicates the words of God at *Horeb*, "Beyond the Jordan in the land of Moab, Moses began to explain this Torah saying: YHWH, our God, spoke to us at the Horeb saying…" (1:5–6), and thus takes all readers back to God's presence at Horeb. The introduction of Deuteronomy emphasizes the fictive character of the spatial concept *Horeb*: it is not possible to locate this exact place with the description of Deut 1:2. The Sinai/Horeb, originally connected with the mountains of Seir (Deut 33:2; cf. Judg 5:4),[60] is located several day trips away from Seir, and its location can no longer be found. Due to the delocalization of the mountain, the way back into the presence of God is only possible by means of the fictional text. The presence of God at Horeb receives gestalt by this fictionality and at the same time is interpreted as the original place of the text. According to Iser, the presence of God belongs to the imaginary, which "attains its concreteness and its effectiveness by way of the fictive"[61] without being absorbed by the fictive. But the "open structures within the linguistic patterning"[62] enable the imaginary to unfold its presence. Iser also formulates a hermeneutic circle: "From this fact we can deduce one last achievement of the fictive in the fictional text: It brings about the presence of the imaginary by transgressing language itself. In outstripping what conditions it, the imaginary reveals itself as the generative matrix of the text."[63] The presence of God, which assumes a gestalt *Horeb*, may be understood simultaneously as generative matrix and ultimate destination of the Deuteronomic fiction. The fictional presence of God may not be placed on the same level as the imaginary; but it is rather the difference between the various spaces in the text and their relation to the reality of the readers which strives for the creative actualization of the imaginary.

60. Cf. L. Perlitt, "Sinai und Horeb," in Perlitt, *Deuteronomium-Studien*, 32–49 (42).
61. Iser, *The Fictive*, 20.
62. Ibid., 21.
63. Ibid.

8. *The Deuteronomic Metafiction:*
"The Book within the Book"[64]

The double function of *Horeb* for the text of Deuteronomy is reflected metafictionally, since the book makes an issue of the formation of its own text. This happens in several steps. The writing of Deuteronomy begins at *Horeb*: after its verbal proclamation (5:6–21), the Decalogue is written down on two tablets of stone (4:13; 5:22; 9:10) by YHWH personally, "with the finger of God" (9:10). After the destruction of the tablets by Moses, YHWH writes it down a second time (10:2, 4). This time, however, the tablets are kept in a wooden ark to protect them and have them ready for transportation (10:5). Sonnet calls this a "translation journey"[65]—the Ten Words are "translated" in their ark, and thus converted from the context of the presence of God at *Horeb* to the context of the *Promised Land*. The ark with the tablets of stone thus represents a material connection with the presence of God at *Horeb*, without being a space where God is present. The logic of Deuteronomy calls for the oral transmission of God's speech at *Horeb* in *Moab*, because Moses as mediator will not cross the *Jordan*. According to Deut 31:9, Moses writes "this Torah" down (cf. 1:5) in *Moab* and hands it over to the Levitical priests. After adding the song of Deut 32 in 31:22, the "book of the Torah" will not be put into the ark of covenant but next to it. The narration about the formation of the book accepts the logical contradiction that the "book" is already completed (31:24), while the Deuteronomic narrator continues reporting about the blessing and death of Moses (33; 34). It is crucial for the Deuteronomic fiction that Moses himself wrote the book of Deuteronomy and gave instructions regarding how to pass it on (31:9–13).

The manner in which the book is passed on links it with its origin at *Horeb*. "This Torah" shall be read every seven years when Israel gathers for the Feast of Booths in the presence of God. The parallel phrasing reminds readers of the assembly at *Horeb* (4:10): the people shall be gathered (הקהל את־העם, 4:10; 31:12), to hear (שמע), to learn (למד) to fear (ירא, 4:10; 31:12, 13) and to preserve (שמר, 4:13; 31:12). The assembly at *Horeb* reaches its aim only with the covenant in *Moab* (5:2, 3; 29:9–14) and this first context of the proclamation is updated by reading it at the *place* to be chosen (31:9–13; cf. the assembly consisting of the elders, women, men, children and foreigners in 29:9, 10;

---

64. Quoting the title of Sonnet's book about writing in Deuteronomy.
65. Sonnet, *The Book Within the Book*, 67.

31:11, 12). The reading of the book of Torah written down by Moses in *Moab* will thus bring to mind the context of the first proclamation of the words to the people, as well as the context of the first writing down of the Ten Commandments by God himself (10:4) and finally the proclamation to Moses at *Horeb*.

Moses' writing will be continued by the writing of the addressed persons. "Moses' command 'you shall write' is an ingenious way of transcending the limitations of time and space… Projecting his words beyond the river Jordan, Moses projects them also beyond his death."[66] Moses' addressees are requested to write "all words of this Torah" (27:3, 8) on limed stones on the Mount *Gerizim* after crossing the River *Jordan* and thereby connecting them to the *land*. Besides the combination of "these words" with the space of all Israel, spatial connections with the smaller social units of *gate* and *house* communities have to be established. Deuteronomy 6:9 requests the writing of "these words…on the doorposts of your house and on your gates" and 6:8 defines the actual *bodies* of the addressed as textual spaces. The king receives a special responsibility for "this Torah" (17:18): he has to write a copy and read it "all days of his life" (17:19). In sum, all textual spaces are repeatedly connected to the central *place* of the presence of God (cf. בית in 12:7).[67]

The metafiction finds a response in another fictional text, 2 Kgs 22:8–14, which narrates, from the perspective of Deuteronomy, how the "book of Torah" (ספר התורה, Deut 1:5; 31:24–26) will be retrieved in a far distant future. The reading of the book and its acknowledgment by the prophet Huldah (2 Kgs 22:14–20) prompts the amanuensis Shaphan and King Josiah to hold an assembly like the one in Deut 31:9–13, in order to renew the covenant before YHWH (לפני יהוה). This fictional narration shows how the Deuteronomic commandments are given a new context and how they are adapted to a changed situation. From the perspective of fictionality, the repeatedly observed differences of the Deuteronomic conception compared to the Josianic reform may be considered as a biblical example of an actualizing interpretation of the commandments. In the book of Deuteronomy, arrangements are made for the process of its tradition. The passing on of the book will take place in reference to the relevant spaces in the *Promised Land* and in connection with the presence of God at *Horeb*. The metafictional staging exceeds the limits of the book: the text of Deuteronomy is not only written on a scroll (31:24),

---

66. Ibid., 95.
67. For the connection between *gates* and the *place* to be chosen, see above, section 6.

but also on tablets of stone (10:4), on huge limed stones (27:2, 4, 8), on the walls of *gates* (6:9) and *houses* (6:9). And finally, the text has to be connected to the very *bodies* of the addressed persons (6:8). The application of the text to particular spaces covers all living spaces so that the readers can develop a relationship to the content of the narration as well as to "these words" themselves. The beginning of the formation of the book is related to God himself and thus subject to great significance.[68] Moses guarantees the tradition "up to its completeness" (31:24). Finally, the celebration of writing serves as a symbolic appreciation of the process of dissemination, which participates in the first formation of the book and thus leads back to the presence of God at *Horeb*.

9. *Conclusion: Fictionality and Space*

As this study has demonstrated, the intertwining of fictionality and space plays a central role for the pragmatics of Deuteronomy. First, the book's spatial dimension provides decisive clues for disclosing Deuteronomy's fictionality. Both the spatial signals of fictionality in the introduction (Deut 1:1–5) and the contradiction between the spatial conceptions of the narrative and the embedded commandments are crucial for the fictional self-disclosure. Moreover, the lucid spatial structure allows the readers to orient themselves between the different time levels of the narration as well as between the book's context and their own.

Secondly, a fictional understanding of Deuteronomy affects the legal hermeneutics. Whereas Deuteronomy aims at shaping the readers' contexts according to the book's spatial theology, fictionality subjects this potentially totalitarian claim to the proviso of contextuality. The Deuteronomic commandments thus attain an inventive character, which exceeds their literal application. Depending on the specific context of the readers, only certain elements of this spatial conception may be implemented, while others are modified by the process of reading in subsequent generations. Yet the fictional character of the book both enshrines the idea of a world entirely shaped by the relationship to God and at the same time submits it to contextual interpretation.

Finally, the analysis of fictionality and space in Deuteronomy leads to the generative matrix of the text, which is linked to the spatial concept *Horeb*. *Horeb* is staged as the origin of the Deuteronomic text, as the reflections on the book's metafictionality have revealed, and

---

68. Wolf, "Metafiktion," 448, denotes the "celebration of the narration or the narrator" as one of the functions of metafictionality.

simultaneously as the origin of the imaginary presence of God, which grounds and enables the whole Deuteronomic conception. In a hermeneutic circle, the Deuteronomic fiction "endows the Imaginary with an articulate gestalt"[69] and traces its theological validity back to the same.

69. Iser, *The Fictive*, 3.

CRITICAL SPATIAL THEORY 2.0

Matthew Sleeman

1. *Introduction*

As a mode of interpretation within biblical studies, critical spatial theory is now over a decade old. From its substantive origins in the SBL/AAR Constructions of Ancient Space Seminar (2000–2005), its rapid evolution evades a single or simple overview.[1] Rather than attempting such a retrospective survey, the present study addresses the present state and future prospects for scholarly exploration of biblical spatialities. In so doing, it projects a continuity and a sea change in such readings, the advent of "Critical Spatial Theory 2.0" (hereafter CST 2.0).

Labeling this maturation within biblical studies as CST 2.0 deliberately echoes "Web 2.0." Rather than replacing the worldwide web that preceded it, Web 2.0, a term originating in 1999, marks a constellation of inter-related but independent developments in software development and use of the web.[2] Initially, this could only be anticipated in part, as a prototypical proof of the concept, but Web 2.0 has transformed the web into more interactive and collaborative user networks.

By analogy, what I propose here is not one singular project, but a shift in perspective and sensibility towards a richer and more dynamic understanding of spatiality within biblical studies. Labeling it CST 2.0 signals both continuity and discontinuity with what has gone before, with what would thus be termed CST 1.0. Such terminology also hints deliberately at subsequent manifestations, at 3.0 and beyond. Equally, many of the developments identified here are already underway, at least in embryonic

---

1. Cf., e.g., J. L. Berquist, "Introduction: Critical Spatiality and the Uses of Theory," in *Constructions of Space I: Theory, Geography, and Narrative* (ed. J. L. Berquist and C. V. Camp; LHBOTS 481; New York/London: T&T Clark International, 2007), 1–12.

2. D. DiNucci, "Fragmented Future," *Print* 53, no. 4 (1999): 32 and 221–22 (32). For a Web 2.0 account of itself, see the Wikipedia entry on "Web 2.0."

form or in isolation from one another: CST 2.0 is a lens to view them together, and to harness the synergies that the parts can offer. Thus, this is an exercise in coalescing existing trajectories around a heuristic label, rather than an individual pioneering of a new line of discourse.

The result, like Web 2.0, will not be driven by central service-providers, by authoritative theoreticians of space. Instead, end-users, Bible interpreters, will generate new spatial readings, which, in turn, will reconfigure wider, broader, deeper, more dynamic spatial discourses than those produced under the conditions of CST 1.0. This will, in turn, generate renewed debate as to what holds such readings together and, indeed, whether such cohesions are to be sought or to be resisted.

Unavoidably, predictions will, in parts, prove to be a failed attempt at crystal ball gazing. First, my view is partial, and leans unapologetically towards the New Testament. This reflects my own research interests, but also I note CST 1.0 making a lesser impact on New Testament studies. That said, I fully anticipate parallel and further developments in connection with the Hebrew Bible. Second, the inevitable time lag in bringing an essay to publication risks hard print appearing outdated from the start. Yet this delay will itself prove illuminating, as will its printed context among other, yet unseen, chapters, so it is not a reason to decline the exercise. Without a doubt, CST 2.0 will prove to be much bigger, much less mappable, than this or any other brief account can contain.

I will address these present realities and future prospects under three sections. The first section travels back into the spatial turn, the broad spatialization of many scholarly disciplines since the mid-1990s. It revisits the works of three key spatial theorists who informed its impact in biblical studies, namely Henri Lefebvre, David Harvey and Edward Soja. It seeks out more nuanced appropriations of their work, probing how biblical spatialities might themselves reflexively reshape spatial theory. In so doing, this section inhabits the original spaces of CST 1.0, but also strains their paradigmatic bounds.

The second section recircles the wider spatial turn, especially the aquifers of human geography from which it sprang. CST 2.0, I suggest, needs a wider and more on-going reconnection with the geographical and other spatial disciplines, since there is much more within these discourses, which can and should be drawn into reading biblical texts for their spaces. Simultaneously these discourses are neither static nor neutral: thus, a reflexive interdisciplinary sensibility needs to be fostered and developed.

The final section indicates some wider interstices within biblical studies where spatial readings can multiply. Such pluralist sites mark CST 2.0's resistance to discursive delimitation. Simultaneously, this calls for a comprehensive rethinking of the spatial and triggers consideration as to whether there is a singularity of thought that can be labeled CST 2.0. Recognition of this tension is something that the 2.0 label is intended to encapsulate, but not control.

2. *Looking Back at the Spatial Turn*

The first wave of critical spatial theory within biblical studies was part of a wider, transdisciplinary awakening to the importance of space within the humanities and social sciences since the mid-1990s, now known as the spatial turn.[3] This retrospective labeling and narration provokes CST 2.0 to make an on-going reassessment of the trajectory of this turn, and the place of biblical studies within it.

CST 1.0 drew strongly on the legacy of Henri Lefebvre, both directly and through two influential spatial theorists, who built on his work, David Harvey and Edward Soja.[4] With that in mind, CST 2.0 will need to revisit these original "fathers" of spatial theory, to reappraise their ongoing contributions to this field. Lefebvre specialist Stuart Elden comments, "It would be harsh, but perhaps not unfair, to suggest that Lefebvre's work may have suffered as a *result* of being…appropriated for a certain type of academic work by certain types of scholars."[5] Although beyond Elden's scope, I suggest that biblical scholars should *properly* be implicated in his carefully balanced charge. Yes, Lefebvre's work deserves respect but, also, it needs critiquing *by* biblical texts and scholarship.

3. For a survey of the reach and progress of the spatial turn, see B. Warf and S. Arias, eds., *The Spatial Turn: Interdisciplinary Perspectives* (London: Routledge. 2009).

4. Biblical scholars have made some occasional use of other geographers. For an extended and insightful appropriation of Robert Sack's geographical theory, see B. Bruehler, *A Public and Political Christ: The Socio-Spatial Characteristics of Luke 18:35–19:43 and the Gospel as a Whole in Its Ancient Context* (Eugene: Pickwick, 2011), as well as his "Reading Zechariah with Soja and Sack," a paper presented at the SBL Annual Meeting, New Orleans, November 21, 2009. Although not a geographer, Michel Foucault provides biblical studies with spatial sensibility which helps avert an ongoing danger for CST 2.0, namely, "crowning space at the expense of an impoverished historical understanding," so S. Elden, "Politics, Philosophy, Geography: Henri Lefebvre in Recent Anglo-American Scholarship," *Antipode* 10, no. 2 (2001): 809–25 (817).

5. Elden, "Politics," 820.

a. *Henri Lefebvre*

Lefebvre's death in 1991 coincided with an English translation of his most significant work on space.[6] "Most significant" is an Anglophone assessment, since the vast majority of this wide-ranging and influential thinker's nearly seventy books remain untranslated and, to my knowledge, no biblical scholar has made substantial use of Lefebvre's broader *oeuvre*.[7] This reflects, in part, that *The Production of Space* remains a dense text, even in translation, and the breadth of Lefebvre's interests and perspectives appears daunting.[8] It assumes Lefebvre's decades of prior writing and reflection, and is best understood within his ongoing works. For those willing to explore further, his posthumously published *Rhythmanalysis*, with its focus on holding space and time together within everyday life, is promising for CST 2.0 especially where it focuses on Mediterranean cities, both modern and ancient, and thus comes close to biblical urban forms.[9]

Always, however, Lefebvre retains a distance from biblical texts. In his youth, he rejected the Roman Catholic Church, which had informed his upbringing.[10] A limited appreciation of it remained, albeit within a Nietzschian frame of reference, as frequently the only public space, a political and social hub as well as a religious center, for rural communities.[11] Time might still belong to religion, long after the secularizing impulses of progress and revolution had plucked space from its grasp,[12]

---

6. H. Lefebvre, *The Production of Space* (trans. D. Nicholson-Smith; Oxford: Blackwell, 1991 [1974]).

7. For surveys, see R. Shields, *Lefebvre, Love and Struggle: Spatial Dialectics* (New York: Routledge, 1999); A. Merrifield, *Henri Lefebvre: A Critical Introduction* (New York: Routledge, 2006).

8. Elden, "Politics," 816, criticizes Soja (through whom many biblical scholars approach Lefebvre), for presenting too narrow a reading of Lefebvre, focused excessively on the first chapter of *The Production of Space*. Cf. Shields, *Lefebvre*, which Elden, "Politics," 818–20, judges to provide a better introduction to Lefebvre than that offered by Soja.

9. H. Lefebvre, *Rhythmanalysis: Space, Time and Everyday Life* (trans. S. Elden and G. Moore; London: Continuum, 2004 [1992]), 87–100. This section, co-authored with Catherine Régulier, Lefebvre's wife, was originally published as "Essai de rythmanalyse des villes méditerranéens," *Peuples Méditerranéens* 37 (1986).

10. See, e.g., Merrifield, *Lefebvre*, xxviii, 6, 116, 167.

11. S. Elden, *Understanding Henri Lefebvre: Theory and the Possible* (London: Continuum, 2004), 138–39, 170–72.

12. H. Lefebvre, *Introduction to Modernity: Twelve Preludes* (trans. J. Moore; London: Verso, 1995), 68.

but, for him, biblical ideas reflect an inferior dualistic analysis outdated and overwhelmed by dialectical thought.[13]

Thus Lefebvre's mercurial aperture for life renders religion and religious texts as marginal actors, residual influences, primarily rural spaces. Religion is silenced in his work on urban space, the very juncture at which biblical scholars have encountered him. This does not negate Lefebvre's influence in biblical studies, but does caution against an uncritical appropriation of it. The disjuncture may be a creative, generative one, but it is a dissonance that is best held consciously in view.

b. *David Harvey*

Like Lefebvre, David Harvey's influence on CST 1.0 rests on one publication within a wider corpus of works, and typically, he is cited within CST 1.0 for his similarities with Lefebvre's tripartite schema of space.[14] Yet arguably, Harvey has been the most influential human geographer of the past 40 years, and he does not simply replicate Lefebvre's thought. Given these observations, do Harvey's ongoing writings provide further sustenance for CST 2.0?

Initially, like Lefebvre, Harvey appears to offer no sustained interactions with biblical spaces. Nevertheless, his many writings show isolated instances, which integrate biblical concerns (*qua* biblical concerns) within his formulations of space.[15]

Admittedly, such instances remain isolated from the mainstream of Harvey's argumentation, which remains "secularist,"[16] but biblical texts are sometimes momentarily foregrounded. Thus, *Justice, Nature and the Geography of Difference* opens with Harvey reflecting on his juxtaposed experiences of two events sharing the same hotel: a meeting of Pentecostal preachers, and a conference on globalization.[17] Interestingly, the

---

13. Lefebvre, *Rhythmanalysis*, 11. Cf. p. 94, regarding religious rites within the Mediterranean city.

14. D. Harvey, *The Condition of Postmodernity* (Oxford: Blackwell, 1990), 219–22.

15. For now dated examples, see M. Clark and M. Sleeman, "Writing the Earth, Righting the Earth: Committed Presuppositions and the Geographical Imagination," in *New Words, New Worlds: Reconceptualising Social and Cultural Geography* (ed. C. Philo; Lampeter: Social and Cultural Geography Study Group, 1991), 49–60 (50–51).

16. G. McLennan, "Postsecular Cities and Radical Critique: A Philosophical Sea Change?," in *Postsecular Cities: Space, Theory and Practice* (ed. J. Beaumont and C. Baker; London: Continuum, 2011), 15–30 (16; cf. 28–29).

17. D. Harvey, *Justice, Nature and the Geography of Difference* (Oxford: Blackwell, 1996), 1–15.

former provides a critique of the latter, via a critique filtered through the parable of the sheep and the goats in Matt 25:31–46. While restricted to the book's introduction, even this would be unimaginable from Lefebvre. Other allusions, whether witting or unwitting, also occur: thus, paralleling Ecclesiastes, Harvey laments that "nobody quite knows what "the right time and place for everything" might be," elsewhere claiming that "the common-sense notion that there is 'a time and a place for everything'" still carries weight.[18]

The metaphor of weight is appropriate for the historical (and geographical) materialist impulse, which Harvey never deserts. It runs through to his search for "a better cosmopolitan theory,"[19] casting him as a fellow traveler, working alongside biblical texts even if not within them.

c. *Edward W. Soja*

Compared with Harvey, Soja has engaged in far more sustained dialogue regarding biblical concerns. In general, this has been with theologians rather than biblical scholars, but the insights are informative for CST 2.0. Also, these interactions cast retrospective light back onto Lefebvre, the initial spur for Soja's formulations.

As was the case with Lefebvre and Harvey, CST 1.0 has focused on one of Soja's works, but *Thirdspace* is the middle part of a trilogy. Both it and *Postmetropolis* build, deliberately, on a first volume, *Postmodern Geographies*, which offers much to CST 2.0.[20] *Postmetropolis* has proved the least influential within biblical studies. Tracing at length Soja's projections regarding Los Angeles as the archetype for the post-modern urban future, its interests travel away from the predominant gaze of biblical studies.[21]

Although these divergences have led CST 1.0 to show limited interest in Soja after *Thirdspace*, his more recent writings can rejuvenate CST 2.0. Here, two inter-related trajectories inform spatial readings of biblical

---

18. Harvey, *Postmodernity*, 239, 216, respectively.

19. D. Harvey, *Cosmopolitanism and the Geographies of Freedom* (New York: Columbia University Press, 2009).

20. E. W. Soja, *Postmodern Geographies: The Reassertion of Space in Critical Social Theory* (London: Verso, 1989); *Thirdspace: Journeys to Los Angeles and Other Real-and-Imagined Places* (Oxford/Malden, Mass.: Blackwell, 1996); and *Postmetropolis: Critical Studies of Cities and Regions* (Malden, Mass.: Blackwell, 2000).

21. Cf. Beaumont and Baker, eds., *Postsecular Cities*, 256–58. For a concise overview of *Postmetropolis*, see E. W. Soja, "Beyond *Postmetropolis*," *Urban Geography* 32, no. 4 (2011): 451–69 (454–55).

texts. First, he has engaged directly with theologians, in conference and in print. Second, Soja has—with substantial reason—reflected on his own part in provoking the spatial turn and its role in his own ongoing maturation as a spatial theorist. Engagement with biblical studies has informed this reflection, marked by a surprise at the interest in his work among biblical scholars.[22] Both these trajectories can empower CST 2.0 for new and creative engagements with Soja.

The retrospective narration of the spatial turn has already been noted; also, inescapably, it occurs from a particular standpoint. By its very nature, it is an influence "from somewhere," impacting differently in different locales, and so an inevitable positionality attaches to any telling of its process and progress. This intensifies when Soja addresses the spatial turn within biblical studies. Soja, although a deliberate disciplinary nomad, observes biblical studies as an outsider. Without privileging the emic perspective, his etic standpoint regarding CST 1.0 merits a heightened rhetorical sensibility.

Such a sensibility problematizes a taken-for-granted hierarchy and core-periphery that position "more specialized spatial turns" within the (otherwise capitalized) Spatial Turn.[23] Singularity and capitalization infers substantive emphasis and, potentially, a colonizing core. While Soja readily acknowledges that the spatial turn decenters disciplinary privileges,[24] a rhetorical marginalizing of biblical and theological studies remains. For instance, his surprise at eschatology's spatial awareness, an area that he separates from biblical studies, confirms its assumed marginalization, via rhetorical questions and wordplays.[25]

As a second and related observation, Soja's construal of critical spatiality makes its own implicit ultimate claims. These do not remain

22. E. W. Soja, "Taking Space Personally," in Warf and Arias, eds., *The Spatial Turn*, 11–35 (28). Soja also expressed such surprise in response to my thesis concerning the spatial implications arising from Jesus' ascension into heaven as recounted in Acts 1:6–11 (personal communication, November 2005). Cf. M. Sleeman, *Geography and the Ascension Narrative in Acts* (Cambridge: Cambridge University Press, 2009), 68–81.

23. Soja, "Personally," 26, referring to Jewish spatialities.

24. Ibid., 24–25.

25. Ibid., 28: "I had become aware that my work was being widely used in Bible [*sic*] studies...but eschatology? What was going on here?... The Spatial Turn had seemingly reached its outer limits." Eschatology is both inherently biblical and unavoidably spatial. T. J. Gorringe, "The Decline of Nature: Natural Theology, Theology of Nature, and the Built Environment," in *Without Nature? A New Condition for Theology* (ed. D. Albertson and C. King; New York: Fordham University Press, 2010), 203–20 (215), asserts, provocatively: "What geographers call the 'spatial turn' was, curiously, already anticipated by Karl Barth in 1937."

neutral when brought into contact with biblical spatialities: they declare
their own presuppositional hierarchy which both contacts and conflicts
with the presuppositions arising within the biblical texts themselves. Just
as Soja has been criticized for his localized particularism,[26] so too a
biblical critique can appropriate and amend his work.[27] These presuppositions remain submerged in Soja's earlier works, but emerge in his more
reflective recent writings. For instance, his assertion of "urban causality"
renders the city as a transcendental force in its own right.[28] As such, it
becomes one of the "powers," subjected to sustained theological critique
at numerous junctures within the Hebrew Bible and the New Testament.
Concurrently, Soja's adoption of "first nature" (the biosphere) and
"second nature" (the urban) reveals a Deistic construal of space.[29]

On one level, this is unsurprising. It fits with the predominantly
secular worldview which Soja shares with Lefebvre and Harvey, even as
his grand narrative of urbanization mirrors (mimics?) the biblical space–
time drama.[30] Yet, on another level, Soja's theological construal of space
is critically unsettling in a manner, which CST 2.0 needs to accommodate or address.

It is now widely recognized that even the most stridently secular
theory rests on ultimate, unprovable, assumptions.[31] In this light, it is
telling that Soja's projected first and second natures lack a *third* nature,
one akin to biblical divine agency. Clearly, its absence fits with his
schema's Hegelian precursors, but it also stands at odds with biblical
eschatologies.

These eschatological promissory incursions by God, which continually
impinge into human space, refuse to remain in either Soja's Deistic
framework or Lefebvre's construal of dualistic categories. Far from
being an esoteric add-on, these eschatological impulses assume and
demand a different "thirding" within their construals of space. This is
variously expressed, whether it be the "new song" of the Psalms, the

---

26. Cf. Elden, "Politics," 816, concerning Soja's focus on Los Angeles.

27. Cf. a call for such a self-conscious biblical perspective within an earlier
postmodern turn in human geography by Clark and Sleeman, "Writing," 49–60.

28. See, e.g., Soja, "Beyond," 410 n. 6.

29. See E. W. Soja, "Seeing Nature Spatially," in Albertson and King, eds.,
Without Nature?, 181–202 (195–96). On p. 195 he states: "Raw, physical nature
may be naively or even divinely given to begin with, but once urban society comes
into being, a new nature is created that blends into and absorbs what existed before."

30. See, e.g., Soja, "Beyond," 457, likening the sites of initial ancient urbanization to the Garden of Eden.

31. E.g. McLennan, "Radical Critique," 16.

"new thing" of Isaiah, the coming "kingdom," or Paul's "second Adam." Other instances multiply freely, within both biblical texts and spaces construed according to them. Thus, eschatological trajectories which might appear initially to remain at the margins, the "outer limits" of the spatial turn, instead reflexively curve back to reconfigure the center. Biblical eschatologies variously restructure spatial relations and, within their texts' persuasive frames, reflect an inbreaking which is both within and from beyond earthly, secular spaces. By their own claims, such knowledge cannot be isolated from, nor reduced to, either real or imagined space. As such, these eschatological impulses qualify or "third" the anthrocentricism for which Soja has been criticized[32] and supply a more biblically sensitive foundation than McFague's panentheism from which to address urban and ecological crises.[33]

For Soja, however, there is no such alien third nature. Instead, he posits first and second nature interacting to form a third entity. It remains questionable, however, whether this provides a genuinely additive transformation, within "a process of recursive hybridization…a critical 'thirding,' that is the creation of something new and different from the breakdown and reconstitution of binary distinctions."[34] The same critique coheres to the "and more" in Soja's oft-quoted formulation of thirdspace as "simultaneously real and imagined and more."[35] Perhaps this "and more" is no more than an "and more than we have previously produced or foreseen." If so, then it remains moot as to whether its thirding can, ultimately, be truly emancipatory and produce "another nature" or, whether, it is ultimately illusory in that regard.[36] Continuing, Soja describes this "another nature" as "significantly different from either of the originals," but this raises the question as to whether either of the original natures are ever known or experienced in isolation from the other. If not, then the degree of "difference" remains elusive. It is telling that the 2009 entry on "third space" in the *Dictionary of Human Geography* expands the 2000 entry by conceding that "third spaces are not always emancipatory formations," noting extraterritorial-liminal places such as

32. Cf. Albertson and King, eds., *Without Nature?*, 179.
33. Soja claims that "One might say that the City *re-places* nature"; cf. Soja, "Nature," 195–96. McFague responds with a panentheistic reformulation of nature; cf. S. McFague, "The Body of the World: Our Body, Ourselves," in Albertson and King, eds., *Without Nature?*, 221–38. This stands at odds with biblical theology and ignores a playful multivalence within Soja's italics.
34. Soja, "Nature," 196.
35. Soja, *Thirdspace*, 11.
36. Soja, "Nature," 196.

detention camps like Camp X-Ray at Guantánamo Bay.[37] Of course, such spaces of exemption are not an invention of the opening years of this century: perhaps, though, these years have tarnished any uncritical shine regarding third spaces, and have highlighted the need for a deeper critique of their construction and maintenance.

Simultaneously, Soja's schema fears any termination of reconceptualization: it desires a ceaseless continuation, a "continuous expansion."[38] A telos would imply and impose violent closure on space, and is to be resisted. Again, reversing the analytical and critical flow, the Bible's eschatological impulses allow for, even desire, a telos. Far from fearing anything beyond a Deistic spatiality, this telos promises divine resolution, restitution, and restoration of space. If CST 2.0 is to make properly critical use of Soja's schema, this dissonance requires closer reflection, even reformulation.

Thus, as a third and consequent element of this critique, Soja's engagement with theology provokes a counter-assertion of genuinely biblical productions of space. Lefebvre resisted such assertions as "mythomania," denying that his triadic dialectics bore any substantive connections with "the uses (and abuses) of this sacred number" by "metaphysics and theology" evoking "the trinity of the image, the three reference points of the universe (hell, the earth and the sky)."[39] Yet biblical spatialities have been articulated long and far, and continue to be formed and formative: also, as the final section of this essay will demonstrate, there exists already a broad coalition of scholarly spatial reading within biblical studies, both within and beyond CST 1.0. This might not render biblical studies as a net "exporter" of theoretical ideas,[40] but it will mark its spatialities as theoretically informative and, potentially, as increasingly critical. This counter-assertion will, in turn, "provincialize" the more typically secular, non-eschatological formulations of spatiality arising from the spatial turn, whether they emerge in Paris, Los Angeles, or elsewhere.[41]

---

37. D. Gregory et al., eds., *The Dictionary of Human Geography* (5th ed.; Malden, Mass.: Wiley-Blackwell, 2009), 754.

38. Soja, "Nature," 196.

39. Lefebvre, *Rhythmanalysis*, 11. Lefebvre's equating of these "myths" with Nietzsche's camel–lion–child periodization and Joachim de Flore's millenarian schema of ages reflects his ideological reductionism. Cf. also, e.g. Lefebvre, *Modernity*, 66.

40. Cf. human geography as having "moved decisively from being an importer of ideas from other fields to an exporter," so Warf and Arias, eds., *Spatial Turn*, 1.

41. For the strategy of provincializing, see D. Chakrabarty, *Provincializing Europe: Postcolonial Thought and Historical Difference* (Princeton: Princeton

d. *Summary*

These ambivalences arising from the biblical texts regarding the "fathers" of the spatial turn suggest that spatiality involves more than these theoreticians have imagined or allowed. Far from precluding biblical spatialities, the spatial turn is—I suggest—more theologically charged than many realize. The attenuated emancipatory spaces outlined above reflect a mysticism to which Soja retreats when likening third-space to Borges' literary *Aleph*,[42] but it, too, remains a view "from somewhere," from a theological stance: its embodied viewers maintain an inherent positionality. In addition, there are other, unnoted connections between the spatial and the theological. The spatial turn within accounting, for instance, coheres with its theological turn, both arising from Ken McPhail's innovative work.[43] Such coinherent ontologies speak against Lefebvre's isolation of the theological from the spatial as mythomania, as does the religious turn beyond narrowly "religious" disciplines of knowledge.[44] Instead, such connections cry out for further development within CST 2.0, a need only intensified by various spatial crises facing this century.

Soja marks the way forward with his deliberately conversational stance aimed at maintaining spatiality in ongoing dialogue and interdisciplinary formation. His own formulations are intended as initial points of contact, not reified privileged discourse, remaining subject to change on engagement with others.[45] The map, after all, is not the territory. Thus,

---

University Press, 2000). See also S. Levinson and D. Wilkins, eds., *Grammars of Space: Explorations in Cognitive Diversity* (Cambridge: Cambridge University Press, 2006). As discourse analysis indicates, such spatial "grammars" also constitute the biblical texts themselves.

42. Soja, *Thirdspace*, esp. 54–60. Perhaps Borges nurses a Buddhist impulse—so J. Wilson, *Jorge Luis Borges* (London: Reaktion, 2006), 15–19—but this does not completely locate his thought.

43. Cf. K. McPhail, "Accounting as Space: Accounting and the Geo-politics of Social Space," (Department of Accounting and Finance, University of Glasgow, Working Paper 99/4, 1999) <http://dspace.gla.ac.uk/bitstream/1905/144/1/99–4%5b1%5d.pdf>, and, introducing a themed journal issue, K. McPhail et al., "Accounting and Theology, an Introduction: Initiating a Dialogue Between Immediacy and Eternity," *Accounting, Auditing, and Accountability Journal* 17, no. 3 (2004): 320–26. Soja, "Beyond," 453 n. 6, and "Personally," 25, mentions accounting's spatial turn. He appears to be unaware of its theological turn.

44. See, e.g., K. McPhail, "A Review of the Emergence of Post-Secular Critical Accounting and a Provocation from Radical Orthodoxy," *Critical Perspectives in Accounting* 22 (2011): 516–28 (517–18).

45. See, esp. Soja, *Thirdspace*, 1–2.

as will be shown below, these matters are best supplemented and critiqued by a wider range of conversational voices, both within and beyond biblical studies.

3. *Looking Further Into the Spatial Turn*

As well as critiquing and refining the relatively small group of spatial theorists who have dominated CST 1.0, CST 2.0 also engenders an enhanced sensibility for interaction with a wider variety of spatial insights.

For a wider array of geographical interpretive lenses to flourish within biblical studies, the sources and sites of such readings must be widely known. Herein lie two challenges for spatial readings of biblical texts. First, such dialogue partners are increasingly diverse, spread out across multiple disciplinary fields. Second, there are no stable taxonomies which map this terrain.

To face these challenges head on, an obvious and important entrée-point for such wider interaction is the *Dictionary of Human Geography*. This work is an entrée-point rather than a center-point but, now in its fifth edition, it remains the barometer of the academic discipline known as human geography, providing the best overview of the progressions and niches which constitute what its editors' preface calls the "restless tradition" of this discipline.[46] Its successive prefaces provide sharp reorientation for any still nursing the misapprehension that geography is an untheoretical domain focused on maps and colouring. A critical reading of these prefaces also illuminates the scope for CST 2.0 to engage productively with the discourses of human geography.[47] There, the editors repeatedly survey what they recognize as a lively "trans-disciplinary, even post-disciplinary, space,"[48] seeking to provide "both mirror and goad" for "the emergence of new themes, approaches, and concerns within human geography." As such, they remain focused on human geographers, whom they see as "moving with considerable critical intelligence" within these spaces,[49] thus providing an entrée-point for CST 2.0 seeking wider critical engagement with human geography.

---

46. Gregory et al., *Dictionary*, vi. The earlier editions appeared in 1981, 1986, 1994, and 2000.

47. Space does not allow here even a listing of the articles originating in the 2009 edition. Its preface provides such a list. Here and elsewhere, the *Dictionary* provides a reservoir of approaches to space which can and should inform biblical studies.

48. This and the following quotations are from Gregory et al., *Dictionary*, vii, and are repeated from the 2000 preface.

49. Cf. the less congratulatory view of Soja, "Beyond," 453 n. 6.

Yet such exchanges need a critical edge. In homage to Raymond Williams,[50] the editors themselves remain keenly aware "of the slipperiness of our geographical 'keywords': of the claims they silently make, the privileges they surreptitiously install, and of the wider webs of meaning and practice within which they do their work."[51] Thus a combined hermeneutics of representation and suspicion remains an imperative for CST 2.0. Whereas the editors assert a desire to resist privileging or normalizing "the modern" in their search for "more cosmopolitan geographies,"[52] this cosmopolitan hospitality has its limits within the inscribed bounds of their work. While "religion" has been addressed since at least its second edition, this category remains confined to subject-specific entries, maintained as a reified concept lacking internal differentiation.[53] The pervasive, even ubiquitous, spaces of "implicit religion" are airbrushed out by a domesticated explicit religion.[54] This reflects a normalized but significant ordering of the world within the *Dictionary*'s predominantly modern-Western-secular worldview. This unremarked marginalizing of religion (and, with it, biblical spatialities), replicated from edition to edition, reflects the disciplinary divisions of an imperialist Anglo-American scholarship which marginalizes other scholarships. Dialogue, "while nobly attempted," remains "regrettably limited."[55] This confronts any critical geography aspiring to "internationalism and solidarity, reflexivity, and the analysis of power."[56]

These fracture-points within the discourse of human geography both invite and repulse biblical spatialities. CST 2.0 can gain helpful footholds here, but it is hard to parse out the extent to which this kind of bias reflects and reproduces the isolated and limited attempts by geographers to explore biblical texts for their productions of space. Perhaps such

50. R. Williams, *Keywords: A Vocabulary of Culture and Society* (rev. ed.; London: Fontana, 1983 [1976]).

51. Gregory et al., *Dictionary*, vii.

52. Ibid., vii–viii (viii).

53. The 1986 edition contained a predominantly dismissive entry on "Religion, Geography of." The 1994 and 2000 editions saw a new entry, describing it more sympathetically as "a subfield of cultural geography." The 2009 edition replaced it with a shorter entry on "Religion."

54. Cf. L. Kong, "Global Shifts, Theoretical Shifts: Changing Geographies of Religion," *Progress in Human Geography* 34, no. 6 (2010): 755–76 (756–57), regarding the rise of the "unofficially" sacred, such that religion is "neither spatially nor temporally confined to 'reservations'…"

55. Beaumont and Baker, eds., *Postsecular Cities*, 3.

56. N. Bromley, "The Spaces of Critical Geography," *Progress in Human Geography* 32, no. 2 (2008): 285–93 (290).

forensic appraisals are less useful than constructive agendas to pursue such spatialities, and it is worth noting the relatively high access point required for investigating biblical texts within their original languages. Indirectly, the editors acknowledge this: "we must also recognize that this edition, like its predecessors, remains focused on English-language words, terms and literatures… [W]e know that there are severe limitations to working within a single-language tradition (especially in a field like human geography). The vitality of other geographical traditions should neither be overlooked nor minimized."[57]

Certainly, there are geographers who engage with biblical texts and biblical agendas. There are, for instance, political geographers who have explored Christian geopolitical imaginations, specifically premillennial eschatologies, for their influence upon contemporary American politics.[58] A panel discussion entitled "The Future of Religious Geopolitics" at the 2010 Meeting of the American Association of Geographers (AAG) expressed interest in exploring other geopolitical imaginations beyond the premillennial, citing Richard Bauckham's work for future attention. Here lies a very fruitful area of dialogue for CST 2.0. Likewise, post-secular geographies are a growing field of interest.[59] Whether the sacred has "re-emerged" or has simply continued need not be mutually exclusive options: the re-engagement is what matters and what will feed CST 2.0.[60]

There remains, however, a characteristic resistance within human geography to consider the theological, let alone the biblical. CST 2.0 needs to be alert to both the opportunities and constraints within its interactions with human geography. A fear of the "god-trick" (that is, of disembodied, unsituated knowledge) pervades critical human geography, and is applied with particular rigor to matters pertaining to God. Thus the editors of the *Dictionary* know their text risks being "a textual performance" of this "god-trick" and invite their readers "to consider how these other voices might be heard from other positions, other places, and to think about the voices that are—deliberately or unconsciously—silenced or marginalized."[61] Ironically, God is largely and notably absent from its pages, as are texts which claim to speak in his name, even while

---

57. Gregory et al., *Dictionary*, viii.

58. See J. Dittmer and T. Sturm, eds., *Mapping the End Times: American Evangelical Geopolitics and Apocalyptic Visions* (Aldershot: Ashgate, 2010).

59. See the spread of trajectories and readings pursued in Beaumont and Baker, eds., *Postsecular Cities*.

60. Cf. Kong, "Shifts," 764–65.

61. Gregory et al., *Dictionary*, viii.

the surrounding rhetoric downplays such exclusions. The reified catchall term of "religion" has no direct manifestation within empirical life, thus confirming the perceived marginalization of instantiated religions and their particular texts but at the cost of distancing geography from a rich and pervasive dimension of everyday spatialities.[62]

From the perspective of the geographical mainstream, biblical studies remains a subset of a subset within one distant corner of the spatial turn. Yet working on the margins *is* creative, and can be subversive. That much is clear throughout Soja's *Thirdspace*. While, as mentioned above, biblical studies is unlikely to become a net exporter of spatial theory in the foreseeable future, this need not bother its practitioners. As well as any connections formed with human geography, there exist other explorers of the spaces of antiquity to help reconfigure modern(istic) construals of space.[63] Together with biblical scholars undertaking spatial readings, but not identifying with CST 1.0, the margins are rich with opportunity.

In addition, from the margins, CST 2.0 can engage productively with the centers of the spatial turn. Professional bodies such as the AAG provide openings for biblical scholars beyond their normal spheres.[64] The AAG's Bible Geography Specialty Group offers some crossover for biblical scholars, albeit using the Bible as a source of geographical information for studying the geography of ancient Israel. The Geography of Religions and Belief Systems (GORABS) Specialty Group offers a

---

62. Cf. J. Corrigan, "Spatiality and Religion," in Warf and Arias, eds., *The Spatial Turn*, 157–72; Kong, "Shifts," 769–70; R. Henkel, "Are Geographers Religiously Unmusical? Positionalities in Geographical Research on Religion," *Erkunde* 65, no. 4 (2011): 389–99. Instead, "Geographers need to allow religion to speak back," as E. Yorgason and V. Della Dora, "Geography, Religion, and Emerging Paradigms: Problematizing the Dialogue," *Social & Cultural Geography* 10 (2009): 629–37 (629), argue.

63. E.g. Y. Shahar, *Josephus Geographicus: The Classical Context of Geography in Josephus* (Tübingen: Mohr Siebeck, 2004); M. Scott, *Delphi and Olympia: The Spatial Politics of Panhellenism in the Archaic and Classical Periods* (Cambridge: Cambridge University Press, 2010); I. De Jong, ed., *Space in Ancient Greek Literature: Studies in Ancient Greek Narrative*, vol. 3 (Leiden: Brill, 2012). Also, for a review of Jewish topographies, see C. Fonrobert, "The New Spatial Turn in Jewish Studies," *AJSR* 33, no. 1 (2009): 155–64.

64. Other professional groups include the Arbeitskreis Religionsgeographie within the Deutsche Gesellschaft für Geographie <http://religionsgeographie.de/> and the Royal Geographical Society's Geographies of Religion, Spirituality and Faith Working Group. Conversely, Kong, "Shifts," 770, encourages geographers of religion to move beyond their own spheres.

latent niche for emergent biblical spatialities.[65] Also, as noted above, "mainstream" groups within AAG provide opportunities for biblical scholarship beyond biblical studies.

4. *Looking Around, Beyond the Spatial Turn*

So far, CST 2.0 might be criticized for merely accruing more theory. Nevertheless, mere mass is not, in itself, enough. CST 2.0 also acquires more gravity by asserting self-conscious and strategic links with other existing spatial readings of biblical texts which do not position themselves within CST 1.0. Some of these interpretive approaches are already in place; some remain to be formed and established; still others will come into being as the spatialization of biblical studies continues to unfold through an increasingly pluriform CST 2.0. Within all this, spatial readings can diffuse further down all levels of education. CST 2.0 will not remain the domain of the academic conference, the doctoral paper, or the specialist monograph: increasingly it will infuse all biblical scholarship.

Connecting with wider, existing biblical disciplines will help avoid a narrow and self-referencing corpus, a parochial turn within CST 2.0. CST 1.0 already connects with the broad amalgam of approaches labeled feminist, postcolonial, and social-scientific criticisms,[66] and a deliberately pluralistic CST 2.0 brokers new intersectionalities, such as with postsecular spaces.[67] Likewise, CST 2.0 engages spatial readings of biblical texts which are not explicitly connected with CST 1.0's critical spatialities. In this way archaeological, ethnographic, minority criticism and topographic approaches to Bible texts provide scope for CST 2.0,[68] as does the deliberate spatializing of other discourses.[69] Thus, for

---

65. See <http://www.gorabs.org>.

66. Berquist, "Introduction," 6–7, identifies these connections.

67. E.g. H. Moxnes, "Identity in Jesus' Galilee: From Ethnicity to Locative Intersectionality," *BibInt* 18, nos. 4–5 (2010): 390–416; Beaumont and Baker, eds., *Postsecular Cities*.

68. E.g. P. Oakes, *Reading Romans in Pompeii* (London: SPCK, 2009); L. Lawrence, *The Word in Place: Reading the New Testament in Contemporary Contexts* (London: SPCK, 2009); U. Kim, "To the Ends of the Earth? Minority Biblical Criticism in Motion," *Reviews in Religion and Theology* 18, no. 1 (2011), 4–12; J. Charlesworth, "Background I: Jesus of History and the Topography of the Holy Land," in *Handbook for the Study of the Historical Jesus*. Vol. 3, *The Historical Jesus* (ed. T. Holmén and S. E. Porter; Leiden: Brill, 2011), 2213–42.

69. See, e.g., M. Sleeman, "Mark, The Temple and Space: A Geographer's Response," *BibInt* 15, no. 3 (2007): 338–49, and "The Vision of Acts: World Right Way Up," *JSNT* 33, no. 3 (2011): 327–33.

example, intertextualities invite a spatial sensibility. Texts are produced somewhere, and are consumed somewhere, and they seek to portray and persuade particular productions of space. Projecting interspatialities requires a more maximalist aperture for intertextuality, anticipating varying forms among fulfillment, mimicry, parody, irony, and subversion. A new register of such strategies remains to be mapped. In each instance, broader coalitions of approaches can generate new spatial readings as CST 2.0 creatively blurs and bridges methodological divides, seeking novel alliances, new interpretive spaces.

Having affected both theology and biblical studies, the spatial turn presents a platform for greater rapprochement between these related but often isolated scholarly agendas. Theology has been a more prominent interlocutor with Soja and postsecular geographers, but these exchanges highlight the frequently limited direct exegesis of biblical texts undertaken by theologians.[70] Close readings of these texts can only enhance and refine existing debates and provoke new questions, and a reflexive critique of spatial theory's theological presuppositions will depend upon forging new partnerships with theology.

5. Conclusion

This may be the best of times to be a spatialized reader of biblical texts.[71] The spatialization of biblical studies is irreversible and ongoing, both within and away from the spatial turn. Now that the question of space has been raised, awareness of it is increasing. The question is how far this will spread within biblical discourses, not whether it will survive. Biblical studies cannot remain space-blind, or retain a positivistic limitation on space. Space is not an optional extra, and critical spatial theory need not be a niche nor a constraining label; instead, it can be a coalescing locus. CST 2.0 heralds growth and innovation to come throughout biblical studies.

Spatialization faces, and resists, the risk of being co-opted as just another "criticism": indeed, it reframes biblical discourse. Because of its material, emplaced demands, space forces biblical texts which seek to persuade to turn toward themselves and judge their own claims: space is

---

70. Cf., e.g., those reviewed in S. Bergmann, "Theology in Its Spatial Turn: Space, Place and Built Environments Challenging and Changing the Images of God," *Religion Compass* 1, no. 3 (2007): 353–79.

71. Cf. Soja, "Beyond," 451: "This may be the best of times to be an urban geographer... Today, no scholar of any stripe can afford not to be, to some degree, an urban geographer."

the terrain of the Bible's questioning par excellence. Nowhere is the internal dynamic between the universal and the particular in biblical texts more forcefully tested than in space. Space brings an awareness of (other) spaces, both within and significantly beyond the reach of these texts. Space, if taken seriously in biblical studies, as in legal philosophy, must be properly theorized "in its complexity as both an opportunity and a threat, a guest and a host," both a product of text as well as a production that goes beyond the text.[72] In sum, CST 2.0 heralds a radical conception of scripture, of *spatial* scriptures.

72. A. Philippopoulos-Mihalopoulos, "Law's Spatial Turn: Geography, Justice and a Certain Fear of Space," *Law, Culture and the Humanities* 7, no. 2 (2010): 187–202 (197).

Part II

SACRED SPACE AND THE FORMATION OF IDENTITY

The Implied Transcendence of Physical and Ideological Borders and Boundaries in Psalm 47

Jo-Marí Schäder

1. *Introduction*

Critical spatiality has indicated that our notion about space is the result of social constructions. The purpose of this study will be to understand the relationship between experience, (b)ordering and othering, and the (re-)construction and (re-)representation of reality as Second- and Third-space practices. To summarize all perspectives on boundary research in the extent of a single essay is impossible and it is not my endeavor to do so. Here the focus falls specifically on how boundaries operate in personal relations.

As critical spatiality builds on postmodern themes, it stands to reason that they are not immediately applicable to the biblical context due to the great temporal and geographical distance from the respective representative cultures. However, by emphasizing the value system of the biblical peoples, one will find that there are nevertheless some striking parallels in the manner in which people experience and construct borders and boundaries. This study is based specifically on theories from postmodern and humanist geography and political boundary studies regarding borders and boundaries. Psalm 47 will be discussed as an example of where the typical borders or boundaries that are innately part of human experience and reality construction apparently transcend or cross the boundaries of culture, the sacred and tradition. This study builds on an intratextual analysis of Ps 47.[1]

---

1. For a complete intratextual analysis of Ps 47, cf. J. Schäder, "Psalm 47—How Universal is Its Universalism? An Intra-, Inter- and Extratextual Analysis of the Poem" (M.A. diss., Pretoria: University of Pretoria, 2008), 6–49.

2. *Critical Spatiality*

Critical spatiality understands different aspects of space as human constructs that are socially attested and it concentrates primarily on the sociology of space. Two names that have become synonymous with the theory of critical spatiality are those of Henri Lefebvre and Edward W. Soja.[2] Soja attempts to apply spatial theory to a post-modern intellectual context and focuses on three spatial categories, which are "epistemologically triune," namely, Firstspace ("geophysical realities as perceived" or physical space), Secondspace ("mapped realities as represented" or mental space) and Thirdspace ("lived realities as practised" or social space).[3]

Space that is conceived through the spoken or written word is constructed through the word and, therefore, Secondspace. It is a space of domination as those in power make the "maps" through which Firstspace can be experienced. They design and control it and validate their right to be able to do so. "This would be particularly true of canonical literature, given its apparent status as the record of the winners."[4] But to classify any text only as Secondspace would not require any further analysis.[5]

---

2. H. Lefebvre, *The Production of Space* (trans. D. Nicholson-Smith; Oxford: Blackwell, 1991); E. W. Soja, *Thirdspace: Journeys to Los Angeles and Other Real-and-Imagined Places* (Oxford: Blackwell, 1996).

3. C. V. Camp, "Storied Space, or, Ben Sira 'Tells' a Temple," in *"Imagining" Biblical Worlds: Studies in Spatial, Social and Historical Constructs in Honor of James W. Flanagan* (ed. D. M. Gunn and P. M. McNutt; JSOTSup 359; Sheffield: Sheffield Academic, 2002), 64–80 (65).

4. Ibid., 66.

5. Even though it appears that definitions of First-, Second and Thirdspace convey a clear differentiation that exists between these spatialities, Camp has indicated how they collapse if applied to biblical texts such as the book of Sirach: "One could already appeal, against that assumption, to the notion of the text 'creating a world,' that is, a space in which the reader as well as the characters 'live.' Human 'living,' both inside and outside texts, inescapably involves language and concepts. So one issue of spatial analysis—is it First? is it Second? is it Third?—is not decided on the basis of 'is it written?'" (ibid., 67–68). The kind of literature involved will also play an important role. Narrative literature supplies a potential model for thinking Thirdspatially and a site of Thirdspace from which lived First- and Secondspatial possibilities can be abstracted and analyzed. In this manner, a window is provided into the ancient world (ibid., 67–68). Maier also cautions that narrative texts are not solely classifiable as Secondspace. Instead of representing realities of space, a trialectic epistemology of spatiality indicates different representations or perspectives; cf. C. M. Maier, "Daughter Zion as a Gendered Space in the Book of Isaiah," in *Constructions of Space II: The Biblical City and Other*

"[A]ny search for space in literary texts will find it everywhere and in every guise; encoded, described, projected, dreamt of, speculated about."[6] Space also forms an intricate part of any narrative's focalization or point of view as it contributes to the "perception" created by the narrative.

3. *Experience, (B)Ordering and Othering, and (Re-)Constructions and (Re-)Presentations of Reality*

In this section an overview will be given on how the relationship between experience, (b)ordering and othering, and the (re-)construction and (re-)representation of reality should be understood as Second- and Thirdspace practices. Here the focus falls specifically on how boundaries operate in personal relations.

a. *Experience as Mode for Constructing Reality*

Yi-Fu Tuan emphasizes that "experience is a cover-all term for the various modes through which a person knows and constructs a reality" and that "emotion tints all human experience, including the high flights of thought."[7]

People of different cultures may differ in how they divide up their world, assign value to its parts and even measure them, but certain cross-cultural similarities do exist as humans are the measure of all things. Tuan indicates that there are two kinds of facts that form fundamental principles of spatial organization: the posture and structure of the human body and the relations (be it close or distant) between human beings.[8] Humans therefore tend to organize space to conform to their biological needs and social relations due to the intimate experience with our bodies and other people. The result is that humans impose a schema on space by

Imagined Spaces (ed. J. L. Berquist and C. V. Camp; LHBOTS 490; New York/London: T&T Clark International, 2008), 103–23 (104). Flanagan also briefly discusses how Firstspace would collapse into Secondspace if Secondspace images were to be taken seriously; Firstspace would become a substitute for Secondspace. He also indicates how Soja emphasizes the importance of distinguishing the first two spatialities from Thirdspace and he stresses lived space as a neglected one; cf. J. W. Flanagan, "Mapping the Biblical World: Perceptions of Space in Ancient Southwestern Asia," in *Mappa Mundi: Mapping Culture, Mapping the World* (ed. J. Murray; Windsor, Ont.: Humanities Research Group, University of Windsor, 2001), 1–18 (3).

6. Lefebvre, *Production*, 15.

7. Y.-F. Tuan, *Space and Place: The Perspective of Experience* (6th printing; Minneapolis: University of Minnesota Press, 2008), 8.

8. Ibid., 34.

their mere presence.[9] "Man is the measure. In a literal sense, the human body is the measure of direction, location, and distance."[10] As a result, all spatial prepositions, in humankind's attempt to order the world, are necessarily anthropocentric, whether derived from parts of the human body or not.

"The prestige of the centre is well established. People everywhere tend to regard their own homeland as the 'middle place,' or the centre of the world. Among some people there is also the belief, quite unsupported by geography, that they live at the top of the world, or that their sacred place is at the earth's summit."[11] This differentiation in spatial organization is intrinsically imbedded into language. Tuan indicates that the demonstratives "this" and "that" are a pair that lack locational range and has thus become polarized and carry high emotional charge.[12] The members of the we-group are close to each other, and, as a result, distant from members of the outside they-group. The meanings of "close" and "distant" "are a compound of degrees of interpersonal intimacy and geographical distance."[13] Social distance may be the inverse of geographical distance. "[T]he small worlds of direct experience are fringed with much broader fields known indirectly through symbolic means."[14] This then forms the sphere of the mythical.

b. *(B)Ordering and Othering*
Michèle Lamont and Virág Molnár wrote an article in which they summarize various research agendas and perspectives on boundaries and borders from disciplines in the social sciences, such as anthropology, history, political science, social psychology, and sociology.[15] They also indicate how "boundaries" have been associated with research on cognition, social and collective identity, commensuration, census categories, cultural capital, cultural membership, racial and ethnic group positioning, hegemonic masculinity, professional jurisdictions, scientific controversies, group rights, immigration, and contentious politics, to mention but a few. Lamont and Molnár's work surveys some of the developments in literature on the following subjects: social and collective identity; class,

9. Ibid., 36.
10. Ibid., 44.
11. Ibid., 38–39.
12. Ibid., 47.
13. Ibid., 50.
14. Ibid., 50, 88.
15. M. Lamont and V. Molnár, "The Study of Boundaries in the Social Sciences," *Annual Review of Sociology* 28 (2002): 167–95.

ethnic/racial, and gender/sex inequality; professions, knowledge, and science; and communities, national identities; and spatial boundaries.[16] They also indicate that more work is still needed to integrate the psychological, cultural, and social mechanisms involved in the process of boundary construction.

Henk van Houtum and Ton van Naerssen stress that bordering processes do not begin or stop at demarcated lines in space and that borders do not represent fixed points in space and time.[17] They rather symbolize a social practice of spatial differentiation. Central to the notion of border as process and institution is the process through which borders are demarcated and managed.

Sociologically, border categorization has been expressed through a series of binary distinctions, which highlight borders as constituting a sharp edge or line of separation between two distinct, or even opposed, entities. Borders therefore contain a sense of sharp dislocation and separation and of a cut-off point between two polarities.[18] Examples are expressions such as "here" and "there," "us" and "them," "include" and "exclude," "self" and "other," and "inside" and "outside." These terms reflect that borders exist in almost every aspect of society, categorizing humanity into those who belong to the group (or compartment) and those who do not. This border demarcation then consists of precise criteria for determining on which side of the border one is located.[19] The cut off points between these opposites are not always observable in the construction of walls and fences.[20]

According to Van Houtum and Van Naerssen, (b)ordering rejects as well as erects othering.[21] The paradoxical character of bordering processes entails borders being erected to erase territorial ambiguity and ambivalent identities in order to shape a unique and cohesive order, thereby, however, either creating new differences or reproducing latently existing ones in space and identity. This is a way of marking and making a differentiation in social space and in people beyond the border and of rejecting differences within the bordered. "It thus seems justified to neglect (or to be indifferent about) what is beyond the border. The other

16. Ibid., 169–85.

17. H. van Houtum and T. van Naerssen, "Bordering, Ordering and Othering," *Tijdschrift voor Economische en Sociale Geografie* 93 (2002): 125–36 (126).

18. D. Newman, "The Lines That Continue to Separate Us: Borders in Our 'Borderless' World," *Progress in Human Geography* 30 (2006): 143–61 (148).

19. D. Newman, "Borders and Bordering: Towards an Interdisciplinary Dialogue," *European Journal of Social Theory* 9, no. 2 (2006): 171–86 (176).

20. Ibid., 177.

21. Van Houtum and Van Naerssen, "Bordering," 126.

is imaginatively there, but not present. The constructed border is an imaginative, mental border…but therefore not less real in its effects and consequences."[22] If much of the traditionalist geographic border discourse was characterized by tangible demarcation criteria, contemporary border discourse is then characterized by the more abstract notions relating to difference and othering. Some even experience the other as an indifferent or hostile reality out there. Strategies of ordering, bordering and othering are territorial and often, although not necessarily, take place at the spatial scale of states; otherness is then reproduced by national education programs.[23]

Border scholars of the first half of the twentieth century saw borders as the result of political decision-making processes so that the criteria determining where and how the border is to be constructed in society and/or space are drawn up by societal managers, usually acting in their own political, economic or institutional interests.[24] As a result, the normative values of differential social systems meet at borders. They function as the spatial mediators of (often latent) power and governance discourses and practices of places in society. Borders thereby represent the governing and preserving of values.[25]

Our social identity is the product of the social relations we are imbedded in. "Identities must be understood as social processes of continuous 're-writing' of the self and of social collectives."[26] It is difficult to change or break with our social relations and it would be hard to change or leave our identity behind when migrating from one place to another.[27] People who try to make a living and a home elsewhere, even temporarily, will change their identities to some degree to accommodate what is going on around them.[28] People are therefore not passive receptors but play active roles in bordering and identity construction.[29] "[I]t is people's habitus (practices and performances) that (re)produces their habitat… These practices are performed in order to impose one's

22. H. van Houtum and A. Strüver, "Borders, Strangers, Doors and Bridges," *Space & Polity* 6 (2002): 141–46 (142).

23. Van Houtum and Van Naerssen, "Bordering," 126. According to Van Houtum and Van Naerssen a state territory might claim to represent an imagined homogeneous population, although this is hardly ever the case.

24. Newman, "Borders and Bordering," 175.

25. Van Houtum and Van Naerssen, "Bordering," 129.

26. Ibid., 132.

27. Ibid.

28. K. D. Madsen and T. van Naerssen, "Migration, Identity, and Belonging," *Journal of Borderlands Studies* 18 (2003): 61–75 (61).

29. Ibid., 62.

own vision of the world and to (re)claim one's socio-spatial identity."[30] It is then the utopian dream of an ordered, consistent and stabilized unity that asks for a non-stop monitoring of control of access and a close examination of those entering.[31] "The traditional function of borders has been to create barriers to movement rather than bridges enabling contact. Borders are normally perceived as institutional mechanisms aimed at protecting what is inside, by excluding whatever originates from the outside."[32]

The opening of borders does not, automatically, result in the hybridization of ethnic and national identity,[33] called transnationalism by Kenneth D. Madsen and Ton van Naerssen.[34] Transnationalism (or continued connections not only with others of similar heritage, but others continuing to reside in one's place of origin) continues to integrate economies and cultures in vastly dispersed locations while challenging traditional notions of nation states and territorial identities. The crossing of borders does not necessarily take place at the "edge" of space, where the border is expected to be found. Physically crossing the boundary can be considered the easy part of the crossing process.[35] Where one border (the physical) can be crossed, a new one (cultural) presents itself—it may never be crossed successfully in a lifetime.[36]

Henk van Houtum and Anke Strüver argue that overcoming borders is mainly about overcoming the socially constructed imaginations of belonging to a certain place and of the need for a spatial fixity.[37] As imagination has the potential of dividing people as a deconstructive power, it also has the potential of uniting people as a constructive one. Overcoming borders then requires the reimagining of borders and the reimagining of outsiders as insiders.

30. Van Houtum and Strüver, "Doors and Bridges," 143.

31. Van Houtum and Van Naerssen, "Bordering," 128.

32. Newman, "Lines," 150. "Bridges are perceived as phenomena of connections, while doors are understood as the blocking *and* permitting effects of borders. Doors are constructed to be able to exclude the world outside, as well as to open for the world outside. Hence, it is not the door itself that should be a topic of study, it is *people* who limit, separate and border" (Van Houtum and Strüver, "Doors and Bridges," 143).

33. Newman, "Lines," 150. "[A]s people succeed in moving from one category to another, they may experience a period of transitional hybridity, adopting new customs from the other side, while retaining, at one and the same time, many of their customs from the place of origin" (Newman, "Borders and Bordering," 180).

34. Madsen and Van Naerssen, "Migration," 68.

35. Newman, "Borders and Bordering," 178, 179.

36. Ibid., 179.

37. Van Houtum and Strüver, "Doors and Bridges," 141, 142.

c. *(Re-)Constructions and (Re-)Presentations of Reality*

From a postmodern cartographic perspective, John B. Harley indicates that all maps are representations of power.[38] According to the theory of critical spatiality, any representation or reconstruction of reality, such as texts,[39] or any other Secondspace realities, share this characteristic with maps. It then stands to reason that the same theories applicable to the mapmaking process are applicable to literary sources as well.

Regarding the mapmaking process, Harley writes that the scientific rules of mapping are influenced by rules governing the cultural production of the map. "To discover these rules, we have to read between the lines of technical procedures or of the map's topographic content. They are related to values, such as those of ethnicity, politics, religion, or social class, and they are also embedded in the map-producing society at large."[40]

Harley identifies two rules that manifest in the cultural production/construction of world maps. The purpose of these rules is not to indicate an assumed underlying universality, but to indicate interesting correlations between constructions of world maps. The first is the "rule of ethnocentricity"—many historical societies tend to place themselves and their own territories at the center of cosmographies or world maps.[41] The second is the "rule of social order" or the hierarchicalization of space—these rules appear to be inserted as smaller codes and cartographic inscriptions on maps, in verbal texts and in commentary that convey social and political factors beyond the physical human landscape. The rules of society and those of measurement are mutually reinforcing in the same image. This can be deemed as a conscious act of cartographic representation. As a representation of social geography, maps operate behind a mask of seemingly neutral science.[42]

---

38. J. B. Harley, "Deconstructing the Map," *Cartographica* 26 (1989): 1–20 (1).

39. Harley, ibid., 7–8, states: "The word 'text' is deliberately chosen. It is now generally accepted that the model of text can have a much wider application than to literary texts alone. To non-book texts such as musical compositions and architectural structures we can confidently add the graphic texts we call maps. It has been said that 'what constitutes a text is not the presence of linguistic elements but the act of construction' so that maps, as 'constructions employing a conventional sign system,' become texts… Maps are a cultural text. By accepting their textuality we are able to embrace a number of different interpretative possibilities."

40. Ibid., 5–6.

41. Ibid., 7–8; cf. Flanagan, "Mapping," 2.

42. Harley, "Deconstructing," 6–7.

James W. Flanagan adds a third rule: "Maps reflect the social worlds of both the peoples being mapped and the cartographer, sometimes more the latter than the former."[43]

All the steps involved in making a map (or any reconstruction of reality) are rhetorical. These include selection, omission, simplification, classification, the creation of hierarchies, and "symbolization." Harley points out that "the freedom of rhetorical manoeuvre in cartography is considerable: the mapmaker merely omits those features of the world that lie outside the purpose of the immediate discourse."[44] Maps therefore also reflect specific power or knowledge matrices by certain individuals, organizations or states. When ordered by governments, maps can "extend and reinforce the legal statutes, territorial imperatives, and values stem-ming from the exercise of political power."[45] In this sense, maps also have and are concerned with politics and one of their "liabilities" is that they express an embedded social vision since they are mass produced and stereotyped images.[46]

Flanagan linked up with Harley's work in his exposition on mapping in the biblical world. The thesis for Flanagan's essay can be expressed in three statements: (1) "Maps, as representations of space, are governed by rules that allow map makers—cartographers—to control or influence the way maps are read"; (2) "Accurate or informed readings of maps require knowledge of social theory that sometimes challenges assumptions of scientific accuracy"; and (3) "Recent studies on critical spatiality in fields such as geography, cartography, philosophy, and religion are expanding our understanding of social space and spatial practice."[47]

Flanagan rightly questions which reality is being mapped. How does one map Thirdspace, and avoid reading it as Firstspace?[48] As spatiality is constructed through social practice, it stands to reason that there is more than one kind of space at work in peoples' lives and therefore physical and material space is not always the most important. To assume explicit borders and boundary lines on maps is problematic—in the end, we are dealing with maps on segmentary systems.[49] As space is socially

---

43. Flanagan, "Mapping," 2.
44. Harley, "Deconstructing," 11.
45. Ibid., 12.
46. Ibid., 13, 14.
47. Flanagan, "Mapping," 1.
48. Ibid., 2, 6.
49. In such a segmented social system it is not the locality (where people are) that is important, but who their kin and enemies are. Some have suggested that "territoriality" in such societies depends more on kinship relations than land. It then

constructed, the way it is experienced affects the way it is perceived. Flanagan writes that "space is a subtext or presupposition that we bring to our view of the world" and that boundaries are formed from people's experiences.[50] Like texts, maps portray the preferences of the cartographer.[51] It ought to be clear as well that advancements in technology that aids in "accurate" recordings of world maps do not assure greater equality or objectivity.

4. *Psalm 47 and the Implied Transcendence of Borders and Boundaries*

Here follows a literal translation of Ps 47:

[1] *For the supervisor. By the sons of Korah. A Psalm.*
[2] *All the nations, you must clap your hands,*
    you must shout to God with a voice of joy.
[3] *For Yahweh Almighty is fearsome,*
    a great king over all the earth.
[4] *He subjugates nations under us*
    and peoples under our feet.
[5] *He chooses for us our inheritance,*
    the glory of Jacob, whom he loved. Selah.
[6] *God has gone up with a shout,*
    Yahweh with the sound of a ram's horn.
[7] *You must praise God, you must praise.*
    You must praise our king, you must praise.
[8] *For the King of all the earth is God,*
    you must praise with insight.
[9] *God has reigned over (gentile) nations,*
    God has sat on his holy throne.
[10] *The nobles of the nations have been gathered*
    with the nation of the God of Abraham.[52]
    For to God are the shields of the earth.
He has been greatly exalted.

stands to reason that space in a segmented society means something different from space in a centralized society. It is important to note that biblical societies were mostly segmented societies (ibid., 7).

50. Ibid., 4.
51. Ibid., 5, 6.
52. There is a text-critical note on v. 10 which states that the Septuagint and the Peshitta read עִם עַם ("with the people") instead of the Masoretic text עַם (ʿam, "people"), influencing the reading as "with (as?) the people of the God of Abraham." The assumption is made that עִם (ʿim) was accidentally omitted by copyists due to haplography. The omission of עִם (ʿim) drastically influences the meaning of the text,

In this section the emphasis falls on how the role-players, holy space or the temple and the Patriarchal and Promised Land traditions represent borders or boundaries on physical and ideological levels that are implicitly transcended or crossed in Ps 47.

a. *The Role-players in Psalm 47*

A notable characteristic of the morphology of Ps 47 is that the person and gender of words and suffixes clearly refer to three distinct persons or groups, namely, the nations ("you"),[53] God or Yahweh,[54] and Israel ("us"—the "in-group").[55] From this it can be deduced that what concerns the author of Ps 47 is the relationship between these role-players.

whether the nobles of the nations are to be considered part of the people of the God of Abraham or not. For the purpose of this study, the explanation of the omission of עם is considered to be correct and the variant reading of v. 10 is preferred; cf. A. A. Anderson, *The Book of Psalms*, vols. 1 and 2 (NCB; London: Oliphants, 1972), 366. D. Schneider, *Das Buch der Psalmen, Teil 1: Psalm 1 bis 50* (Wuppertaler Studienbibel; Wuppertal: R. Brockhaus, 1995), 310, prefers the vocalization *'im* above the Masoretic vocalization indicting the nations. The translation he proposes then reads "bei dem Gott Abrahams." But what is important here is that for the first time in the psalm there is no longer a distinction between "we" and "the nations"; cf. F.-L. Hossfeld and E. Zenger, *Die Psalmen: Psalm 1–50* (NEchtB; Würzburg: Echter Verlag, 1993), 291; S. Terrien, *The Psalms: Strophic Structure and Theological Commentary* (Eerdmans Critical Commentary; Grand Rapids: Eerdmans, 2003), 378.

53. There is a preference for nouns in the absolute state masculine plural form to refer to the nations ("you") and imperative second masculine plural verbs to refer to the actions of the nations (or what they are exhorted to do). Muilenburg writes that the view that "all the nations/peoples" refer to the peoples of Palestine is contradicted by the content of the psalm. The writer of Ps 47 also mentions three times (vv. 3, 8 and 10) that the whole earth is the range of his vision, cf. J. Muilenburg, "Psalm 47," *JBL* 63 (1944): 235–56 (244).

54. אלהים ("God"), יהוה ("Yahweh"), עליון ("Almighty" or "Elyon") and מלך ("king") are all used to refer to God. Third masculine singular verbs are used to refer to the actions of God. God is mentioned a total of eleven times in Ps 47. In eight instances אלהים is used and in two instances יהוה; cf. J. S. Sabinga, "Some Observations on the Composition of Psalm xlvii," *VT* 37 (1988): 474–80 (475).

55. Israel ("us") is indicated by the use of first person plural suffixes. In v. 10 the members of the "in-group" are referred to as עם אברהם ("nation of Abraham," masculine singular) and מגני ("the shields of," masculine plural); all nations are now part of or "with" the nation of Israel. Israel is not referred to once as doing any specific action—the first person plural suffix does not appear attached to any verb. The assumption can be made that Israel exhorts the nations to praise God and that they also praise him, but this is not explicitly stated in the text itself. The fact that they speak of "our inheritance," which also seems to be "the glory of Jacob," is reason to view this group as Israel. Craigie states that "the peoples" in v. 2 refer to

There are a number of nouns, verbs, prepositions, conjunctions, and articles that occur often in Ps 47. It is important to take note of the repetition of כל in כל־עמים ("all the nations," v. 2) and כל־ארץ ("all the earth," vv. 3 and 8), which emphasizes the universal theme of Ps 47. The function of these verses is to give the reasons for the exhortations to praise God, namely, that he is the universal king.[56] Another particle that often occurs in Ps 47 is על ("over, on," v. 3 and twice in v. 9). It corresponds to the use of עליון ("Almighty" or "Elyon," v. 3), עלה ("he has gone up or ascended," v. 6) and נעלה ("he has been exalted," v. 10). The repetition of the particle על, and the verbal stem עלה also emphasizes the theme of Yahweh as universal king.[57]

In Ps 47 Israel serves as the intermediary between God and the nations; by calling on the nations to exhort God, they attempt to convince the nations to subject themselves to God in a peaceful manner. Verse 4 also serves as a reminder that Israel can accomplish nothing without God aiding them in their pursuit, not even vanquishing their enemies. For subduing their enemies under them, Israel's proper response towards God as patron would be to acclaim his honor by praising his name and by submitting themselves to the covenant stipulations in thanksgiving.

In Ps 47 God functions as Israel's patron when he subdues nations (v. 4) and chooses Israel's inheritance (v. 5) for them. Israel responds to this act of grace by proclaiming God's honor and even compelling the nations to do so as well, for not only did God look after the interests of Israel, but he is also the creator, sustainer and king of the whole earth. It follows that all living beings are indebted to God.[58] This applies to Israel and "the nations" as the fact that God is praiseworthy reflects positively on Israel and God's honor.

b. *Holy Space or the Temple in Psalm 47*

The overall unity of Ps 47 is evident in its use of the following words: עם ("nations," vv. 2, 4, 10), מלך ("king," vv. 3, 7, 8, 9), and ארץ ("earth," vv. 3, 8, 10). Psalm 47 elaborates on the words "I am exalted on the earth" at the end of Ps 46. Frank-Lothar Hossfeld and Erich Zenger state

both Israel and foreign nations that are exhorted to praise God's kingship. From the above it is clear that there is a distinction to be made between Israel and the nations who are exhorted to praise, cf. P. C. Craigie, *Psalms 1–50* (WBC 19; Waco: Word Books, 1983), 347.

56. W. S. Prinsloo, "Psalm 47: Partikularisme en Universalisme. Jahwe Is Ons Koning én Koning oor die Hele Aarde," *SK* 17 (1996): 388–401 (390–91).

57. Ibid., 391.

58. D. A. DeSilva, *Honor, Patronage, Kinship and Purity: Unlocking New Testament Culture* (Downers Grove, Ill.: InterVarsity Press, 2000), 126–27.

that Ps 47 is a "*Fortführung*" or continuation of Ps 46. The theme here shifts from God coming from heaven to deliver his people to his returning to his throne in v. 6.[59] The temple was regarded as the most important location of God's presence on earth and an earthly representation of his heavenly abode, and the most likely place to where he would ascend. It was also the place where the horizontal and vertical spheres intersected. Regarding the representation of the horizontal axis in Ps 47, Israel exhorts the (surrounding) nations to praise. The reference to Jacob in Ps 47 brings to mind the tradition of how Israel gained its land and of Abraham as the father of all the nations and his divinely instituted covenant with God (Gen 12). As king of all the earth and the nations, God is depicted as the universal sovereign. On the vertical axis, God is represented as ruling from heaven over all the earth.

It is important to note that the temple in Jerusalem functions as the earthly counterpart of God's heavenly dwelling. Psalm 47:6 may indicate an ascent up to God's earthly sanctuary. In the temple, heaven and earth come together.[60] It is therefore necessary to consider that the procession to Zion is at the same time an ascent to heaven. On psalms containing the Divine Warrior theme, Harold Ballard writes that the tradition-history probably arose from the concept of the inviolability of Zion. The temple was a place where Israel could experience the presence of God, and it represented the deity physically as well.[61]

In Ps 47 God is depicted as the great king ruling over all his vassals. The nations in turn become Israel's more immediate vassals. Peter Craigie states that "the actual occasion for the acknowledgement would have been some ceremony in Jerusalem, where Israel and its vassals were pledged to God, the great King…"[62] The reference to "our king" in Ps 47:7 is the manner in which Israel specifically refers to the close relationships it has with God as its covenant partner. In v. 9 the reign of God appears to be extended over the nations as well, as they are considered to be just like Israel in God's eyes. Psalm 47 is therefore concerned with Yahweh as the ultimate great king.[63]

59. Hossfeld and Zenger, *Psalmen*, 290.
60. Anderson, *Psalms*, 363.
61. H. W. Ballard, *The Divine Warrior Motif in the Psalms* (Bibal Dissertation Series 6; Texas: Bibal, 1999), 88. Keel writes that temples were constructed in such a manner that in times of need they could serve as places of refuge; cf. O. Keel, *The Symbolism of the Biblical World: Ancient Near Eastern Iconography and the Book of Psalms* (trans. T. J. Hallett; Winona Lake: Eisenbrauns, 1997), 179–80.
62. Craigie, *Psalms 1–50*, 350.
63. Anderson, *Psalms*, 362.

Since time immemorial, the ark has been regarded as the throne of Yahweh—an *empty* throne upon which Yahweh was invisibly present. Yahweh sits enthroned on the cherubim in Ps 99:1. It is likely that his throne was initially associated with these figures and later on with the ark. In Jer 3:16 we read that Yahweh's throne is Jerusalem, while other writers of the Old Testament view it as being in the heavens (cf. 1 Kgs 22:19; 2 Chr 18:18; Ps 103:19; Isa 66:1). It is highly unlikely that Ps 47:9 refers to Jerusalem as his throne, but it should not be discredited as a possibility.[64]

The Israelites believed that nothing created is inherently holy, but that it receives that quality through some relation to Yahweh. The temple in itself is not holy, but because Yahweh dwells there or has established it, it becomes so.[65] Therefore, when we read in Ps 47:10 that "God has sat on his holy throne," we can surmise that he rules from his temple or from heaven. This is also to where he apparently ascended in v. 6. Yahweh enthroned is the great universal king to whom all honor is due as he is the patron of the universe, which is indebted to him for defeating the forces of chaos.

c. *The Patriarchal and Promised Land Traditions in Psalm 47*

In v. 5 "our inheritance" and "the glory of Jacob" (two parallel aspects) refer to the inheritance that Israel has received, namely, the Promised Land.[66] The word בחר is closely connected to the concept of the divine election in the Old Testament.[67] The reference to the nations being gathered together as with the nation of the God of Abraham is the result of the fulfillment of God's promise of a land to Abraham in Gen 12. The impression is given that Israel acknowledges the status of the nations as being descendants of Abraham as well.

In comparison to the nations, Israel is God's main client in Ps 47. Thus there is a distinction between the status of Israel and that of the nations. It is only in v. 10 that there is no longer a difference between "us/we" (Israel as "in- group") and "you" (the nations as "out-group").

The generally accepted literal meaning of נחל (v. 4) is as a reference to the division of the land within Israel's kinship structure, and it signifies

---

64. Ibid., 365.

65. Keel, *Symbolism*, 174.

66. Anderson, *Psalms*, 363; cf. H. Gunkel, *Die Psalmen* (6th ed.; Göttingen: Vandenhoeck & Ruprecht, 1986), 203.

67. E. Nicole, "בחר," in *New International Dictionary of Old Testament Theology and Exegesis* (ed. W. A. VanGemeren; 5 vols.; Grand Rapids: Zondervan, 1997), 1:638.

the permanent allotment to various families, clans and tribes. There is a "triangular" usage, which signifies the land as Israel and Yahweh's inheritance, Israel as Yahweh's inheritance and Yahweh as Israel's inheritance.[68] This allotted land was the place of a family's security, to which one returned after battle and where one was eventually buried. It was not owned by the present generation, but held "from the fathers" for the sake of posterity, thus the land remained in family patrimonies for many generations. In Israel's kinship structure, the extended family or the "father's house" was the basic unit of the clan and the tribe. The land of Canaan is viewed as the inheritance of all of Israel and is associated with the divine promise to Israel's ancestors (Exod 32:23; Josh 1:6; Ps 105:11; cf. Deut 4:21; 26:1).

Living in the Promised Land naturally brought with it certain responsibilities, such as doing no evil and obedience to the covenant demands.[69] Yahweh's sovereignty over the nations was such that he could promise to return them to their own inheritances after the Babylonian exile if they turn to him (Jer 12:14–17). While citing Ps 47 as an example, Christopher Wright writes that the ultimate purpose of this was that the nations would eventually belong to the people of Abraham themselves.[70]

It is unclear whether the leaders of the nations come willingly to worship Yahweh in Ps 47:10 or if they are captives of Israel. It is possible that they were foreign representatives present at the pilgrimage festival. There were times when foreigners were incorporated through conquest or conversion into Israel. When Israel conquered an enemy, that territory became a vassal to Israel and leaders of such nations would have been obliged to attend cultic festivals.[71] It was believed that Yahweh was the sovereign over all the nations and that he could restore Israel to their inheritance after the exile.

As the patron of Israel, God is expected to act in a specific manner, namely, by looking after Israel's interests. He does this by not only subjugating the nations under Israel's feet (v. 4), but it is also stated in Ps 47:5 that he loves Jacob, which implies that he would look after the interests of Jacob's descendants as well by supplying them with a land to live on and by protecting them from foreign threats.

---

68. C. J. H. Wright, "נחל," in VanGemeren, ed., *New International Dictionary of Old Testament Theology and Exegesis*, 3:77.
69. Ibid., 77–78.
70. Ibid., 78–79.
71. Anderson, *Psalms*, 365.

The homage of "the nobles of the nations" before the Judaic king on Zion (v. 10) would be a tribute to Yahweh.[72] It is ironic that in Ps 47:10 the nobles or "honorable ones" of the nations are gathered together to praise the God of Israel, that is, to proclaim his world-wide honor.[73] Perhaps this is what makes these representatives noble in the first instance—they realize that they are subject to their conquerors and to their God's will and so offer themselves freely to the inevitable instead of shaming their new-found patron and their God which would only result in retribution and revenge by Israel.

An important contextual item in Pss 46–48 is the focus on the Jerusalem temple. Whether the writer(s) actually lived in the city as he/they wrote is unclear, but the climax of these psalms is Yahweh's ascension to heaven in Ps 47:6. Horizontally, these psalms read the Patriarchal textual tradition as a story line. The settlement narrative describes the story of a people who are physically outside a Firstspace (namely, Canaan or the land of Israel) who long to be inside that Firstspace, described according to their Secondspace perceptions (namely, it being the Holy and Promised Land). Before the settlement, Canaan was the Thirdspace of other "outsider" peoples. These psalms refer to events; often only by allusions, of what happened in the history of Israel. Since this line tends to move chronologically through points in time, I therefore call it a horizontal line.

Underlying the writing down of Ps 47 lays the experience of reality of some individual or group that is (re-)constructed within the wording of the poem. The distinct entities or groups referred to in the poem reflect a schema that has been imposed on a (re-)constructed reality within the text. Even though the representation of Israel and the nations implies distinct homogenous groups, a distinct ethnic categorization between peoples and cultures can be problematic and overly simplistic. The psalm can be considered as someone's representation of the opening of doors and crossing of bridges to cross the cultural divide between what was considered as not necessarily competing, but different, cultural or ethnic groups.

In this poem, Israel's identity is strongly defined in terms of its relationship between itself, its deity, surrounding nations or foreigners and its traditions. Considering the Patriarchal and Promised Land traditions, it is clear that the land was prominent with regards to Israel's identity. This text also reflects how a nation such as Israel might have

72. Keel, *Symbolism*, 268.
73. P. J. Botha, "The 'Enthronement Psalms': A Claim to the World-Wide Honour of Yahweh," *OTE* 11 (1998): 24–39 (24).

experienced great tribulations, such as the Exile, the longing for a physical locale to call the homeland and the traditional associations with such a location and how this can be integral to identity formation, and even reinforcing thereof, during long periods of forced migration in the past.

This text represents a constructed ideal and not necessarily a reflection of (historical) reality. The perspective or focalization of the author is that of a universal perspective on the kingship of God and its transcendence of imposed borders and boundaries between different groups. It also presents an ethnocentric perspective as the author implies patronage of the nations to Israel and then via them to God. There is clearly a social order imposed on this reality—Israel and its deity are in the center of this constructed world. The resulting, yet unintentional, processes are (b)ordering and othering. It does raise the question whether the author of the text has purposely and intentionally sketched a reality of universalism that he/they desire to be reflected in reality.

This psalm is therefore clearly occupied with the establishment and transcendence of boundaries. The privileged status of the in-group determined how near or far one is from sacred space. This is extended to the nations when they are gathered with the people of the God of Abraham in front of his throne and in his presence (Ps 47:10). The limited access they had to Yahweh is now increased as their status changes. Where Ps 46 celebrates the nation's deliverance from peril, Ps 47 extols the power of God, Ps 48 describes the glory of the city, which God has preserved. In Pss 46–48, especially Ps 47, one gets the impression that the author/redactor is concerned with reform—religious or ideological—of nature. This is reinforced by the belief that Zion was the central locus for the Israelite faith.

5. Conclusion

From the preceding, it is clear that the experience of humans permeates their wording and the construction of their worldview and that this worldview or reality has an imposed schema due to a natural differentiation between peoples and places. The practices of (b)ordering and othering are the result of imposed values and identity scripts, which are strongly influenced by social and group relations. Both experience and the practices of (b)ordering and othering then influence the manner in which humans communicate about their world view or reality. There appear to be rules that permeate these constructions, such as the rule of ethnocentricity, that of social order or hierarchicalization. Maps (or texts) reflect not only the worldview or reality of the people being mapped or communicated about, but also that of the cartographer or author. It then stands to reason that mappers or writers control or influence the way in which a particular reality is perceived.

In Ps 47, the theme shifts from God coming from heaven to deliver his people to God returning to his throne. Yahweh has made a place for his people among the nations and the nations are included as his people (Ps 47:5, 10). One can conclude that the author of Ps 47 made use of imagery that was familiar to him from the Syro-Palestinian context. The semantic domains of patronage in Ps 47 indicate that the reader is encountering war terminology where Yahweh is depicted as warrior, or at least as a conqueror who acts on the behalf of Israel, and as universal patron. It could be argued that a universalistic perspective developed either during or after the Babylonian exile, which caused the Israelites or Hebrews to have greater tolerance for cultural diversity. Because of this patron-client relationship between Israel and the nations, the nations also became the clients of God. Universalism is a prominent theme in Ps 47. The nations are exhorted by Israel to praise God for the mighty deeds that he has done for his people. The content of Ps 47 indicates that the nations become part of the nation of the God of Abraham and that the shields of the earth (princes or kings of the nations) belong to God (v. 10). The reference to Jacob and Abraham recalls the Patriarchal and Promised Land traditions and the covenant instituted by God.

The separation between Israel and the nations is transcended when the nations are to be treated as Israel. The relationship between Israel and the nations, as well as the nations' relationship with God, takes on the form of patronage. According to Ps 47, God's rule resonates on all planes of existence, as from his heavenly throne he rules over all the earth, namely, Israel and the nations.

To praise God is an indication of being voluntarily subject to him and accepting his rule over oneself. The call by Israel to the nations for them to praise him thus reinforces the notion of their subjugation and willing subjection to him. To be gathered in the presence of God implies being where he is physically present, namely, the holy mountain, holy city or the temple. This in turn implies that the nations will be able to move into the territory of Israel, which would normally be forbidden as they risk profaning the holy sphere of where God rules and lives. It is clear that if the nations are considered as part of Israel and if God rules over all the earth, then God's rule knows no boundaries and physical and ideological boundaries are crossed. The nations are no longer depicted as an entirely separate entity to Israel. The Patriarchal tradition and promise of the holy land is therefore also extended. The temple is no longer the locus of the Israelite faith alone, but even the nations can have a relationship with Yahweh, albeit it through the vassalage of Israel.

JERUSALEM, THE HOLY CITY:
THE MEANING OF THE CITY OF JERUSALEM
IN THE BOOKS OF EZRA–NEHEMIAH

Maria Häusl

1. *The Problem of the "Holy City"*

In compiling the Old Testament references for Jerusalem as עיר הקדש,
one encounters the books of Ezra–Nehemiah, or rather Neh 11:1 and
11:18.[1] Although Jerusalem has the title "Holy City" here, in the exegesis
of Ezra–Nehemiah the city of Jerusalem does not receive much consideration with respect to its theological meaning. The books of Ezra–
Nehemiah, however, are seen as an important outline of the formation of
post-exilic Israel, and key elements of the concept of identity can be
drawn from the two books. Such key elements usually are the observance
of the Torah, the temple cult, and the isolation from foreigners/others.[2]
The city of Jerusalem does not receive much attention in this context.

2. *Short Research Overview*

Until now, only few scholars, like Eskenazi,[3] Karrer[4] and Böhler,[5] for
example, have noticed that the city takes on an important role in

---

1. See O. Keel, *Die Geschichte Jerusalems und die Entstehung des Mono-*
theismus (2 vols.; OLB 4; Göttingen: Vandenhoeck & Ruprecht, 2007), 1:72–73.
2. See, e.g., J. L. Wright, *Rebuilding Identity: The Nehemiah-Memoir and Its*
Earliest Readers (BZAW 348; Berlin: W. de Gruyter, 2004), or R. Rothenbusch,
"Die Auseinandersetzung um die Identität Israels im Esra- und Nehemiabuch," in
Die Identität Israels: Entwicklungen und Kontroversen in alttestamentlicher Zeit
(ed. H. Irsigler; HBS 56; Freiburg: Herder, 2009), 111–44.
3. T. C. Eskenazi, *In an Age of Prose: A Literary Approach to Ezra–Nehemiah*
(SBLMS 36; Atlanta: Scholars Press, 1988).
4. C. Karrer, *Ringen um die Verfassung Judas: Eine Studie zu den theologisch-*
politischen Vorstellungen im Esra-Nehemia-Buch (BZAW 308; Berlin: W. de
Gruyter, 2001).

establishing post-exilic Israel's identity in Ezra–Nehemiah. Eskenazi suggests "that in Ezra–Nehemiah, the building of the wall is an extension of building the temple."[6] This means that the house of God is not identified with the temple but with the city and "temple-like sanctity is extended to the city as a whole."[7] Karrer and Böhler recognize the important relationship between city and Torah which is reflected in the composition of the book of Nehemiah. The proclamation of the Torah (Neh 8–10) is framed by the description of how the city wall is rebuilt and the city is settled. Karrer argues:

> The construction of the city wall and the observance of the Torah form a thematic pair which designates the foundations for the formation of the Judaean community. They include an external and an internal aspect of the community, both of which are different, but in the perspective of the overall concept have to be seen as closely connected.[8]

Böhler describes the relation between the wall and Torah as follows: "The Nehemiah narrative forms a concentric structure with the city wall as the outer frame, the colonization of the city as the inner frame and Ezra's Torah as the core... The wall constitutes the outer skin, God's people stand for the living flesh, and the Torah is the soul."[9]

In comparison with Karrer's differentiation between the external and internal perspectives of a community, the imagery of the body used by Böhler does not seem to be very helpful: the relationship between the city wall and the community can hardly be described through body imagery. In their definition of the relationship between temple and city, Karrer and Böhler mainly follow the almost unanimous opinion that the city of Jerusalem does not draw its theological importance and dignity from anything else except the fact that the temple is located there.[10] At first, Karrer defines the relationship between temple and city carefully

---

5. D. Böhler, "Das Gottesvolk als Altargemeinschaft: Die Bedeutung des Tempels für die Konstituierung kollektiver Identität nach Esra-Nehemia," in *Gottesstadt und Gottesgarten: Zu Geschichte und Theologie des Jerusalemer Tempels* (ed. O. Keel and E. Zenger; QD 191; Freiburg: Herder, 2002), 207–30.

6. Eskenazi, *In an Age of Prose*, 83.

7. Ibid., 188–89.

8. Karrer, *Ringen um die Verfassung Judas*, 357 (author's translation).

9. Böhler, "Das Gottesvolk als Altargemeinschaft," 209–10 (author's translation).

10. Other Old Testament conceptions show clearly that Jerusalem is not perceived as only the location of the temple, and that the city's theological meaning is not derived only from this. Remember, for example, the concept of Ezek 40–48, which separates temple and city, or Zech 1–8, which sees the city as the "house of YHWH."

and—in my opinion—accurately, when she parallels temple and city:
"With respect to the overall composition [of Ezra–Nehemiah], the
construction of temple and city wall belong together. Both of them are
concerned with the 'external perspective' of the formation of the
community."[11] Why the temple is then seen as the center, which is to
shape our understanding of the city and its walls,[12] is neither convincing,
nor is it substantiated. Böhler describes the relationship between temple
and city as follows:

> The temple is not only the first thing, which must be reconstructed during
> Israel's restoration after the exile, but it also remains Israel's core consti-
> tuent. The Torah as the house rules and the Holy City as the society,
> which lives according to these house rules, are both oriented towards this
> core. In the vital body of the *civitas*, the temple appears as the pulsating
> heart that supplies the body with life. So much for the internal structure of
> Ezra–Nehemiah.[13]

While I would not call into question the fact that the temple is one of the
core constituents of the concept of identity in the books of Ezra–
Nehemiah, I find it difficult to determine the relationship between temple
and city. Is the house of God identified with the city in Ezra–Nehemiah,
as Eskenazi argues? Alternatively, is the temple really the core of the city
according to Ezra–Nehemiah, as Karrer opines? In Böhler's interpretation, the city is even identified with its population, thus ultimately
losing its meaning with reference to a concept of identity, whereas the
temple is recognized as a constitutive element thereof.

Although Eskenazi, Karrer, and Böhler realize the importance of the
city of Jerusalem in the books of Ezra–Nehemiah, their theses are not
convincing. One must therefore explore anew and more deeply the theological meaning of the city of Jerusalem within the concept of identity in
the books of Ezra–Nehemiah. That the city of Jerusalem cannot simply
be identified with its population, as Böhler does, has been proven by
various studies that analyze the portrayal of Jerusalem in other Old
Testament texts.[14] In fact, Jerusalem should to be seen as a symbol that

---

11. Karrer, *Ringen um die Verfassung Judas*, 359 (author's translation).
12. Ibid., 361.
13. Böhler, "Das Gottesvolk als Altargemeinschaft," 214 (author's translation).
14. See M. Häusl, *Bilder der Not: Weiblichkeits- und Geschlechtermetaphorik im
Buch Jeremia* (HBS 37; Freiburg: Herder, 2003); C. M. Maier, *Daughter Zion,
Mother Zion: Gender, Space, and the Sacred in Ancient Israel* (Minneapolis:
Fortress, 2008); R. Zimmermann, *Geschlechtermetaphorik und Gottesverhältnis:
Traditionsgeschichte und Theologie eines Bildfelds in Urchristentum und antiker
Umwelt* (WUNT II/122; Tübingen: Mohr Siebeck, 2001).

creates identity and community spirit. Though some aspects of the temple are ascribed to the city of Jerusalem, the city is not simply identical with the house of God, as Eskenazi opines. The following questions arise: Which aspects that actually fulfill a symbolic function does the city have in the books of Ezra–Nehemiah? Does Jerusalem only function as a symbol because the temple is located there, as Karrer suggests?

The following literary approach to the books of Ezra–Nehemiah[15] will demonstrate that aspects of space, especially of urban space are important for the designation of Jerusalem as Holy City. Based on the theoretical considerations of Berquist and Camp about space in biblical texts,[16] one may consider the description of Jerusalem in the books of Ezra–Nehemiah as mental space (Secondspace). This mental space uses aspects only characteristic of a city, as well as aspects that mark Jerusalem as a place in the greater geographical space of the Persian Empire.[17]

Regarding the urban aspects of the city highly reflects the center–periphery concept, which is part of the ancient Near Eastern cosmology.[18] On the other hand, the greater geographical space of the Persian Empire, which also comes into play, depends on the perspective of the Diaspora. The spatial concept of a Diaspora group implies not only the actual living space, but also a fictional or actual relationship towards the country of origin.[19]

3. *Texts and Topics Regarding the City of Jerusalem in Ezra–Nehemiah*

To start with, I would like to present some statistics that not only provide an initial overview, but, at the same time, underline the meaning of Jerusalem in the books of Ezra–Nehemiah. The term "Zion" is not used,

---

15. The results are based on structural and narrative analyses of those parts of the books Ezra–Nehemiah which mention Jerusalem. I thank Diana Edelman for her critical and stimulating response to an earlier draft of the present study.

16. See J. L. Berquist and C. V. Camp, eds., *Constructions of Space I: Theory, Geography and Narrative* (LHBOTS 481; New York/London: T&T Clark International, 2008), and *Constructions of Space II: The Biblical City and Other Imagined Spaces* (LHBOTS 490; New York/London: T&T Clark International, 2007).

17. See J. L. Berquist, "Spaces of Jerusalem," in Berquist and Camp, eds., *Constructions of Space II*, 40–52 (47–48).

18. See B. Janowski, "Das biblische Weltbild: Eine methodologische Skizze," in *Das biblische Weltbild und seine altorientalischen Kontexte* (ed. B. Janowski and B. Ego; FAT 32; Tübingen: Mohr Siebeck, 2001), 3–26 (20–21).

19. See R. Mayer, *Diaspora: Eine kritische Begriffsklärung* (Cultural Studies 14; Bielefeld: Transkript, 2005), 8–14.

but the name "Jerusalem" is mentioned 85 times in all.[20] Compared to other Old Testament books, this is a remarkable number of references.[21] The nouns קריא and עיר refer to Jerusalem 14 times and pronouns refer to Jerusalem ten times.[22] As such, Jerusalem is mentioned almost as frequently as the temple in the books of Ezra–Nehemiah.

Taking a closer look at the syntactical constructions of the name "Jerusalem" or the above-mentioned lexemes and the pronouns referring to Jerusalem, one recognizes four features.

1. Jerusalem is often used significantly in constructions as the destination of a movement.[23]
2. Equally often, the prepositional construction בירושלם is used as a predicate for locating the temple.[24]

Special constructions of Jerusalem are, however, limited to certain passages of the text.

3. In Neh 1–7, Jerusalem is used as the object of actions.[25] Correspondingly, this passage also refers to the walls and gates of Jerusalem.[26]
4. Only in Neh 11 is the city used in the construction ישב ב.[27]

This specific syntactical distribution of the name "Jerusalem" corresponds to four topics:

1. Jerusalem is the place to which people from the Golah or the Diaspora go.
2. Jerusalem is the location of the house of God, especially in the book of Ezra.

---

20. Thirty-eight times in Nehemiah, 24 times in the Hebrew and 23 times in the Aramaic part of Ezra.

21. Jerusalem is mentioned in comparable frequency only in Kings, Chronicles and Jeremiah. They all are concerned with the pre-exilic, destroyed city or with the building of the First Temple respectively.

22. Cf. קריא: Ezra 4:12, 13, 15, 16, 19 and 21; עיר: Neh 2:3, 5, 8; 7:4; 11:1, 9, 18; 13:18; suffixed pronouns: Ezra 4:15, 16; Neh 1:3; 2:3 (×2), 5, 17; 7:4 (×2). The בירה mentioned in Neh 2:8; 7:2 has no decisive significance in the texts.

23. Cf. Ezra 1:3, 7, 11; 2:1; 3:8; 7:7, 8, 9; 8:30, 31, 32; Neh 2:11; 7:6; 12:27; 13:7, 15; in the Aramaic parts: Ezra 4:12, 23 and 7:13.

24. Cf. Ezra 1:2 (as an apposition), 4, 5; 2:68; 7:27; in the Aramaic parts: Ezra 4:24; 5:2, 14, 15, 16, 17 (as an apposition); 6:3 (as an apposition), 5 (×2), 12, 18 (sacrificial service); 7:15, 16, 17.

25. Cf. Neh 2:17; 3:8; 4:2.

26. Cf. חומה 24 times in Neh 1–7; שערים eight times in Neh 1–7; this must be complemented by the dedication of the city wall in Neh 12:27–43.

27. Cf. Neh 11:1, 2, 3, 4, 6.

3. The walls and gates of Jerusalem, according to Neh 1:1–7:3, are reconstructed.[28]
4. According to Neh 7:4–5 and ch. 11, Jerusalem is the place that is resettled.

a. *The Way to Jerusalem*

In the books of Ezra–Nehemiah, Jerusalem is the destination of movement of various kinds.[29] Four of these are especially prominent. In the following, starting-points and destinations of movements will be analyzed.

Regarding textual chronology, the first reference to movement occurs in Ezra 1:5 and 1:11. According to Ezra 1:11, Sheshbazzar and the Golah go up (עלה) to Jerusalem together and bring the vessels of the temple. The preceding edict of Cyrus (Ezra 1:3) and Ezra 1:5 state that the reason for going up to Jerusalem is to rebuild the temple of YHWH there.[30] Ezra 5:14–16 refers back to Sheshbazzar who brought the temple vessels from Babylon to the Jerusalem temple and laid the foundations of the temple.

The second movement is connected to Zerubbabel and Jeshua. The headline of the list in Ezra 2 indicates the movement as עלה, "to go up" (Ezra 2:1), but also as שוב, "to return" (Ezra 2:1). Ezra 2:1 thus creates the idea that Zerubbabel's and Jeshua's people will return. In other contexts, however, this "return" is also called עלה, "to go up,"[31] or בוא, "to come."[32] This movement, labeled a "return," is not only limited to Jerusalem; its destination is rather Jerusalem *and* Judah with all its cities (Ezra 2:1). As the first concrete destination of the movement—indicated as בוא, "to come"—the Jerusalem temple is named in Ezra 2:68. Thereafter, Ezra 2:70 finally states that all people and groups (as well as all of Israel) settled in their cities.

---

28.   The rebuilding of the city wall is completed by the dedication in Neh 12:27–43. The reconstruction of the city is also mentioned in Ezra 4:12–16, when the leaders of Samaria try to prohibit the rebuilding.

29.   This statement cannot be found in only one passage of the books of Ezra–Nehemiah, nor in one redactional layer only. Rather, "going up to Jerusalem" introduces a new topic; it therefore serves as a means of structuring the text on the final textual layer and is characteristic for the books of Ezra–Nehemiah.

30.   Ezra 1:5 lists those who go up: the heads of the families of Judah and Benjamin, the priests and Levites, and everyone whose spirit God has stirred will go up to rebuild the house of YHWH in Jerusalem.

31.   עלה Ezra 2:59 (par. Neh 7:61); Neh 12:1.

32.   בוא Ezra 3:8; Neh 7:7.

In Ezra 7:6–9, the third movement under the scribe Ezra is described in a similar way to the first one under Sheshbazzar. Ezra also goes up (עלה) from Babylon to Jerusalem;[33] he is accompanied by the Israelites, priests, Levites, singers, gatekeepers, and temple servants, all of whom are listed in Ezra 8:1–20.[34] There is, however, no mention of the fact that they settle down anywhere. This movement has Jerusalem as its only destination, although Artaxerxes' decree refers not only to Jerusalem, but also to Judah (Ezra 7:14) or "the province beyond the river" (7:25).

The fourth movement is Nehemiah's: in Neh 2:11a, he comes (בוא) to Jerusalem alone, and does not bring a group of Israelites with him.[35] Where his journey started can only be deduced from the context. In 1:1, it is said that he stayed in Susa. According to 13:6–7, he comes to Jerusalem a second time after having returned to King Artaxerxes in the interim.[36]

In reviewing all four movements of Sheshbazzar. Zerubbabel and Jeshua, Ezra and Nehemiah to Jerusalem, it is striking that only one of the four movements is called a "return" (שוב).[37] Otherwise, it is called עלה, "to go up,"[38] בוא, "to come,"[39] or הלך, "to go."[40] In three of the four cases, other people or groups from the Golah come to Jerusalem or Judah together with the protagonist. But only Zerubbabel's and Jeshua's movement, which is called a "return," does in fact lead to a settling in Judah. At the same time, this movement is the only one that is not the result of a direct Persian order. The other three moves to Jerusalem are the result of a decree of a Persian king. Sheshbazzar is supposed to rebuild the Jerusalem temple for the God of Heaven and therefore has to bring the temple objects to Jerusalem. Ezra receives an order to

---

33. עלה Ezra 7:7, 28; בוא Ezra 7:8, 9; 8:1, 30 (hiphil), 32; הלך Ezra 8:31; Aram. Ezra 7:13.

34. In Ezra 8:35, the people coming from captivity together with Ezra are called בני הגלה, "sons of the Golah."

35. See also Neh 2:10; in 2:9, a royal escort for Nehemiah is mentioned.

36. See also Neh 2:6 with Artaxerxes' question when Nehemiah will return (שוב).

37. Beyond that, שוב is used only in Ezra 6:21 and Neh 8:17 to indicate the coming out of captivity. Both texts are summaries, which do not refer to a specific "wave of returnees."

38. Cf. Ezra 1:3, 5, 11; 7:7, 28; Neh 12:27 (hiphil); 13:7, 15 (hiphil); Aram. Ezra 4:12.

39. Cf. Ezra 2:2; 3:8; 7:8, 9; 8:1, 30 (hiphil), 32; Neh 1:9–10 (hiphil); 2:11; Aram. Ezra 4:12; 5:16.

40. Cf. Ezra 8:31; Aram. Ezra 7:13.

investigate the law of God in Judah and Jerusalem as well as to bring more money to the Jerusalem temple. Nehemiah's assignment is to rebuild the city wall. There is no Persian decree for resettling Judah. Zerubbabel's and Jeshua's movement, which in Ezra 2:2 is called a "return" and which results in a settlement in Judah, is significantly different from the other movements. This movement alone introduces to the books of Ezra–Nehemiah the idea that the population of Judah or "the whole of Israel," respectively, are to be identified with the returnees from the Golah.[41] As a result, most scholars so far have regarded the other three movements—or at least Sheshbazzar's and Ezra's—as movements of returnees, or even waves of returnees. One should be careful to speak of a return, however, because only Ezra 2:1 speaks of a "return": Not all movements can be qualified as a "return."

If one starts the interpretation with the verb עלה, which, in fact, is used most frequently, the movements to Jerusalem are to be understood differently. At first, the basic meaning of עלה, "to go up to a higher destination," has to be taken into account, so that movements to Jerusalem appear as journeys to this destination. It is possible, however, to assume allusions to theological contexts of the use of עלה; one could think of the motifs of exodus or of pilgrimage. Nevertheless, for the exodus motif, there is hardly any textual evidence. Only Ezra 2 explicitly mentions people going up from captivity (Ezra 2:1) and eventually settling in Judah (Ezra 2:70).[42] Much more significantly, the movement of going up most often has the goal of rebuilding the Jerusalem temple or bringing offerings there.[43] Yet one should not interpret these goals as pilgrimages in the strict sense of the word,[44] even though there is a connection between עלה and cultic activity in Ezra 1 and 3–6. In these texts, the movement to Jerusalem does not only result in the rebuilding of the temple, but primarily in the re-installation of sacrifice, which should be seen as the proper goal of Ezra 1 and 3–6.[45]

41. See Karrer, *Ringen um die Verfassung Judas*, 73, 108–9.
42. See ibid., 77–78.
43. See ibid., 332.
44. Similarly, O. Dyma, *Die Wallfahrt zum Zweiten Tempel: Untersuchungen zur Entwicklung der Wallfahrtsfeste in vorhasmonäischer Zeit* (FAT II/40; Tübingen: Mohr Siebeck, 2009), 304–6.
45. See Karrer, *Ringen um die Verfassung Judas*, 346; M. Häusl, "Feste feiern— Zur Bedeutung der Feste im Buch Esra/Nehemia," in *Kulte, Priester, Rituale: Beiträge zu Kult und Kultkritik im Alten Testament und Alten Orient* (ed. S. Ernst and M. Häusl; Festschrift T. Seidl; St. Ottilien: EOS, 2010), 231–51.

In sum, "returning" is not the primary goal of the various movements to Jerusalem.[46] Rather, the Eastern Diaspora wants to exert formative influence on Jerusalem, by making donations, for example, or promoting the rebuilding of the temple and the city.[47] As such, various theological motivations guide the Diaspora. Jerusalem is understood as the legitimate location of the YHWH-temple and of sacrifice, and further as the place of one's own origin in Neh 2:3–5. The Eastern Diaspora sees the city of Jerusalem as a place that is theologically highly charged and one, too, which acquires its dignity in part from being the legitimate dwelling place of YHWH. The first topic is followed immediately by the second topic: Jerusalem is where the temple is located. Here we expect the text to determine more precisely the relationship between the temple and the city of Jerusalem.

b. *The House of God, Located in Jerusalem*

The above-mentioned prepositional construction בירושלם is frequently used to describe the location of the temple in Jerusalem,[48] but it does not explain either the dignity of the city or that of the temple fully. Instead, the phrase בירושלם raises the question as to what may be the function and meaning of the location of the temple in Jerusalem with regard to both the city and the temple. Syntactically, the construction בירושלם is the predicate of a nominal sentence,[49] which is a relative clause, and as such an attribute to a nominal group designating the temple. The construction

---

46. In Ezra 1:3; Neh 1:3 and 13:6 the idea of a permanent Diaspora appears. Throughout the structure of the books of Ezra–Nehemiah, with their repeated journeys to Jerusalem, it is made equally clear that the crucial point is the "relationship" of the Eastern Diaspora to Jerusalem/Judah and not the return. The Diaspora's dominance can first of all be seen in the Hebrew parts of Ezra 1–6 and Ezra 7–10, whereas the main actor in the Aramaic parts of Ezra 1–6 and also Neh 1–7 is the local Judaean population.

47. The books of Ezra–Nehemiah are dominated in total by the Diaspora perspective. Christiane Karrer, however, has pointed to the fact that the Aramaic part of Ezra 1–6 and Neh 1–7 is focused on the Judaean population with no interest in the Golah; only the Hebrew parts of Ezra 1–6 and Ezra 7–10 speak of a dominance of the Golah.

48. All references come from the book of Ezra, which narrates the rebuilding of the temple and the new installation of the sacrificial cult. These events cannot be assigned to one specific layer or redaction. We find the constructions in the Aramaic part of the narrative about the building of the temple (Ezra 4:7–6:15) as well as in the later, framing parts of the Hebrew text (Ezra 1–6*) and in the Ezra narrative (Ezra 7–10).

49. This is constructed as an apposition in Ezra 5:17 and 6:3.

therefore clearly serves as a clause that specifies the temple. The city of Jerusalem is the well-known entity that identifies the temple. This relation between the temple and the city nullifies Eskenazi's thesis that the house of God is identified with the city of Jerusalem in the books of Ezra–Nehemiah.

This result is confirmed by the way in which the construction is integrated into the context, as the temple is mostly localized in Jerusalem when the perspective of the Persian Empire is "quoted" in decrees or letters.[50] This external perspective requires an exact location, so that one can distinguish this "house of God" from other such houses in the Persian Empire. First, this is the case in King Cyrus's edict in Ezra 1:2–4,[51] and secondly, the same applies to the correspondence between Tattenai and Darius in Ezra 5:6–6:12. In this passage, the house of God is placed in Jerusalem eight times.[52] Both the builders of the temple and Cyrus emphasize that the temple has to be rebuilt at its original site. This means that it is important to maintain or to re-establish the continuity of the houses of God (and the places of sacrifice).[53] A third Persian view of the house of God in Jerusalem can be found in the letter of King Artaxerxes in Ezra 7:11–26, although its focus is not the house of God in the first place.[54] Aside from these references to the temple being located in Jerusalem, the letters of Cyrus and Artaxerxes also express a direct relationship between the deity and Jerusalem without mentioning the house of God.[55] Perhaps the frequent placement of the temple of YHWH in the letters of Persian kings not only has the intention of clarifying exactly which temple is meant, but also has the aim of letting the highest authority of Persia legitimate and acknowledge this temple.[56] Yet, the latter only makes sense if there were alternatives to Jerusalem for locating a temple. In the Persian and early Hellenistic period, such alternative places for the worship of YHWH would have been Mizpah, Bethel, Elephantine or Mount Gerizim, all of which are discussed in

50. There are five references that cannot be explained this way: Ezra 2:68; 3:8; 4:24; 5:2 and 7:27.

51. In Ezra 1:5, the localization is taken up again in the narration. In Ezra 1:3 God himself is located in Jerusalem.

52. Cf. Ezra 5:14, 15, 16, 17; 6:3, 5, 12.

53. Cf. Ezra 6:18.

54. Cf. Ezra 7:15, 16, 17.

55. Cf. Ezra 1:3; 7:19.

56. It is interesting that there are no assertions to the uniqueness of the Jerusalem temple in Ezra–Nehemiah aside from Ezra 9:8 and Neh 1:9, which form part of prayers influenced by Deuteronomistic language and thought.

research. This is also true for an Aramaic ostracon from Idumaea inscribed with the words *byt yhw*.[57]

c. *Building the Jerusalem City Wall*

For most parts of the book of Nehemiah, the city of Jerusalem is a key issue. One can thereby distinguish the building of the city wall in Neh 1:1–7:3 and the settling of the city in 7:4–5 and ch. 11. The topic of the city wall ends with the ceremonial dedication of the wall in Neh 12:27–43. Furthermore, the city of Jerusalem is central to Ezra 4.[58]

The main text about the building of the city wall is found in Neh 1:1–7:3, the plot of which mentions two problems at the beginning: "The survivors there in the province who escaped captivity are in great trouble and shame," and: "The wall of Jerusalem is broken down, and its gates have been destroyed by fire" (1:3). The subsequent narrative centers on the solution of the second problem, whereby the first problem is also eventually solved.

Analyzing the syntax of the sentences and of the whole text, the shift of place and time as well as the constellation of the characters reveal the following structure in Neh 1:1–7:3.[59] The delimitation of 7:4 is due to a

57. For Bethel, see M. Köhlmoos, *Bet-El—Erinnerungen an eine Stadt: Perspektiven der alttestamentlichen Bet-El-Überlieferung* (FAT 49; Tübingen: Mohr Siebeck, 2006); E. A. Knauf, "Bethel: The Israelite Impact on Judean Language and Literature," in *Judah and the Judeans in the Persian Period* (ed. O. Lipschits and M. Oeming; Winona Lake: Eisenbrauns, 2006), 291–349, and U. Becker, "Jakob in Bet-El und Sichem," in *Die Erzväter in der biblischen Tradition* (ed. A. C. Hagedorn and H. Pfeiffer; Festschrift M. Köckert; BZAW 400; Berlin: W. de Gruyter, 2009), 159–85; for *byt yhw*, written on an Aramaic ostracon, see A. Lemaire, *Nouvelles inscriptions araméennes d'Idumée* (Paris: Gabalda, 2002), 149–56; L. L. Grabbe, *Yehud: A History of the Persian Province of Judah* (LSTS 47; New York/London: T&T Clark International, 2006), 215–16.

58. Regarding literary history, I assume that there was a basic narrative in Neh 1:1–7:3 which did not include ch. 5 and ch. 3; see T. Reinmuth, *Der Bericht Nehemias: Zur literarischen Eigenart, traditionsgeschichtlichen Prägung und inner-biblischen Rezeption des Ich-Berichts Nehemias* (OBO 183; Freiburg: Vandenhoeck & Ruprecht, 2002). It has to remain open here as to whether the basic narrative was originally resumed in Neh 7:4–5 or in 12:27–43, because the later redactional revisions in chs. 7–12 are too strong.

59. Neh 1:1a is not a part of the narration itself, but of the headline to the book of Nehemiah. In Ezra–Nehemiah, this headline does not rank as a superior structural element. Furthermore, ויהי in Neh 1:1 is only a relative segmentation, and the date of the twentieth regal year in Neh 1:1 points to Ezra 7:1. See Karrer, *Ringen um die Verfassung Judas*, 300–303.

thematic shift and is not largely based on formal criteria,[60] since the problem mentioned in 1:3 finds a permanent solution: guard duty and the use of the city gates have been organized. At the same time, 7:4 approaches a problem which was not previously perceived—there is hardly any population in the city, and practically no houses have been built.

Exposition   Neh 1:1–11
     identifying the problem in 1:3[61]

Main part   Neh 2:1–6:14: the city wall is built against hostile attacks
  1. 2:1–10
     Nehemiah is sent by the king to rebuild the city (2:5)[62]
     —anticipated mention of the opponents Sanballat, Tobiah, and Geshem[63]

  2. 2:11–20
     Nehemiah motivates to build the city wall (2:17)[64]
     —Sanballat's, Tobiah's, and Geshem's mockery

  3. 3:1–32
     building of the city wall; the involved persons (groups) and sections of the wall are named[65]

  4. 3:33–38[66]
     again, mockery by Sanballat, Tobiah, and Geshem—building of the wall is continued[67]

  5. 4:1–8
     conflict with Sanballat, Tobiah, and Geshem—preparation for defense[68]

  6. 4:9–17
     thwarting of the enemy's attack—building of the wall is continued[69]

---

60. Neh 7:4 does not proceed with the narration, but uses nominal sentences to address new problems.

61. Structuring features: in 1:1, the month of Chislev in the twentieth year as date; in 1:1, Susa as place; an interruption of the narrative flow with ויהי in 1:1.

62. Structuring features: in 2:1, the month of Nisan in the twentieth year of Artaxerxes as date; an interruption of the narrative flow with יהי in 2:1.

63. Structuring features: introduction of new names.

64. Structuring features: in 2:11, Jerusalem as place; introduction of new groups.

65. Structuring features: a different genre of a list of builders, which is embedded into the narrative by a *wayyiqtol* form.

66. The NRSV differs from the Hebrew text in its numbering of the verses of Neh 3 and 4.

67. Structuring features: an interruption of the narrative flow in 3:33 with ויהי.

68. Structuring features: an interruption of the narrative flow in 4:1 with ויהי.

69. Structuring features: an interruption of the narrative flow in 4:9 with ויהי.

7. 6:1–14
Sanballat's and Tobiah's intrigues against Nehemiah—intrigues repelled

Conclusion   Neh 6:15–7:3
1. 6:15
finishing of the city wall[70]

2. 6:16–19
reaction of the enemies [added: Tobiah's position][71]

3. 7:1–3
setting up of the gates and appointment of the guard duty[72]

The structure of Neh 1:1–7:3 is determined by the shift of individual episodes that are separated by the repeated element ויהי. The individual episodes include the corresponding activities of two groups of people. These groups are, on the one hand, Nehemiah and the builders, and on the other hand, their enemies Sanballat, Tobiah, and Geshem. Therefore, in the course of the narrative, there is a constant change between both of these groups. In the first two episodes, the enemies react on Nehemiah's initiative, and in the following four episodes, the enemies are active while Nehemiah and the builders react. Beginning with 3:33, the enemies' agitations become more prominent in the text than the building work. In 6:1–7:3, the latter retreats completely to the background. After the third episode, the initiative shifts from Nehemiah to the enemies. This episode, however, is not a narrative in the strict sense, but a separate list of the people and groups involved in the building activities.

A closer look at the antagonistic groups makes it possible to recognize the intentions connected with the city. Except for Neh 3, the narrative in 1:1–7:3 is formulated as a first-person account of Nehemiah presenting himself as the main character. In 1:11, he is introduced as the cupbearer of the Persian king in Susa and granted authority by the Persian king to rebuild the city of his ancestor's graves (2:5). Nehemiah is the one who takes the initiative; he travels to Jerusalem, motivates the persons in charge of building the city wall and organizes the guard duty at the gates. It is also Nehemiah who initiates the defense against hostile agitation and attacks; in ch. 6, he himself is targeted.

---

70. Structuring features: in 6:15, "on the twenty-fifth day of the month Elul, in 52 days" as date.

71. Structuring features: an interruption of the narrative flow in 6:16 with ויהי; and a date in 6:17.

72. Structuring features: an interruption of the narrative flow in 7:1 with ויהי.

The most prominent group among those involved in building the city wall is the יהודים. The importance of this group is clearly expressed by the fact that Nehemiah's narrative "I" is replaced by "we" starting at Neh 3:33.[73] The project of building the city wall thus is a project of the entire Judaean population. The word יהודים is a geographical denotation of the Judaeans; it does not refer to religious or cultic criteria.[74] Except for Nehemiah himself, no person from the Diaspora participates in the building of the city wall.[75] When 2:16 speaks of סגנים, "officials," כוהנים, "priests," and חרים, "nobles," it means leading groups of this population.[76] In 7:1–3, other people are introduced: Hanani, a brother of Nehemiah, who is already mentioned in 1:2 and given charge over Jerusalem, and Hananiah, who is the commander of the guard. Additionally, ch. 6 refers to prophets and 4:7 to clans. The account of the building in ch. 3, however, divides the population with respect to status, professional groups, and individuals.

Nehemiah's interpretations and prayers, which finally characterize the theological interpretation of the city, permeate the activities of Nehemiah and the builders.[77] As I have stated elsewhere, the prayers, in particular Neh 1:5–11, serve the function of ascribing to God the initiative of the action, and of making clear that God actually is the agent.[78] The respective explicit statements from Nehemiah confirm this. In this way, the following actions are ascribed to God: the king's consent (2:8, 18); the plan to renew the city wall (2:12); the success of the building of the wall (2:20); the thwarting of the enemies' plan (4:9); the defense (4:14); and the fact that Shemaiah has not been sent (6:12). All these interpretations lead to the statement in 6:16 that God himself completed the building of the wall. Both the success of the building of the wall and the defense of the enemies are attributed to God's work. In the course of the narrative and in Nehemiah's interpretations, the rebuilding of the Jerusalem city

---

73. Karrer, *Ringen um die Verfassung Judas*, 177–79.

74. Ibid., 149–53, clearly substantiates that in Neh 1:1–7:3 יהודים characterizes the Judaeans as population of Judaea and as part of Israel (2:10).

75. Ibid., 116: "In the course of the text, the returnees and other parts of the Judaean population are not distinguished; it lacks any terminology which could point to a return from exile" (author's translation).

76. Cf. also Neh 4:8, 13; 6:17. See ibid., 116–20, 161–62.

77. Neh 1:5–11; 3:36–37; 6:14; the narration of a prayer in 2:4, 5; 4:3.

78. See M. Häusl, "'Ich betete zum Gott des Himmels' (Neh 2,4): Zur kontextuellen Einbettung der Gebete in Neh 1–13," in *Der über Seine Weisung nachsinnt bei Tag und bei Nacht (Ps 1,2)* (ed. C. Diller et al.; Festschrift H. Irsigler; HBS 64; Freiburg: Herder, 2010), 47–64.

wall is seen as the solution to both problems mentioned in 1:3. The city wall, now restored, represents the end of the population's trouble (רעה) and of shame/disgrace (חרפה). Nehemiah 2:17, in particular, confirms this interpretation by arguing that the city's troubles are rooted in the destruction of the city and, therefore, the city wall's rebuilding ends the disgrace. This interpretation is also confirmed by 3:36, which identifies the shame/disgrace with the mocking of the wall's rebuilding by the enemies.

In the narrative, the enemies seem to be as important as the builders are, for both groups are mentioned alternately. Sanballat, Tobiah, and Geshem are specifically mentioned by name. They are not characterized by their political offices, but by *nomina gentilicia*. "Sanballat was presumably the Samaritan governor. In the account of Nehemiah, however, this can only be recognized from 3:34, where it is said that Sanballat speaks in the presence of the Samarian army."[79] The enemy group is distinguished in two respects from the group of the builders. In 2:20, Nehemiah states that Sanballat, Tobiah, and Geshem shall have no share or claim or memorial in Jerusalem. Unlike Ezra 4:2, Nehemiah's statement does not exclude the three persons from participating in the building activities, because they did not have the intention of participating. In the context of the narrative, this statement of Nehemiah can only be understood as an attempt to reduce the influence of these persons in Jerusalem and Judah. They are implicitly excluded by a narrative strategy that characterizes them as enemies of the building project, since their attitude is marked by a fundamental rejection of Nehemiah and the Judaeans even *before* Nehemiah takes the initiative in Jerusalem (Neh 2:10). After that, their exclusion is reflected in mockery and anger (2:19; 3:33–35), in conspiracy and plans of attack (4:2) and in intrigues against Nehemiah himself (ch. 6). The structure of the narrative clearly emphasizes these hostile "attacks."

Yet, the enemies are given the opportunity of voicing their interpretation of the building activities, namely, that the building of the city wall is a rebellion against the Persian king (Neh 2:19). The opponents argue that the builders intend to fortify the city for themselves (3:34) and even that Nehemiah wants to become king and therefore has restored the city (ch. 6). By this argumentation, the enemies presuppose that it is the duty and the prerogative of a king to rebuild the city and its wall.

79. Karrer, *Ringen um die Verfassung Judas*, 107 (author's translation).

Discussing the coding of the city or the dignity ascribed to it, one has to look more closely at the narration and at the interpretations expressed by the enemies. The narration focuses on the building of the wall and the insertion of the gates against hostile attacks and invasions.[80] The wall and the gates mirror the way in which the ancient Near East sees a city, since a city—compared to other types of settlements—is characterized by a wall with gates.[81] Rebuilding the city wall, therefore, means creating a new protected space in which the population can live.

By contrast, the enemies consider the wall to be a sign for the Judaeans' intention to claim Jerusalem for themselves, to rebel against the king, and especially for Nehemiah to become king. Seen from the outside, a walled city is perceived as politically independent or rebellious and dangerous. This is especially true with regard to Ezra 4, where the letter of the Persian king prohibits the rebuilding of the city (Ezra 4:21) based on the argument that he would lose this land, because Jerusalem has always been a rebellious and seditious city (Ezra 4:12, 15, 19).

In response to these interpretations, Neh 2:5 states that the Persian king allows the building of the wall. In 2:17, Nehemiah argues that the rebuilding of the wall would end the shame/disgrace and thus restore the Judaeans' reputation in the view of the surrounding peoples. Further-more, when Nehemiah calls the construction of the city wall a work of God (6:16), he primarily interprets the city's existence religiously. The building of the wall as the distinguishing feature of the city takes on a religious quality,[82] which is expressed clearly in the ceremonial dedication of the city wall in 12:27–43.[83]

d. *The Settling of Jerusalem*
Immediately after the completion of the city wall in Neh 7:1–3, the problem arises that Jerusalem is not sufficiently populated (7:4, 5).[84] In

---

80. See the distribution of references of חומה and שערים. חומה: Neh 1:3; 2:13, 17; 4:1; 12:27; שערים: Neh 1:3; 2:3, 17; 7:3; 13:19; cf. Aramaic שור: Ezra 4:12, 13, 16.

81. Zech 2:5–9 is one example for alternative concepts of cities without a city wall. See P. Marinkovic, "Stadt ohne Mauern: Die Neukonstitution Jerusalems nach Sacharja 1–8" (Ph.D. diss., University of Munich, 1996), who refers to Persian imperial cities without walls.

82. Karrer, *Ringen um die Verfassung Judas*, 177: "In the narrative about the building of the wall, the act of building has a clearly integrative function for the Judaeans, and it is qualified religiously" (author's translation).

83. See Häusl, "Feste feiern," 246–50.

84. Structuring features: an interruption of the narrative flow in 7:4, achieved by nominal sentences and by the introduction of a new topic.

the narrative, this problem is not solved until ch. 11[85] and thus chs. 8–10[86] stand between the problem's identification and its solution.[87] If one wants to understand the meaning of the city in Ezra–Nehemiah as a whole— more precisely, the meaning of its settling and its designation as עיר הקדש in 11:1, 18—the overall structure of 7:4–11:36 needs to be examined more closely.[88] Nehemiah 7:4–11:36 consists of narrative passages and lists, and is structured as follows:

1:1–7:3	Rebuilding of the city wall
	list of builders/course of the wall (ch. 3)
7:4–5	problem: the city is not populated sufficiently
	list of returnees (7:6–72a [par. Ezra 2:1–70])
ch. 8	reading of the Torah; feast of the Torah reading and Feast of Booths[89]
ch. 9	day of penance and prayer of repentance
ch. 10	making of a "firm agreement"[90] and oath on the Torah
	list of people who made the firm agreement (10:1–29)
11:1–2	settling of Jerusalem
	list of the population of Jerusalem/Judah (11:3–36)
12:27–43	dedication of the city wall
	route of festival choirs/course of the wall (12:31–42)

The topic of settling forms a double frame around the activities that take place in Jerusalem according to Neh 8–10: the first frame in 7:4–5 and 11:1–2 uses narrative means, and the second one consists of the lists in chs. 7 and 11.[91]

In 7:4, the problem is raised that there is only a sparse population and few fortified houses. As a first step to a solution, Nehemiah intends to register the nobles, the officials and the people (חרים, סגנים, עם, cf.

85. Cf. n. 27.

86. The composition of the texts in Neh 7–12 is unanimously ascribed to the final redaction of the books of Ezra–Nehemiah (see, e.g., Karrer, *Ringen um die Verfassung Judas*, 289–91). It is debated, however, which texts were written by the redactors, which existed before and which were inserted later.

87. The resettling of Jerusalem is literally framed by the construction of the city wall in Neh 1:1–7:3 and by its dedication in 12:27–43. See Böhler, "Das Gottesvolk als Altargemeinschaft," 209–10.

88. Neh 12:1–26 offers lists of the families of priests and Levites; these lists are connected to similar ones in ch. 11, but they do not refer to the topic of settlement.

89. The narrated introduction to Neh 8 in 7:72–8:1 (up to כאיש אחד) also parallels Ezra 3:1.

90. The firm agreement (אמנה) is not called covenant (ברית).

91. One may even discern a "third" frame, comprised of the construction and dedication of the city wall, both of which also contain some list-like material.

7:5).[92] Yet, instead of narrating the execution of this registration, 7:6–72 presents a list of persons who came back from the Golah under Zerubbabel and Jeshua. After this list of returnees, chs. 8–10 recounts the reading of the Torah in Jerusalem, the subsequent feasts and the making of the firm agreement with YHWH. The agreement is complemented by the list of the persons who approved it (10:1–29). Nehemiah 11 resumes the issue of Jerusalem's settling, in 11:1–2 as a narrative and in 11:3–36 in the form of lists.[93] With regard to the population ch. 11 differentiates—in contrast to 7:5, but parallel to chs. 9–10 and 12:27–43—between inhabitants who are involved in the cult and those who are not.[94] The lists in ch. 11 resume the structure of the lists in 7:6–72a and 10:1–29. They do not only mention that Jerusalem is resettled, but also add information about Judaean settlements.[95] Therefore, 7:4–11:36 forms a composition the parts of which are correlated in a sophisticated manner.

The meaning that is connected to the settling of the city can be discovered by asking two questions: What do the people do in the city? And: Who lives in the city? And finally it can be explained why Jerusalem is called "Holy City" in this context.

In Neh 8–10, the city is the public space where the reading of the Torah, the liturgical and cultic feasts, as well as the conclusion of the agreement with YHWH take place. These activities are not located at the

---

92. The names of the groups refer to Neh 2:11.

93. Structure of Neh 11 (see Eskenazi, *In an Age of Prose,* 111–12):

11:1–2   narrated frame with reference to 7:4 and 5
   11:3   two-part overall superscription: inhabitants of Jerusalem and the Judaean cities
   11:4   superscription: inhabitants of Jerusalem
      11:4b   of the sons of Judah
      11:7a   of the sons of Benjamin
      11:10a   of the priests
      11:15a   of the Levites
      11:18   conclusion: term "holy city"
         11:19   addition: gatekeepers
   11:20   superscription or linkage—inhabitants of the Judaean cities
         11:21–24   uncertain
      11:25   sons of Judah
      11:31   sons of Benjamin
12:1–26   superscriptions of lists; no narrative embedding.

94. Neh 11:1–2 as well as the lists speak of שׂרים and not of חרים or סגנים.

95. See U. Kellermann, "Die Listen in Neh. 11: Eine Dokumentation aus den letzten Jahren des Reiches Juda?," *ZDPV* 82 (1996): 223–25. He demonstrates that the cities mentioned form a ring of fortress towns around Jerusalem.

temple, but in the city: 8:1 locates them at the Water Gate, and according to 8:16 the activities involve the whole township. Thus, as a location for these religious activities, the temple is of no relevance.

The city, however, is not only the public space for performing these religious activities. Living in the city as such is also theologically charged: first, according to the lists, the representatives of the groups that signed the agreement with YHWH live in the city. Second, according to Neh 11:1, aside from the שׂרים, "the leaders of the people," one tenth of the Judaean population lives in Jerusalem. The tenth corresponds to the tithe as a levy, an offering to the deity.[96] In my opinion, it is not sufficient to explain the settling of Jerusalem as synoikism,[97] because the religious context and the designation of Jerusalem as עיר הקדש remain unexplained. After all, Jerusalem has been correctly described before in chs. 8–10 as a public space in which all religious activities take place, and it is now called עיר הקדש. As such, a religious interpretation of the tenth part of the population living in Jerusalem as an offering to the deity is more plausible than as a synoikism.[98]

4. *Conclusions*

By interpreting the designation of Jerusalem as Holy City, taking into account the near and distant literary context is crucial. The context of Neh 7–11 does not suggest that the designation of Jerusalem as Holy City qualifies the city as the location of the sanctuary. Rather, the city is characterized in chs. 8–10 as a public place of meeting with God: it is the city and not the temple where reading and teaching of the Torah, the Feast of Booths and the conclusion of the agreement with God take place. First and foremost, living in the city is understood as an offering to the deity. In chs. 1–7, the city wall is a symbol of the protected living space and qualified as a work of God at the same time. Therefore, the designation of Jerusalem as Holy City is strongly related to urban aspects and the idea of holiness is expanded beyond a specific cultic meaning.

96. See Deut 14:22–27.

97. See K.-D. Schunck, *Nehemia* (BKAT 23/2; Neukirchen–Vluyn: Neukirchener, 2009), 228, and Karrer, *Ringen um die Verfassung Judas*, 121.

98. Eskenazi, *In an Age of Prose*, 113–14, also criticizes the synoikism as a relevant model and says: "The volunteering of one tenth of the population is a form of tithing for Jerusalem, the holy city, the house of God." Cf. also J. Clauss, "Understanding the Mixed Marriages of Ezra–Nehemiah in the Light of Temple-Building and the Book's Concept of Jerusalem," in *Mixed Marriages: Intermarriage and Group Identity in the Second Temple Period* (ed. C. Frevel; LHBOTS 547; New York/London: T&T Clark International, 2011), 109–31 (121–24).

Although all important religious activities are located in the city, and the city wall and dwelling are connected with God, the city is not identified with the temple, because living in the city does not mean to serve God as priestly or cultic personnel. Therefore Jerusalem's theological dignity does not (only) derive from the temple. This is also confirmed by function of the city for the placement of the temple in the book of Ezra. The city is the well-known entity that clarifies which temple is meant, a fact that is underlined by the movements to Jerusalem and by the Diaspora's interest in Jerusalem. The books of Ezra–Nehemiah show Jerusalem as a well-known place in the greater geographical space of the Persian Empire. All these observations demonstrate that in the books of Ezra–Nehemiah Jerusalem serves as an important theological topos for the construction of identity of post-exilic Israel.

WHOSE MOTHER? WHOSE SPACE?
JERUSALEM IN THIRD ISAIAH

Christl M. Maier

Jerusalem is considered a "holy city" in Judaism, Christianity, and Islam.[1] In the Hebrew Bible, this city is often personified as a woman bearing the title "Daughter Zion" or "Daughter Jerusalem." Such personification intertwines the idea of a city as a space—an assembly of buildings, streets, and squares—with the idea of a human collective, the inhabitants of a settlement. Thus, the literary device of personification, a sub-category of metaphor, allows the creation of relations between the city, its population, and the deity; it also allows viewing these relations from different angles.

The present study aims at analyzing the link between a spatial depiction of Jerusalem and her female embodiment in order to explore the city's significance for the circles of redactors who shaped the book of Isaiah. My thesis is that in the postexilic texts of Third Isaiah Zion/ Jerusalem serves as a mediating figure in two respects. First, the city resumes the mediating role that the king held in pre-exilic times; second, the city offers a space for contacting the Divine and thus resumes the earlier Zion-theology without focusing solely on the temple. In the following, I will introduce my methodology and then interpret four passages of Third Isaiah (60:1–22; 62:1–12; 66:5–14; 57:1–13) with special regard to the interweaving of spatial and gendered aspects of the city's portrait.

1. Space as a Social Product and the Female City

In my studies of texts about Jerusalem, I use the spatial theory of the French Marxist sociologist Henri Lefebvre (1901–1991) as a heuristic

---

1. The history of Jerusalem in antiquity and the development of monotheism has been explored in detail by O. Keel, *Die Geschichte Jerusalems und die Entstehung des Monotheismus* (2 vols.; OLB 4; Göttingen: Vandenhoeck & Ruprecht, 2007).

tool.[2] Lefebvre's epistemology of space focuses on the interrelation of spatial practice, conceptualization, and human experience of space. He argues that space is socially produced and "'incorporates' social actions, the actions of subjects both individual and collective."[3] His theory analyzes the production of space from three dimensions that are intrinsically intertwined. First, Lefebvre holds that space is produced by spatial practice (*pratique spatiale*), for example by architecture and urban planning as well as by daily life and routine that encompasses both production and reproduction.[4] From the viewpoint of an individual, any spatial practice presupposes the use of the body, that is, hands, sensory organs, and gestures, so that space is *perceived* as physical space, the materiality of space (*l'espace perçu*).[5]

The second dimension is named "representations of space" or "conceptualized space"[6] and comprises the ideology of space. Lefebvre here refers to the results of social processes of planning, naming, and inscribing of significance, thus to space as mentally constructed or ordered, a process that is often shaped by a certain political strategy in society and thus dominates the concepts and ideas about space. On the individual level, this is space as *conceived* space (*l'espace conçu*) by scientific knowledge of anatomy, physiology, and so on.[7]

The third dimension analyzes the social significance of a society's space by focusing on "spaces of representation,"[8] which embody complex symbolisms, communal values, traditions, metaphors, dreams—that is, a different, often nonverbal collective experience. This is space as

2. H. Lefebvre, *La production de l'espace* (Paris: Editions Anthropos, 1974), published in English as *The Production of Space* (trans. D. Nicholson-Smith; Oxford: Blackwell, 1991). The following references and citations are taken from the English edition. For an evaluation of Lefebvre's theory on space and its influence on other fields, see E. W. Soja, *Postmodern Geographies: The Reassertion of Space in Critical Social Theory* (London: Verso, 1989), 43–75; J. L. Berquist, "Critical Spatiality and the Construction of the Ancient World," in *"Imagining" Biblical Worlds: Studies in Spatial, Social and Historical Constructs in Honor of James W. Flanagan* (ed. D. M. Gunn and P. M. McNutt; JSOTSup 359; Sheffield: Sheffield Academic, 2002), 14–29; and J. W. Flanagan, "Ancient Perceptions of Space/ Perceptions of Ancient Space," *Semeia* 87 (1999): 15–43.

3. Lefebvre, *Production*, 33.

4. Cf. ibid., 33, 38.

5. Cf. ibid., 40.

6. Ibid., 38. Lefebvre (p. 45) uses the term *representation* as a broader notion that subsumes the area where *knowledge* and *ideology* are barely distinguishable.

7. Cf. ibid., 40.

8. I prefer this term to the translation "representational spaces" used by D. Nicholson-Smith; the French reads "les espaces de représentation."

experienced or *lived* (*l'espace vécu*), *"lived* through its associated images and symbols, and hence the space of 'inhabitants' and 'users'."[9] Lefebvre employs the plural, pointing out that various simultaneous representations may exist as different groups or individuals appropriate space in various ways through imagination and symbolic use. This third dimension, space as experienced or lived, is important since it covers any use of space that challenges the dominant conceptualized space and thus counteracts hegemonic spatial patterns.

While one has to keep in mind that Lefebvre analyzed modern societies dominated by a capitalist mode of production in the 1960s, I also find his theory useful for investigating the production of space in an ancient society and culture, even if common knowledge of such society is mainly mediated through texts. I further argue that space as described in biblical texts comprises all three dimensions of space: such "narrated" space is produced by spatial practice that makes use of its materiality as well as by certain ideology and experience of living in it.

With regard to "representations of space," the ideology of space, gender analysis is vital since the female personification of Jerusalem is not only based on specific ideas about gender but also shapes perceptions of gender in the readers of these texts.[10] In the last decades, the feminist theorizing of the body has demonstrated that ideas about body and gender are, like ideologies or symbolisms of space, closely tied to the cultural and historical circumstances of a given society.[11] This corresponds to Lefebvre's insight that the human body as space is subject to the production of space in a given society.[12] Therefore, the use of the body in literary personifications is tied to societal norms and has to be interpreted in relation to their socio-historical context. As the feminist theologian Paula M. Cooey demonstrates, female personification serves two ends: it presents the female body as a cultural artefact and generates a relation between the personified figure and the imagining subject who also has a body.[13] Cooey attributes to the body a major epistemological role as a medium in art and in texts, a role that is ambiguous because it is twofold:

9. Lefebvre, *Production*, 39.
10. For the social-historical context of the female personification of city and land, see my study *Daughter Zion, Mother Zion: Gender, Space, and the Sacred in Ancient Israel* (Minneapolis: Fortress, 2008), 61–74.
11. Cf. ibid., 21–28.
12. Cf. Lefebvre, *Production*, 172–74.
13. P. M. Cooey, *Religious Imagination and the Body: A Feminist Analysis* (New York: Oxford University Press, 1994).

> Its ambiguity lies in its double role as *site* and as *sign*. Viewed as *site*, "body" focuses conceptually upon sentience as a field of pain and pleasure, experienced by imagining subjects. Viewed as *sign*, "body" forces the attribution or denial of agency to another, and therefore serves as a building block in the social construction of subjectivity.[14]

Cooey's exploration of agency at the margins of the dominant ideology correlates to Lefebvre's search for *lived space* that resists *conceived space*. Cooey includes the viewer of art or reader of texts and thus explores the function of the body in the production of meaning within the reception process. The keywords *sentience, agency,* and *subjectivity* relate Cooey's theoretical work to the political goals of the feminist movement, which strives to establish as political subjects women who are marginalized because of their sex, race, class, age, and so on.

2. *Jerusalem in the Book of Isaiah and in Third Isaiah*

a. *Texts and Contexts*

Texts mentioning Zion/Jerusalem mark a common thread throughout the book of Isaiah. Ulrich Berges argues that the name "Jerusalem" is more frequently used in political contexts and thus more often connected to the topic of judgment, while "Zion" stands for the restoration of postexilic Israel, especially from ch. 40 onwards.[15] However, both terms refer topographically to the same entity, namely, the city including its temple precincts. In seventeen instances, "Zion" and "Jerusalem" are mentioned parallel to each other and thus appear as synonyms.[16] In many of these passages, Zion/Jerusalem is personified, characterized as a woman, entitled "Daughter Zion," or "Virgin," and often addressed as a female person. Interestingly, Isaiah does not explicitly narrate the city's destruction since at the dramatic point where the reader expects the burning of Jerusalem to take place, the book talks about the destruction of Edom (Isa 34) as vengeance on Zion's behalf (34:8) and proclaims the salvation of Zion (35:10).[17] In a moment of utmost threat to Zion's body and status, when the Assyrian army gathers around the city wall, "Virgin,

---

14. Ibid., 90 (italics mine).

15. U. Berges, "Personifications and Prophetic Voices of Zion in Isaiah and Beyond," in *The Elusive Prophet: The Prophet as a Historical Person, Literary Character and Anonymous Artist* (ed. J. C. de Moor; OTS 45; Leiden: Brill, 2001), 54–82 (54–55).

16. Cf. Isa 2:3; 4:3, 4; 10:12, 32; 24:23; 30:19; 31:9; 33:20; 37:22, 32; 40:9; 41:27; 52:1, 2; 62:1; 64:9.

17. Cf. Berges, "Personifications and Prophetic Voices of Zion," 63.

Daughter Zion" emerges as a proud young woman who despises and scorns her enemy (37:22). In contrast, chs. 40–55 clearly reflect the exilic disaster in prophetic oracles announcing that she will be comforted, brought up from the dust, reconstructed and re-established in her former status. Chapters 56–66, however, presuppose the restoration of city and temple and thus point to a postexilic situation.

In his commentary published in 1892, Bernhard Duhm was the first to distinguish First, Second, and Third Isaiah, assuming three different prophets as originators of the book's message.[18] In recent scholarship, there are mainly two different models regarding the development of Isa 56–66. Klaus Koenen and Seizo Sekine argue that the core of these chapters can be traced back to a prophet who was active in postexilic Jerusalem.[19] Wolfgang Lau, who explores inner-biblical allusions and literary parallels of chs. 56–66 to other texts in Isaiah, understands chs. 56–66 as successively written comments—the German term is "*Fort-schreibungen*"—by scribes who interpreted Second Isaiah's message of salvation for a postexilic audience.[20] This model of subsequent additions has been elaborated by Odil Hannes Steck, who connects the development of texts in Third Isaiah with redactional layers that span the whole book.[21] Interestingly, all four scholars see chs. 60–62 as the core and starting point of the collection in Third Isaiah, since these chapters include numerous allusions to and have strong literary parallels in chs. 40–55.[22] In my view, the model of successively written comments is more plausible since form, contents, and the intertextual references of

18. B. Duhm, *Das Buch Jesaia* (5th ed.; Göttingen: Vandenhoeck & Ruprecht, 1968), 18–19. Duhm assumed a fourth person as author of the so-called servant songs in Isa 40–55.

19. K. Koenen, *Ethik und Eschatologie im Tritojesajabuch: Eine literarkritische und redaktionsgeschichtliche Studie* (WMANT 62; Neukirchen–Vluyn: Neu-kirchener, 1990), 215–21; S. Sekine, *Die Tritojesajanische Sammlung (Jes 56–66) redaktionsgeschichtlich untersucht* (BZAW 175; Berlin: W. de Gruyter, 1989), 182, 230.

20. See W. Lau, *Schriftgelehrte Prophetie in Jes 56–66: Eine Untersuchung zu den literarischen Bezügen in den letzten elf Kapiteln des Jesajabuches* (BZAW 225; Berlin: W. de Gruyter, 1994).

21. See O. H. Steck, *Bereitete Heimkehr: Jesaja 35 als redaktionelle Brücke zwischen dem Ersten und dem Zweiten Jesaja* (SBS 121; Stuttgart: Katholisches Bibelwerk, 1985); idem, *Studien zu Tritojesaja* (BZAW 203; Berlin: W. de Gruyter, 1991).

22. See Koenen, *Ethik*, 215; Sekine, *Tritojesajanische Sammlung*, 101–4; Steck, *Studien zu Tritojesaja*, 14–19, 119–39; Lau, *Schriftgelehrte Prophetie*, 22–117, esp. 90–112.

chs. 60–62 hint at scribal activity and initially written annotations of earlier texts. In the following, I will demonstrate that these literary links are underscored by a gradual enhancement of the female personification, which adds more traits to the figure and adjusts her role to altered situations.

The text collection in Third Isaiah is concentrically structured: chs. 60–62 are framed by the thematically similar chs. 56–59 and 63–66. Isaiah 56:1–8 serves as a prologue, 66:5–14 as an epilogue. Since 66:15–24 encompasses intertextual relations to all three parts of Isaiah, this last passage concludes the whole book.[23]

The name "Zion" occurs seven times in Third Isaiah, twice as a place name (Isa 59:20; 61:3) and five times as a name for the city, whereas the title "Daughter Zion" is used only once (62:11). "Jerusalem" has nine references in Third Isaiah and is used synonymously to "Zion" in chs. 62, 64, 66.[24] Starting with the core of the collection, my interpretation of relevant passages in Third Isaiah will explore the interlinkage between the spatial description and the female embodiment of Zion/Jerusalem.

b. *Zion as a Center of Commerce and Pilgrimage: Isaiah 60:1–22*
Isaiah 60 describes a stream of people and goods flowing to Jerusalem. The prophetic speech of twenty-two verses addresses a female figure, which in v. 14 is named "city of YHWH, the Zion of the Holy One of Israel." The chapter is framed by verses that announce a light, that is, the glory of YHWH, rising over the city like the sun (vv. 1–3 and vv. 19–22).[25] This focus on YHWH's glory recalls Isaiah's vision of YHWH's epiphany in the first temple (6:1–5) and thus promotes a "conceptualized space" based on divine presence. Isaiah 60:1–3 is peculiar in making Zion mirror the divine radiance, which renders the city valuable in the eyes of the nations. What is called "light" in the frame is described in

---

23. For a concordance of terminological parallels between Isa 1 and 65–66, see W. A. M. Beuken, "Isaiah Chapter LXV–LXVI: Trito-Isaiah and the Closure of the Book of Isaiah," in *Congress Volume Leuven 1989* (ed. J. A. Emerton; VTSup 43; Leiden: Brill, 1991), 204–21 (218–19). Steck, *Studien zu Tritojesaja*, 263–65, attributes Isa 66:5–24 to the last book redaction.

24. For "Zion" as city name, cf. Isa 60:14; 62:1, 11; 64:9; 66:8; for "Jerusalem," cf. Isa 62:1, 6, 7; 64:9; 65:18, 19; 66:10, 13, 20.

25. The concentric structuring of Isa 60 in five stanzas is argued by G. J. Polan, "Zion, the Glory of the Holy One of Israel: A Literary Analysis of Isaiah 60," in *Imagery and Imagination in Biblical Literature: Essays in Honor of Aloysius Fitzgerald* (ed. L. Boadt and M. S. Smith; CBQMS 32; Washington: Catholic Biblical Association of America, 2001), 50–71 (55–56).

three stanzas as a stream of wealth and glory (vv. 4–9), as the splendor of the newly built city (vv. 10–14), and as the abundance of material and people in the city (vv. 15–18)—a situation of peace and righteousness, as v. 17 concisely summarizes.

Analyzing the chapter with Lefebvre's three perspectives of space reveals a discrepancy between the spatial practice (*perceived space*) and representations of space (*lived space*).

With regard to the first, the city is portrayed as filled with people and merchandise from all four points of the compass and thus mirrors the re-establishment of the temple and its cult: The "abundance of the sea" (v. 5) and the "ships of Tarshish" (v. 9) come from the west, since the latter are merchant vessels that cruise the Mediterranean Sea from Tarshish in Southern Spain to the Levantine coast (cf. Ps 48:8). From the north, the lumber of Lebanon is imported as building material for the sanctuary (v. 13). The herds of the Northern Arabic tribes of Kedar and Nebaioth (v. 7) serve as animals for sacrifice. Midian and Ephah (v. 6) represent the trading desert people east of the Gulf of Aqaba; Sheba in Southern Arabia is legendary for its gold and spices (cf. 1 Kgs 10:1–13). Crowds of people enter the permanently open city gates (v. 11): they are foreigners who work as masons (v. 10) and merchants, but also Zion's exiled sons and daughters return with their silver and gold (v. 9), an announcement that alludes to an oracle of Second Isaiah (49:18–22). In sum, the spatial practice in Isa 60 describes Jerusalem as a center of commerce and pilgrimage.

Lefebvre's second perspective, "conceptualized space" or *conceived space*, ties in with the pre-exilic idea of God's presence in this city and enforces it by the concept of ownership. The honorary name of this space, "Zion of the Holy One of Israel" (v. 14), expressively labels this ideology. It is YHWH who navigates the stream of goods (v. 17), implants the people in the land again (v. 21) and calls himself Zion's "savior" and "redeemer" (v. 16). With the key words צדקה, "righteousness" (v. 17), and צדק, "righteous" (v. 21), Isa 60 resumes the pre-exilic idea of Jerusalem as a righteous city (1:21, 27).

Yet, the "spaces of representation," collective experience as well as the individual's *lived space* appear less glorious in Isa 60. The imperatives "arise" (v. 1), "lift up your eyes" (v. 4) and Zion's skeptical question "Who are these that fly like a cloud, and like doves to their windows?" (v. 8), as well as the "days of mourning" (v. 20), show that the female addressee of the prophetic announcement is still not convinced. The personified city appears as struck by God (v. 10), forsaken, hated, without visitors (v. 15); violence and destruction are still an issue (v. 18). At present, the addressees share the collective experience of a ruined and abandoned city—the gates are not yet built (v. 10), but the temple and altar already exist (vv. 7, 13). Only in the near future will the city be resettled and re-established as a center. Thus, a spatial analysis demonstrates the discrepancy between the present and the future, between the city's real situation and the idea of her new role.

The female personification underlines this focus on the near future. In Isa 60, Zion serves as *site* and *sign* for a time of salvation. Zion is characterized both as a mother who awaits the homecoming of her children (v. 9) and as an infant who will soon suck the milk of the nations (v. 16). As a *site*, the female body communicates the sentience of pleasure, relief, and satiation to the readers who are supposed to associate with these feelings while reflecting the text. At the same time, the figure of the mother and the suckling infant serves as a "sign" in anticipating the agency of Jerusalem's inhabitants: they are supposed to welcome the returning exiles and to enjoy the merchandise and gifts that will stream to the city. The transfer between the mother metaphor that presents Zion as a counterpart to her inhabitants, and her identification with the population in the infant metaphor does not reflect a lack of precision on behalf of the author, but pertains to the creative force of the female personification.

c. *Zion as a Crown and Bride: Isaiah 62:1–12*
In Isa 62:1–12, a prophetic voice explicitly addresses Zion and announces her salvation for the near future (cf. עַד, "until," in vv. 1, 7).[26] As in ch. 60, Jerusalem is not yet fully rebuilt and the sentinels on her walls still have to remind YHWH to re-establish the city in its former prominence (vv. 6–7). The oracle shares keywords such as "righteousness," "light," "glory" with ch. 60, yet this time the light and glory pertains to Jerusalem herself and not to God. Moreover, parallel motifs are the homage of the nations (v. 2), the existence of the temple (v. 9), and a new name for Zion (vv. 2, 4, 12). The peculiar message of ch. 62, however, is a change in God's relationship to the city: she will be a crown in YHWH's hand (v. 3) and he will honor and receive her like a bride (v. 5).

---

26. For a discussion of the speaker's identity, see Koenen, *Ethik*, 123–24. J. Blenkinsopp, *Isaiah 56–66* (AB 19B; New York: Doubleday, 2003), 233–34, takes the self-referential phrasing as a clue for a prophetic anxiety about the non-fulfillment of the prophecies. Since I regard the text of Third Isaiah as written comments to Second Isaiah's oracles, I use the term "prophetic voice."

The passage contains at least two interpretive problems in v. 5 and v. 3. The idea of Jerusalem's sons marrying their mother (יִבְעָלוּךְ בָּנָיִךְ) expressed in the Masoretic text seems inappropriate and contradicts vv. 4–5, which insinuate a marriage relationship between the city or land and YHWH. While the Masoretic reading is supported by the ancient versions, the editors of *BHS* suggest the reading יִבְעָלֵךְ בֹּנֵךְ, "so will your builder marry you," which follows a proposal of Robert Lowth in 1833 and refers to Ps 147:2, where YHWH is called "the builder of Jerusalem." This reading is also adopted by the NRSV. An emendation is, however, unnecessary if one assumes a wordplay on the double meaning of the Hebrew verb בעל, "to marry, rule over."[27] With this reading, the Masoretic text circumvents a direct identification of YHWH with Zion's husband while at the same time mentioning Jerusalem's repopulation and resurgence as a capital city.

Verse 3 poses another problem since it interrupts the topic of renaming and identifies Jerusalem with the crown, although Jerusalem is supposedly the bride to be crowned.[28] Moreover, a crown belongs on the head and not in the hand. The alleged confusion is due to the female personification of Zion, which creates a triangular relationship between the city, its population, and God. Based on the metaphor, multiple roles emerge, especially since the female city not only represents the people as a collective but also the place that has been destroyed. On the one hand, the city is related to the surrounding land, which in this passage is also personified as female (v. 4). Since in ancient Israel the marriage meta-phor connotes a hierarchical relationship, the "married" land now has a new master, Zion's homecoming sons. On the other hand, the motif of the crown in v. 3 alludes to the prediction of Second Isaiah that Jerusa-lem's foundations, walls, and gates will be rebuilt with precious stones (Isa 54:11–12). Viewed from afar, a city wall with towers and pinnacles resembles a crown, and in neo-Assyrian iconography such a stylized city wall, called a "mural crown," serves both as an emblem for a city and as a crown for the king's spouse.[29] Jerusalem as the crown in YHWH's hand borrows this symbolism, leading to two possible interpretations: with regard to the gendered aspect that connotes her social function, the city will be exalted like a queen. With regard to the spatial aspect, the city

27. Cf. Blenkinsopp, *Isaiah 56–66*, 233.
28. Cf. Koenen, *Ethik*, 122 n. 388.
29. For a more detailed interpretation, see C. M. Maier, "Daughter Zion as Queen and the Iconography of the Female City," in *Images and Prophecy in the Ancient Eastern Mediterranean* (ed. M. Nissinen and C. Carter; FRLANT 233; Göttingen: Vandenhoeck & Ruprecht, 2009), 147–62.

will be rebuilt like a precious mural crown. Both characteristics, the queen and the crown, allude to the royal status of the city, and so Isa 62 re-establishes Jerusalem's role as capital of Judah even if the Judaean monarchy is no longer an option. The authors of ch. 62 envision YHWH retaking the role of a patron deity of Jerusalem and compare God's joy with the rejoicing of the bridegroom. Contrary to Isa 54:5, however, they hesitate to call YHWH Jerusalem's husband and thus use the marriage metaphor in a more subtle way.

The perspectives on space in 62:1–12 are similar to those in ch. 60. The spatial practice (*perceived space*) described in this chapter depicts an inhabited city and its hinterland, both of which prosper so that other nations have to acknowledge the city's resurrection from the dust. "Conceptualized space," or *conceived space*, builds on the close relationship between the city and its patron deity and signifies royal status and glory. The new names for the city ("My Delight Is in Her") and the land ("Married") in v. 4 underline the ideas of protection and divine rule. Since 62:1–12 announces this change of status for the future, the portrait of the city does not cover the actual experience of space or *lived space*. At present, the city wall is rebuilt, but the space seems unpopulated (vv. 6–7, 12), those who labor for grain and wine do not yet relish the fruits (vv. 8–9). At present, Zion only anticipates her new status and thus serves as a *site* of joy and glory. At the same time, the city conveys agency to her inhabitants—the *sign* aspect—that they would not yield to despair but constantly remind God of his promise (vv. 6–7).

d. *Zion's Motherly Role Between Universalism and Particularism: Isaiah 66:5–14*

Isaiah 66 offers a collection of short sayings introduced by different prophetic rubrics, which scholars differentiate into three to seven pericopes.[30] The interpretation of 66:5–14 hinges on the range of verses that scholars assume belong together. An announcement of universal peace for Zion in vv. 7–14a is framed by verses that sharply distinguish between two groups. One group is directly addressed, called "servants" of God (v. 14b) and portrayed as those "who tremble at his word" (v. 5); they will receive blessings. In contrast, v. 6 announces God's wrath over "people who hate you and reject you for my name's sake" (v. 5). They are also called God's "enemies" (v. 14b). God's retributive actions against these enemies begin at the temple (v. 6).

---

30. Cf. the list of scholarly divisions in Blenkinsopp, *Isaiah 56–66*, 292.

In my view, the call to listen to God's word in v. 5 marks the beginning of a new unit; its addressees are the people who are called to rejoice with Jerusalem in v. 10. Since there is no reason for a source-critical separation of v. 14a and b,[31] the distinction between both groups cannot be regarded as a later redaction. Thus, the universal outlook on Zion in vv. 7–14a and its particularistic framing originally belong together. As a literary unit, 66:5–14 generates a written comment and epilogue to Third Isaiah by using keywords and motifs of ch. 60, and even some ideas of Second Isaiah, while shifting the prospects of salvation.[32] Whereas 60:4, 9 announce the homecoming of Zion's exiled children who are carried in nurses' arms or arrive on merchant ships,[33] 66:12–13 no longer talk about homecoming but use the same terminology to portray Zion as a happy mother who carries her children in her arms and caresses them on her knees. Zion's body is described as a motherly body with a womb (v. 7) and breasts full of milk (v. 11). In vv. 7–9, Zion is clearly personified as a mother of newborns, an idea that is unique within the book of Isaiah. Zion's birthing without pain is a counter image of the "woman in labor" metaphor, which often appears in prophetic writings to express a situation of war and inimical attack (e.g. Jer 4:31). The new role of Zion as breastfeeding mother of newborns (v. 11) alludes to the promise in 60:16 that she shall suck the milk of nations and the breasts of kings. The stream of goods and offerings gushing into the city, which ch. 60 describes in detail, is summarized in 66:12 by God's statement "I will extend prosperity to her like a river and the wealth of the nations like an overflowing stream." In comparison to ch. 60, Zion's role in ch. 66 shifts from the addressee of the promise to a mediator who transfers God's blessing to her inhabitants.[34]

While the relationship between God and Zion is not explicitly stated, 66:9 characterizes the deity as master of the womb in the role of a midwife who assists at a smooth birth. God is named neither the father of the infants nor the husband of female Zion. Yet, Zion's ability to feed her children resembles God's ability to provide food (cf. Isa 55:1–2). Thus, Zion's role merges with the role of God, which is explicitly stated in v. 13: "As a mother comforts her child, so I will comfort you; you shall

---

31. As argued by Koenen, *Ethik*, 201–4.

32. Blenkinsopp, *Isaiah 56–66*, 293, and Beuken, "Isaiah Chapter LXV–LXVI," 218–19, read Isa 66:7–14 as epilogue to Third Isaiah.

33. Isa 60:4, 9 refer back to the initial announcement of homecoming in Isa 49:20–23.

34. Cf. also U. Berges, *Das Buch Jesaja: Komposition und Endgestalt* (HBS 16; Freiburg: Herder, 1998), 525.

be comforted in Jerusalem" (NRSV). While most translations translate בירושלם with "*in* Jerusalem," the preposition can also be interpreted as instrumental insofar as the comfort will be mediated *by* or *through* Jerusalem. Thus, Zion's maternal body, not the temple, becomes the mediator of divine blessing and salvation.

Zion's fertile female body is the *site* of salvation for her children. Zion's role as nurturing mother underlines the imagination of a city full of people and conveys the sentiments of satiation, protection and comfort. At the same time, Zion's body is a *sign* of the coming time of salvation since it symbolizes the relationship between the addressees and God.

This great vision, however, does not include all inhabitants of the city and thus raises the question of who are the recipients of Zion's and thus God's motherly care. The addressees of the prophecy are characterized as people who closely adhere to God (v. 14b) and "tremble at his word" (v. 5), who love Jerusalem and have mourned over her (v. 10); they are "poor and broken-hearted" (v. 2), hated and rejected by others (v. 5), thus in a minority position and in need of consolation. According to 66:1–4, these "tremblers" seem to have abandoned the temple cult, claiming that heaven is God's throne while their opponents offer the customary sacrifices. The keyword "servants of YHWH" borrows a title that is frequently used in Second Isaiah, where Israel or Jacob are called "servant" (Isa 41:8–9; 44:1–2, 21; 45:4; 48:20). Moreover, there is the anonymous servant of God in the so-called servant songs.[35] Willem Beuken plausibly argues that the servants and their vindication is the predominant theme of chs. 56–66 and that the title in the plural builds on the singular renderings.[36] These servants consider themselves to be the true remnant of Jacob that suffers from oppression by fellow Judaeans. The latter are described as leading circles in Jerusalem (56:9–12) who make the pious perish (57:1–2), act relentlessly against the hungry and marginalized (58:1–8), and engage in crime and deception (59:1–8, 13) as well as in illegitimate cults (57:6–13; 65:1–5).

With regard to Lefebvre's theory of space, I observe in the portrait of Jerusalem two competing views that belong to two different perspectives of "spaces of representation" or *lived space*. While both views presuppose Jerusalem's rebuilding and restitution as capital city (*perceived space*) and its significance as a place in which God's glory dwells

---

35. The servant songs comprise Isa 42:1–4; 49:1–6; 50:4–9, 52:13–53:12.

36. Cf. Isa 56:6; 63:17; 65:8–9, 13–15; 66:14, and W. A. M. Beuken, "The Main Theme of Trito-Isaiah: The 'Servants of YHWH'," *JSOT* 47 (1990): 67–87 (68).

(*conceived space*), they diverge on their understanding of *lived space*, especially on the question of who are to be the real beneficiaries of Zion's nourishment and comfort. Whereas the oracles of salvation in Isa 40–55 and their reinterpretation in chs. 60–62 portray Zion as the former mother of all Judaeans, who return from exile and as a dwelling place open to everyone of the postexilic community, in 66:5–14 the marginalized group reclaims Zion's motherhood for itself and denies it to others who are associated with the temple. Significantly, the authors of 66:5–14 claim themselves and their addressees to be newborn children of Zion, a designation that opens up the possibility of including people of non-Judaean descent to the group of YHWH-followers (cf. 56:1–8). The image of Zion's miraculous child-bearing resumes the promise of blessed offspring for the servants of YHWH in 65:13.[37]

Joseph Blenkinsopp rightly points out that the designation חרדים/חרד "the one/those who tremble" at the word/commandment of God is used only in Isa 66:2, 5; Ezra 9:4 and 10:3.[38] In the story of Ezra's failed attempt to divorce the foreign wives of Golah members, that is, returned exiles,[39] "the tremblers" seem to support Ezra's rigorous interpretation of the law and Ezra is described as a devout ascetic like them (Ezra 9:1–5; 10:1–3). In Mal 3:13–21, Blenkinsopp sees a similar rift between "the devout and the reprobate."[40] The parallels in Ezra 9–10 and Mal 3 point to a schism in the postexilic community at the end of the fifth or the beginning of the fourth century B.C.E. While the "tremblers" in Isa 65–66 may have been part of the Golah group, the main criterion of their self-distinction is not, or more precisely, no longer, Judaean descent, but loyalty to YHWH's word, be it delivered in the Torah or through a reinterpretation of earlier prophecy.[41] In re-using the old divine warrior metaphor (Isa 66:6), they claim that YHWH will side with the afflicted and oppressed and punish those who worship YHWH among other deities.[42] There may be an overlap between the "tremblers" and a dissident group of "servants" of YHWH, whose voice appears in the Songs of

---

37. Cf. ibid., 83.

38. Blenkinsopp, *Isaiah 56–66*, 299.

39. The Masoretic text of Ezra 10:44 does not state that the Golah members actually divorced their foreign wives, and only the priests swear to do so (Ezra 10:18–19). See H. G. M. Williamson, *Ezra, Nehemiah* (WBC 16; Nashville: Word Books, 1985), 145, 159–62.

40. Blenkinsopp, *Isaiah 56–66*, 301.

41. Berges, *Das Buch Jesaja*, 545, argues in a similar way that in Isa 56 and 66, ethos, not ethnicity, is the key to belong to the community of servants.

42. For the divine warrior metaphor, cf. Blenkinsopp, *Isaiah 55–65*, 316–17.

Ascent, that is, Pss 120–134. Gert Prinsloo sees the latter as Levites who have been expelled from the temple service by the temple aristocracy in the late Persian period.[43] In Third Isaiah, their particularistic perspective on mother Zion has even generated another text, in which the female city is associated with the "other" group.

e. Jerusalem's Alter Ego, the "Whore": Isaiah 57:1–13
The only passage in Isa 40–66 that sheds a negative light on a personified female figure is 57:1–13. Starting with a lament that the righteous perish and the devout are taken away, while no one takes notice (vv. 1–2), the prophetic voice addresses a group named "children of the sorceress, offspring of an adulterer and a whore" (v. 3) and "offspring of deceit" (v. 4). In v. 6, the prophetic voice abruptly turns to a feminine singular addressee by listing her vices (vv. 6–10) and announcing the divine verdict on her (vv. 11–13). The chapter concludes with a salvation oracle (vv. 14–21) for those who are "contrite and humble in spirit" (v. 15). Given the distinction between the two groups discussed above, it is obvious that this passage polemically characterizes the opponents of "YHWH's servants." With regard to the negative portrait of the unnamed female figure, which is depicted as the group's mother, the question arises whether this entity can be identified with Zion, and if yes, what the function of this passage within Third Isaiah may be.

Any reader familiar with the whore metaphor may recall similar prophetic scolding from Jer 2–3 as well as Ezek 16 and 23. These parallels insinuate that the female person addressed is none other than personified Jerusalem. The accusations against her are threefold: she offers sacrifices at illegitimate cultic sites both in the valley (v. 6) and on the hill (v. 7); she venerates other gods (v. 9); and she plays the whore (vv. 8, 10). Since the identity of the male lovers is not disclosed, all of these activities seem to be related to other deities, who are again not named. The charge against the plural addressees that they "slaughter" their children in the valleys (v. 5) most probably refers to Molek sacrifices in the valley of Ben-Hinnom south of Jerusalem, which Jeremiah harshly condemns (Jer 7:31–34; 19:5–6, 11–13; 32:35) and Ezekiel lists among Jerusalem's abominations (Ezek 16:20–21; 23:37, 39). The cult seems to have flourished during the Judaean monarchy despite King

---

43. See G. T. M. Prinsloo, "The Role of Space in the שירי המעלות (Psalms 120–134)," *Bib* 86 (2005): 457–77 (476). For common views on Zion and similar theological goals of the "servants" in Third Isaiah and the Psalter, see U. Berges, "Die Knechte im Psalter: Ein Beitrag zu seiner Kompositionsgeschichte," *Bib* 81 (2000): 153–78.

Josiah's reform, which destroyed the site (2 Kgs 23:10).[44] In this context, the "king" (MT: מלך, v. 9) probably refers to the god Molek[45] who is associated with these rites and with Sheol, the underworld. Theodore Lewis argues for a royal cult of the dead as background of Isa 56:9–57:13, in which libations and offerings may be brought to the deceased who are buried in the valleys.[46]

The description of the personified female figure carries strong sexual overtones: she uncovers her bed for others and plays the whore for money (v. 8, cf. Ezek 23:17). The sign at the door (v. 8) is reminiscent of the crimson cord in the window of Rahab, the prostitute (Josh 2:18). The sigh of the woman in v. 10, "it is useless," cites the female figure in Jer 2:25 who is said to love strangers. The site on the "high and lofty mountain" (v. 7) is ambiguous because it alludes to the Temple Mount (cf. Isa 2:2; Ezek 40:2) as well as to the high places that Jeremiah denounces (Jer 2:20; 3:6). In my view, this ambiguity is deliberate, since the polemic against the "whore" in Isa 57 ends with a reference to YHWH's mountain (v. 13). The prediction that whoever takes refuge in YHWH "shall possess the land and inherit my holy mountain" (57:13b) mirrors a situation in which the access to and control over the Temple Mount of Jerusalem is disputed. YHWH's verdict on personified Jerusalem fully reveals that "his holy mountain" represents the ultimate counter-space to all sites of an illegitimate cult.

Mark Biddle has called this portrait of Jerusalem one of "Lady Zion's alter Egos."[47] Isaiah 57:11 includes a citation of 47:7 and thus identifies the activities of Jerusalem with those of haughty Babylon described in 47:1–15. According to Biddle, 57:6–13 signifies the "old" Jerusalem, "the disloyal, immoral, untrustworthy harlot" and thus a reality that is beyond cure but has to be replaced by a new heaven and a new earth (66:22).[48] Yet, in my view, 57:6–13 combines both old and new accusations and attests to religious challenges in postexilic Jerusalem. While the passage downplays the power of other deities besides YHWH—they can be carried off by a wind (v. 13)—their cults apparently pose a

---

44. For a reconstruction of the rites, see J. Day, *Molech: A God of Human Sacrifice in the Old Testament* (Cambridge: Cambridge University Press, 1989).

45. While the ancient versions do not render a name, Blenkinsopp, *Isaiah 56–66*, 160–61, assumes that the consonantal text once referred to this deity.

46. T. J. Lewis, "Death Cult Imagery in Isaiah 57," *HAR* 11 (1987): 267–84.

47. M. E. Biddle, "Lady Zion's Alter Egos: Isaiah 47:1–15 and 57:6–13 as Structural Counterparts," in *New Visions of Isaiah* (ed. R. Melugin; JSOTSup 214; Sheffield: Sheffield Academic, 1996), 124–39 (135–39).

48. Ibid., 139.

significant threat for the authors of the passage and their addressees. In contrast to the universal message of hope emphasized in chs. 60 and 62, 57:1–13 and 66:5–14 mirror a sharp divide within the community.

In sum, the rehearsal of the whore metaphor in Isa 57:6–13 challenges the positive portraits of Jerusalem in chs. 60, 62, and 66. While the passage only vaguely alludes to the Temple Mount without mentioning a temple building, the description implies that there are cultic sites including the Temple Mount as well as a re-established city life. Thus, the narrated spatial practice or *perceived space* is a rebuilt and populated city. The intertextual connections to the whore metaphor repeat the negative evaluation of Jerusalem in some prophetic texts and thus construct *conceived space* as a defiled sacred space, a counter-image to the Zion theology of temple and city as sites of divine presence. Like in the other passages discussed, a debate about "spaces of representation" or *lived space* is also obvious in 57:6–13: while the authors of 57:1–13 oppose a specific use of certain valleys and hills as cultic sites, they claim that the Temple Mount of Jerusalem is reserved for themselves as true followers of YHWH (v. 13). Taken together with other passages in Third Isaiah that reflect a divide in the community on religious and social concerns, 57:6–13 demonstrates that the situation in postexilic Jerusalem is a far cry from the glorious expectations formulated in chs. 60 and 62. In the polemical portrait of Jerusalem in 57:1–13, I see the starting point for the distinction between a Jerusalem on earth and the heavenly Jerusalem, which becomes prominent in later apocalyptic writings.[49]

3. *Construct and Reality:* *Jerusalem as a Space for Israel's Hope*

In this essay I try to interpret different portraits of Zion/Jerusalem in Third Isaiah with the help of Henri Lefebvre's three perspectives on space and Paula Cooey's evaluation of the personified female body as an ambiguous medium that conveys both sentience and agency to the readers of these texts. In my view, the passages collected in Isa 56–66 successively comment on Second Isaiah's oracles of salvation and simultaneously adjust their grandiose outlook to a later situation.

Isaiah 60 presupposes the existence of the Second Temple while not yet the rebuilding of the city wall. The passage alludes to the announcement of the exiles' homecoming in 49:18–22 and reconfigures it in the

---

49. See also the essay by Carla Sulzbach in the present volume.

prediction of a constant stream of merchandise and offerings to Jerusalem. The city is portrayed as repopulated and splendidly rebuilt in the near future since YHWH's light is said to shine upon the city already. Zion appears as a mother who rejoices over the homecoming of her lost children and as a city that provides space for Judaeans, but also for foreign merchants and pilgrims.

Isaiah 62 increases this hope for Jerusalem's impeding glory by depicting the city and its hinterland as repopulated and even crowded. The chapter comments on the idea that Jerusalem will be rebuilt with precious stones (54:11–12) by envisioning the city as a beautiful crown in YHWH's hand. Zion anticipates her new status as a queen and as a city ruled again by her former children. This portrait of the city conveys the message to her inhabitants not to yield to despair but to remind God of his promise constantly.

At first sight, Isa 66:5–14 offers another culmination by announcing a swift birth of new children to Zion and by heightening the city's image to that of nurturing mother. Whereas 60:16 portrays Zion as an infant suckling the wealth of the nations, in 66:11 she assumes the role of a breastfeeding mother and as a mediator of God's motherly care and protection. Yet, this heightened message of peace and fruitfulness is confined to only one group of the city's inhabitants. The authors of the passage perceive themselves and their addressees as a minority group of true YHWH-worshippers oppressed by those who organize the temple cult in Jerusalem and who belong to the leading circles. The universal message of chs. 60 and 62 is thus interpreted in a particularistic way.

Whereas in 66:5–14 the minority group of God-fearing "servants" claim to be the true children of Zion, in 57:1–13 they argue that cults for other deities and the oppressive social behavior of the majority perverted even Zion and the Temple Mount. The differences in the portrayal of Zion in chs. 66 and 57 respectively may point to an aggravation of the struggle about who are the true "children of Zion" and who can claim to be the recipients of the great message of hope. The strong differentiation among Zion's inhabitants and the polemics against the majority group hint at a successively aggravating divide in the postexilic community.

In all passages discussed so far, the female personification of the city serves not only as a literary device with which the authors describe their own attachment to the place. It also allows the circumscription of the relations between the city, its patron deity, and its inhabitants. While in pre-exilic times the Judaean king served as a representative of YHWH and as the mediator between God and the people, now Zion assumes this role in her capacity as a mother who protects and nurtures her children or her inhabitants, respectively. Yet, the personified city, whose splendid rebuilding is predicted in Third Isaiah passages, also advances to a space for contacting the Divine and receiving God's blessing. While Zion does not fully replace the temple as a sacred space, the separation between different groups of citizens hints at a fierce debate about who can access and control the space among those who worship at the Second Temple. The particularism articulated in 66:5–14 and 57:1–13 appears as a first sign of the later differentiation of an earthly and a heavenly Jerusalem. That there are also other voices in the postexilic community is witnessed in Ezra–Nehemiah and its portrayal of the city.[50] Reconstructing this inner-Judaean debate from today's perspective seems to assert that the debate is still not settled: to this day different groups are struggling over access to the sacred space and over the heritage of this ancient city.

50. See the essay by Maria Häusl in the present volume.

THE MEANING OF THE CITY OF JERUSALEM IN THE BOOK OF TOBIT: AN ANALYSIS OF THE JERUSALEM HYMN IN TOBIT 13:8–18

Johanna Rautenberg

The research to date on the book of Tobit is characterized by its focus on the individual fate of the protagonist and his family in the Diaspora. "Thus, the book attempts to tell the story of a 'true Israelite' in the threatening situation of the exile."[1] As an example of Jewish narrative theology, the story tries "to express that God answers prayers, that he accompanies people who run into dangers on the road of life, and that he is no further away from them in times of unhappiness and in the Diaspora than in pleasant times and in the Holy Land."[2] The story thus presents a model of how Jewish life can succeed in a foreign land. The threat of the foreign environment is managed successfully, and the life of the protagonists comes to a happy end. The fact that this process takes place in exile and not in the home country leads to the realization that Jewish life can also evolve outside Palestine.

This interpretation leads to the question of the meaning assumed by the topos Jerusalem in such a concept of Jewish self-understanding. According to the ancient Near Eastern worldview, the temple city is the center of the cosmos with the site of the temple representing the axis mundi.[3] From an exilic Palestinian perspective, the rebuilding of

---

1. P. Deselaers, *Das Buch Tobit: Studien zu seiner Entstehung, Komposition und Theologie* (Göttingen: Vandenhoeck & Ruprecht, 1982), 61 (author's translation). Cf. also A.-J. Levine, "Teaching Jews How to Live in the Diaspora," *BR* 8 (1992): 42–64 (42), and the commentaries mentioned in n. 4.

2. H. Engel, "Das Buch Tobit," in E. Zenger et al., *Einleitung in das Alte Testament* (7th ed.; Stuttgart: Kohlhammer, 2008), 287–88 (288).

3. Regarding the ancient Near Eastern concept and its spatial orientation, cf. B. Janowski, "Das biblische Weltbild. Eine methodologische Skizze," in *Das biblische Weltbild und seine altorientalischen Kontexte* (ed. B. Janowski and B. Ego; FAT 32; Tübingen: Mohr Siebeck, 2001), 3–26; A. Berlejung, "Weltbild/Kosmologie,"

Jerusalem and its temple could restore the relationship between God and the Israelite people.

The prayer of Tobit (13:1–18) provides a clear indication that the city of Jerusalem indeed plays an important role in the lives of believers away from home. On the one hand, the city is included in the invitation to the sons of Israel to praise and extol God (13:10a), and on the other hand, Tobit presents a future vision of Jerusalem as a city built of precious stones to which the people will make pilgrimages (13:11–12). Yet, how can one explain the relationship between the view of a future Jerusalem as a gathering place of nations, and the experience described by the narrated world which confirms that life as a Jew is possible without actually living in the city?

An interpretation that concentrates solely on geographical aspects can hardly resolve this tension. The text itself refers to a different perspective, which in Tob 13 portrays Jerusalem and the narrative within one conceptual context.[4] Thus, the author uses the terms "captivity" and "dispersion" (1:2, 10; 3:4) to describe the experience of foreignness. Conversely, however, "dwelling" is not used in the sense of a local positioning, but in the constitution of a new community: the actors of the narrative experience the positive turn of their destiny in the marriage of Tobias and Sarah, and in the healing of Tobit's blindness which leads him out of his isolation. In contrast to what one would expect with regard to the ancient Near Eastern concept of the temple-city, it is not the return to Jerusalem, which brings salvation, but the growing together of a new community, a social process that leads the story to a positive end while geographical references fade into the background. The book of Tobit does not address the question of where Jewish life can be lived, but how and under what conditions the faith community is constituted. The thesis

in *Handbuch theologischer Grundbegriffe zum Alten und Neuen Testament* (ed. A. Berlejung and C. Frevel; Darmstadt: Wissenschaftliche Buchgesellschaft, 2006), 65–72.

4. The Jerusalem hymn is connected with the narrative part by numerous keywords. Commentators who use a diachronic method suggest that the hymn is a later addition; see, for example, F. Zimmermann, *The Book of Tobit* (New York: Eisenbrauns, 1958), 24–27; Deselaers, *Das Buch Tobit*, 413–17; M. Rabenau, *Studien zum Buch Tobit* (Berlin: W. de Gruyter, 1994), 67–93. Recent approaches forego a literary-critical analysis (in the framework of traditional historical criticism) and read the book as a unified text; see, for example, P. J. Griffin, *The Theology and Function of Prayer in the Book of Tobit* (Ann Arbor: Catholic University of America, 1984), 224; J. Fitzmyer, *Tobit* (Commentaries on Early Jewish Literature; Berlin: W. de Gruyter, 2003), 42–45; C. Moore, *Tobit* (AB 40A; New York: Anchor Bible, 1996).

of the present study is that the narrative develops its own approach to the constitution of the Jewish community and is not limited to the representation of the individual fate of a devout Jew in exile.[5] Against this background, the following questions should be investigated: In what way does the hymn in 13:8–18 perceive the city? What function does Jerusalem play in the process of community building?

1. The Jerusalem Hymn and Its Embedding in the Entire Prayer

The manuscript transmission of the story of Tobit is quite complicated and has been rendered even more so by the discoveries of the text fragments of Qumran. Today three Greek translations are known. The *Short Recension* (G^I) is mainly found in the MSS Vaticanus (B) and Alexandrinus (A). This version of the book has been used by the Christian church almost from the beginning. The longer version of the *Long Recension* (G^{II}) is represented in the MS Sinaiticus (S), which was not known until the nineteenth century. To a great extend the fragments found in Qumran agree with G^{II}. The third version, G^{III}, is basically related to G^{II}. Since the priority of G^{II} or G^I is not decided yet, the present study offers both text versions:[6]

G^I	G^{II}
[1] And Tobit wrote his prayer in exultation and said: Praised be God who lives forever, and (praised be) His kingship	[1] And he said: Praised be God who lives forever, and (praised be) His kingship
[2] because He flogs and shows mercy. He brings down to Hades and brings back. There is no one who will escape His hand.	[2] because He flogs and shows mercy. He brings down to Hades far below and brings back from the great abyss. There is nothing that will escape His hand.

---

5. See my article, "Stadtfrau Jerusalem und ihre Kinder—zur Bedeutung der Stadt Jerusalem im Gemeinschaftskonzept des Buches Tobit," in *Tochter Zion auf dem Weg zum himmlischen Jerusalem: Rezeptionslinien der „Stadtfrau Jerusalem"* von den späten alttestamentlichen Texten bis zu den Werken der Kirchenväter (ed. M. Häusl; Dresdner Beiträge zur Geschlechterforschung in Geschichte, Kultur und Literatur 2; Leipzig: Leipziger Universitätsverlag, 2011), 51–101 (51–78).

6. The translation of Tob 13:1–8 is based on the Greek text versions edited by R. Hanhart, *Tobit* (Septuaginta: Vetus Testamentum Graecum auctoritate Academiae Scientiarium Gottingensis VIII/5; Göttingen: Vandenhoeck & Ruprecht, 1983).

³ Acknowledge Him, sons of Israel, in the sight of the nations, for He has scattered us among them,
⁴ there show His greatness. Exalt Him in the sight of every living being because He (is) our Lord and God, he himself (is) our father forever and ever.

⁵ And he will flog us for our wicked deeds, and He will show mercy again and gather us from the nations among which you have been scattered.
⁶ When you turn to Him with all your heart and all your soul to act in faithfulness to Him, then He will turn to you and will no longer hide His face from you. Consider now what He will do for you and gratefully acknowledge Him with your full voice. Praise the Lord of righteousness, exalt the King of eternity!
In the land of my captivity I gratefully acknowledge Him and make known His might and His majesty to a sinful nation. Turn, sinners, and do what is righteous before Him. Who knows whether He will welcome you or pardon you?
⁷ I extol my God, and my soul (extols) the King of Heaven, it will rejoice in His majesty.
⁸ All shall speak and acknowledge Him in Jerusalem.
⁹ Jerusalem, holy city, He will afflict (you) because of the deeds of your sons, and he will again show mercy to the sons of the righteous.
¹⁰ Acknowledge the Lord in goodness and praise the King of eternity! That once again His tent will be built with joy within you, that He may cheer in you those who are captives and love in you those who are miserable for all generations.

³ Acknowledge Him, sons of Israel, in the sight of the nations, for He has scattered you among them,
⁴ and there He has shown you His greatness. And exalt Him in the sight of every living being because He is our Lord, He (is) our God, He (is) our father, and He (is) God forever and ever.
⁵ He will flog you for your wicked deeds, and He will show mercy to all of you from all nations among which you have been scattered.
⁶ When you turn to Him with all your heart and all your soul to act in faithfulness to Him, then He will turn to you and hide His face no longer. Consider now what He has done for you and gratefully acknowledge Him with full voice. And praise the Lord of righteousness and extol the King of ages!⁷

¹⁰ And once again your tent will be built for you with joy, that He may cheer in you all those who are captives and love in you all those who are miserable for all generations.

7. Verses 6b–10a are missing in MS Sinaiticus.

[11] Many nations from afar will come to the name of the Lord God, bearing gifts in their hands, gifts for the King of Heaven. Generation after generation will present you with rejoicing.

[12] Cursed be all who hate you; blessed forever will be all who love you.

[13] Rejoice and exult over the sons of the righteous because they will all be gathered together and will praise the Lord of the righteous.

[14] O blessed are those who love you; they will rejoice over your peace. Blessed (are) those who have grieved over all your afflictions, for they will rejoice over you when they see all your glory and will be cheered forevermore.

[15] Let my soul praise God, the great King!

[16] For Jerusalem will be rebuilt with sapphire and emerald, and your walls with precious stone; its towers and parapets with finest gold.

[17] The squares of Jerusalem will be paved with beryl, garnet, and stone of Ophir.

[11] A bright light will shine unto all the ends of the earth. Many nations will come to you from afar, inhabitants from the most remote parts of the earth to your holy name, bearing gifts in their hands for the King of Heaven. Generation after generation will present in you a joyful offering, and the name of the chosen one will last eternally for generations.

[12] Cursed be all who will speak harshly against you; cursed be all who will destroy and pull down your walls and all who overturn your towers, and all who set fire to your dwellings. But blessed will be all who fear you to all eternity.

[13] Go then and rejoice over the sons of the righteous because they will all be gathered together and will praise the Lord of eternity.

[14] Blessed are those who love you, and blessed are those who rejoice over your peace. Blessed are all people who will grieve over you because of all your afflictions, for they will rejoice in you and witness all your joy forever.

[15] Praise the Lord—my soul—who is the great King!

[16] For Jerusalem will be rebuilt as a city to be His dwelling-place for all ages. Blessed shall I be if a remnant of my offspring will see your glory and gratefully acknowledge the King of Heaven! And the gates of Jerusalem will be built of sapphire and emerald, and all your walls of precious stone. The towers of Jerusalem will be built of gold and their parapets of finest gold.

[17] The squares of Jerusalem will be paved with garnet and stone of Ophir.

¹⁸ All her alleys will say: Hallelujah, and they will give praise, saying: Praise be to God who has exalted all forever!

¹⁸ The gates of Jerusalem will speak with hymns of joy, and all her houses will say: Hallelujah, praised be the God of Israel! And the blessed will praise His holy name for all eternity and even longer.

In his prayer in 13:1–18, Tobit praises his God and his actions. His praise is not directed toward the wonderful turn that his own destiny has taken, but instead focuses on the fate of his people and invites the listeners to commit themselves to God and to proclaim his greatness (13:3, 4, 6). Tobit interprets the current scattering of the children of Israel as a punishment from God (13:3, 5), which will cease if God, in his mercy, turns toward the people in Jerusalem again (13:6, 10). As such, the three decisive entities of this text are identified: *God* acts upon his people by chastising them and then having mercy on them. Tobit refers to him as πατὴρ ἡμῶν (13:4).[8] The title "father" as a metaphor for God is used in the book of Tobit only once, namely in this passage. The characterization of God as father represents an exclusive and personal relationship between God and Israel, manifested in the aspects of "upbringing" and "kindness."[9] The pedagogical acts of God are intended for the addressees of the song of praise, who are called as υἱοὶ Ισραηλ (13:3), or the υἱοὺς τῶν δικαίων (13:9). The *Israelites* thereby receive the role of the children in need of upbringing,[10] whose behavior determines whether God turns toward them or away from them. Based on the experience that God's punishment is followed by his benevolence and faithfulness, Tobit calls upon the Israelites to commit themselves to God and to praise him (13:3, 6). This father–child relationship is expanded by an address to *Jerusalem* as a person who is assigned the role of the mother (13:9). She too is summoned to praise and rejoice (13:10, 13). Her own destiny is intertwined in a special way with that of her dwellers (13:9, 10, 12–14). The result is an interrelationship that corresponds to that of the family constellation as it is encountered in the book of Tobit: the family consists of a father (Tobit, Raguel), a mother (Anna, Edna) and a child (Tobias, Sarah). The hymn depicts the relationship between God, Jerusalem, and Israel according to this family model. What significance does the "mother"

8. Regarding the paternity of God in the book of Tobit, cf. A. Strotmann, *"Mein Vater bist du!" (Sir 51,20): Zur Bedeutung der Vaterschaft Gottes in kanonischen und nichtkanonischen frühjüdischen Schriften* (Frankfurt a.M.: Knecht, 1991), 24–58.
9. Cf. ibid., 24–58.
10. Regarding the aspect of punishment in the father–son relationship, cf. Prov 3:12; 29:17; Sir 30:1–13.

Jerusalem assume in this context? Is she also perceived in her topographical dimension? The focus of the following interpretation of Tob 13:8–18 is on the meaning and function of Jerusalem as topos in the present context. The lines are being read as a psalm[11] with special regard to aspects of literary composition on a synchronic level. Therefore, an analysis of the history of tradition is of little relevance here.[12]

2. Tobit 13:8–11: Jerusalem as a Personal and Spatial Entity

The prayer reveals a clear dichotomy: the first part (vv. 2–6 or 2–7) describes the chastising and merciful treatment of God toward his people in the role of the father; the second part (vv. 10–18 or 8–18) deals with the city of Jerusalem as a personalized entity and her relationship to the community and to God. Both sections invite the addressees to rejoice and to praise. The four eternity formulas in the second part of the prayer (vv. 10, 11, 14, 18) indicate a structure of four stanzas:

v. 8 (G[I])	=	Transitional introduction			
vv. 9–10	=	1st stanza	v. 11	=	2nd stanza
vv. 12–14	=	3rd stanza	vv. 15–18	=	4th stanza

All verses address the city of Jerusalem, each with different facets of meaning. Although the structure of the individual units does not seem to follow any overall structural scheme, two pairs of stanzas can be identified: stanzas 1–2 and stanzas 3–4.

Starting from v. 9, there is a change of addressees: in the first part of the psalm, Tobit speaks to the people of Israel; in the second part, he appeals to the city of Jerusalem. In v. 9a, Jerusalem is addressed directly in the second person; the vocative is followed by the apposition Ἱεροσόλυμα πόλις ἁγία, "Jerusalem, holy city."[13] Being holy puts Jerusalem in the sphere of the divine; that is, with the concept of holiness a connection to the cult is created, which is otherwise not mentioned in the entire psalm.[14] The verbs refer to vv. 2 and 5, and "he" refers to God who

---

11. Regarding the reading of Tob 13:8–18 as a psalm, cf. Griffin, *Prayer*, 297–98.

12. Cf., for example, the extensive studies of P. Söllner, *Jerusalem, die hochgebaute Stadt: Eschatologisches und himmlisches Jerusalem im Frühjudentum und im frühen Christentum* (Texte und Arbeiten zum neutestamentlichen Zeitalter 25; Tübingen: Francke, 1998), 43–76, and Griffin, *Prayer*, 283–348.

13. Regarding the Aramaic text in the Qumran fragments, cf. M. Hallermayer, *Text und Überlieferung des Buches Tobit* (Deuterocanonical and Cognate Literature Studies 3; Berlin: W. de Gruyter, 2008), 74. Cf. also Neh 11:1; Isa 52:1.

14. With regard to the close connection between the city and the temple within the ancient Near Eastern worldview, cf. Berlejung, "Weltbild/Kosmologie," 67.

is active as the educative "father." As the acting subject, he is mentioned only indirectly, while the objects of the action are clearly identified with υἱοὺς τῶν δικαίων, "sons of the righteous," and the pronoun σοῦ. Verse 9b (Gᴵ) specifies the personhood of Jerusalem, where Tobit perceives the city as the mother of the sons. The pronoun τῶν υἱῶν σοῦ makes this role assignment clear. Jerusalem is punished because of the deeds of her sons. Verse 10 begins with a present-tense imperative, which is aimed at Jerusalem and prompts the city to praise and worship in the present. This invitation corresponds to the expectation formulated to Tobit and Tobias earlier in the narrative by the angel Raphael in Tob 12:18. The conditional conjunction ἵνα in v. 10b (Gᴵ) makes the presence of God in the city dependent on her praise while Gᴵᴵ connects the parts of the sentence with καί. Particularly striking in v. 10c is the abrupt change of imagery. In the context of urban images used with regard to Jerusalem, the "tent" as the place of God's presence comes across as a foreign element from the world of the nomads. Tobit does not use the term ναός, "temple"; cf. Tob 1:4) or οἶκος τοῦ θεοῦ ("house of God"; cf. Tob 14:4), but plays with the designation σκηνή[15] used for, among other things, the tent of meeting in Exod 33:7–11. The adverb πάλιν implies that there will be such a tent again in the future. By combining σκηνή, "tent," with the verb οἰκοδομέω, "to build," the encounter with God receives a cultic character, since this verb is typically used with regard to the construction of religious buildings. In the LXX, this word combination is unique.[16] The construction as *passivum divinum* suggests that God will be the builder of the tent, and will rebuild it for the city. Gᴵᴵ emphasizes the special relationship between God and Jerusalem by speaking of σκηνή σου. Both text versions have one thing in common: they pick up on the spatial aspect by using ἐν σοί. In v. 10d, the pronoun "he" again refers to God, who is again the active agent. Tobit wishes that God may give joy to the prisoners and show love to the poor. In this interaction, the city of Jerusalem plays a role as a person and gains meaning in her spatial dimension. *In and through her*, God will turn lovingly towards the people.

In the second unit of the psalm the motifs change; now Tobit talks of light and nations on pilgrimage. The introductory declarative statement v. 11a (Gᴵᴵ) clearly alludes to Isa 60:1–3 and underlines that the expression φῶς λαμπρὸν, "a bright light," refers to God, and his light will shine upon Jerusalem. With the personal pronoun σοί in the following verses, the city of Jerusalem is addressed. As in the verses before, the

---

15. Regarding the tent in Jerusalem, cf. Isa 54:2; Jer 10:20, and the name אהליבה, "my tent (is) in her," for Jerusalem in Ezek 23:4.

16. Cf. Griffin, *Prayer*, 306.

text does not directly identify God as an acting agent, but replaces his name with the metaphor of light. The motif of light is of central importance in the book of Tobit: the blindness (darkness) is an obvious expression of the crisis of the hero Tobit (Tob 2:9–10), which is overcome through the recovery of his eyesight (Tob 11:10–13).[17] In v. 11b (G[I]: v. 11a) the subject changes: the many peoples act upon Jerusalem. They will come from afar with a goal: to reach τὸ ὄνομα τὸ ἅγιόν σου, "your holy name." The "holy name" of Jerusalem as a destination only occurs in G[II]; G[I] speaks of τὸ ὄνομα κυρίου τοῦ θεοῦ, "the name of the Lord God." Verses 11a and 11b-c describe an opposing movement: the light radiates out from the city and the people enter the city. Jerusalem thus forms a spatial center from which a movement emanates, and which simultaneously attracts such a movement as well. With the formulation that the generations ἐν σοὶ will cheer (v. 11d), G[II] continues to express the spatial perspective, while in G[I] the city appears more clearly as a person who receives gifts and is cheered. Verbs formulated in the future tense indicate that the shining of the city and the pilgrimage of the peoples will occur in the future. A striking feature of v. 11 (G[II]) is the name for Jerusalem; Tobit speaks of "her holy name" and ὄνομα τῆς ἐκλεκτῆς, "the name of the chosen" (v. 11e). The feminine form of this term refers to a female dimension that is to be applied to Jerusalem, because this city is the place in which God will rebuild his tent and let his light shine again.[18]

With regard to the interrelations between God, Israel, and Jerusalem, vv. 9–10 deal exclusively with the relationship of Jerusalem to God. Because of her holiness, she enjoys a special closeness to God, though this does not protect her from being punished. But she is not only an object of divine action; in her role as messenger, her praise and laud bring about the presence of God (G[I]: conditional). This renders her actions salvific and correlates to the spatial level: Jerusalem is the place where the tent of God will be built and a space for God's action will be prepared. Furthermore, Jerusalem appears as a person or mother who plays a crucial role in the aforementioned relationship.

Verse 11 steers attention from God to the people by focusing on their relationship to Jerusalem. With the ἔθνη πολλὰ, "many nations" (cf. Isa 2:3), apparently not only Jews but also non-Jews approach Jerusalem. The image of the pilgrimage of the nations in v. 11b is preceded in G[II]

---

17. Cf. the fate of Ahikar in Tob 14:10.

18. With regard to Jerusalem as elected by God, cf. 1 Kgs 8:16; 11:13, 32; 2 Kgs 21:7; 2 Chr 6:6; see more extensively Söllner, *Jerusalem*, 60.

by the motif of light, which stands for God's presence in the city. Jerusalem appears as a shining light, and thus as a visually perceptible entity which can be seen from afar. Interestingly, however, it is not only the spatial entity Jerusalem to which the peoples come; the target of the pilgrimage is τὸ ὄνομα τὸ ἅγιόν σου, "your holy name." Jerusalem as a sacred city (v. 9a) carries her own holy name. The privilege of being called "holy," which normally belongs to God alone, indicates the special status of Jerusalem in this text. G¹ is not as bold in its theological assessment of the city and describes the nations' pilgrimage to τὸ ὄνομα κυρίου τοῦ θεοῦ, "the name of the Lord, of God." In v. 11b (G¹) not only God receives gifts and cheers, but also Jerusalem (v. 11c). G¹¹, however, does not mention any recipients (v. 11d), and instead emphasizes the spatial dimension of the city: people will rejoice "in her." In the eternity formula v. 11e, which is absent in G¹, the name is addressed once again: ὄνομα τῆς ἐκλεκτῆς, "the name of the chosen one," will stand the test of time. Thus, the entire v. 11 underlines the high esteem of Jerusalem in the eyes of the foreign nations. The city's charisma attracts people from everywhere, who will praise her and bestow gifts on her. Therefore, in this section as well, the city is viewed as a personal entity; she is the recipient of gifts and celebration. In addition, she represents the space in which the praising takes place (G¹¹). Noteworthy in v. 11 (G¹¹) is the name-giving, which suggests the rudiments of a name theology.

In summary, in the first two stanzas, the city is addressed as an entity which enables an encounter with God. As a person, her praising and extolling brings about the rebuilding of the tent (v. 9), in her spatial dimension she prepares a space for God's presence (v. 10d–e) and for the praising of the people (v. 11). This space is defined by positive interactions (God's love, joy, gifts), from both the divine and the human side. Because room in the city is designed as a social space, the structural description is of less importance. After all, the pilgrimage of the nations does not have the goal of reaching the city itself, but rather strives toward the "holy name of Jerusalem" or the "name of the Lord."

3. *Tobit 13:12–18: Jerusalem as a Personal and Structural Entity*

The second pair of stanzas is clearly distinguished from the previous pair in terms of formal design and imagery. In vv. 12–13 and 14–18 God and the people are not named as acting subjects, while the city of Jerusalem continues to be addressed in the second person.

The third stanza focuses on two contrasting attitudes that people can take towards the city. They either confront her with hatred or meet her with loving care. The structure of this verse follows a mirror-image pattern: the three curses in v. 12 (A) are contrasted with the three macarisms in v. 14 (A'), with v. 13 as the mirror axis (A–13–A'). The accumulation of destructive verbs in v. 12 (G^II) brings about a strong contrast to the image of the peaceful folk going on pilgrimages in v. 11. Jerusalem has enemies, whose potential for violence is described quite vividly. Tobit first curses those who ἐροῦσιν λόγον σκληρόν, "speak harsh words." Since the phrase refers to verbal violence, it is an attack on a mental level, which can only affect a person, and thus, Jerusalem is viewed as a personal entity; the verbs in v. 12 b–c, in contrast, refer to the city's structural dimension. While the harsh words of the people in v. 12a are considered to be a future action, the author uses present tense participle forms to describe Jerusalem's destruction in v. 12b–d. The curse is intended for the enemies of the city, but Tobit praises those who fear Jerusalem. It is noticeable that there is semantic change from the destructive verbs in v. 12 to the verbs in v. 14 which stand for positive emotions. Tobit labels those who feel empathy towards the city as blessed: they love Jerusalem; they will be pleased with her peace and will be saddened by her afflictions. The present-tense participle ἀγαπῶντές refers to the current love of Jerusalem that will manifest itself in the future in the caring for the welfare of the city. In contrast to v. 12, the behavior of the people in v. 14d is substantiated. Its positive attitude is rooted in the certainty that they are happy in the city and they will see her joy. Both in A and in A', Jerusalem is the object of the action and does not react herself. Verse 13, which calls Jerusalem to action, is inserted between the two parts A and A': the city shall rejoice over the sons of the righteous (v. 13a). The reason for the appeal to rejoice is stated in v. 13b: ὅτι πάντες ἐπισυναχθήσονται, "they all will be gathered." The reason for the joy is the future gathering of the people, which will once again form a new community. G^I shortens the third stanza by omitting the destruction of Jerusalem, and thus leaves out the physical aspects. Instead, this version describes the destructive violence with the verb of relation μισέω, "to hate." As a corresponding antonym, the verb ἀγαπάω (cf. v. 10e) is used instead of φοβέω in G^II (v. 10). Here, too, the author chooses the present participle, that is, the people react emotionally toward the city in the present time in one way or another. In v. 14d with ἐπὶ σοί, "because of you," G^I once again addresses the more personal entity, whereas G^II sees the city rather as a place for joy: ἐν σοί, "in you."

The fourth stanza (vv. 15–18) retains the same urban imagery as the previous section, but instead of destruction it deals with the rebuilding of the city, which will take place in the future. On the formal level, there is a change of perspective: Tobit does not summon the others to offer praise but rather speaks of his own act of praising. This stanza thus exhibits a slightly altered form of the structure of a thanksgiving psalm.

This thanksgiving psalm starts in both text variants with the praising by Tobit. The imperative to praise in v. 10, which is aimed at Jerusalem, is put into action by the psalmist himself. The occasion and reason for the praising is the rebuilding of the city. According to G^{II}, God's house will be rebuilt as well. In the macarisms in v. 16c-d, which are absent in G^{I}, Tobit hopes that his descendants will experience the rebuilt Jerusalem and see the glory of the city. Verses 16–17 describe the reconstruction by naming—similar to v. 12—the urban details and by listing the precious materials from which they are to be made. There is no information provided on architectural design or construction details. The walls and towers in v. 12 are included, the houses are replaced by gates, parapets and squares (G^{I}: walls, towers, parapets, squares). The author does not develop an overall view of the city in terms of a description of the layout or the architecture of Jerusalem. Rather, he enumerates the various elements that enable the city's protection and defense. Verse 16 names structural elements that are noticeable from outside of the city, while v. 17 offers a glimpse inside the city by mentioning the squares. In both versions, Jerusalem is referred to in the third person with the exception of v. 16c, f (G^{II}) or v. 16b (G^{I}). In the latter, the psalmist again addresses Jerusalem directly by speaking of τείχη σου, "your walls." The possessive pronoun only relates to the walls, while the other buildings in the city are preceded by the article. The vow of praise in v. 18 does not talk about people, as one would infer from v. 15, where Tobit himself commences to praise God. There are construction components (G^{II}: gates,[19] houses, G^{I}: alleys[20]) which as living entities talk and sing. The feminine form αὐτῆς in v. 18 (G^{I}) and v. 18b (G^{II}) refers to the female figuration of Jerusalem. The city will not praise God either in her entirety or as an abstract entity, but rather her individual members fulfill this task. In terms of the complete psalm, v. 18 forms an inclusion to v. 1b: The psalm begins and ends with the praising and extolling of God.

Despite the abrupt change of imagery and of subject starting with v. 12, there is still a recognizable connection to the previous stanzas. The salvific relevance of Jerusalem in v. 10, which is based on the presence of God, is resumed in vv. 12–14 and described in its direct consequence for the people. It is not the city's behavior towards God that is the central

---

19. Regarding the social function of gates as places of encounter and exchange, cf. Deut 22:1; Isa 29:21.

20. Cf. the idea presented in Amos 5:16 that, instead of joy, there will be grief in the squares and lamentations in the alleys.

theme, but rather the behavior of people towards the city. Their hostile or loving attitude determines the fate of their lives; they will either be cursed or blessed. The positive attitude of people to the city does not aim at the protection or the restoration of the buildings but manifests itself in an empathic relationship with Jerusalem. The spatial dimension of Jerusalem is mentioned again in v. 14d: since the people will rejoice ἐν σοί, the city is a place of joy, and such happiness is the reason for the macarisms (v. 14). The motivation for the joy of the city also stems from a relational process: Jerusalem should celebrate not because the city will be rebuilt, but because the sons of the righteous will be gathered again. The gathering of the people who will thus form a new community represents a social process that constitutes the reason for the jubilation. As a new aspect, the third stanza describes the structural dimension of the city: her buildings and walls are the object of negative interactions; as a person, she receives joy and love. Jerusalem thus becomes a mediator of blessings, since she plays a crucial role in the fate of the people: their attitude toward the city decides whether their life is cursed or blessed. In G¹, the personal perception of the city is exclusively predominant; no statements regarding room or building designs are made. Notably, in v. 14d, the people will see the δόξα of Jerusalem (cf. Isa 62:2). Since in the Old Testament tradition this term is exclusively used in reference to God, Tobit expresses the almost God-like status of the city by transferring this divine attribute to her.

The fourth stanza (vv. 15–18) refers to the third stanza by describing the structural reconstruction of the city. As in v. 10c, the author points to the close connection between the city and the place of God's presence, which is initially created for Jerusalem. This special closeness to God is further emphasized in v. 16c, where the author, as in G¹, speaks of the δόξα of the city. Starting in v. 16e, there is a list of construction materials from which the future city is to be built. The text does not describe the appearance and design of these urban details; instead, it focuses on the valuable materials from which the buildings and structures are to be made. Jerusalem will be built of precious stones (cf. Isa 54:11–13). Apart from the glory that will emanate from such a city, these materials represent a distinct stability and durability: buildings made of precious stones cannot be destroyed; the city cannot be conquered ever again, it regains its defensive and protective function. As in v. 12, first the elements that represent these functions are named: the gates, walls, towers, and parapets. Then, the text draws attention to the structural elements located in the city: alleys and houses. Interestingly, only the walls are provided with a possessive pronoun. These works stand for a construction element that first creates the space; within its boundaries the city can develop. A function can be attributed even to the "buildings in the city" or the constructions leading into the city: Gates, alleys and houses are places that allow encounters and stand for social life. In v. 18, the gates and houses are personified as living entities that sing and talk.

The magnificent city of precious gems, which will be built in the future, does not correspond to realistic standards. It is not a construction model for the historic city of Jerusalem. The exceptional accouterments rather point to a metaphorical meaning of the individual components. They allow Jerusalem to appear as a lively space, in the walls of which love and joy will shape the togetherness of the people. Jerusalem is a "social" space, which constitutes itself through positive, empathetic relations. This space is qualified as "sacred" in the text, because it maintains a place for the presence of God. The behavior of the personified city will decide whether God will again set up his tent and turn his attention to the people. She constitutes an independent entity next to God in a nearly God-compliant status: she is holy, bears a holy name, is the chosen one and has glory. The female figuration stands for the special relationship between Jerusalem and the people—she appears as their mother, who has a reciprocal relationship with her children: on the one hand, she bears the consequences of their actions; on the other hand, Jerusalem decides their fate. As a relational entity, she can be addressed directly and is emotionally accessible. Thus the city takes on a tangible salvific meaning, because, as a mediator, she plays a decisive role in the encounter between God and the people. At this metaphorical level the topography recedes to the background.

4. *Jerusalem, the City as Woman*

With regard to the meaning and function of the topos Jerusalem in the overall context of the book of Tobit, it may be concluded that the city is less important in terms of her geographical dimension, but instead plays a significant role as a relational entity. Analogous to the model of the family as a viable basis for the Jewish community in the interrelations between God, Israel, and Jerusalem, Jerusalem takes on the role of the mother. The female personification of the city allows her to be addressed on an emotional level, and intensifies the potential for identifying with her. Jerusalem, however, not only stands for a personal, relational entity, but also for a specific space. This habitat, which is equipped with urban elements, is described with positive verbs of relation. As a "social" space, she is constituted in the loving care of God toward the people and the people toward Jerusalem. In connection with the social group processes that are depicted in the book of Tobit, Jerusalem fulfills a dual function: on the one hand, she provides a decisive identification figure; on the other hand, one can read in the image of the "spatial" Jerusalem how the coexistence of the people will be shaped. Jerusalem is a symbol for a future, successful community of believers (and nations) who amicably communicate with each other and with God; by allowing this vision of the city to oscillate between urban and feminine metaphors, the text creates an image of the city as woman. The observation that the readers learn nothing about architecture, layout, dimensions, and so on, except for rather general information about construction materials, underscores the clear perception of the city as a social entity. The present participles and imperative forms point to the existing city of Jerusalem in an ambivalent situation of threat and devotion. Thus even in the Diaspora the authors of the book of Tobit as well as its readers position themselves with respect to Jerusalem.

After Tobit finishes his prayer in 13:18 the narrative proceeds by recalling Tobit's blindness, his recovery and his deeds of charity. Before he dies he calls his son Tobiah to leave Nineveh and to move to Media with his family, for in 14:3–11 Tobit predicts the destruction of Nineveh and the devastation of Jerusalem and the temple. He also foresees the later rebuilding of both the temple and the city. Mentioning the city at the beginning (1:4) and at the end of the book (14:4) indicates the importance of Jerusalem as a topographic element. This view of Jerusalem and the temple corresponds with the conventional ancient Near Eastern concept of the temple-city as axis mundi. Identity-forming for the Jewish community that reads the book of Tobit is not, however, any actual spatial relationship to the city, but the perception of Jerusalem as a female entity that provides a space for the encounter between God and believers, as well as between Jews and the nations. In this sense, Jerusalem does not stand for a territorially defined space, but for an open, universally oriented community.

Part III

PLACE, SPACE, IDENTITY:
THEORY AND PRACTICE

From the Walls of Uruk: Reflections on Space in the Gilgamesh Epic

Gerda de Villiers

1. *Introduction*

Any attempt at interpreting literature from ancient times in terms of modern concepts or theories should be approached with caution. The ancients themselves had no such term as "literature," nor did they distinguish between different literary genres like "prose," "poetry," "myth," "epic," and so on. Furthermore, the purposes for which they wrote were certainly different from those of present day authors. To complicate matters even more, the texts were written in languages that are no longer spoken. Although the words and syntax may be understood perfectly, the same cannot be said for many of the subtle nuances and idiomatic expressions. The very old texts, like the Gilgamesh Epic, were written on clay tablets, which have been much damaged, and many of the parts have been lost. All these reservations should be kept in mind, especially with regard to the discussion in the present study, which attempts to apply two modern spatial theories to the Gilgamesh Epic. The first comes from Edward Soja's geographical background as understood by various biblical scholars and the second is mainly Nicholas Wyatt's theory on space and time, based on his understanding of the ancient Near Eastern worldview.

2. *Uruk: Secondspace—Soja's Ideas*

The building blocks of a story are characters, time and place[1]—or, to put it differently, something happens to someone somewhere and sometime. Narratologists are also paying attention to another dimension, namely, "space." Whereas "place" may be conceived of as a physical location, "space" is more abstract, carrying emotional undertones and is present in

---

1. M. Bal, *De Theorie van Vertellen en Verhalen: Inleiding in de Narratologie* (Muiderberg: Couthino, 1986), 101.

every narrative, even if "place" is not named at all.[2] Biblical scholars find "space" an interesting dimension to explore and they draw particularly on the theories of "critical spatiality" as advanced by Henri Lefebvre and Edward Soja.[3] It is interesting that Soja is a geographer, but especially his notions of Firstspace, Secondspace and Thirdspace are applied to biblical narrative.[4] Firstspace applies to what is commonly understood to be place, something real, material and concrete. Secondspace becomes more abstract and pertains to ideas and ideologies about place, in other words, that which place is imagined to be. Thirdspace is lived space, that is, "lived realities." The moment something is recorded in writing, however, it becomes a literary construct. In terms of Soja, a written text would be Secondspace, as imagined by someone who is called the author.

a. *The Literary History of the Gilgamesh Epic in a Nutshell*
To retrieve the author of the Gilgamesh Epic is no easy task, as this epic has a long and intricate literary history. Its origins can be traced back to Sumerian times,[5] where it consisted of individual poems of which five are extant[6]—there may have been more. These poems are not connected by theme, for each one recounts a different individual incident. The only matter that they do have in common is their reference to the same place, namely, the city Uruk, and the two main characters, King Bilgames (the

2. A. P. Brink, *Vertelkunde: 'n Inleiding tot die Lees van Verhalende Tekste* (Pretoria: Academica, 1987), 107–8.

3. See the contributions in D. M. Gunn and P. M. McNutt, eds., *"Imagining" Biblical Worlds: Studies in Spatial, Social and Historical Constructs in Honor of James W. Flanagan* (JSOTSup 359; Sheffield: Sheffield Academic, 2002).

4. For example, J. L. Berquist, "Critical Spatiality and the Construction of the Ancient World," in Gunn and McNutt, eds., *"Imagining" Biblical Worlds*, 14–29 (20), and, in the same volume, C. V. Camp, "Storied Space or Ben Sira 'Tells' a Temple," 64–80 (65).

5. A. Kuhrt, *The Ancient Near East c. 3000–330 BC*, vol. 1 (Routledge History of the Ancient World; London: Routledge, 1995), 29–30, provides a useful time chart for the various periods under discussion.

6. J. H. Tigay, *The Evolution of the Gilgamesh Epic* (Philadelphia: University of Pennsylvania Press, 1982), 13; D. Damrosch, *The Narrative Covenant: Transformations of Genre in the Growth of Biblical Narrative* (San Francisco: Harper & Row, 1987), 98; M. van de Mieroop, *Cuneiform Texts and the Writing of History* (Approaching the Ancient World; London: Routledge, 1999), 29; A. R. George, *The Epic of Gilgamesh: A New Translation* (New York: Barnes & Noble, 1999), 141–208, provides excellent translations of these poems; see also George's *The Babylonian Gilgamesh Epic: Introduction, Critical Edition and Cuneiform Texts*, vol. 1 (Oxford: Oxford University Press, 2003), 7–18.

Sumerian name for Akkadian Gilgamesh) and his faithful slave Enkidu. These poems were initially oral compositions recited, or more probably sung, in the royal courts of the Sumerian city-states. Only much later were they written down, possibly during the Ur III period or the Sumerian Renaissance.[7]

The first longer composition in which the name Gilgamesh appears was compiled several centuries later, during the Old Babylonian period.[8] To complicate matters further, in the literary history of the Gilgamesh Epic a different language came to be spoken and written: Sumerian was only used for high culture and the courts, but Old Babylonian, an Akkadian dialect, was the vibrant tongue not only spoken, but also the language in which innovative scribes dared to put their skills into practice.[9] Consequently, they also experimented with different literary forms, which scholars nowadays refer to as "epic"—a narrative written in poetic style, that is, a narrative poem. During this stage, the Old Babylonian version of the *Gilgamesh Epic* was composed as a new literary product to address a new audience.[10] Its opening lines are rather triumphant: "Surpassing all other kings."[11]

b. Sîn-lēqi-unninni's *Imagined Space*
However, this was not to be the final text. Towards the latter half of the Middle Babylonian Period (the Late Bronze Age), the Gilgamesh composition underwent yet another transformation and this final literary creation does bear the name of an author: *Sîn-lēqi-unninni.*[12] Most certainly, he was a trained scholar who belonged to an important and well-known family of scribes in Uruk, and perhaps he was an exorcist priest. The

---

7. George, *Epic of Gilgamesh*, xix, and *Babylonian Gilgamesh Epic*, 108–9; R. Schrott, *Gilgamesh: Nachdichtung und Neuübersetzung* (Munich: Carl Hanser, 2001), 11.

8. This is not a historical, but a linguistic terminology. See D. O. Edzard, "The Old Babylonian Period," in *The Near East: The Early Civilizations* (ed. J. Bottéro et al.; London: Weidenfeld & Nicolson, 1967), 177–231 (178); J. N. Postgate, *Early Mesopotamia: Society and Economy at the Dawn of History* (London: Routledge, 1994), 36; George, *Epic of Gilgamesh*, xx.

9. Schrott, *Gilgamesh*, 14, sets the time during the reign of Hammurabi, but this is open to discussion; cf. George, *Babylonian Gilgamesh Epic*, 17, 30.

10. Tigay, *Evolution of the Gilgamesh Epic*, 42–45; George, *Epic of Gilgamesh*, xxi.

11. Ancient literature was known by its opening lines, not by title. See George, *Babylonian Gilgamesh Epic*, 22.

12. Tigay, *Evolution of the Gilgamesh Epic*, 12; George, *Epic of Gilgamesh*, xxiv–xxv; Schrott, *Gilgamesh*, 16–17, and *Babylonian Gilgamesh Epic*, 28–33.

scholars referred to below place him in the late second millennium, somewhere between the thirteenth and eleventh century B.C.E. *Sîn-lēqi-unninni* supplied the existing Gilgamesh Epic with a prologue, starting with the lines: "He who saw the Deep."

By this time, Uruk is no longer Firstspace or Thirdspace. The powerful individual Sumerian city-states have long disappeared to make way for competing kingdoms in Late Bronze Age Mesopotamia: Assyria and Babylonia. New hegemonies built new capitals. From its Sumerian origins the Bilgames/Gilgamesh narrative went through the hands of many authors, most of them completely unknown. It changed its style and its language. Yet, in the final form, nowadays referred to as the Standard Babylonian Gilgamesh Epic,[13] *Sîn-lēqi-unninni* chose to exploit Secondspace possibilities to the fullest.

Why? There is a good reason. Andrew George[14] argues convincingly that the Gilgamesh Epic was an important text in the curriculum for trainee scribes, ever since the time of its Old Babylonian composition. Many copies of parts of the epic were found in the various scribal schools all over Mesopotamia. Probably the young trainees were to memorize parts of the epic and then copy them out in writing. Obviously, the Gilgamesh Epic was appropriated for academic purposes; therefore, *Sîn-lēqi-unninni* had a popular and well-known text at his disposal with which to work.

What did he do? As mentioned above, *Sîn-lēqi-unninni* supplied a prologue to the Standard Version.[15] The closing lines of the prologue in Tablet I are echoed by the closing lines in Tablet XI,[16] spoken by Gilgamesh himself. This creates the impression that the story is actually an autobiography told in the third person, that Gilgamesh is telling his own story by referring to himself as "he." This was a specific literary style—or genre—in ancient Mesopotamia, known as *narû* or wisdom literature,[17]

13. See George, *Babylonian Gilgamesh Epic*, 380–470, for a full discussion of the manuscripts.

14. Ibid., 33–39.

15. *Sîn-lēqi-unninni* wrought some major changes to the Old Babylonian Epic. These are discussed in some detail in my doctoral thesis; see G. G. de Villiers, "Understanding Gilgamesh: His World and His Story" (D.Litt. thesis, University of Pretoria, 2004), 56–102.

16. The Standard Babylonian Epic actually consists of twelve tablets. Many scholars doubt whether Tablet XII should be regarded as part of the narrative. This debate falls outside the scope of the present study. See George, *Babylonian Gilgamesh Epic*, 47–54, for an in-depth discussion.

17. Tigay, *Evolution of the Gilgamesh Epic*, 144; George, *Epic of Gilgamesh*, xxxv, and *Babylonian Gilgamesh Epic*, 32.

and was typical of royal counsel.[18] In the Gilgamesh Epic, history is creatively dramatized and actualized in the present. It is therefore much more powerful than the usual lecturing and moralizing prescriptive texts of codes of conduct. The story of the ancient king Gilgamesh warns Mesopotamian rulers against the pitfalls of the brutal abuse of power, of hubris against the gods, and emphasizes the value of friendship and trust.

However, there is something more. The Gilgamesh Epic reflects deeply on the most profound fear of humanity: death. "He who saw the Deep," the opening lines of the Gilgamesh Epic are not without thought. Suddenly the perspective changes dramatically. The heroic Old Babylonian king who "surpasses all others" is replaced by one who "saw the Deep."[19] An outward show of superiority changes to inward reflection. It is remarkable that the story that is now told is not the usual tale of heroic victory. "There is nothing of war in the Epic of Gilgameš," writes George,[20] "only heroic combat between individuals and between men and monsters, and the grim struggle with death." The hero acquires wisdom through failure, shame and personal suffering. He learns the hard way.

What does he learn? He learns that he is not going to live forever. The search for life everlasting is futile and sooner or later he, like all other human beings, will die. Therefore, the wisdom advocated from the walls of Uruk is much in the vein of the wisdom of Qohelet in the Hebrew Bible. Gilgamesh has learnt and he tells everybody that death is inevitable; therefore, life has to be embraced, here and now, while it lasts.

3. Wyatt's Theory of Space and Time

What separates humans from animals is a notion of time and space. Animals are not aware of the coming of old age and death; nor are they aware of a personal "self" from which point they construct a particular viewpoint. Humans on the other hand know that their life on earth will end; furthermore, their experiences help them to construct the world around them in order to make sense: this is a conscious and subjective endeavor. Concepts of time and space are thus unique to human beings and part of cultural learning.[21]

---

18. The books of Proverbs and Qohelet in the Hebrew Bible are also examples of royal counsel.

19. De Villiers, "Understanding Gilgamesh," 53.

20. George, *Babylonian Gilgamesh Epic*, 33.

21. N. Wyatt, *Space and Time in the Religious Life of the Near East* (Sheffield: Sheffield Academic, 2001), 33.

Reading ancient texts,[22] one immediately realizes that the worldview is completely different from the heliocentric cosmology since Copernicus. The world was imagined as a flat horizontal disk, resting on and surrounded by waters,[23] the so-called cosmic ocean. This disk was stabilized by pillars reaching to the bottom of the waters below, and by two mountains, at the eastern and western ends of the earth where the sun rose and set every day. The city was at the center of the world and at the center of the city stood the temple.[24] This point, the city-center with its temple, was the most sacred spot, for this was also the meeting point between humans and deities, the point of intersection of the human and divine spheres.[25] Furthermore, because the temple was the dwelling place of one or more deities, the city was a place of security where the order of the world was maintained. Opposed to the city were the steppes, or the wilderness,[26] where demons dwelt and danger lurked. Therefore, in addition to the purpose of safeguarding cities from attacks or raids from enemies, thick walls enclosed cities to keep the wilderness at bay.

At the very center of the universe is the human being—the "self"[27] who constructs reality from his or her self-awareness and personal experiences. Wyatt[28] draws two horizontal axes through the self: an east–west axis and a south–north axis. These geographical directions become metaphorical extensions for a temporal axis and a moral–spatial axis with the human body as point of departure.

The temporal axis runs from east to west. A human being's primary orientation is towards the east. That means looking at her or his beginnings, looking at the past, which she/he can see and which consists of memories.[29] Her/his back is towards the west, the future that she/he cannot see. Along this line, the human being is moving backwards away

---

22. The Hebrew Bible is a good and well-known example.

23. A. Berlejung, "Weltbild/Kosmologie," in *Handbuch theologischer Grundbegriffe zum Alten und Neuen Testament* (ed. A. Berlejung and C. Frevel; Darmstadt: Wissenschaftliche Buchgesellschaft, 2006), 65–72 (66); cf. Wyatt, *Space and Time*, 55.

24. Berlejung, "Weltbild/Kosmologie," 67.

25. Wyatt, *Space and Time*, 147.

26. Ibid.

27. Ibid., 35.

28. Ibid., 35–39. Much of his theory is based upon the use of language. This discussion is not relevant for the present study.

29. At first glance this may seem strange to modern Western thought. We look to our future. But the ancients could not "see" their future, only their past. So they directed their face towards that which they could see, namely, the past, that is, the east.

from her/his past towards the unknown future. Consequently, the past becomes more and more distant.

However, this very basic experience is not an individual one, but shared by all human beings who live together in groups or communities. The lives of humans are shaped by events and experiences with others. This includes not only the present, but also the past, even the distant past. Although an individual did not necessarily experience the distant past of his or her ancestors, this past is actualized in the present by means of narrative—whether orally recited or recorded in writing. This is the domain of history and myth, where the ancestors share their experiences and memories; they become vivid and alive and continue to shape the lives of their descendants.

Obviously, then, moving westwards, backwards towards the future, means moving towards the unseen. Two reactions are possible: fear, because something that cannot be controlled may happen, or, on the other hand, creative inventions in order to predict or to control what cannot be known beforehand.

The moral–spatial axis runs from south to north and extends from the body. South means to the "right" and implies exactly what it says: moral conduct, that which is correct and guarantees security and well-being. North of course is the opposite, meaning towards the "left," towards that which is "sinister,"[30] and dangerous. This spatial–moral axis determines the human being's self-centeredness, gives rise to feelings of security, of knowing and doing that which is right and good for the self. Self-centeredness, however, is not to be equated with selfishness. Put differently, the moral-spatial axis keeps the individual upright, at-center with her- or himself. Away from the self "means a progressive approach to the 'end of the world' where reality breaks down."[31]

There is yet another axis: the vertical axis that goes up and down. This axis refers to the world above or below the individual: the world of the gods, those in the transcendent and infernal spheres.[32] A movement upwards is considered positive, and downwards negative. This is not a simple good–evil opposition, as the ancients had no real concept of "hell." Everybody, regardless whether she/he led a good or bad life, went to the Netherworld, which was inhabited by other departed souls and the deities that reigned there. Moreover, the deities of the higher heaven were not always benign towards humans, as is clearly illustrated by the Atrahasis Epic or Babylonian Flood Narrative.

30. Latin *sinister* = "left."
31. Wyatt, *Time and Space*, 39.
32. Ibid., 40.

a. *Sacred Space Inverted*

As indicated above (section 2b), the narrative in the Gilgamesh Epic is introduced by a prologue. A narrator who seems to be anonymous is speaking from the sturdy ramparts of Uruk. From there he invites the reader/listener into the very center of the city, the holy Eanna, the sacred dwelling place of the goddess Ishtar (I.16).[33] One would expect an encounter with the supernatural. After all, the temple is the point of intersection between gods and humans. Here, in the Epic, the reader is instructed to "[s]ee the tablet box of cedar, release its clasp of bronze, lift the lid of its secret, pick up the tablet of *lapis lazuli* and read out the travails of Gilgamesh, all that he went through" (I.24–28). However, what is about to unfold is a very human story, a story of human suffering without divine promises of salvation or redemption. Gilgamesh personally has to work out his life's purpose. The sacred space is inverted: it is not about the gods, it is about one man.

b. *The Horizontal Axis: South–North*

Gilgamesh kicks off with a rather bad start—he bounds to the "north." A Mesopotamian king was supposed to be to his people like a shepherd to his sheep,[34] ruling them with justice, protecting the weak and the poor, providing protection during times of peril and guiding them with wisdom and insight. Gilgamesh does more or less the opposite. As a young king, he abuses his power brutally by harassing his subjects to the point where they can take it no longer. The women-folk complain to the creator-goddess Aruru, asking for the creation of a double for the king, someone equal in strength, who is a match for his energy, someone to keep him occupied so that the people may rest. Consequently, Enkidu is created, initially as a savage primitive human being who roams the wild. Shamhat, the harlot, is sent to instruct him in the ways of civilization and to bring him to Uruk. Ironically, the uncivilized man is the one who brings Gilgamesh back "south." On arrival at Uruk, Enkidu is livid with rage when he is informed that the king insists on nuptial rights with a bride-to-be. A fight breaks out between Gilgamesh and Enkidu, but they appear to be an equal match and eventually become firm friends. Now Gilgamesh is upright, at-center, at Uruk.

---

33. The references to tablets and verses are from George, *Epic of Gilgamesh.*

34. A. Westenholz and U. Koch-Westenholz, "Enkidu—the Noble Savage," in *Wisdom, Gods and Literature: Studies in Assyriology in Honor of W. G. Lambert* (ed. A. R. George and I. L. Finkel; Winona Lake: Eisenbrauns, 2000), 437–51 (443); George, *Epic of Gilgamesh*, xiv.

Being young and restless, Gilgamesh soon wishes to leave his comfort zone—perhaps he became rather bored with his new moral life and too much security? After some time he becomes aware that his friend Enkidu appears depressed because his great strength seems to be ebbing away. Gilgamesh then suggests a death-defying adventure: to slay the monstrous Humbaba, guardian of the cedar forest, appointed by no one less than the god Enlil.[35] Thus, he chooses to venture north once again, doing what he should not do: he challenges the authority of the gods directly. This time the move north, away from center, is more than simply immoral behavior, it is also a move towards that which is sinister and dangerous, because Humbaba's "voice is the Deluge, his speech is fire, his breath is death!" (II.109–110). Despite all the efforts of Enkidu and the elders of Uruk to make him abandon his plan, Gilgamesh continues and eventually persuades his half-hearted friend to come along. The trip is long and exhausting, and when they intrude into his forest, Humbaba is not impressed. He first insults them, and then they start to fight. The whole expedition almost ends in a disaster when Humbaba seems to be winning, but Shamash, the sun god, intervenes, blinds the monster and gives Gilgamesh and Enkidu an opportunity to overcome him. They kill Humbaba, behead him and chop down as many trees as they wish for Gilgamesh to decorate his palace.

c. *A Vertical Interruption—and a Transgression of Boundaries*

As Gilgamesh returns to his palace, washes off the grime of battle and clothes himself in his royal robes, the great goddess Ishtar[36] sees him and falls madly in love with him. In fact, she proposes shamelessly and promises him sex, power and money, all that a man can desire. Strangely enough, Gilgamesh rejects the offer, at first rather politely, but then ending his speech with a number of rude insults. Of course, Ishtar is very much insulted. She demands that Anu, the sky god, head of the gods and her father, gives her the "Bull of Heaven"[37] to smite Gilgamesh in his palace. Ishtar's father warns her that the bull is a celestial beast and its grazing fields are among the stars—on earth, it would create havoc! Yet

---

35. Enlil, also known as "Lord Wind." He is one of the governors of the cosmos, and also the divine ruler of Earth and its living humans. See George, *Epic of Gilgamesh*, 223.

36. Ishtar is the goddess of love and war, known for her insatiable appetite for sex, but also for her vile temper. She is associated with Venus, the morning and evening star. See ibid., 223.

37. The "Bull of Heaven" refers to the celestial constellation of Taurus. See De Villiers, "Understanding Gilgamesh," 3–55.

Ishtar insists and the worst happens. Many citizens of Uruk perish before Gilgamesh and Enkidu intervene and slay yet another monster. Of course Ishtar is both angry and devastated, and when her wails become too much for Enkidu, he tears off the right flank (or penis) of the bull and flings it in her face.

A number of things happen in this scenario: in the first place, as indicated above, a movement downwards is always negative. Both Ishtar and the "Bull of Heaven" descend, with disastrous effect. In the second place, an important boundary is crossed: the boundary between the world of the gods and the world of humans.[38] Ishtar intervenes directly in human affairs, making matters worse by using a celestial beast to wreak her vengeance on Gilgamesh. Enkidu crosses the same boundary when he flings a part of the mutilated beast into the face of the goddess: he taunts the gods and believes his strength matches theirs.[39] The natural and the supernatural should be kept separate.

However, there are allusions to yet another boundary in this text: the boundary between the world of the living and the world of the dead. As Ishtar proposes to Gilgamesh, she says: "Be you my husband, and I your wife" (VI.9). According to Tzvi Abusch[40] this proposal is identical with other proposals from the Netherworld. So, for example, Ereshkigal[41] uses the same words as she proposes to Namtar, her spouse to be. Ishtar's proposal therefore comes from the world of the dead. This argument is further substantiated by her promises. She promises Gilgamesh a chariot of lapis-lazuli and gold drawn by large mules that will bring him to a sweet-scented house (cf. VI.10–13). These promises allude to funerary rites:[42] rather shockingly, Ishtar is therefore inviting him into his tomb and into the Netherworld.

The spiral downwards continues. Gilgamesh and Enkidu celebrate their victory over the "Bull of Heaven" by inviting the people of Uruk to a party at the palace, where everyone more or less passes out. That night Enkidu has a dream—or rather, a nightmare. The great gods sentence him to death, not by means of acquiring honor and an everlasting name, but by means of shame: he is to become ill and die a painful, pitiful death. As he lies ill, hallucinating, he has another dream. He is dragged

---

38. See also Damrosch, *Narrative Covenant*, 107.

39. De Villiers, "Understanding Gilgamesh," 3–56.

40. T. Abusch, "Ishtar's Proposal and Gilgamesh's Refusal: An Interpretation of the Epic Tablet 6, Lines 1–79," *HR* 26 (1986): 143–87 (149).

41. Ereshkigal is Ishtar's sister and Queen of the Netherworld. See George, *Epic of Gilgamesh*, 223.

42. Abusch, "Ishtar's Proposal and Gilgamesh's Refusal," 153, 155.

along lower and lower by a man with a green face until he reaches the bottom of the Netherworld, where he faces Ereshkigal. He dreams of the final boundary all humans will cross, sooner or later.

d. *Horizontal Again: This Time, East–West*

Enkidu then dies. Gilgamesh prepares all the necessary burial rites to ensure that the gods of the Netherworld welcome his friend. However, he also starts becoming aware of his own future: death. He is shocked completely off-center and cast into a deep and dark depression. He realizes that he is pacing slowly but surely towards the west. His one and only obsession is to "overcome time, to neutralize its effects and to become immortal."[43] The only way of achieving this is to look into the past, the very distant past recorded by a very remote ancestor: Utanapishtim,[44] the Distant. Once again, Gilgamesh leaves Uruk, leaves his own center and starts to travel. At this stage, he seems to be going eastward—to the past; he wants to push away the future, to push away death.

His travels bring him to the cosmic end of the earth where his first landmark is the "Mashu Mountains,"[45] or the "Twin Mountains" where the sun rises and sets every day, quite aptly described as mountains "whose tops support the fabric of heaven, whose base reaches down to the Netherworld" (IX.40–41). These mountains are at the very end of the inhabited world, they already touch upon the world of myth when their guardians appear: the scorpion people. At the other side of the Mashu Mountains lies the cosmic ocean, called the "Waters of Death," which Gilgamesh has to cross if he is to reach Utanapishtim.

The scorpion people inform Gilgamesh that the only way that he can travel beyond the mountains is to take "the path of the Sun God" (IX.137). In the Gilgamesh Epic, this appears to be a very dark tunnel below the surface of the earth, even underneath the cosmic ocean below.[46] This path has to be traveled for an exhausting twelve double hours. The reason why this tunnel is shrouded in a thick, tangible darkness is unclear,[47] for the text is very broken. However, it appears that for Gilgamesh this is a race against time, because at twelve double hours he has to come "out in advance of the Sun" (IX.170).

---

43. Wyatt, *Space and Time*, 34.
44. Utanapishtim, also known as Atrahasis, is the survivor of the Babylonian Flood Narrative.
45. W. Horowitz, *Mesopotamian Cosmic Geography* (Mesopotamian Civilizations 8; Winona Lake: Eisenbrauns, 1998), 97.
46. T. Jacobsen, *Treasures of Darkness* (London: Yale University Press, 1976), 204.
47. Horowitz, *Cosmic Geography*, 99.

At this point, an important question arises in terms of Wyatt's theory (explained above). In which direction exactly was Gilgamesh traveling? East or west? Leaving Uruk, he went on a search for life everlasting. He was looking for Utanapishtim, the Distant, who he hoped would disclose to him the secret of defying death. Towards the past seems to be eastwards. Yet this journey was filled with misery and fear. So, perhaps he started in the wrong direction, that is, westwards, towards his own future, towards his own fear of death? Only after traveling the "path of the Sun God"—which is eastwards—does he start venturing towards what he was looking for: the realm of myth. The "path of the Sun" almost serves as a kind of time capsule, projecting Gilgamesh away from the unknown fearful future right back towards the mythical past. It is also remarkable that this travel eastward, recounted in Tablet XI.136–170, is already alluded to in the prologue: Gilgamesh is lauded as one who undertook many adventures—among others, he "crossed the ocean, the wide sea to the sunrise" (I.40).[48] At the end of this race against time, against the future and towards the past, the light breaks through. Gilgamesh arrives in a paradise where trees bear foliage of semi-precious stones.

e. *The Last Boundary—Back to the Future*
The end is not yet. Here, at the seashore of the "Waters of Death" lives Siduri, the wise barmaid. First, she tries to dissuade Gilgamesh from pursuing his quest for life everlasting, but when she realizes that he is determined, she informs him that he still has to cross a last boundary in order to reach Utanapishtim, the survivor of the Deluge. He has to ferry across the "Waters of Death." Urshanabi, the boatman of Utanapishtim, happens to be in the midst of the forest, and he may be willing to ferry Gilgamesh across. Gilgamesh overcomes Urshanabi by surprise, and leaves the boatman no choice but to take him outside the normal boundaries of the cosmos.[49] When Gilgamesh reaches Utanapishtim, he reaches the realm of myth, the very distant past. Paradoxically, this is the meeting point between past and future. Myth, the distant past, also concerns the future of human kind, namely, death. Wyatt[50] is quite clear that myths are "existential tales" that encompass all human experiences, past and future, of which death is the ultimate future experience.

48. Ibid., 97.
49. Wyatt, *Space and Time*, 141.
50. Ibid., 233.

From Utanapishtim Gilgamesh wishes to learn how he can extend his temporal line to the east, for he does not want to die and he does not want to face the future—he wants to learn the secret of life everlasting. Utanapishtim tells him a story of an earth that was flooded from above and below, and that all life would have been wiped out had it not been for a secret disclosed only to one human being: Utanapishtim.[51] However, this was a non-recurrent event and to the advantage of Utanapishtim only. There will not be another deluge, nor another hero. However, if Gilgamesh succeeds in overcoming his own humanity by staying awake for six days and seven nights, there is a chance that he may defy death. However, as could be expected, he fails this test miserably.

There is one last chance. At the bottom of the cosmic ocean grows a thorny shrub. If Gilgamesh retrieves it and uses it, he will not grow older. Thus, he is not granted immortality, but only the ability to postpone old age and death somewhat. With this last piece of information, Utanapishtim instructs Urshanabi to take Gilgamesh back to Uruk, and neither of them may ever return.

It seems that the pace westwards cannot be slowed down, and the direction cannot be changed. As Gilgamesh and Urshanabi camp out for the night, Gilgamesh goes down to bathe in a pool of clear water. Rather carelessly, he leaves the plant on the side of the pool. A snake smells its sweet odors, and Gilgamesh is just in time to see how the creature snatches the precious plant, casts off its old skin, and sails away, young and new. Here, at the end of the world and at the end of his tether, in the realm of myth, he learns a harsh lesson that is to become "indicative for present behavior":[52] all humans die. In the realm of myth, in the very distant past, Gilgamesh is compelled to face his future: death. He returns to Uruk, accompanied by Urshanabi the ferryman.

4. *Uruk: Narrative Pace and Narrative Space*

Every story or narrative, whether ancient or modern, proceeds with a particular rhythm, sometimes moving rapidly forward and at other times slowing down, even coming to a halt. Four basic narrative movements can be distinguished: summary, pause, ellipsis, and scene.[53]

---

51. This is a story within a story. For the purposes of the present study, I am not going to discuss "space" in the flood narrative.
52. Wyatt, *Space and Time*, 233.
53. G. Genette, *Narrative Discourse* (Oxford: Blackwell, 1980), 95–108.

A summary is exactly what it says. In a few sentences or a paragraph, the narrative sums up events that had occurred over a relatively long period, without elaborating on detail or reflecting on dramatic instances. Pauses are there to slow down the narrative, even bringing it to a complete halt by long descriptive passages, which may for example picture the landscape where a character spends a brief moment in the story. In an ellipsis, time vanishes completely into "six years and two months later" or simply "sometime later." Finally, scenes are those dramatic moments in the story, accompanied by vivid and dramatic descriptions.

Twice in the epic, Gilgamesh ventures away from Uruk. In both instances, he journeys towards danger and faces the risk losing his life. First, he and Enkidu head "north" in an effort to slay Humbaba, guardian of the Cedar Forest (see section 3b above). The enemy is tangible: Humbaba is a vicious monster, ready to kill if not killed first. Then, after Enkidu's death he leaves Uruk again, this time westward (see section 3d above). This time the enemy is intangible, invisible, but far more dangerous, because it cannot be killed, it only kills. Its name is Death.

When Gilgamesh journeys away from Uruk, the narrative pace is drawn out by dramatic scenes, alternating with dialogue. However, when he returns, time "pleats." After he and Enkidu had vanquished Humbaba, the period of their return to Uruk ellipses into one brief line.[54] When he realizes that his search for everlasting life is futile, his return to Uruk with Urshanabi the boatman is summarized in two lines, describing a trip that apparently lasted a whole day.[55]

Does the author, *Sîn-lēqi-unninni*, wish to convey something by drawing out the paces away from Uruk, but then sketching the return almost by a snap of the fingers? Is there therefore a relationship between the pace of narration and the space of narration?

To go away from Uruk is dangerous, entails exhausting excursions, up to the point of death. Away from Uruk implies away from a safe, secure space, therefore, the sooner Gilgamesh returns to Uruk, the better. Being at Uruk is where Gilgamesh belongs and where he should stay.

From the walls of Uruk he sees his past. The drama of his life unfolds as he tells his own story. Although he cannot see his future, he is painfully aware of its imminence: death. His present behavior is guided by the failures of his past: to live life here and now as best as he can, because that is all that he has.

---

54. V.302: "and Gilgamesh carried the head of Humbaba."
55. XI.318–319: "At twenty leagues they broke bread, at thirty leagues they stopped for the night."

5. Conclusion

Despite the reservations mentioned in the introduction, the modern spatial theories of Soja and Wyatt appear to have a heuristic function with regard to the Gilgamesh Epic. Uruk is a focal point in the narrative as well as from the perspective of the main character. First, it serves as a Secondspace narrative construct from where wisdom and insight into life issues are reflected. Secondly, it appears to be a central point for Gilgamesh in terms of his self-orientation. When he is at Uruk, he is at-center, at himself, safe and secure. Moreover, from the walls of Uruk he can convey the wisdom of the one "who has seen the Deep."

FAMILY AS LIVED SPACE:
AN INTERDISCIPLINARY AND INTERTEXTUAL READING OF GENESIS 34

Reineth (C. E.) Prinsloo and Gert T. M. Prinsloo

[R]eality is *perspectivistic*... [E]very understanding about reality is relative to the observer's personal history, cultural context, ideology, theoretical framework, choice of focal system, gender, and other personal factors as well as a host of environmental and contextual factors.[1]

1. *Introduction*

Readers accustomed to the concepts of human rights, gender equality, and the honoring of property rights experience the story of the rape of Dinah (Gen 34:1–31) as an unpleasant, disconcerting narrative.[2] Abuse of power, rape, marginalization of the weak, deliberate deceit, murder and plunder abound. God, evidently present before and after the unfortunate incident (cf. Gen 32:23–33; 35:1–15),[3] is surprisingly absent, leaving the reader with the impression that God condones the atrocious behavior of Canaanites and Israelites alike. Interpreting the narrative is problematic and it has attracted several opposing interpretations.[4]

---

1. S. P. Robbins et al., *Contemporary Human Behavior Theory: A Critical Perspective for Social Work* (Boston: Pearson, 2010), 45 (italics original).

2. Cf. D. S. Earl, "Toward a Christian Hermeneutic of Old Testament Narrative: Why Genesis 34 Fails to Find Christian Significance," *CBQ* 73 (2011): 30–49; J. Kugel, *The Ladder of Jacob: Ancient Interpretations of the Biblical Story of Jacob and His Children* (Princeton: Princeton University Press, 2006), 37.

3. Chapters and verses are numbered according to the Masoretic text.

4. M. Sternberg, *The Poetics of Biblical Narrative: Ideological Literature and the Drama of Reading* (Indiana Literary Biblical Series; Bloomington: Indiana University Press, 1985), 441–81; idem, "Biblical Poetics and Sexual Politics: From Reading to Counterreading," *JBL* 111 (1992): 463–88, reads the narrative "with" Dinah's brothers against Shechem and Jacob. D. N. Fewell and D. M. Gunn, "Tipping the Balance: Sternberg's Reader and the Rape of Dinah," *JBL* 111 (1991): 193–211, do exactly the opposite; cf. P. Noble, "A 'Balanced' Reading of the Rape of Dinah: Some Exegetical and Methodological Observations," *BibInt* 4 (1996):

Historical-critical studies propose that an older family narrative with Shechem as protagonist has been incorporated in a tribal narrative with Hamor as protagonist. The family narrative goes back to an oral tradition from patriarchal times, the tribal narrative to the period of the settlement of the land. A redactor then combined the two narratives during exilic or post-exilic times.[5] *Literary approaches* read the text as a single unit composed by one author. Such readings focus upon the repetition of key words or phrases, subtle nuances in the meaning of words at different points in the narrative, and structural patterns discernible when the story is read as a unit.[6] *Feminist scholars* focus on Dinah's silence and the text's patriarchal and androcentric perspective. Dinah is an object of desire, a bargaining chip, and an excuse for her brothers to gain access to resources. Despite the narrative's setting in a patriarchal, androcentric and group-oriented society, Dinah's silence should not become a silent condonation of the violent and unacceptable treatment of defenseless women.[7]

These approaches emphasize the precarious position of Dinah as a lone female in a patriarchal society and the family of Jacob's marginalized status in a hostile environment. We argue that the text should not be read only from a victim's perspective, but also the "other way round," as a metaphorical story casting a long shadow in the ever-growing

173–204. S. P. Jeansonne, *The Women of Genesis: From Sarah to Potiphar's Wife* (Minneapolis: Fortress, 1990), 88 emphasizes the narrative's "permanent ambiguity."

5. Cf. R. Parry, "Source Criticism and Genesis 34," *TynBul* 51(2000): 121–38, for an overview, and H. Gunkel, *Genesis* (8th ed.; HKAT I/1; Göttingen: Vandenhoeck & Ruprecht, 1969), 369–74; G. von Rad, *Genesis* (trans. J. Bowden; rev. ed.; OTL; London: SCM, 1972), 329–35; C. Westermann, *Genesis 12–36* (trans. J. J. Scullion; Minneapolis: Augsburg, 1985), 535–37, for typical historical-critical analyses.

6. Cf. J. G. Janzen, *Abraham and All the Families of the Earth: A Commentary on the Book of Genesis 12–50* (ITC; Grand Rapids: Eerdmans, 1993), 135–38; V. P. Hamilton, *The Book of Genesis* (NICOT; Grand Rapids: Eerdmans, 1995), 351–73; R. Alter, *Genesis* (New York: W. W. Norton, 1996), 189–94; B. K. Waltke, *Genesis: A Commentary* (Grand Rapids: Zondervan, 2001), 349–54, 457–69.

7. Cf. S. Scholz, "Through Whose Eyes? A 'Right' Reading of Genesis 34," in *Genesis: The Feminist Companion to the Bible (Second Series)* (ed. A. Brenner; Sheffield: Sheffield Academic, 1998), 150–71; R. Parry, "Feminist Hermeneutics and Evangelical Concerns: The Rape of Dinah as a Case Study," *TynBul* 53 (2002): 1–28. C. Blyth, "Redeemed by His Love? The Characterization of Shechem in Genesis 34," *JSOT* 33 (2008): 3–18, and "Terrible Silence, Eternal Silence: A Feminist Re-Reading of Dinah's Voicelessness in Genesis 34," *BibInt* 17 (2009): 483–506, advocates a reading "with" Dinah's silent cry.

Israelite/Jehudite meta-narrative of her origins, identity and history.[8] An interdisciplinary and intertextual reading will elucidate the influence of the "Dinah Affair"[9] on the formation of Israelite identity. We emphasize the complex nature of the narrative and its far-reaching influence in the Hebrew Bible, departing from the text in its final form.[10] We read it against the socio-historical background of the late Persian/early Hellenistic period, when the people of Yehud struggled with issues such as political dependence, powerlessness, economic deprivation, and loss of identity.[11] They are strangers in the land promised to them by YHWH. The patriarchal narrative, set in Israel's formative period, becomes a metaphor "for the post-exilic identity-building project."[12]

---

8. S. A. Geller, "The Sack of Shechem: The Use of Typology in Biblical Covenant Religion," *Proof* 10 (1990): 1–15. Geller points to "the rabbinic statement that 'the deeds recounted of the fathers are indicative of what will occur to their descendants'," and remarks: "There are two levels of meaning in Genesis 34. One is that of the narrative itself, a violent incident in the familial history of the man Jacob-Israel. The other level is typological, the significance of the story as foreshadowing events in the national life of later Israel, the people, whose eponymous ancestor is the patriarch" (p. 2). The scope of the present study makes it impossible to trace the development of this ever-growing meta-narrative until it reaches its culmination in Genesis–2 Kings; cf. in this regard the overview in J. C. Gertz, ed., *Grundinformation Altes Testament: Eine Einführung in Literatur, Religion und Geschichte des Alten Testaments* (3d ed.; Göttingen: Vandenhoeck & Ruprecht, 2009), 193–311 (269–79).

9. T. Frymer-Kensky, *Reading the Women of the Bible* (New York: Schocken, 2002), 179.

10. Frymer-Kensky, ibid., 181–82, remarks: "The story piles ambiguity upon enigma by 'gapping' (leaving unsaid) vital elements. The significance of the story depends on the way that readers fill in these gaps."

11. This reading does not, of course, exclude other readings in other epochs. However, it allows for a reading of the narrative against growing tensions in the post-exilic Jewish community and emerging (often contesting) Judaisms. Gen 34, for instance, seems to reflect critique against intermarriage with non-Jewish groups (cf. Ezra 9:1–10:44; Neh 13:23–28). However, it is equally critical of Jacob's inactivity on the one hand and Simeon and Levi's aggressive attack against the Shechemites on the other hand. In this regard I. Hjelm, *The Samaritans and Early Judaism: A Literary Analysis* (JSOTSup 303; Sheffield: Sheffield Academic, 2000), 144, remarks that the story "meets the question of syncretism. With the killing of the Shechemites, although they had become circumcised, the story raises a severe critique against Judaism's expansionist policy, which in the time of the Hasmoneans required all neighbouring people's submission to circumcision and Jewish customs, while formerly they had not been reckoned as belonging to the Jewish race."

12. J. J. Quesada, "Body Piercing: The Issue of Priestly Control Over Acceptable Family Structure in the Book of Numbers," *BibInt* 10 (2002): 24–35 (32). According to Frymer-Kensky, *Reading the Women*, 334, the story of Dinah "demonstrates the

YHWH remains silent while Jacob's clan and the encompassing Canaanite population cross real and imagined boundaries in an endeavor to define their identities. Dinah "goes out" (34:1) to the daughters of the land and this single action results in individual and collective disaster (34:2). Jacob chooses to remain inactive (34:5) and cautious (34:30). The Canaanites try to rectify the social imbalance between the powerful and the powerless via negotiations (34:6, 8–12) while Jacob's sons revert to indignant anger (34:7), deceit (34:13) and violence (34:25–29). None of the efforts are overtly condemned or approved. Read against the uncertainties of the post-exilic period, however, the narrator seems to suggest that only obedience to YHWH (35:1) and faith in his protective power (35:5) can ensure survival "at-center."[13]

2. *Notes on Theory*

Our reading of Gen 34 evolves in phases. A brief intratextual reading of the narrative is followed by an interdisciplinary and intertextual reading,[14] focusing on two important but neglected perspectives related to

intricate difficulties of Israel's destiny among the nations, focusing on the essential question of how Israel should form alliances and how it should grow."

13. The scope of the present study does not allow for a discussion of interpretations of the narrative beyond the Hebrew Bible; cf. R. Pummer, "Genesis 34 in Jewish Writings of the Hellenistic and Roman Periods," *HTR* 75 (1982): 177–88; L. H. Feldman, "Philo, Pseudo-Philo, Josephus, and Theodotus on the Rape of Dinah," *JQR* 94 (2004): 253–77; Kugel, *Ladder of Jacob*, 36–80; J. A. Schroeder, "The Rape of Dinah: Luther's Interpretation of a Biblical Narrative," *Sixteenth Century Journal* 28 (1997): 775–91. The narrative played an important role in defining Yehudite identity with the focus upon Jerusalem and the temple as the only place where YHWH should be worshiped, and Samaritan identity with the city of Shechem as their capital and the temple on Mount Gerizim as the only legitimate place of worship. Cf. in this regard Hjelm, *Samaritans*, 104–82; M. Kartveit, *The Origin of the Samaritans* (VTSup 128; Leiden: Brill, 2009), 106–202.

14. Only texts elucidating family relations in Jacob's clan will be discussed here. Other intertexts (Deut 22:13–29; Judg 19–21; esp. 2 Sam 13:1–39) will be referred to in passing. Cf. D. N. Friedman, "Dinah and Shechem, Tamar and Amnon," *Austin Seminary Bulletin* 105 (1990): 51–63; L. M. Bechtel, "What if Dinah Is Not Raped? (Genesis 34)," *JSOT* 62 (1994): 19–36; E. Fuchs, *Sexual Politics in the Biblical Narrative: Reading the Hebrew Bible as Woman* (JSOTSup 310; Sheffield: Sheffield Academic, 2000), 200–224; I. Kottsieper, "'We Have a Little Sister': Aspects of the Brother–Sister Relationship in Ancient Israel," in *Families and Family Relations as Represented in Early Judaisms and Early Christianities: Texts and Fictions* (ed. J. W. van Henten and A. Brenner; STAR 2; Leiden: Deo, 2000), 49–80; E. van Wolde, "Does *'Innâ* Denote Rape? A Semantic Analysis of a Controversial Word," *VT* 52 (2002): 527–44.

the narrator's point of view. First, the narrative is told from a family-oriented perspective, focusing on the confrontation of a small group of related people with a foreign and potentially hostile environment.[15] Second, the narrative has a distinctly spatial perspective. Emphasis is placed on specific locations, arriving at and departing from those locations, hence suggesting a process of crossing physical and social boundaries.[16]

Principles of general systems theory will be utilized to elucidate the family-oriented perspective.[17] Systems theory focuses upon the inter-relatedness of people and their environments, their interaction with and adaptation to each other.[18] Family, community, social, economic, political and geographical factors affect an individual, and the individual, in turn, affects each of these systems.[19] Systems are elaborately connected to one another and should be viewed holistically, from the micro to the macro level.[20] The physical and social environments are characterized by time and space and can support or fail to support an individual's relatedness to others.[21] By conceptualizing these relations, areas of potential conflict can be identified. Conceptualization is visually expressed by means of a genogram, which collects and organizes data along genealogical lines and represents it using symbols to depict family membership, family

---

15. Words denoting family relationships are key terms in the narrative (see Alter, *Genesis*, 189); cf. בת, "daughter" (34:1, 3, 5, 7, 8, 17, 19); בנות, "daughters" (34:1, 9 [×2], 16 [×2], 21 [×2]); בן, "son" (34:2, 8, 18, 20, 24, 26); בנים, "sons" (34:5, 7, 13, 25, 27); אב, "father" (34:4, 6, 11, 13, 19); אחים, "brothers" (34:7, 11, 25); אחות, "sister" (34:13, 14, 27, 31); אשה, "wife" (34:4, 8, 12); נשים, "wives" (34:21, 29).

16. For explicit locations, cf. הארץ, "the land" (34:1, 2, 10, 21 [×2], 30); שדה, "field" (34:5, 7, 28); שער, "gate" (34:20, 24 [×2]); עיר, "city" (34:20 [×2], 24 [×2], 25, 27, 28); בית, "house" (34:19, 26, 29, 30). בוא, "arrive" (34:5, 7, 20, 25, 27), and יצא, "depart" (34:1, 6, 24 [×2], 26), suggest the crossing of physical and social boundaries.

17. General systems theory is used as a canopy term for approaches "explicating the person-in-environment perspective"; cf. M. E. Kondrat, "Actor-Centered Social Work: Re-visioning 'Person-in-Environment' Through a Critical Theory Lens," *Social Work* 47 (2002): 435–48 (435). System theory emphasizes the tendency of living systems to form multileveled structures of systems within systems. Each system is distinct and is part of a more complex system distinct in its own right; cf. K. Koslowska and L. Hanney, "The Network Perspective: An Integration of Attachment and Family Systems Theories," *Family Process* 41 (2002): 285–312.

18. Robbins et al., *Human Behavior Theory*, 25.

19. According to Robbins et al., ibid., 35, systems are interdependent. People and their environments change constantly, shaping one another in the process.

20. Ibid., 25.

21. Ibid., 35.

structure and composition.[22] Analysis of the family structure may reflect a family's response to the context of culture, community, and society.[23]

To elucidate the spatial perspective, we depart from the notion that all aspects of space are "human constructions that are socially contested."[24] Our reading of Gen 34 is predominantly a *Thirdspatial* reading, utilizing Henri Lefebvre's notion of a spatial trialectics with special focus upon lived space as space experienced through images and symbols, the real life experience of an individual and his/her attempts to make sense of, change and appropriate his/her spatial experience.[25] Edward Soja uses the term Thirdspace when he defines lived space as "the terrain for the generation of "counterspaces," spaces of resistance to the dominant systems arising from their subordinate, peripheral or marginalized positioning."[26] Especially Soja's notion of "Thirding-as-Othering"[27] will be used to interpret actions of characters in Gen 34 as a constant process of creating and transcending boundaries in the movement from being "off-center" to "at-center."[28]

In the last phase, we briefly contextualize the narrative in its remote literary context. This reading is related to our systems theory reading. We indicate that the narrative itself functions in a constant, dynamic set of relationships with its remote context. By engaging in an inter-connected reading, a discerning reader will be sensitive to the subtle nuances displayed in the narrative and their subsequent influence on the perspectives of the final redactors of Genesis–2 Kings.

3. Genesis 34: A Brief Intratextual Reading

Six acts are demarcated, each situated at a specific location. Act 1 (34:1–4) sets the scene for the developing plot: an atrocity is committed in

22. B. Thomlinson, *Family Assessment Handbook: An Introductory Practice Guide to Family Assessment and Intervention* (Pacific Grove: Brooks/Cole, 2002), 57.

23. J. F. Butler, "The Family Diagram and Genogram: Comparisons and Contrasts," *American Journal of Family Therapy* 36 (2008): 169–80 (173).

24. J. L. Berquist, "Critical Spatiality and the Construction of the Ancient World," in *"Imagining" Biblical Worlds: Studies in Spatial, Social and Historical Constructs in Honor of James W. Flanagan* (ed. D. M. Gunn and P. M. McNutt; JSOTSup, 359; London/New York: Sheffield Academic, 2002), 14–29 (15).

25. H. Lefebvre, *The Production of Space* (trans. D. Nicholson-Smith; Oxford: Blackwell, 1991), 38–39.

26. E. W. Soja, *Thirdspace: Journeys to Los Angeles and Other Real-and-Imagined Places* (Oxford: Blackwell, 1996), 68.

27. Ibid., 60–61.

28. Cf. the essay by Gert T. M. Prinsloo in the present volume.

Shechem.[29] Dinah, "the daughter of Leah that she had born to Jacob,"[30] "went out…to look upon the daughters of the land" (34:1).[31] She leaves the security of her own family and enters the city of Shechem, potentially dangerous territory for an unchaperoned, nubile woman. Disaster strikes immediately. Genesis 34:2 records that Shechem, the "son of Hamor, the Hivite, a ruler of the land,"[32] "saw her,"[33] he "took her,[34] raped her and debased her."[35] The contrast between an unprotected woman from a

---

29.   Shechem is the name of a main protagonist in the narrative (Gen 34:2, 4, 6, 8, 11, 13, 18, 20, 24, 26) and the city where the Jacob-clan was encamped (Gen 33:18–20), indicating that the narrative might be "disguised tribal history"; cf. W. Brueggemann, *Genesis* (IBC; Atlanta: John Knox, 1982), 275.

30.   Leah's name, as the first and less loved wife of Jacob (Gen 29:16–30), calls to mind the strained relations in Jacob's family (Gen 29:31–30:23); cf. Waltke, *Genesis*, 461.

31.   The phrase ותצא…לראות בבנות הארץ does not criticize Dinah overtly for her action, but suggests a cautionary tone, cf. G. J. Gevaryahu, "And Dinah the Daughter of Leah Went Out: The Meaning of *Yatz²anit* in Rashi's Commentary," *JBQ* 37 (2009): 121–23; Frymer-Kensky, *Reading the Women*, 180–81. It is uncommon for a girl of marriageable age to move around unchaperoned in an alien city; cf. N. M. Sarna, *Genesis* (JPS Torah Commentary; New York: Jewish Publication Society, 1989), 233. ראה ב suggests that Dinah wants to get acquainted with the Canaanite girls (Alter, *Genesis*, 189). בנות הארץ has definitive negative connotations (cf. Gen 24:3, 37; 27:46).

32.   חמור החוי נשיא הארץ implies that the people of Shechem are part of the Canaanite population (cf. Gen 10:17; 36:2; Exod 3:8, 17; 13:5; 23:23, 28; 33:2; 34:11; Deut 7:1; 20:17; Josh 3:10; 9:1; 11:3; 12:8; 24:11). Hamor was a local chieftain, "ruler" of the city-state of Shechem. נשיא, "prince," instead of the expected מלך, "king," might be an indication that, according to the narrator, Shechem at that time was not yet a fully enclosed city. הארץ refers to the city and its immediate dependent surroundings, that is, a city-state (Sarna, *Genesis*, 233; Waltke, *Genesis*, 462).

33.   Dinah wants to "look upon" (ראה ב) the local women, but becomes the object of Shechem's lustful intentions when he "saw her" (וירא אתה). As son of the local chieftain, Shechem's "seeing" implies "power and position" (Scholz, "Through Whose Eyes," 165).

34.   The nuances of לקח should be noted. Gen 34:2 implies that Shechem "takes" Dinah with force, as does the brothers' threat to "take" Dinah and depart (34:17). Simeon and Levi each "take" a sword to kill every male in the city (34:25) and they "take" Dinah from the house of Shechem (34:26). The brothers "take" the city's possessions (34:28). Other occurrences of the verb refer to marriage negotiations (34:4, 9, 16, 21).

35.   ויקח אתה וישכב אתה ויענה suggests rapid, violent action (Sarna, *Genesis*, 234). Whether it constitutes rape is controversial; cf. R. Clark, "The Silence in Dinah's Cry," *ResQ* 49 (2007): 143–58. Von Rad, *Genesis*, 331, argues that ענה does not denote rape, but the "moral and social degrading…by which a girl loses the expectancy of a fully valid marriage." (Cf., in this regard, Bechtel, "Dinah," 19–36.)

foreign semi-nomadic group and the elevated social status of Shechem emphasizes Dinah's vulnerability and Shechem's power and dominance. Shechem becomes obsessed with Dinah[36] and urges his father to "take for me this girl as wife" (34:4).[37]

Act 2 (34:5–7) transpires at Jacob's field outside Shechem. The contrast between Jacob's silence (34:5) and his son's outrage (34:7) is significant. Initial contact between the two fathers involved in marriage negotiations (34:6) is ominously framed by the silence of the prospective bride's father and the indignant rage of her brothers. Jacob "heard that Dinah his daughter has been defiled,"[38] but because his sons were with the livestock in the field, he "kept quiet until they returned" (34:5).[39] Meanwhile, Hamor "went out to Jacob to speak to him" (34:6). The sons "heard" about their sister's plight and "returned" from the field

According to Van Wolde, "Does *ʿInnâ* Denote Rape?," 527–44, ענה reflects on the *consequences* of illicit sexual intercourse, "the social debasement of the woman in…a social-juridical context, often in relation to the social debasement of the men related to her, and almost always as something which affects the whole Israelite society" (542). We regard the fact that שכב is followed by the *nota accusativi* in 34:2, 7 as significant. It suggests the brutal taking of a woman (i.e. rape), in contrast to שכב + על (Gen 30:15) or עם (2 Sam 13:11; cf. Alter, *Genesis*, 189). 2 Sam 13:11–14 is instructive in this regard. Amnon pleads with Tamar "come lay *with* me" (בואי שכבי עמי, 13:11). When she refuses (13:12–13) "he debased her and laid *her*" (ויענה וישכב אתה, 13:14), that is, he raped her (Waltke, *Genesis*, 462).

36. Three actions denoting lust (34:2) are followed by three positive actions in 34:3 (ותדבק נפשו בדינה...ויאהב את־הנערה וידבר על־לב הנערה). Opinions differ as to whether these verbs indicate genuine love (Bechtel, "Dinah," 27–31) or unhealthy obsession (Scholz, "Through Whose Eyes," 168–71; Blyth, "Redeemed by His Love?," 5–13).

37. Dinah is referred to as הילדה, "the girl." This might imply that "Shechem's desire to marry is also about control" (Clark, "Silence," 149). The use of הילדה is rare. It occurs elsewhere only in late texts (cf. Joel 4:3; Zech 8:5). Shechem is more polite when he addresses the brothers (ותנו־לי את־הנערה לאשה, 34:12; Jeansonne, *Women*, 92).

38. טמא, "defile, desecrate" (piel), is used three times *by the narrator* with reference to Dinah (34:5, 13, 27). In the priestly tradition the term refers to ritual impurity (Lev 5:2; 11:25, 28; 12:2, 5; 15:18; 22:8; cf. Alter, *Genesis*, 275). Dinah is violated as a person and also rendered "ritually unacceptable" (ibid., 276). By extension, her clan has been violated and desecrated. This explains her brothers' outrage (34:7).

39. החרש here points to lack of action rather than silence (cf. Exod 14:14; 2 Sam 13:20). G. J. Wenham, *Genesis 16–50* (WBC 2; Dallas: Word, 1994), 308, points to the stark contrast between this inaction and Jacob's "passionate attachment to Joseph and Benjamin…displayed in the Joseph story."

"outraged" and "exceedingly furious" (34:7)[40] because, according to the narrator, "a sacrilege was done in Israel…and such a thing ought not to be done!"[41]

Act 3 (34:8–17) also transpires at Jacob's field. Hamor and Shechem negotiate with Jacob's sons to establish terms for a marriage between Shechem and Dinah. Jacob plays no active role in the negotiations. Hamor initiates negotiations (34:8–10). He confirms Shechem's attachment to Dinah and pleads "please give her to him as wife" (34:8). He offers a twofold incentive—intermarriage (34:9)[42] and land (34:10).[43] Shechem then respectfully addresses the brothers[44] and adds a third incentive—economic compensation (34:11–12).[45] In the brothers' reply (34:13–17)[46] the narrator adds the ominous note that their reply was "in deceit"[47] because Shechem "defiled Dinah their sister" (34:13). They set

40. ויתיצבו and ויחר indicate strong emotions (cf. Jeansonne, *Women*, 93). יצב is used of God's grief over wickedness (Gen 6:6), יחר of God's anger with various atrocities (Exod 22:23; 32:10; Num 22:22; 25:2).

41. בישראל, "in Israel," is anachronistic. Israel at this stage "existed" only as an alternative name for Jacob (cf. Gen 32:28; 35:10) and by extension could refer to his clan (Alter, *Genesis*, 190; Waltke, *Genesis*, 464). נבלה denotes "folly, stupidity" (1 Sam 25:25); "insult, transgression" (Josh 7:15; Isa 9:17; 32:6; Job 42:8), and often the transgression of sexual taboos (Deut 22:21; Judg 19:23–24; 20:6; 2 Sam 13:12; Jer 29:23). It suggests "the horror of a sacrilege which incriminated the whole cultic community before God" (von Rad, *Genesis*, 332).

42. Such alliances are prohibited in Deut 7:1–6. Gen 34:9 (והתחתנו אתנו בנתיכם ותתנו־לנו ואת־בנתינו תקחו לכם) suggests the exact opposite of Deut 7:3 (ולא תתחתן בם בתך לא־תתן לבנו ובתו לא־תקח לבנך). The intertextual link suggests that Hamor's proposal is a recipe for disaster (Alter, *Genesis*, 191).

43. Both would have been enticing. Intermarriage would broaden the pool of prospective wives for Jacob's sons. The landless, marginalized group would also gain equal access to resources (von Rad, *Genesis*, 332).

44. The phrases אמצא־חן בעיניכם (34:11) and ותנו־לי את־הנערה לאשה (34:12) have a conciliatory, even apologetic tone; cf. H. Bräumer, *Das erste Buch Mose. 2. Teil. Kapitel 12 bis 26* (3d ed.; Wuppertaler Studienbibel; Wuppertal: Brockhaus, 1995), 370. It stands in contrast to Shechem's curt command to his father in 34:4.

45. The מהר is the dowry given by the prospective bridegroom to the father of the bride (Exod 22:16; 1 Sam 18:25). מתן refers to gifts presented by the bridegroom to the bride and her family; cf. R. de Vaux, *Ancient Israel: Its Life and Institutions* (trans. J. McHugh; London: Darton, Longman & Todd, 1976), 26–29.

46. ויענו is a wordplay on ויענה, "and he debased her" (34:2). The ultimate goal of the answer is to reverse the social disadvantage of Jacob's clan. The answer, spoken "in deceit," in effect shames the Canaanites.

47. The noun מרמה describes Jacob's actions in Gen 27:35 and the related verb רמה Laban's actions in Gen 29:25. The sons are like their father and grandfather (Waltke, *Genesis*, 465).

circumcision as a prerequisite for them to consider a marriage proposal because a man with a foreskin is "a disgrace" to them (34:14–15).[48] To the proposal of intermarriage (cf. 34:9) they add the possibility of becoming "one people" (34:16). The scene ends with an ominous remark: "if you do not listen to us…we will take our daughter and depart" (34:17). The reader suspects for the first time that Dinah has never returned to her father's encampment.

In Act 4 (34:18–24) Hamor and Shechem return to the gate of their city to negotiate with their own people. The terms set by the brothers were acceptable to Hamor and Shechem (34:18) and Shechem "did not tarry" to comply with the prerequisite. His position as the "most honored of the whole house of his father" (34:19) ensures successful negotiations in the city gate. Hamor and Shechem put their case before "the men of their city" (34:20). They commence negotiations with the remark that the semi-nomads "have peaceful intentions towards us."[49] Hamor and Shechem entice their subjects by almost, but not quite, repeating the invitation directed to Dinah's brothers (34:21; cf. 34:10).[50] They reiterate the phrase about the taking and giving of daughters as wives (34:21; cf. 34:9), but significantly omit the invitation to "intermarry" (34:9) and "take possession" (34:10) of the land. They repeat the brothers' enticing invitation to become "one people" (34:22, cf. 34:16), but add an incentive not mentioned before, namely, their own economic benefit (34:23).[51] The men of the city accept the precondition (34:24). It is emphasized twice that "all who went from the gates of the city" were circumcised, implying that every able-bodied, battle-ready male was incapacitated.[52]

---

48. Circumcision, in Gen 17 (cf. also Exod 12:43–49) a sign of the special covenantal relationship between YHWH and Abraham's descendants, here is a sign of group identity and solidarity (Waltke, *Genesis*, 465–66). Jacob's sons expect pain to be inflicted upon the offending part of Shechem's body and on those of all the male inhabitants of the city (Waltke, *Genesis*, 466). The offense against a single female relegated the entire clan to a state of being "defiled," therefore retribution will be extracted from all male members of the offending party. To the brothers, in contrast to his social standing with his own people, Shechem is חרפה, "a disgrace" (34:19; cf. 2 Sam 13:13).

49. שלמים picks up the theme of Gen 33:18. By now the reader suspects that these "peaceful intentions" will result in disaster for the inhabitants of Shechem!

50. For a comparative reading of the two conversations, cf. Hamilton, *Genesis*, 366.

51. Von Rad, *Genesis*, 333–34; Waltke, *Genesis*, 466.

52. A. J. Schmutzer, "'All Those Going Out of the Gate of His City': Have the Translations Got It Yet?," *BBR* 17 (2007): 37–52.

Act 5 (34:25–29) transpires in the city. Again (cf. 34:1–4) an atrocity is committed in Shechem, now by Israelites on the inhabitants of the city. Simeon and Levi, "two sons of Jacob" and "the brothers of Dinah," "entered the city undisturbed"[53] on "the third day" after the circumcision, while the male inhabitants "were in pain." They "killed every male" including Hamor and Shechem and "took Dinah from the house of Shechem" (34:25). "The sons of Jacob came upon the slain" and "they plundered the city because they had defiled their sister" (34:27). They "seized" the city's wealth—"their flocks, their herds, their donkeys" (34:28), "all their wealth, all their children and their wives they carried off and plundered" (34:29).

Act 6 (34:30–31) moves to Jacob's field and describes Jacob's outrage at his sons' violence. Jacob specifically singles out Simeon and Levi as the main instigators of the violent attack and accuses them: "You brought ruin upon me by bringing me into disrepute with the inhabitants of the land." Jacob reminds them that the family is "small in number" and that "I and my house will be destroyed" (34:30). The sons, however, remain impenitent and remark: "Should he like a whore have treated our sister?" (34:31).[54]

4. Genesis 34: General Systems Theory Perspectives

> Genesis 34 dramatically illustrates the relationship between "domestic affairs," control over household members, and "external affairs," boundary definition and the relationship with other groups. It involves the intricate connection between the relationship of a girl to her birth family and the relationship of that family to the outside, and between the relationships of individual families to each other and the destiny of the nation as a whole.[55]

Genesis 34 can be read from a family-oriented perspective, with Dinah's experience of *family* as her lived space. In Figure 1 a genogram of Jacob's family is given, based upon information in Gen 29:31–30:24 and 35:16–20.[56]

---

53. On the ambiguity of בטח, cf. von Rad, *Genesis*, 334.

54. It is an "odd and unexpected ending to the narrative" (Waltke, *Genesis*, 278). The sons remain fixated upon issues of defilement and honor and blind to the possible dangers they have unleashed (Waltke, *Genesis*, 279).

55. Frymer-Kensky, *Reading the Women*, 179.

56. Cf. Butler, "Family Diagram," 172. Males are placed on the left and females on the right when describing relationships. Children are listed from the left to the right in order of their births and are placed beneath their parents. Squares represent males and circles represent females.

Figure 1. *A Genogram of Jacob's Family*

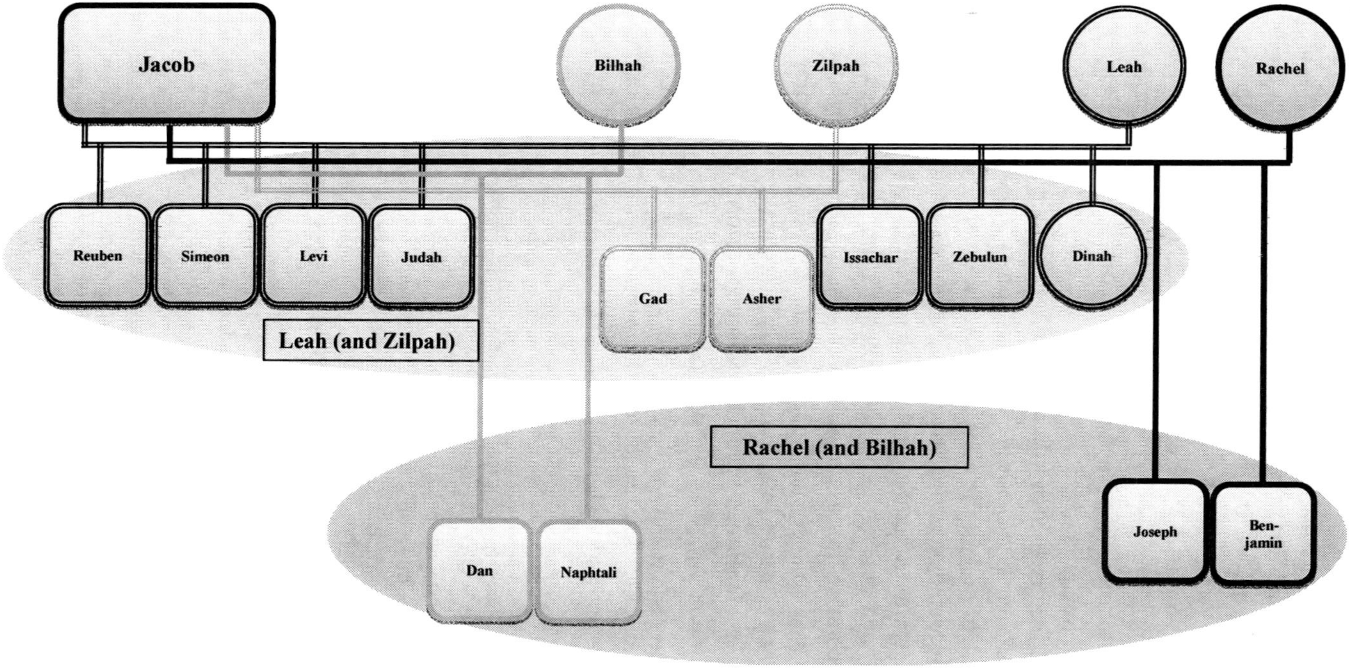

The genogram predicts problems on all levels of family functioning and graphically illustrates Dinah's insignificant position in a male-dominated and internally divided family. Dinah is the only daughter among eleven brothers, the only daughter of Leah, the less favored wife.[57] She is the seventh of Jacob and Leah's biological children, the ninth child in the Leah group, the eleventh in the Leah and Rachel groups. Dinah is the last child before the favorite son, Joseph, is born to the favorite wife, Rachel. The birth of the last son, Benjamin, coincides with Rachel's death.

Dinah is an insignificant member of Jacob's family. In the birth narrative (Gen 29:31–30:24), Dinah is conspicuous for two reasons. First, the birth of nine of the eleven sons is described by the phrase "and she conceived and gave birth to a son."[58] Dinah's birth (30:21), however, comes as an afterthought after the birth of Leah's sixth son (Zebulun; cf. 30:19–20) and before the birth of Rachel's first son (Joseph; cf. 30:22–24).[59] Second, in the case of all eleven sons, Leah or Rachel names the son and gives a folk etymological explanation of the meaning of the name.[60] Dinah is named without any etymological explanation (30:21). Dinah is not mentioned when Jacob's clan returns to Canaan. The text only mentions Jacob's "two wives, his two maids, and his *eleven* children" (32:23).[61] When Esau approaches with an armed force (33:1–2), Jacob divides the children among the women, with the maidservants' children in front, Leah's children next, and Rachel and Joseph at the back.[62] Dinah

---

57. The etymological explanation of the names of the two brothers directly involved in Gen 34 is telling. Simeon receives his name "because I am hated" (Gen 29:33) and Levi because "this time my husband will love me" (Gen 29:34). The animosity in Jacob's household determines relationships within and without the family; cf. M. Reiss, "The Family Relationship of Simeon and Dinah," *JBQ* 34 (2002): 119–21.

58. ותהר...ותלד בן, cf. 29:32, 33, 34, 35; 30:5, 7, 17, 19, 23. In the case of the two sons of Zilpah, Leah's maid, the phrase is reduced to ותלד...בן.

59. The phrase ואחר ילדה בת, "afterwards she gave birth to a daughter," introduced by a temporal adverb, can indeed be construed as an afterthought.

60. Cf. קרא שמו in 29:32, 33, 34, 35; 30:6, 8, 11, 13, 18, 20, 24. The explanation usually precedes the naming (cf. 29:33, 34, 35; 30:6, 8, 11, 13, 18, 20). In the case of the first son (Reuben), it follows upon the naming (29:32), and in the case of the eleventh son (Joseph) an explanation occurs before and after the naming (30:23–24).

61. Gen 32:23 explicitly mentions אחד עשר ילדיו, "his eleven children," not בניו, "his sons."

62. Jeansonne, *Women*, 91, indicates that this action of Jacob influences the reader's response to Gen 34: "The reader is now led to wonder if Jacob will ignore Dinah as he did Leah. Will Dinah live as neglected an existence as did her mother?"

is ignored in the list of Jacob's children in Gen 35:22–26.[63] In the list of the Jacob-clan who went down to Egypt (Gen 46:8–27) "Dinah his daughter" (Gen 46:15) is mentioned for the last time in the Hebrew Bible. Dinah is not conceived, not perceived, and not counted![64]

The six references to Dinah in Gen 34 are therefore conspicuous.[65] Dinah acts only in 34:1 by going out among "the daughters of the land." Throughout the narrative she is defined by her family ties.[66] Only once is her name alone mentioned: "they took Dinah from Shechem's house and left" (34:26). Dinah remains silent, the object of Shechem's obsession (34:3). Her father remains silent when he hears about her ordeal (34:5). She becomes a bargaining chip in negotiations between the Shechemites and Jacob's clan (34:6–17), a catalyst for Simeon and Levi's attack on the incapacitated male inhabitants of Shechem (34:25–26) and for her brothers' raid upon the city (34:27–29). When Jacob belatedly reprimands Simeon and Levi for their violent behavior (34:30), their curt answer (34:31) emphasizes their shame, but does not acknowledge Dinah's pain. What the genogram predicts is confirmed by these intertexts: the lone daughter of the "hated" wife (Gen 29:31, 33) has no voice in her dysfunctional family—not as far as her father is concerned, not as far as her brothers are concerned, and seemingly not as far as the narrator(s) of the patriarchal narratives is (are) concerned.

But appearances can be misleading. A careful reading of the family narrative in the context of Israel's great meta-narrative of its history reveals that the "Dinah Affair" was in actual fact a significant event of major importance. Gerhard von Rad maintains that the single action of this insignificant girl (34:1) "loosened the stone which became a landslide"[67] of reactions affecting not only Dinah as individual, but every system involving her and her family. In the patriarchal family setting, Dinah's "going out" implies the worst nightmare for the male members of her clan. Neither her father nor her brothers are capable of protecting her.[68] Whatever happens to her has serious implications for the whole clan. Her liaison with a Canaanite prince, illicit or legitimate, jeopardizes

63. In this case they are explicitly called בני יעקב, "the sons of Jacob."

64. Hamilton, *Genesis*, 353.

65. Cf. 34:1, 3, 5, 13, 25, 26.

66. Cf. דינה אחותם (34:5), דינה בתו (34:3); דינה בת־יעקב (34:1); דינה בת־לאה (34:13), אחי דינה (34:25).

67. Von Rad, *Genesis*, 331.

68. Frymer-Kensky, *Reading the Women*, 180, remarks: "To a patriarch, 'going out' can strike terror. It means leaving the family domain, leaving both the protection and the control of the head of the household."

family structures, family possessions, and meaningful partnerships with other groups, indeed the very existence of Israel.[69] That she is taken by force and kept in the city of the perpetrator only increases the shame of her father and brothers. Significantly, after this event Jacob's influence declines and his sons become the main actors in the development of the patriarchal narrative (cf. Gen 37–48).[70] Jacob only regains his "voice" on his deathbed (49:1–28), and then to curse Dinah's two brothers for their violent actions (49:5–7).

5. *Genesis 34: Spatial Perspectives*

> The human quest for identity, competence, self-direction and self-esteem has an impact on one form of universal spatial behaviour—the search for a community, which is both a social and physical setting.[71]

Genesis 34 can be read from a spatial perspective, with Dinah's family as her *lived space*. Jacob returns to the land promised to Abraham by YHWH, and this poses a theological problem, namely "survival and faithfulness *in the land*"[72] by a marginalised group without any real economic and political power. Three spatial perspectives are important.

First, questions of space, identity and being at-center permeate the patriarchal narratives. In Gen 12:6–9 Abram arrives at Shechem, conspicuously the first named location in the country promised to him and his descendants. YHWH appears to him and reminds him of the divine promise. Abram claims the new territory for his God by erecting an altar (Gen 12:7). Arrival at a new location, theophany, repetition of divine promises and the construction of an altar are crucial elements in the patriarchal narratives.[73] Divine promise and patriarchal reaction imply a process of "othering." The patriarchs are demarcating "our" people, "our" land, and "our" God from the surrounding Canaanite population. It suggests tension between the patriarchal families living on the margins of Canaanite society, yet at the same time striving to be at-center in the divine presence. Each altar becomes an access point between the divine and human spheres in the context of a hostile and foreign environment. The patriarch is at-center when he experiences YHWH's presence

69. Cf. ibid., 189–90.

70. Wenham, *Genesis*, 317.

71. Robbins et al., *Human Behavior Theory*, 36.

72. Brueggemann, *Genesis*, 274 (italics original).

73. For Abraham, cf. Gen 12:7–8; 13:4, 18; 22:9. For Isaac, cf. Gen 26:24–25. For Jacob, cf. Gen 35:1, 3, 7.

and proclaims YHWH as the only God *in* the polytheistic Canaanite environment.[74]

Two deviations from the pattern appear in the Jacob cycle. In Gen 28:10–22 an off-center Jacob is fleeing before his brother, leaving the protective environment of his family and his God (cf. 26:23–25). At Bethel he has an encounter with YHWH (28:13). The promise of land is reiterated (28:13–15) and Jacob proclaims YHWH's presence at the location (28:16–17) by erecting a מצבה (28:18). He promises to return and make the place a בית אלהים, a permanent meeting point with the divine sphere (28:22). However, he does not erect a מזבח. The encounter without an altar symbolizes Jacob's off-center position when he departs from Canaan. In 33:18–20 Jacob has returned to the land promised to him by YHWH. His meeting with Esau (33:1–17) had a positive outcome. However, Jacob does not return to Bethel, as implied in Gen 28:20–22.[75] He remains in Succoth for an unknown period of time (33:17). Then he returns, but locates at Shechem (33:19), conspicuously in the "land of Canaan" (33:18).[76] There he erects an altar and calls it אל אלהי ישראל, "God/El is the God of Israel"[77] (33:20). However, there is no encounter with YHWH. Jacob is concerned with questions of "land" and "God," but on his initiative. The divine voice remains silent while Jacob is living in the margins.[78]

In 35:1–15 Jacob is reprimanded for "enforcing" contact with the divine sphere on his own terms and by his own initiative. God commands Jacob to "go up to Bethel and settle there, and build an altar there to God, who appeared to you when you were fleeing from your brother Esau" (35:1).

---

74. Read against the background of the late post-exilic period "Canaanite" is an anachronism. Geller, "Typology," 5, remarks with reference to Josiah's reforms in 621 B.C.E.: "If 'Canaanites' had an actual, contemporary reference it was not to any foreign group, but to Judean 'Canaanizers,' the heretical priests of the *bamot* and their licentious congregations." By extension, "Canaanite" could refer to everyone "outside" the strict monotheistic developments of the post-exilic period.

75. Cf. Waltke, *Genesis*, 461.

76. Waltke (ibid., 460) regards the specific reference as a reminder "to the wickedness of the area (see Gen 19), foreshadowing the trouble to come."

77. That Jacob equates El, the highest deity of the Canaanite pantheon, with the God of Israel and appropriates the Canaanite deity for his clan (30:18) with their monotheistic religion should be taken seriously; cf. A. van Selms, *Genesis Deel II* (POut; Nijkerk: Callenbach, 1967), 152; C. Westermann, *Genesis 2. Teilband Genesis 12–36* (BKAT I/2; Neukirchen–Vluyn: Neukirchener, 1981), 645.

78. Waltke, *Genesis*, 459, argues that the "omission of God in the rape episode is an intentional gap, not an unintentional blank. Had Jacob pushed on to fulfill his vow at Bethel…this tragedy would not have happened."

Living "at-center" in a hostile environment is possible only when YHWH's promise is the point of departure. Significantly, Jacob commands his clan to "get rid of the foreign gods" and to "purify yourselves and change your clothes" (35:2) before they can depart for Bethel. These are left at Shechem (35:4), a clear indication of a new beginning, reaffirmed by the repetition of the new name Jacob received upon entering the land (35:9–10) and the divine promise of descendants and land (35:11–13). Most significant, however, is the divine presence's shielding of Jacob's clan as they depart from Shechem (35:5), thus nullifying Jacob's fears of reprisal from the Canaanite population for his sons' violence against them (34:30).

Second, Gen 34 has a decidedly spatial character. Jacob's field and the city of Shechem become two focal spaces with יצא, "to depart," and בוא, "to arrive," as key terms describing movement between these spaces. Two fatal movements occur, both indicated by יצא and both suggesting the crossing of real and imagined boundaries. In 34:1 Dinah crosses the real boundary between her clan's encampment and the Canaanite city. At the same time, this is a crossing of imagined boundaries: between the safety of her patriarchal family and the dangers lurking in Canaanite society; between Israel's belief in YHWH and the polytheistic religion of the Canaanites. In 34:26 Simeon and Levi take Dinah from Shechem's house and cross the real boundary between the Canaanite city and Jacob's encampment. This too, however, implies the crossing of an imagined boundary: the ostensibly peaceful relationship between the Canaanites and the patriarchs becomes one fraught with danger.[79] Dinah's crossing causes a permanent rift in social relationships, a process of continuous "othering" and marginalization for both the powerful and the powerless. The stark contrast between the arrival of Jacob's clan in peace at the gates of Shechem (ויבא יעקב שלם, 33:18) and his sons coming upon the slain to plunder (בני יעקב באו על־החללים ויבזו העיר, 34:27) emphasizes the inevitable confrontation and the lasting enmity. In the quest for ארץ, a spiral of "othering" leads to increasing violence, culminating in the final rhetorical question: הכזונה יעשה את־אחותנו (34:31).[80]

79. Sarna, *Genesis*, 406, remarks that the incident stands in contrast with "the generally idyllic biblical picture of peaceful relationships between the patriarchs and the local peoples."

80. Reiss, "Family Relationship," 120, remarks: "They acted to a concept of honor that justified them in taking revenge on the perpetrator and all his tribe."

Third, the narrative transpires at a specific location with important Thirdspatial connotations in the meta-narrative of Israel's history, namely, the city of Shechem.[81] "Real" Shechem[82] was located on a major crossroad in the valley between Mount Ebal and Mount Gerizim in the central hill county of Ephraim, about 67 km north of Jerusalem and 10 km south-east of Samaria. It had been inhabited fairly consistently from Chalcolithic times up to its destruction by John Hyrcanus in 107 B.C.E.[83] "Imagined" Shechem[84] plays a crucial role in Israel's perception of its identity and is especially associated with "northern" tribal heroes like Jacob and Joseph.[85] Apart from being the first Canaanite site mentioned in the patriarchal narratives (Gen 12:6) where YHWH revealed himself as well as the site of Jacob's first encampment upon his return to the land (33:18–34:31), it also plays an important role subsequently. Joseph sought his brothers in the vicinity of Shechem (37:12–15), setting the scene for the Joseph narrative and Israel's sojourn in Egypt. In several Deuteronomic passages Moses instructed the Israelites to participate in a ceremony in the vicinity of Shechem by proclaiming on Mount Gerizim the covenantal blessings and on Mount Ebal the curses (Deut 11:26–32; 27:1–26), an instruction adhered to when they entered the land (Josh 8:30–36). After the Israelite conquest Joshua called for a renewal of the covenant ceremony at Shechem (Josh 24:1–28) and Joseph's bones were buried there (Josh 24:32). It becomes the site of a first failed attempt to set up a kingdom in Israel (Judg 8:28–9:56). After Solomon's death, the people of the north rejected Rehoboam at Shechem and made Jeroboam king (1 Kgs 12:1–19; 2 Chr 10:1–11). Shechem served first as capital of the northern kingdom (1 Kgs 12:25) before Jeroboam relocated his capital to Penuel and established sanctuaries at Bethel and Dan (1 Kgs 12:26–33). From this point onwards these locations in the northern kingdom became places to be avoided and destroyed, as Josiah actually did a

---

81. Sarna, *Genesis*, 404–7. In spite of Shechem's prominent "imagined" role, there is no account in the Hebrew Bible of Israel occupying the city by force (ibid., 406).

82. "Real" refers to a Firstspace (physical) location; cf. E. F. Campbell, "Shechem *Tell Balâtah*," in *The New Encyclopedia of Archaeological Excavations in the Holy Land* (ed. E. Stern; 4 vols.; New York: Simon & Schuster, 1993), 4:1345–54.

83. Cf. W. Harrelson, "Shechem in Extra-Biblical References," *BA* 20 (1957): 2–10; G. E. Wright, "The Archaeology of the City," *BA* 20 (1957): 19–32.

84. "Imagined" refers to a Secondspace (abstract) and/or Thirdspace (lived space) notion of spatiality; cf. J. A. Thompson and J. J. Bimson, "Shechem," in *Illustrated Encyclopedia of Bible Places* (ed. J. J. Bimson; Leicester: Inter-Varsity, 1995), 279–81.

85. B. W. Anderson, "The Place of Shechem in the Bible," *BA* 20 (1957): 10–19.

century later (2 Kgs 23:15–20).[86] In post-exilic times Shechem became an important city of the Samaritans and they erected a temple on Mount Gerizim, probably during the Persian period.[87] Enmity between the Samaritans and the people of Yehud echoes throughout this period and well into the New Testament (John 4:1–42).[88]

6. *But Her Name is Dinah!*

We have already pointed to a conspicuous characteristic of Dinah in the Jacob cycle of narratives. Dinah is the only one of Jacob's children not "conceived" or "perceived" in the birth narrative (Gen 30:18), and not "counted" when the clan re-enters the land promised to Abraham (32:23). But her name is Dinah, and it means "judgment"![89] On a broader intertextual level the "Dinah Affair" reverberates through the history of Israel.[90]

86. For Deuteronomistic views on the sanctuary at Bethel, cf. J. S. Burnett, "'Going Down' to Bethel: Elijah and Elisha in the Theological Geography of the Deuteronomistic History," *JBL* 129 (2010): 281–97.

87. For the history of the Samaritans, cf. R. T. Anderson and T. Giles, *The Keepers: An Introduction to the History and Culture of the Samaritans* (Peabody: Hendrickson, 2002); cf. Kartveit, *Origin*, 1–15, for an overview of the difficulties in reconstructing the history of the Samaritans.

88. From a spatial perspective a reading of Gen 34–35 in the late post-exilic period opens interesting possibilities. As a Firstspace location Bethel then ceased to exist, but two rival Jewish sanctuaries existed at Gerizim and Jerusalem. Gen 34 might have been interpreted at that time as a critique against the perceived syncretism of the Samaritans of Shechem (in ideological [Secondspace!] terms identified as "Canaanites") while true Jews abandon their idols there and depart to בית אל, "the house of God" (i.e. the temple in Jerusalem), to worship there. Y. Amit, *Hidden Polemics in Biblical Narrative* (trans. J. Chipman; BIS 25; Leiden: Brill, 2000), 187–211, argues that the present form of Gen 34 should be attributed to the so-called Holiness School and that it contains overt and hidden polemics against the Samaritans.

89. J. K. Salkin, "Dinah, the Torah's Forgotten Woman," *Judaism* 35 (1986): 284–89. Salkin (p. 284) remarks "that the theme of judgment moves throughout the entire story…and the implications of its re-telling."

90. A detailed discussion of the intertexts mentioned in this section is not possible. Some of the most controversial texts in the Hebrew Bible are involved. Our very cursory references to these intertexts will of necessity be oversimplifications of very complex redaction- and composition-critical issues. Jeansonne (*Women*, 87) remarks with reference to Dinah: "Although her appearance is brief and her characterization elusive, her legacy is significant. This daughter of Israel illustrates the fragile nature of the promise of descendants, and also of the equally important promise of land."

In Gen 49:1–28 Jacob calls together his sons to give to each "the blessing appropriate to him" (49:28).[91] The three oldest are reprimanded: Reuben (49:3–4) for going up "onto your father's bed" and thus defiling it (49:4; cf. 35:22), Simeon and Levi (49:5–7) for their violence.[92] "Their swords are weapons of violence" (49:5), hence Israel should not "enter their council" (49:6). They indeed receive no blessing from their father: "Cursed be their anger, so fierce, and their fury, so cruel! I will scatter them in Jacob and disperse them in Israel." In the end Judah (49:8–12) receives a blessing worthy of the oldest son and Joseph (49:22–27) and Benjamin (49:27) blessings worthy of the sons of the favorite wife.

The tribe of Levi twice plays a crucial role in correcting the wrongs of Israel when the people engage in idol worship and the resulting illicit sexual behavior.[93] In Exod 31:18–32:35 the tribe of Levi is called upon to execute those who worshiped the golden calf (32:27) and this opens the possibility of making atonement for Israel's sin (30:30). In Num 25:1–18 YHWH condemns Israel while they were staying at Shittim for indulging in sexual immorality with Moabite women and worshipping the Baal of Peor. While Moses and the leaders were weeping at the entrance of the Tent of Assembly (25:5) a leader of a Simeonite family brought a Midianite princess (25:14–15) to his family. Phinehas, a Levitical priest and grandson of Aaron killed both of them with a spear (25:7–9) and is commended by YHWH for his zeal for YHWH's honor (25:10–11) which made atonement for the Israelites (25:13). In Gen 34 Simeon and Levi execute Shechem. In Num 25 "the sibling partnership disintegrates over a similar bone of contention."[94] Levi is vindicated, Simeon not.[95]

---

91. Cf. R. de Hoop, *Genesis 49 in Its Literary and Historical Context* (OTS 39; Leiden: Brill, 1999).

92. Reiss, "Family Relationship," 121, speculates that the fact that Joseph chose Simeon as the brother to hold hostage in Egypt (Gen 42:24) might indicate that he played a leading role in the initial assault on Joseph (Gen 37:18–30).

93. Cf. J. Grossmann, "Divine Command and Human Initiative: A Literary View on Numbers 25–31," *BibInt* 15 (2007): 54–79 (58–61), for a comparative reading of Exod 32 and Num 25.

94. H. Z. Sivan, "The Rape of Cozbi (Numbers XXV)," *VT* 51 (2001): 69–80 (74). Sivan concludes her intertextual reading of Gen 34 and Num 25 with the remark: "In hindsight it is best, perhaps, to regard the rapes of Dinah and Cozbi as two bookends, one signalling the demise of the last matriarch, the other effecting the elimination of a potential matriarch" (p. 80).

95. Cf. Reiss, "Family Relationship," 121. In Num 31:9 vengeance is taken upon the Midianites. It is an "almost word-for-word" repetition of Gen 34:29, but in reverse order. The parallels emphasize the ambiguous nature of Gen 34. The 'brothers' action…is not viewed as unequivocally evil" (Wenham, *Genesis*, 316).

When Moses blesses the tribes of Israel before his death (Deut 33), Simeon is not mentioned at all. The tribe of Levi (33:8–11), however, is an honored tribe, keepers of the Thummim and Urim (33:8), watching over YHWH's word, guarding his covenant (33:9), teaching Israel YHWH's precepts and law and offering incense and burnt offerings on YHWH's altar (33:10). Significantly, when the land is divided among the Israelite tribes (Josh 13–19) the Levites receive no land (13:14, 33; 14:4) and the Simeonites a small portion of land actually in the territory of Judah (19:1–9).[96] Simeon is also conspicuously absent in the list of Leah tribes mentioned in Judg 5:1–31.[97]

7. *Conclusion*

Systems theory and critical spatiality complement each other in an interdisciplinary and intertextual reading of the Dinah story. An insignificant girl in a patriarchal family, a victim of her time and space, sets in motion a series of incidents with significant consequences for her family, the Canaanite population, and the people of Israel generally. Read against the background of the post-exilic identity-building project, the "Dinah Affair" holds an important message. Neither Dinah's crossing social borders to the Canaanites, or her brothers' violent defense of these borders, or Jacob's silence, will ensure a life "at-center." Taking YHWH at his word and acknowledging his promises ensures contact with the divine sphere and a sustainable future. Reading Dinah from this perspective allows her silent cry to reverberate throughout Israel's history and beyond. Dinah becomes a "metaphor" for illustrating that living in the margins can be meaningful in contact with the divine sphere. Genesis 34 concluded with an open-ended question. We conclude our study with open-ended questions as well: Could it be that Dinah, whose name means "judgment," is much more significant in the developing plot of Israel's history than it appears at face value? Can we hear the "judgment" of the "Dinah Affair" reverberating throughout biblical history when the boundaries of acceptable behavior are crossed and "a sacrilege is committed in Israel?" (Gen 34:7).

---

96. Salkin, "Dinah," 288, remarks: "the Levites will have no land of their own; they will be dependent on the other tribes for support."

97. For a detailed exegetical study of Deut 33 and Judg 5, cf. H. Pfeiffer, *Jahwes Kommen von Süden: Jdc 5, Hab 3, Dtn 33 und Ps 68 in ihrem literatur- und theologiegeschichtlichen Umfeld* (FRLANT 211; Göttingen: Vandenhoeck & Ruprecht, 2005).

(Re-)Siting Space and Identity of Gibeonites and Japanese Americans

Johnny Miles

In 1993 the Deutsches Historisches Museum featured the *Chapters of Life in Germany, 1900–1993* (*Lebensstationen in Deutschland, 1900–1993*) exhibition as a means of constructing a shared national identity between former East and West Germans after the dismantling of the Berlin Wall. Described as a "family reunion" of sorts, the exhibit's normative representation of the nation excluded some social groups as "typical" Germans. Its narrative created a singular voice to speak for the "imagined community" of Germany where "we" was defined by "exclusive notions of kinship."[1] The exhibit heavily influenced K. Till's observations about museums. She noted that museums are "staged spaces" or "inscapes" where space, place and identity converge and authors transform the fluidity of time into a static representation of history with select stories about the past. "Exhibition authors interpret the past by relating spaces, objects, and written texts." As a complex place, the museum "localizes and spatially communicates narratives of time and identity."[2]

Similarly, the Bible compares to an ancient museum of sorts. It is a staged space where its writers have carefully and selectively displayed a spatial representation as part of its cultural memory based on difference in order to construct a collective identity, or "imagined" community. And we who arrange and display its diverse literary artefacts with our interpretations are no less the curators of its diverse exhibits. This essay fixes its gaze particularly on the biblical exhibit of the Gibeonites (Josh 9) while relying principally on Edward W. Soja's trialectic spatial

---

1. K. Till, "Reimagining National Identity," in *Textures of Place: Exploring Humanist Geographies* (ed. P. Adams, S. Hoelscher, and K. Till; Minneapolis: University of Minnesota Press, 2001), 273–99 (287). See the further discussion of "imagined communities" in B. Anderson, *Imagined Communities* (London: Verso, 1983), 204. Anderson explores dramatic changes in a nation's notion of identity. In the process of this profound change in consciousness where new narratives are forged, aspects of the past (and present) are forgotten in a cultural amnesia.

2. Till, "Reimagining National Identity," 276–77.

theory supplemented by Arjun Appadurai's postcolonial construct and sociological insights about identity construction in order to explore the interstices of space, place and identity vis-à-vis the social space of Gibeonites and Japanese Americans.

1. *A Space Construct(ion)*

Much has been written concerning Soja's spatial construct in prior *Constructions of Space* volumes. I therefore feel no compunction to traverse familiar ground by explicating principal tenets in his model. Admittedly, Soja constructs his model following Henri Lefebvre's spatial theory. Like so many of my colleagues applying Soja's construct to biblical studies, I find myself with more numerous questions than answers. There are, however, several facets to Soja's spatial theory that I feel need emphasizing within the larger discussion: (1) his theory intends simply to be a heuristic device for understanding different types of spaces, their relation to one another and to a trialectics of ontology; (2) his concept of Thirdspace receives the focus it does because of reality's myopic view of space as merely physical; and (3) social space in praxis comprises all three spaces and is ultimately the *telos* of his theoretical construct. In other words, Soja's construct foregrounds space in all its permutations to conjoin theory with praxis, an objective that any biblical interpretation true to Soja's spatial trialectic would do well to achieve.

That Soja privileges Thirdspace and his concept of "Thirding-as-Othering" naturally lends itself to criticism. After all, do not those in power experience Thirdspace, too?[3] Granted, but Thirdspace as the space of representation, or the dominated or subjected space as Soja describes it, is an inescapable web of power relations duly noted by critics. Yet, no dominated or subjected space can exist without the power necessary to participate in the construction of said space. Soja's theoretical construct acknowledges this reality but highlights Thirdspace as it does because that facet of lived space often gets overlooked.[4] Integrating postcolonial

---

3. C. V. Camp, "Storied Space, or, Ben Sira 'Tells' a Temple," in *"Imagining" Biblical Worlds: Studies in Spatial, Social and Historical Constructs in Honor of James W. Flanagan* (ed. D. M. Gunn and P. M. McNutt; JSOTSup 359; London/ New York: Sheffield Academic, 2002), 64–80 (68).

4. Though no one particular form of space and, by extension, spatial knowledge possesses ontological privilege or is inherently privileged *a priori*, the longstanding tendency in reality confines spatial knowledge to Firstspace and Secondspace epistemologies while ignoring the lived spaces of representation. See E. W. Soja,

insights into the discussion moves beyond this critique because focus on the colonized and the cultural politics of difference and identity considers the colonizer as part of the process. Thus Thirdspace for the oppressed is not isolated from that of the oppressors though the experience of that space will be perceived differently. Appadurai notes: "One man's imagined community is another man's political prison."[5]

Appadurai's postcolonial construct isolates five dimensions, or *scapes* (comparable to Soja's Thirdspace and Gloria Anzaldúa's *borderlands*). These *scapes* form the building blocks of *imagined worlds* where people may contest, even subvert, the imagined worlds of the official mind that surround them. They are the space of marginality that can ultimately transcend a modernist cultural politics of difference by eschewing essentialist notions of identity like "otherness," which is based on the center–margin binarism. Two of Appadurai's *scapes*, ethnoscape and ideoscape, are germane for this essay's postcolonial spatial perspective in that they (1) provide a rich array of detail-specific features in breadth commensurate with social praxis and (2) concretize Soja's overtly theoretical and nebulous constructs of Firstspace, Secondspace and Thirdspace. By ethnoscape, Appadurai refers to the landscape of persons who constitute the shifting world in which we live. It is the warp of stability (indigeneity) shot through with the woof of human movement (migrations). By ideoscape is meant the "concatenations of images" that are "often directly political and frequently have to do with the ideologies of states and the counter-ideologies of movements explicitly oriented to capturing state power or a piece of it"[6] (e.g. numerous ideas of the Enlightenment master-narrative dominant throughout England, France and the US in the eighteenth and nineteenth centuries).

Soja notes how the utilization of his spatial triad demands the necessity to negotiate a fine balance between the double illusions of objectivism (realistic illusion), a Firstspace concern, and subjectivism (transcendental illusion or illusion of transparency), a Secondspace focus.[7] With biblical

---

Thirdspace: Journeys to Los Angeles and Other Real-and-Imagined Places (Malden, Mass.: Blackwell, 1996), 64, 74.

5. A. Appadurai, "Disjuncture and Difference in the Global Cultural Economy," *Public Culture* 2 (1990): 1–24 (6).

6. Ibid., 7–10.

7. "Realistic illusion" is the illusion of "opacity" where only objective things have more reality than "thoughts." The material world and natural objects are what constitute reality. By contrast, the transcendental illusion, or illusion of transparency, assumes reality to be confined to "thought things" comprehended through its representations. See Soja, *Thirdspace*, 63–64.

studies in particular, social space easily becomes an encrypted reality where the illusive presumptions in the text of what are re-presented as real become just that…real. Imagined geography, for instance, becomes "real" geography, the re-presentation (Secondspace) defining and ordering physical reality (Firstspace). And this leads me to several nagging questions of utilizing a spatial trialectics in biblical studies analysis. How can an interpreter accurately speak of First- and Thirdspace elements when the text itself is a Secondspace filter? Can Second- and Thirdspace be so easily disentangled when exploring identity? And to what extent can we speak of space vis-à-vis the biblical text as anything beyond "imagined" such that biblical spatial analysis has contemporary relevance? In terms of theory Soja's construct makes sense, though "real life" rarely presents itself so neatly in such easily distinguishable categories. In fact, "real life" gets messy as these identifiable spaces easily blend one into the other. Soja recognized this reality since Thirdspace for him encompasses the other two spaces while itself being distinct.[8] While the present essay identifies various spatial elements in its analyses, it does so relating each space to the other through concrete details as a part of social space.

A postcolonial perspective proves beneficial at this point because drawing on the lived experience of a dominated group attends to "real life" while helping to fill in Thirdspace blanks by demonstrating the interrelatedness of these spaces, especially when interpreting the Secondspace phenomena of biblical texts. In this essay, the lived, and voiced, experience of Japanese Americans helps to elucidate the voiceless, yet lived, experience of the Gibeonites. The varied nuances of postcolonial critique, according to Soja a form of Thirdspace, focus on the cultural politics of difference and identity, thus addressing colonizer and colonized alike. However, the social space of marginality also becomes a Thirdspace site of resistance, whereby to establish an identity undefined by "otherness" established by an essentialist politics.

The essentialist perspective of fixing identity drives the process of identifying and naming peoples and their spaces. David Chidester noted from his observations of South Africans and their European colonizers that the fixed, ethnographic knowledge of the indigenous was necessary to sustain the colonizer and enable them to configure local control.[9]

---

8. Ibid., 67–69.

9. This ethnographic knowledge extended to religion as well and was, most importantly, constructed knowledge. Before coming under subjugation, Africans were regarded as having had no religion. Those who lacked religion lacked any recognizable human right or entitlement to the land on which they lived. Only after

"Spatiality and people are organically linked." claimed James W. Flanagan.[10] In segmentary societies like that of ancient Israel identity and space become inextricably linked where identity and space derive from membership in a particular group rather than simply from territoriality.[11] Space as experienced affects the way it is perceived, and vice versa. In addition, spaces, and identity, become nodal points socially constructed in a complex system of power relations. Paula M. McNutt's study of artisan groups in traditional African societies for understanding similar groups in Middle Eastern societies concluded that those groups with power used it to construct difference in terms of identity via strategies of social and spatial divisions.[12] A non-essentialist perspective, however, recognizes identity and, by extension, spaces as socially constructed and, thus, open for renegotiation.[13] Homi Bhabha's concept of hybridity assumes this non-essentialist stance toward identity/space by opening up sites or spaces where identity can be renegotiated even if in terms of resistance. "All forms of culture are continually in a process of hybridity." Thus, Thirdspace is this site; "hybridity is...the 'third space'."[14] This essay's postcolonial spatial analysis of both Gibeonite and Japanese American narratives will reveal them to accomplish the same, that is essentializing identity at Secondspace and thereby denying them land

local control of the indigenes was established were they found to have had a religious system after all. See D. Chidester, *Savage Systems: Colonialism and Comparative Religion in Southern Africa* (Charlottesville, Va.: University Press of Virginia, 1996), 14, 20.

10. J. W. Flanagan, "Mapping the Biblical World: Perceptions of Space in Ancient Southwestern Asia," in *Mappa Mundi: Mapping Culture, Mapping the World* (ed. J. Murray; Windsor, Ont.: Humanities Research Group, University of Windsor, 2001), 1–18 (13).

11. J. W. Flanagan, "Ancient Perceptions of Space/Perceptions of Ancient Space," *Semeia* 87 (1999): 15–43 (35–36).

12. P. M. McNutt, "'Fathers of the Empty Spaces' and 'Strangers Forever': Social Marginality and the Construction of Space," in Gunn and McNutt, eds., *"Imagining" Biblical Worlds*, 30–50 (38–41).

13. This relational process immediately elicits questions of hegemony—for example, who has the power to construct the "other"; and how this power fixes identifications around "nodal" points for constructing "identity." Non-essentialist identity politics recognizes no identity/space to be so colonized to disallow the reconfiguration of these nodal points of both identity and space. See W. Natter and J. P. Jones III, "Identity, Space, and Other Uncertainties," in *Space and Social Theory: Interpreting Modernity and Postmodernity* (ed. G. Benko and U. Strohmayer; Oxford: Blackwell, 1997), 141–61 (146, 148, 155).

14. H. Bhabha, "The Third Space," in *Identity: Community, Culture, Difference* (ed. J. Rutherford; London: Lawrence & Wishart, 1990), 207–21 (211).

(Canaan for one; US for the other) as their lived space at Thirdspace while simultaneously re-siting both space and identity.

2. *Ethnoscape: Space and Identity*

The Josh 9 exhibit on the Gibeonites foregrounds matters of space and identity with the presence of diverse ethnic groups prepared for conflict. And what is at stake? Well, space and…identity, since the two are linked together in segmentary societies. Immediately, the issues of indigeneity, real (Gibeonites) and imagined (Israelites), and immigration, real (Israelites) and imagined (Gibeonites), run headlong into each other in this ethnoscape contention not too dissimilar to that of the American ethnoscape. From 1891–1900 Japanese immigration increased in the US to 24,326, with a population reaching 72,157 by 1910. By 1924, 200,000 Japanese had arrived in Hawaii and 180,000 to the mainland.[15] Control over the one meant control over the other. Certainly identity within the Canaanite ethnoscape mattered such that the narrator makes the ethnic identity of Gibeonites as Hivites a point,[16] not once but twice (vv. 1, 7). This twice-repeated identification of Gibeonites as Hivites may have several purposes: (1) to distance Israel from Hivites and other Canaanite groups in terms of character since the Hivites and other Canaanite groups clearly have violence in mind by preparing for armed conflict against Israel; and (2) to reinforce ethnic boundaries by demarcating Gibeon as "other." The Gibeonites knew that their only fate based on Israel's ethnic

---

15. Reasons sparking this immigration explosion vary, but two are prominent. First, farmers all over Japan encountered economic hardships. Second, the contract-labor period (1885–1894) especially targeted Japanese farmers in the southwestern prefectures with opportunities for success. Third, the higher wage advantage with a favorable dollar–yen exchange appealed to many Japanese. See R. Daniels, *Concentration Camps: North America: Japanese in the United States and Canada During World War II* (repr.; Malabar, Fla.: Robert E. Krieger, 1989), 6.

16. The biblical text associates the Gibeonites with both Hivites (Josh 9:7; 11:19) and Amorites (Josh 10:5), both groups doomed to extinction. Ascertaining the ethnic origins of the Gibeonites remains a speculative matter with no definitive conclusion in sight, but see the monograph of J. Blenkinsopp, *Gibeon and Israel: The Role of Gibeon and the Gibeonites in the Political and Religious History of Early Israel* (SOTSMS 2; Cambridge: Cambridge University Press, 1972); the essay by J. Day, "Gibeon and the Gibeonites in the Old Testament," in *Reflection and Refraction: Studies in Biblical Historiography in Honour of A. Graeme Auld* (ed. R. Rezetko, T. Lim, and W. B. Aucker; VTSup 113; Leiden: Brill, 2007), 113–37; and the discussion in G. Mitchell, *Together in the Land: A Reading of the Book of Joshua* (JSOTSup 134; Sheffield: Sheffield Academic, 1993), 175–76.

prejudicial terms was death. And their only fault?—being the wrong ethnicity in the right place. "They," who are clearly not "us," are "other," and the standard punishment for Otherness was death.[17]

Reinforcing Gibeonites as "other" is their re-presentation as deceitful, with their worn-out clothing, patched sandals, stale bread, old wineskins, and story of a long journey. The motif of Gibeonite deception marks Gibeonite social space as Israelite, though *not quite* Israelite. The Gibeonites threaten Israel, not by their stature or might, but by their *difference*. Despite their *difference*, Gibeonite assimilation within Israel marks a significant ethnic boundary crossing by blurring the lines of demarcation.[18] Despite exclusivist boundaries established in Deuteronomy, this particular story (and that of Rahab) where Canaanites as "other" who transform into marginal Israelites, outsiders becoming insiders, may "argue for flexibility in the determination of Israel's boundaries" though the boundaries "must nevertheless be preserved."[19] Yet how does the inclusion of Canaanites as part of the spoil along with goods devoted to the *ban* preserve boundaries? Gibeonite assimilation into Israelite culture would have resulted in a shared social space working and living among Israelites. Their physical presence within the symbolic center of Israelite identity, the Temple complex, best emblematizes this paradoxical presence of "other" within Israel. The enemy is no longer simply "out there," but is now within (Israel). This Secondspace re-presentation of Gibeonites as deceitful and "other," albeit *imagined*, essentializes or fixes their identity and furthermore marks their social space as Israelite, though *not quite* Israelite, while siting potential Thirdspace resistance (discussed below), thus maintaining (social) boundaries.

---

17. L. Rowlett perceives the function for the book of Joshua's rhetoric of violence as "to make examples of Others while controlling the lines of authority within the community." The rhetoric becomes a means of self-reconstitution where outsiders can become insiders, and insiders can become outsiders just as easily simply by failing to submit to the rules and norms of the king (identified as Josiah). See L. Rowlett, "Inclusion, Exclusion and Marginality in the Book of Joshua," *JSOT* 55 (1992): 15–23 (17).

18. The connotation of ethnic boundary-crossing semantically links with the geographic boundary-crossing earlier in the book, where the phrase ויהי מקצה שלשת ימים, introducing the Jordan crossing (3:1), reiterates that and is emphasized by thrice-repeated references to Gibeonites living "in the midst of" Israel (vv. 7, 16, 22). See L. D. Hawk, *Joshua* (Berit Olam; Collegeville, Minn.: The Liturgical Press, 2000), 144.

19. L. D. Hawk, "The Problem with Pagans," in *Reading Bibles, Writing Bodies: Identity and the Book* (ed. T. Beal and D. M. Gunn; New York: Routledge, 1997), 153–63 (154, 162).

The same concerns of a fixed identity dogged Japanese Americans who found their early twentieth century lived experience as American, though *not quite* American. The racial prejudice of the Occident would never let them forget that they would always remain Japanese.[20] Nonetheless, Japanese immigrants were a welcome sight for the railroad and agricultural industries of the US mainland and the Hawaiian plantations if only for the labor their bodies would provide. After having left the railroads and mines, the Japanese increasingly entered the agricultural sector as farm laborers only to experience segregation within the labor market. Japanese efforts to climb the ladder of success met with racial discrimination as the swirling politics of prejudice fomented "yellow peril" fears.

"Yellow peril" fears were widespread among the American public by 1905 to indicate an imminent invasion by the Japanese.[21] As example, newspaper publisher William Randolph Hearst launched a 35-year war against Japan in his San Francisco *Examiner* in 1906 with headlines such as "JAPAN SOUNDS OUR COASTS: BROWN MEN HAVE MAPS AND COULD LAND EASILY" and "JAPAN MAY SEIZE THE PACIFIC SLOPE."[22] "Yellow peril" fears led to numerous discriminations of the Japanese in the American ethnoscape. Japanese were segregated in First-space sites like schools and theatres and in isolated ghettoes dubbed "Little Tokyos." Legislative discrimination targeted Japanese as well with the notable Alien Land Law (1913) in California that prohibited "aliens ineligible to citizenship" from owning land. Restrictive land laws hinged on the ineligibility of the Japanese to naturalized citizenship reinforced by the 1922 US Supreme Court *Ozawa* case ruling that Takao Ozawa was ineligible for naturalized citizenship because "he was

20.   Racial slurs such as "Jap Go Home," "Goddamn Jap," "Yellow Jap," "Dirty Jap," "Japs Go Away," "Yellow Bastards," "Yellow Monkeys," "Japs We Do Not Want You," "No More Japs Wanted Here," and "Keep California White" and other ugly graffiti spewing anti-Japanese sentiments plastered storefront windows and signs, sidewalks, railroad stations, and public restrooms and contributed to the racially charged American ethnoscape.

21.   Originally associated with the Chinese, the "yellow peril" stereotype gravitated toward the Japanese when the 1882 Exclusion Act put to rest the Chinese question of immigration, at least legally. Exclusionary tactics used against the Chinese eventually targeted the Japanese. For thorough treatment of the "yellow peril" stereotype, see G. Y. Okihiro, *Margins and Mainstreams: Asians in American History and Culture* (Seattle, Wash.: University of Washington Press, 1994), 118–47.

22.   R. Daniels, *The Politics of Prejudice: The Anti-Japanese Movement in California and the Struggle for Japanese Exclusion* (2d ed.; Berkeley: University of California Press, 1977), 70–71.

'clearly' 'not Caucasian'." "Yellow peril" fears clearly demarcated the lived space of Japanese in an ethnoscape where their identity was constructed as deceitful and *not quite* American, and their Firstspace work and residences relegated to the agricultural labor sector and segregated businesses within isolated ghettoes. Despite the residential and economic confinement of Japanese social space, prejudice and mis-representations, including "fifth element" claims, continuously targeted Japanese Americans.

When we read closely the Josh 9 narrative at its seams, we find the expressions "on that day" and "to this day" (v. 27), which indicate that this story is not simply about Joshua and the Gibeonites, but is also about the presence of Gibeonites as slaves among a group from a much later time period imagining its shared heritage as that of Joshua.[23] Thus, this story creates a temporal-spatial nexus wherein pre-monarchic concerns over space and identity maintain in a post-exilic ethnoscape of human stability paired with human movement. References to Gibeonites among the temple servants in the post-exilic literature (Neh 7:25; 3:7; cf. 1 Chr 9:2; Ezra 2:43, 58, 70; 7:7, 24; 8:17, 20; Neh 3:26, 31; 7:46, 60, 73; 10:28 [MT 10:29]; 11:3, 21)[24] reveal just how low down the pecking order within the Temple labor sector they were. At this point, two factors—boundedness and exhaustiveness—noted by sociologists are integral in understanding the process of establishing social space and reinforcing identity.[25] Boundedness refers to "the extent to which the

---

23. R. Sutherland's redactional approach to Josh 9 posits three strata on the basis of Israelite principles in the negotiation processes with the Gibeonites: the איש ישראל, Joshua and the נשיאי העדה. Each stratum reveals different leadership processes for a particular era, the most notable difference being between the איש ישראל passages of the pre-monarchic era (vv. 4–6, 7, 11–14, 16), where all adult males took part in the decision to make the treaty, and the נשיאי העדה of the post-exilic era (vv. 15b, 17–21), where an elite leadership cadre makes the decision. See R. Sutherland, "Israelite Political Theories in Joshua 9," *JSOT* 53 (1992): 65–74.

24. Jewish rabbis simply equated the two groups in the Talmud (*b. Yeb.* 71a, 78b–79a). Modern scholars, however, remain divided: Are the Gibeonites and Nethinim one and the same? Or were the Gibeonites one of several foreign ethnic groups absorbed within the Nethinim? Or do the Gibeonites bear no connection whatsoever to the Nethinim, having been absorbed into the "sons of Solomon's servants," often listed immediately after the Nethinim and also comprising a significant foreign element (see Day, "Gibeon and the Gibeonites," 136–37)? The high plausibility of Day's proposal assumes the Gibeonites to belong to various Canaanite groups enslaved by Solomon (1 Kgs 9:20–21), as well as the "sons of Solomon's servants" to be descendants of these Canaanite groups.

25. Factors such as jobs, discrimination, pricing, and personal choice definitely play into residential space and ultimately the construction and reinforcement of

positions in the labor or residential markets available to group members
are available only to them and not to non-members." A high degree of
boundedness means an inordinate concentration of group members to the
practical nonexistence of non-group members, for example, diamond-
selling Jews in New York City. Exhaustiveness refers to "the extent to
which a particular position is the only opportunity available to group
members."[26]

For the Gibeonites, their Thirdspace in Yehud comprised high
boundedness and exhaustiveness factors. When both boundedness and
exhaustiveness factors are high, the residential boundary naturally
coincides to reinforce group boundaries as indicated by Gibeonite
residential confinement to the Firstspace Ophel district in Jerusalem
(Neh 3:26, 31; 11:21). High boundedness and exhaustiveness factors for
Gibeonites within the labor sector (as "wood cutters and water drawers")
additionally fixed both their social space and identity: ethnically as
Gibeonite/Hivite, sociologically as "other." While maintaining boundaries, the Joshua narrative simultaneously accounts for the presence of
the "other" within those boundaries, especially in a post-exilic ethnoscape where a migrant group would particularly be concerned about
establishing an identity. The Golah "imagined" its community as "Israelite" in a way that reinforced social boundaries between an "us" and
"them" in terms of ethnic kinship, never mind their own identity amnesia.
As this group reconstituted its identity, the virulence of difference
precluded a trace of the indigenes in proximity to "Israel" (Josh 7:1–26;
cf. 8:19–20; 12:29–32). Regardless of the presence of outsiders, cement-
ing social relations and forming a state identity necessitated the creation
of "others." Ethnic border crossings and encounters with those of different ethnic backgrounds are experiences central to identity formation.[27]
High boundedness and exhaustiveness factors contributed to the culturally hybrid status of Gibeonites and Japanese alike despite their border
crossings. Thirdspace identity encompasses First- and Secondspace
elements. In terms of Firstspace work and residence: for the Japanese, it
was the agricultural sector, segregated businesses and "Little Tokyos";

ethnic identity. Migrants to a particular place tend to concentrate in one area; for
example, the nineteenth-century Chinese of America resided in ghettoes called
"Chinatowns," generally because of limited opportunities available to them within
the larger society. See S. Spencer, *Race and Ethnicity: Culture, Identity and
Representation* (New York: Routledge, 2006), 176.

26. S. Cornell and D. Hartmann, *Ethnicity and Race: Making Identities in a
Changing World* (2d ed.; Thousand Oaks, Calif.: Pine Forge, 2007), 184–85.

27. See Spencer, *Race and Ethnicity*, 13–21.

for the Gibeonites, it was the Temple sector and the Ophel district of Jerusalem. In terms of Secondspace re-presentation, both are portrayed as sneaky, deceitful, *not quite*, and "other."

While narratives of ethnic identity ascribe a value to their subjects—Japanese and Gibeonites as deceitful—they also indicate something about those constructing the stories. The language that a society uses to describe a group not itself and the action that a society engages in due to that language signal primary clues about that society's self-understanding.[28] For example, the craftiness and savvy of the Gibeonites that should characterize Israel, according to its own story, does not. Gibeonite identity reflects back something of Israelite identity because the image of the "other" always originates within the "self." Thus, Gibeonite identity as migrant and deceitful reflects back that of Israelite identity as migrant and not indigenous in terms of space, hybrid not homogeneous in terms of identity, and colonized. So what if the Gibeonites are *not quite* Israelite. Who *really is* within this "imagined" community? In addition, ethnicity narratives imply "we are the people who...," in contrast to "...and you are not."[29] Thus, the shared story of Israelites–Gibeonites exclaims "we are not a people willing to resort to deception to obtain peace," while alternatively admitting, but "we are a people capable of being deceived to ensure peace." Colonizer narratives may create the enemy without; but it is the enemy without whose presence unveils the true enemy within.

28. The "other" is always created and in a social context of groups too much alike in close proximity to one another, hence the necessity to differentiate. When using a term to describe the "other" and to symbolize difference, a group has to reach deep within itself to find that quality that will induce a response, whether good or bad, admired or hated, to project onto the other. See W. S. Green, "Otherness Within: Toward a Theory of Difference in Rabbinic Judaism," in *"To See Ourselves as Others See Us": Christians, Jews, "Others" in Late Antiquity* (ed. J. Neusner and E. Frerichs; Scholars Press Studies in the Humanities; Chico, Calif.: Scholars Press, 1985), 49–69 (49–50). The act of projection becomes integral to the process of demonization whereby a group transfers some moral weakness to the outside to avoid any culpability. Demonizing the "other" preys on ethnocentrism in order to displace evil beyond group boundaries, an act that also encourages group narcissism and even killing, a far more unsettling enterprise if the "other" is considered human. See H. Befu, "Demonizing the 'Other'," in *Demonizing the Other: Antisemitism, Racism and Xenophobia* (ed. R. Wistrich; repr.; London: Routledge, 1999), 17–30.

29. S. Cornell, "That's the Story of Our Life," in *We Are a People: Narrative and Multiplicity in Constructing Ethnic Identities* (ed. P. Spickard and W. J. Burroughs; Philadelphia: Temple University Press, 2000), 41–53 (50).

3. *Ideoscape: Colonization and Resistance*

How does a politics of prejudice circumscribing space and essentializing identity on the ethnoscape front materialize into a Thirdspace lived experience of colonization? With Japanese American colonization, theories range among historians from military culpability to President Roosevelt to public pressure.[30] Morton Grodzins' *Americans Betrayed: Politics and the Japanese Evacuation* (1949) first advanced the theory of public pressure as decades of anti-Asian sentiment had shifted to open animus against the Japanese.[31] Anti-Japanese feelings ran deep despite improved relations from 1924–1941 as certain agricultural and business groups (e.g. Western Growers Protective Association, Grower-Shipper Vegetable Association) seized upon the attack on Pearl Harbor to expel Japanese from the agricultural sector. Other pressure groups (e.g. American Legion, Native Sons of the Golden West, the Pacific League, and labor unions) also remained unapologetic about the economic benefits gained by Japanese removal as they unabashedly publicized their positions.

But could such acrimony at ground level actually affect federal government policy? The strongest critiques against Grodzins' theory are twofold: (1) the theory of regional pressure assumes public policy to emanate from the ground up, and (2) that the military shared the same racial attitudes as the public does not *de facto* suggest that their decisions were motivated by public attitude. Granting the theoretical value of both critiques, their contextualization does not render them ironclad. In the first place, public policy develops from a rather complex process of interaction between politicians and their constituents; somewhere along this spectrum of the top down and the ground up policies emerge. Secondly, evidence of numerous letters to federal officials by regional pressure groups demanding Japanese removal bear out public influence on federal policy. It is completely inconceivable that Lieutenant General John De Witt, commander of the Western Defense Command headquartered in San Francisco, the "man on the ground" with his own racist prejudices against the Japanese, had no knowledge of public animus or

---

30. See the detailed discussion of divergent theories in G. Y. Okihiro, *The Columbia Guide to Asian American History* (New York: Columbia University Press, 2001), 100–127.

31. M. Grodzins, *Americans Betrayed: Politics and the Japanese Evacuation* (Chicago: University of Chicago Press, 1949).

remained uninfluenced by a growing movement calling for Japanese removal as he shaped what would become public domestic policy.[32]

Joshua and the Israelite political echelon were likewise not that far removed from public opinion suspicious of the "other" within. Having been sought out by the shrewd Gibeonite ambassadors, Joshua and the leaders conducted their own summit talks. They accepted the gifts of their newfound political friends (vv. 9–10), and established terms of peace and a covenant (vv. 6–7, 14–15).[33] The Gibeonites acknowledged YHWH and YHWH's deeds whereas Israel seems to have forgotten YHWH. Nonetheless, the public intuits something askew with their initial query, "perhaps you live among us…"? (v. 7). When the public does find out the "immigrant" status of the Gibeonites, a social outcry permeates the community exacerbated only by a pre-existing foreign policy allowing their immigration in the first place. Swayed by public opinion the Israelite leaders cannot simply revoke their treaty. Instead, they engage in damage control, spinning the situation as a boon to the community who will reap the economic benefits from Gibeonite labor, that is, internal colonization (vv. 20–21). The leaders' quick response aborts sure social chaos wrought by mob vigilantism (vv. 18, 26). The propensity for wide-scale physical violence by the masses bespeaks an ethos of prejudice requisite for the expression of such violence. The attitudes toward "them" within "us" enable "us," when feeling threatened by the enemy alien, to justify violence against "them." Joshua and the political intelligentsia do just that, as do the Golah leaders of Yehud to justify the presence and treatment of the Gibeonites, not with the violence of bloodshed but with that of colonization (vv. 22–23). Moreover, the

---

32. On the role of General De Witt in federal public policy and his contributions to President Roosevelt's Executive Order 9066 mandating Japanese removal, see the thorough treatment of Daniels, *Concentration Camps*, 42–73, 81–90.

33. The formal structure of vv. 14–15 with bracketing elements stresses their central emphasis:

> A   the leaders partook of their provisions
> B   *(the leaders) did not ask direction from* YHWH
> A'   Joshua made peace with them

Though the lexemes of A and A' are not identical, they nonetheless intimate the establishment of a covenant treaty since a meal was always a part of the diplomatic proceedings. Hawk (*Joshua*, 144) suggests a vassal treaty on the basis of the language employed and other elements in the encounter; cf. the discussions in J. M. Grintz, "The Treaty of Joshua with the Gibeonites," *JAOS* 86 (1966): 113–26, and F. C. Fensham, "The Treaty Between Israel and the Gibeonites," *BA* 27 (1964): 96–100.

speech of the Israelite leaders regards them as *the* victims. Because the Gibeonites deceived Israel, the leaders' righteous indignation leads them to feel justified in enslaving the Gibeonites (vv. 19–20). Only after the insistent pressure of public animus do the cognoscenti implement the social institution of slavery to circumscribe Gibeonite social space within. Established social space boundaries and an essentialist Gibeonite identity altogether actualize an ideoscape with one group as dominant and with a divine right to land control over that of the "other" unfit to do so.

No iconic symbol best emblematizes the lived social space of Japanese Americans than their internment in concentration camps.[34] The linguistic deception with preferred euphemisms by the federal government enabled it (1) to sidestep legal and/or constitutional challenges since two-thirds of Japanese detainees were American citizens, (2) to co-opt the victims' willing participation, and (3) to ensure a decent public image. Nevertheless, the linguistic deception failed to capture the reality of barbed wire compounds surrounded by guard towers and armed sentries in order to accurately shape that reality in the minds of casual observers.

Some of the concentration camps housing the Japanese[35] were noted for their brutally harsh weather conditions (e.g. winter temperatures as low as minus 30°F at Heart Mountain, Minidoka and Topaz, and summer temperatures easily reaching upwards of 106°F at Topaz); all, however, were noted for being safely distant from strategic installations and were godforsaken, desolate, uninhabitable areas with dust all around that turned to mud after rain, creating an ideal breeding ground for mosquitoes.

34. Official memoranda of the American government preferred language like "evacuation," "relocation," "assembly centers," "transit camps," and "protective custody camps," among others, to that of "concentration camps." Dillon Meyer, the director of the War Relocation Authority (WRA), advised his civilian staff: "The term 'camp' when used to refer to a relocation center is likewise objectionable... The evacuees are not 'internees.' They have not been 'interned'... [E]mployees of the War Relocation Authority should refer to persons who have been evacuated from the West Coast as evacuees, and the projects as relocation centers." R. Okamura, "The American Concentration Camps: A Cover-Up Through Euphemistic Terminology," *The Journal of Ethnic Studies* 10 (1982): 95–109 (99–100).

35. Manzaar, California, and Poston, Arizona [also functioning as Assembly Centers]; Tule Lake, California, Minidoka, Idaho, and Heart Mountain, Wyoming [these areas were undeveloped federal reclamation projects]; and Gila River, Arizona, Granada (Amache), Colorado, Topaz, Utah, and Jerome and Rohwer, Arkansas.

Unfit living conditions matched their surroundings. Each family lived in an "apartment," basically an 8 foot × 20 foot section in a long, barracks-like one-story building with the largest "apartment" being 20 foot × 24 foot for a family of six. Partitions separated these "apartments," though offering little privacy since the partitions did not extend to the ceiling. None of the apartments had running water, furnishings (save army-style cots) and cooking facilities. Everybody ate in the mess hall where they received three meals a day, usually starchy, cheap food. These concentration camps were the apotheosis of "Thirding-as-Othering" in that Firstspace qualities (the physical, material nature of the camps), Secondspace re-presentations (these camps' power and ideology) and Thirdspace experience (domination and subjugation) altogether comprise the social space of Japanese Americans as very much Japanese and very little American.

What details of Gibeonite colonization that do exist are quite meagre. But did the lived social space in the Ophel district of the Gibeonites as Israelite though *not quite* Israelite also open up a site for resistance within the interstices of the *real* and the *imagined*? Details of any resistance are more miniscule than those of their colonization. Yet, despite the narrative presentation of their assimilation, one indicator of resistance presents itself with the motif of Gibeonite deception. Deception, according to James C. Scott in *Weapons of the Weak*, is one of many *everyday* forms of passive non-compliance by the powerless. Deception is a form of Thirdspace resistance "intended to mitigate or deny claims made by super-ordinate classes or to advance claims vis-à-vis those super-ordinate classes" in the struggle over, in this case, land rights.[36] To identify other potential tells of Gibeonite resistance, I turn to the Thirdspace site of Japanese resistance for assistance.

Prior to the Japanese' iconic experience of colonization, they had already begun to resist discrimination against them on a variety of fronts. Unfair land laws in California that targeted the Japanese sprang up in surrounding states as far east as Missouri. But the Japanese found loopholes within such racially driven legislation either by leasing or owning

---

36. J. C. Scott, *Weapons of the Weak: Everyday Forms of Peasant Resistance* (New Haven, Conn.: Yale University Press, 1985), 27–47 (32). Though the object of struggle between those in power and those relatively powerless groups may vary (e.g. extraction of labor, rents, food, taxes, and interest), as may the weapons of resistance (e.g. foot dragging, dissimulation, feigned ignorance, slander, false compliance, subtle sabotage, evasion, and so forth), they nonetheless signal the *everyday forms of resistance* in class struggle that, when reaching a crisis point, will explode into overt acts of rebellion.

land under the names of their American-born children, entering into unwritten arrangements with their white landlords, or borrowing the names of American citizens. From an economic standpoint, the social isolation of the Japanese enabled them to build their own economy by not funneling their revenue into the American market.

Instances of Japanese resistance within the camps did occur, though scholars debate their interpretation. The orthodox view construes the Japanese as defenseless, dependent, totally compliant, and submissive. Any resistance was sporadic and uncharacteristic and dismissed out of hand as mere "incidents" (note the official documentation referring to the Manzanar "incident"[37]). "Normalization" followed these outbreaks with some amiable—yet sometimes uncertain—resolution, resulting in a peaceful, "happy" camp. The revisionist view, on the other hand, contends that internee resistance, both active and passive, preceded evacuation and intensified within the camps. Internees were in conflict with their keepers and with each other.[38]

37. The Manzanar event occurred on December 6, 1942 after the assault of Fred Tayama, a well-known JACL leader who was regarded as an *inu* ("a dog," a collaborator), by Harry Ueno, president of the Kitchen Worker's Union and a Kibei (those Nisei who had been to Japan and returned to America), who was arrested the day after the attack. A crowd of some 3,000 to 4,000 gathered to demand the release of the popular Kibei, as well as to call for investigations into camp conditions. Many felt Ueno was framed and called for a strike the next day if he was not released that night. Evacuee representatives followed by a crowd of about one thousand went to the administration building on December 6 to meet with the project director only to be confronted by military police armed with submachine guns, rifles, and shotguns. Soldiers initially fired tear gas into the crowd to disperse it. But when the crowd reformed that evening, soldiers fired tear gas and bullets into the crowd, leaving one Nisei dead, another dying, and about a dozen wounded. That night the bells tolled continuously as the people held meetings and the soldiers patrolled the camp. To refer to this riot with the term "incident," claim Hansen and Hacker, trivializes the cultural significance of the event "by scaling down the affair to commonplace proportions." See A. Hansen and D. Hacker, "The Manzanar Riot: An Ethnic Perspective," *Amerasia Journal* 2 (1974): 112–57 (113–15); G. Y. Okihiro, "Japanese Resistance in America's Concentration Camps: A Re-Evaluation," *Amerasia Journal* 2 (1973): 20–34 (24–25).

38. For example, conflict occurred between newcomers from Sacramento, California and those from Washington and Oregon already at the Tule Lake camp over good jobs, scrap lumber, and various scarce resources. Cf. Okihiro, *The Columbia Guide to Asian American History*, 167. Okihiro augments the revisionist perspective throughout a series of articles where he identifies the result of the conflict, whether between generations, groups, or of politics expressed as pro-Japan or pro-American, as basically the struggle for civil liberties and human dignity. This

Japanese resistance did not principally manifest itself in overt acts of aggression but rather took on the quiet struggle for "possession of the children's minds and habits."[39] In short, it became a struggle to resist the manipulation of Japanese lives and "the erasure of their ethnic identity."[40] Resistance reflects a "response to endangered ethnicity."[41] Japanese religious belief played no small role, as Gary Y. Okihiro notes: "religion and culture...were both a vehicle for and an expression of the people's resistance."[42] The rise of Buddhism and an increase in religious activity within the Japanese American community paralleled that of the camps, an indication that religious activity increases in relationship to stresses brought on by the uncontrollable, unknown, or threatening. As time progressed in the camps, the Japanese block, consisting of fourteen barracks, took on the characteristics of the family to bolster ethnic solidarity. Block organizations such as The Young People's Association emerged and the slogan "Keep Children within the Block" widely circulated. Thus the psychological stresses of Japanese internment yielded responses at cross-purposes with the "Americanization" program, a Secondspace ideological move, which especially targeted filial piety by dislocating the family through evacuation. Japanese response countered "Americanization" attempts to essentialize their identity.

Cultural aesthetic expressions like landscape gardening, bonsai, *sumo*, art, music, drama, and poetry collectively created a common "Japanese spirit" whereby ethnic beliefs and practices rechanneled Japanese resistance away from open aggression. Representative examples of cultural resistance include the collection of personal reminiscences in Lawson Inada's *Only What We Could Carry* (2000), the diverse artistry and crafts in Chiura Obata's *Topaz Moon* (2000), Delphine Hirasuna's *The Art of Gaman* (2005), and the Online Centre for the Study of Japanese American Concentration Camp Art (http://www.lib.iastate.edu/internart-main/6786).

Cultural resistance began prior to internment as the social prejudice behind each anti-Japanese attack precipitated further retreat into

was certainly the case with Japanese resistance at Tule Lake. See Okihiro's "Tule Lake Under Martial Law: A Study in Japanese Resistance," *The Journal of Ethnic Studies* 5 (1977): 71–85.

39. Okihiro, "Japanese Resistance in America's Concentration Camps," 26, 31–32.

40. Okihiro, *The Columbia Guide to Asian American History*, 172.

41. Hansen and Hacker, "The Manzanar Riot," 122, 133, 141.

42. G. Y. Okihiro, "Religion and Resistance in America's Concentration Camps," *Phylon* 45 (1984): 220–33 (233).

traditional Japanese culture. In addition, the high boundedness and exhaustiveness factors in the labor and residential sectors together with incarceration faced by the Nisei undermined their growing "Americanization" as they returned to the Japanese American community. With the growing restoration of ethnicity and maintenance of group solidarity by the heightened determination to punish informers, boundary markers became more defined, thus illumining the deconstructive nature of colonization efforts to "Americanize" Japanese. Though the Nisei struggled with their culturally hybrid identity, it did open up a site for resisting an essentialist identity.

And what of the Gibeonites possible cultural resistance? Certain tells exist that may indicate Gibeonite cultural resistance to their own colonization—for example, the persistence of Gibeonite ethnic identity into the post-exilic era; the high boundedness and exhaustiveness factors in both labor and residential spaces for Gibeonites within the post-exilic era; their close proximity to Temple rituals in the post-exilic era coupled with the overt influence and proliferation of Canaanite religion (a marker of cultural resistance) on Israelite practices throughout its history well into the post-exilic era.

4. *Conclusion*

With the known colonization of Japanese Americans, the admittedly modest objective of this essay has been to explore the confluence of space and identity in Gibeonite colonization utilizing the postcolonial spatial constructs of Soja and Appadurai. Sociological insights identified high boundedness and exhaustiveness factors present in the narrative *ethnoscape* of Gibeonites and Japanese Americans delimiting their social space and fixing their identity at the *ideoscape* site. But their ostracism to a culturally hybrid status as "other," or Thirdspace, additionally opens up a site of resistance whereby to reconfigure identity from a non-essentialist stance utilizing cultural traditions.

As I close, I return to some of my nagging questions: How well does a trialectic, spatial theory work with biblical studies? Is this model on spatiality too limited in its perspective on space? How well, if at all, does it synchronize with the current, growing social media space in its diverse forms? And what of the ramifications of that for biblical studies? How can a triadic, spatial theory be utilized in an effective manner to move biblical studies beyond a First- or Secondspace preoccupation to a Thirdspace concern with "real life"? In other words, how can it move biblical studies beyond virtual reality to that of contemporary relevance?

As I understand Soja and the distinct nuances of trialectic spatiality, focus moves beyond just the physical or material (Firstspace) and the "imaginary" or virtual (Secondspace) to directly lived or experienced space (Thirdspace). If the foci of biblical studies simply remain at First- or Secondspace, then biblical studies unwittingly entraps itself in either a realistic or transcendental illusion. How can biblical text spatial analyses move to Thirdspace concerns of social praxis without simply being an attribute of "mental" space when we know so very little socially about these groups? This may pose the greatest obstacle for biblical studies' spatial analyses utilizing Soja's model.

When coupled with other reading strategies, however, biblical studies' spatial analyses show some promise and may potentially engage contemporary Thirdspace social praxis (note, for example, Nutt's essay relying on social-scientific analyses of artisan groups in African and Middle Eastern societies). With the contemporary lived experience of Islamophobia, including but not limited to illegally detained Muslims at Guantánamo Bay, it is as if the fear of the incarcerated Japanese Americans that the same thing could happen again has indeed happened again. The Japanese temporal-spatial experience has simply been displaced onto that of Arab Americans and other American Muslims in twenty-first-century social space. The enemy is indeed a threat and does pose a danger. But the "enemy other" does not merely reside among us, and nor is he/she simply out there; rather, the "enemy other" resides "within," because it is the enemy "within" who essentializes identity and space.

NARRATIVE SPACE AND THE CONSTRUCTION OF MEANING IN THE BOOK OF JOEL

Mary Mills

1. *Introduction*

This essay focuses on a single prophetic book, using the concept of religious geography as a lens through which to analyze the text and its construction. The text of Joel opens out to a spatial interpretation because it visibly links land, city and shrine and deals with sacred space as the means of controlling events in the natural and human worlds; the narrative of the book constructs space through its depiction of the places of land, city and temple, all of which are governed by transcendent activity. The aim of the present study is to explore the manner in which the imaginative universe of a literary text creates an ordered response to chaotic events through its deployment of religious geography.

In developing a reading lens for the biblical text under the heading of religious geography I am mainly concerned with a spatial approach to textual commentary. I pick up on the concept of mythical space and then work with the definitions of space made by Wesley Kort in his recent essay.[1] Kort develops a schematic reading tool in which three spatial levels—cosmic, communal and personal—are cross-referenced with the states of physical and spiritual reality. These perspectives allow for an interrogation of how the use of spatial location helps to focalize the meaning of events narrated by the text. In particular I address the topics of geo-piety and geopolitics. I suggest that the land is a major theme of the book of Joel and that the value of land and land-based identity is explored through a reader's engagement with the narrative space constructed by the biblical text.

---

1. W. A. Kort, "Sacred/Profane and an Adequate Theory of Human Place-Relations," in *Constructions of Space I: Theory, Geography, and Narrative* (ed. J. L. Berquist and C. V. Camp; LHBOTS 481; New York/London: T&T Clark International, 2007), 32–50.

In Joel 1:6–7, for instance, the reader is led to view a fertile agricultural land visited by a vast destructive force.[2] The ultimate response to this event is found in the call to gather at a ritual site in order to perform a lament ceremony (vv. 13–14). This textual movement renders the performance of lament as a powerful tool for restoring order to the cosmos. Behind this inter-action lies an urban setting; ch. 2 refers to the images of Zion and Holy Hill and thus engages also with the city of Jerusalem (v. 1). Implicitly, both the city and its land are ravaged by invaders and the same pattern is seen in the reverse theme of divine pity—land, Zion, Jerusalem (vv. 18, 23, 32). Insofar as Joel provides a visionary answer to human problems of survival it does so through the alignment of places and sites from earth to temple-city to the heavenly spaces. It is this combination of city and land, subsumed to the theme of religious praxis, which provides the fundamental level of the religious geography of Joel.

2. *Religious Approaches to Geography*

Thomas Dozeman notes the overlap of geography and religion in the ancient world, with a focus on religion's role in shaping human perceptions of the world.[3] In support of his views he turns to theorists such as Yi-Fu Tuan; in his 1977 work on space and place, Tuan stresses that the modern separation between myth and reality is too clear-cut and fails to do justice to the continuing life of myths in human thought as vehicles for a yearning to identify that which exists beyond experienced geographical borders.[4] In mythical space there is continuity between the material context of daily life and the realm of the divine, creating a link between lived space and perceived space which underlines the fact that all map-making is at heart a social activity and reflects existing social perceptions of the world.[5]

2.   It is to be noted that the numbering of verses from the book of Joel follows the usage of most modern commentaries rather than that of the Hebrew text, which makes Joel 2:28–32 into 3:1–5 and thus turns ch. 3 into ch. 4. See here, L. C. Allen, *The Books of Joel, Obadiah, Jonah and Micah* (Grand Rapids: Eerdmans, 1976), 39–42.

3.   T. B. Dozeman, "Biblical Geography and Critical Spatial Studies," in Berquist and Camp, eds., *Constructions of Space I*, 87–108 (91–92).

4.   Y.-F. Tuan, *Space and Place: The Perspective of Experience* (Minneapolis: University of Minnesota Press, 1977).

5.   This is to use the terminology of Edward Soja in his development of a theory of spatial trialectics: Firstspace is that of the material (perceived) reality, while Thirdspace (lived) consists neither of the material nor the intellectual approach to

Mark George takes this idea further by discussing the ways in which symbolic, mythological spaces convey the social values of a community. He argues that symbolic spaces have socially significant meaning and that they perform the task of ordering material space in a socially authoritative manner. Examination of the use of public space provides a means of studying communal values[6] since there is no gap between secular and religious meaning for "sacred and profane are social constructs."[7] George's work offers a mode of textual exegesis in which the literary account of worship sites such as temples and shrines is examined in the light of its function as a tool for managing cultural values. The combination of space and ritual act reflects the society so engaged, allowing symbolic meaning to emerge. At the center of this is an emotional, rather than an intellectual, uptake: social space deals with the actual hopes and fears of the population.[8]

Applying George's perspective to Joel 1–2 provides the following insights. The text deals with the emotional responses of a religious culture to the fears of a catastrophe, which it is facing, and seeks to provide a suitable reply to this threat by stressing the relevance of religious activity. In chs. 1 and 2 the call to use mourning as a symbolic action, which balances exactly the nature of the threat, is set out by repeated commands to sections of the population to become part of this activity. In Joel 1:9, for instance, the central group in any such public act is named as that of the priests. This makes engagement with the symbolic space of the cult the proper way in which this society deals with threats to its survival. The references to a material site as the necessary location for religious acts in aid of land renewal in Joel 2:15–17 create a double spatial layer in which the historical worship site is run together with the symbolic space of the narrative. The performance of lament draws on mourning as a rite of passage between life and death. This transforms fear to hope and permits the desire for compassion to be realized insofar as a ritual space brings together congregation, priests and God in order to re-shape the destiny of people, animals, land and city, as seen in the shift

spatiality but of the socially constructed lived environment. See E. W. Soja, *Postmetropolis: Critical Studies of Cities and Regions* (Oxford/Malden, Mass.: Blackwell, 2000), 10–12.

6. M. K. George, "Space and History: Siting Critical Space for Biblical Studies," in Berquist and Camp, eds., *Constructions of Space 1*, 15–31 (16). George's essay situates the treatment of space with regard to its value for biblical studies, using the concept of critical spatiality in which space per se becomes a topic of interest. He stresses the conceptualization of space as a social activity.

7. Ibid., 25.

8. Ibid., 29.

of mood and speakers between v. 18 and v. 19. The text creates a setting in which land provides an image of symbolic space, twinned with that of the temple-city.

3. *Cosmic Space and Threats to the Land*

There is, then, a close connection made by the text of Joel between land and religion. The spatiality of land is commented upon by the cosmic space which worship places access. Joel opens in the divine sphere, since Joel 1:1 moves from the voice of the prophet to that of divine speech;[9] hence, the major spatial frame of the book is one in which narrative sites such as land, worship site and army on the move are contained within the sacred cosmos. The role of God in this opening scene is to draw human attention to the locusts.[10] Verse 8 introduces the idea that lament is the suitable response to their presence. This pattern is repeated in the following verses, but the new climax in v. 14 moves from a generic call to mourn to the specific act of a public rite. In this sequence the locust advance, the failure of land and the need for lament are held together by the Day of the Lord image in v. 15.

The imagery of locusts as deadly enemies is certainly one which draws on historical experience in the ancient Near Eastern region, but here it takes on an extra dimension, becoming symbolic of divine presence and an impending judgment. The space of the locust journey over fields and city is defined as that also of the deity, since the insects are a form of divine army, which signify a transcendent attack on Jerusalem and condemn the inhabitants to annihilation both on natural and transcendent levels. This vision enacts a religious geography in which the land is presented as subject to serious attack, and whether any human value can be attached to attempts to own and cultivate land is uncertain. Indeed, the text depicts a double threat to land-value, with locust activity paired with the drought caused by the dry season. The work of insects in bringing about famine is thus joined with that of fire as a second icon of agricultural collapse.[11]

---

9. This is true overall even though ch. 2 does offer a third-person slant in, for instance, vv. 18–19.

10. Cf. R. Mason, *Zephaniah, Habakkuk, Joel* (OTG; Sheffield: JSOT, 1994), 105, where Mason refers to the overlap between a vast cloud of locusts and the use of cloud cover as an apocalyptic image. This comment is part of the treatment of the complex imagery which links both army and locusts to the Day of the Lord, with a blurring of borders between historical and cosmological aspects of events.

11. Cf. R. Murray, *The Cosmic Covenant: Biblical Themes of Justice, Peace and the Integrity of Creation* (London: Sheed & Ward, 1992), 51–56. Murray focuses his

Since Joel 3:1 clearly moves to human enemies, the text may be deliberately mixing images from the natural and human worlds. In Joel 2:3–9, for instance, it is not clear which of the two hostile forces is described as like warhorses. The use of "like" may imply that locusts are the focus, although the language of rumbling chariot wheels, scaling of walls, climbing into the city is drawn very clearly from the behavior of a besieging force.[12] In ch. 3 the emphasis on human enemies sharpens with the reference to the hope that Zion and Jerusalem be delivered from attack—a topic which introduces the topic of the judgment of other nations. The core message stresses the social significance of land, since v. 2 defines the nations as the force which scattered the people and divided their land. The land is also described as the "homeland" of the Judahite population which has been separated from its social identity by being sent from its own place in v. 6. In v. 12 land is more narrowly defined as the "valley" of battle, and whereas earlier passages dealt with the land as barren, what is at stake now is a land newly made fertile.

The connection made between fire and a cosmic Day of the Lord in Joel 2 provides a religious understanding of climate as ultimately controlled by self-conscious transcendent energy and places this alongside the understanding that historical events of human history are likewise controlled by transcendent space. These alignments produce a complex notion of space and place, in which ordinary events such as the effect of the dry season are mixed with historical events such as the appearance of foreign troops, and both types of event are aligned with the divine sphere. The biblical geography thus produced is a map of territory where the graphic symbols of insects, sun and soldiers are held together by the storm-image of the Lord's Day and all converge on the space of the land, raising the issue of land as profit or loss for the inhabitants and their herds and flocks.

4. *Exploring Narrative Space*

Wesley Kort's spatial theory offers a useful tool for gaining a deeper understanding of this unity between land and social identity.[13] He

---

study of Joel on the drought caused by the burning heat of the midday sun, which is likened to the activity of demonic forces.

12. Cf. H.-W. Wolff, *Joel and Amos* (trans. W. Janzen, S. D. McBride and C. A. Muenchow; Hermeneia; Philadelphia: Fortress, 1977), 46. The sound of chariot wheels rumbling indicates a mixing of symbolism between locust and human forces.

13. I have treated this subject, from the perspective of ritual space, in my book, *Urban Imagination in Biblical Prophecy* (LHBOTS 560; New York/London: T&T Clark International, 2012).

develops three levels and two modes of spatiality which are operative in human place-relations.[14] The three levels of space are the cosmic or comprehensive, the social and the personal.[15] Cosmic space directs our attention to that which precedes and comprehends humanly-constructed places,[16] while social space is oriented both to the present material reality and to future goals.[17] Personal space emerges from the interaction of both cosmic and social levels and all three levels have both a physical and spiritual mode.[18] Physicality "grants space value because it grounds and steadies human life,"[19] while the visionary element is "crucial to the possibilities for human creativity in social space."[20]

Kort's perspective provides a lens for examination of how social constructions of space bring the widest possible spatial plane which can be imagined to bear upon the fortunes of the group and of the individual. In addition, his theory is helpful in that it highlights the complementary perspectives of space as that which grounds human endeavor and as that which encourages a creative development of fresh responses to the material environment. For Kort the central aspect in space-management is "accommodation," a term which indicates a positive engagement between the aspects of space/flexibility/relationship/non-finality. Accommodation expresses both a capacity for space to be delineated as place of residence and a role for that mobility which is "crucial to human place-relations because...it allows movement"[21] between the cosmic/social/personal and the physical/spiritual.

a. *Comprehensive Space*
So how does Kort's paradigm of spatiality enable the reader to work with the text of Joel? At the level of comprehensive space God and the text are coterminous and the fullest example of this reality is found in the motif of the "Day of the Lord," an event which comprehends all disasters, locust and human armies, together with the burning up of the land.

---

14. Kort, "Sacred/Profane," 38–40. Kort refers to the manner in which treatments of time and history took priority over space and place in modern Western culture, only to lose their primacy as society became less optimistic about its values. However, the return of interest in space is problematic and the topic of "sacred space" needs much unpacking.
   15. Ibid., 38–42.
   16. Ibid., 38.
   17. Ibid., 41–42.
   18. Ibid., 41.
   19. Ibid.
   20. Ibid., 42.
   21. Ibid., 44.

The deity and the day form a spatial continuity in which a transcendent Being is revealed within metaphors of threats to human survival. Religious meaning is thus found in the events of the natural world as these manifestations impact on human beings.[22] This model of comprehensive space aligns the deity with specific icons on the biblical map of Joel—the person of the deity is fleshed out by his location at the head of an army—an imaging which is dependent on the presentation of two historical enemies as constituting the transcendental army which God leads.

This movement of the text has the effect of uniting the disembodied presence of a transcendent energy with spatial location and hence with a bounded spatial "body."

The deity is in this sense a spatial reality, as noted by Timothy Gorringe, whose work on the theology of the built environment discusses the potential separation between material and spiritual space. Gorringe rejects the view that material space must be divided from abstract space, since physical places exist within the framework of divine creativity. Hence all space is potentially sacred, "waiting for the moment of encounter in which it mediates God."[23] "To fully appreciate our own spatiality we need a theology of the 'eminent spatiality' of God" since space provides a sacramental reality of access to the divine.[24] Application of these ideas to the deity of the book of Joel allows for a two-way communication between the disasters and benefits which occur in nature and society and a powerful supernatural force. The "Day of the Lord" motif brings disasters inside divine purpose, as part of God's own space, while also providing counter-arguments to the view that natural evil is purely random and that human beings are powerless in the face of such events.

b. *Social Space*
This unitive approach to nature and society, expressed through the iconography of land, allows for enabling power to be transferred from God-space to the social space of sacred activity. Human religious practice has an influence on what happens, even on the implacable advance

---

22. This is to continue with an anthropocentric approach to the text. However, an earth-focused approach has been produced, which counters this viewpoint. See L. J. Braaten, "Earth Community in Joel: A Call to Identify with the Rest of Creation," in *Exploring Ecological Hermeneutics* (ed. N. C. Habel and P. Trudinger; SBLSymS 46; Atlanta: Society of Biblical Literature, 2008), 63–74.

23. T. J. Gorringe, *A Theology of the Built Environment: Justice, Empowerment, Redemption* (Cambridge: Cambridge University Press, 2006), 40.

24. Ibid.

of insect destroyers. In this context Robert Murray has made valuable contributions to understanding the text[25] when he suggests that Joel 1:8–20 is evidence of a ritual practice for controlling and disabling hostile forces, whether supernatural or earthly[26] and that the space of the text is the equivalent of a temple-site.[27] Murray argues that the hostile forces envisaged include both locusts and the effect of the summer drought with a resultant focus on what "seemed to be an outbreak of cosmic disorder."[28] Since the book goes on to cite the thirst-filled land receiving its fill of rain, Murray argues that "after due intercessions and fasting, the gift of rain has returned cosmic *tsedaqah*."[29]

Here ritual space leads to ritual action and together they produce a social space in which the growth of vegetation replaces loss of land value for the community. In turn this shift impacts on the meaning attached to comprehensive space, ensuring that it too is understood as a site of nurture. In Joel 3, key activity is located in the space of the valley, which becomes a divine judgment seat. The agricultural image is not fertility/barrenness, but the theme of the harvest. The armies of the nations are ripe for cutting and threshing, a topic, which also leads to prosperity for the home nation, since it allows the people to regain land control through the beneficial acts of the divine reaper. Thus it can be argued that the space of the text is performative in bringing about the removal of threats: by taking part in the situation narrated by the prophet the reader can share in the prevention of urban catastrophe through an act of attentive reading accompanied by religious assent to the over-arching frame of land and cult which the book provides.

c. *Personal Space*

Kort suggests that cosmic and social space together provide the context for personal space and in Joel 2:15–16 there is a direct address to the reader in the form of the voice of command: "Sanctify a fast, call a solemn assembly, gather the people, sanctify the elders, gather the children." This address sums up the whole of society by naming the youngest and oldest cohorts, emphasizing that the centrality of ingathering to focus on ritual events is the proper social action at this stage. The space of the

25. Murray, *Cosmic Covenant*, 44–67. In this study Murray deals with texts whose content focuses on breaches in Covenant and their effect. In particular he argues that social, cultural interests and the praxis of religious belief are conjoined in the topic of cultic activity.

26. Ibid., 51–56.

27. Ibid., 71.

28. Ibid., 55.

29. Ibid.

personal is occupied in this manner by a call to action which gathers
human energy and purpose to the support of the social good. This also
includes movement through the symbolic space of the text to arrive at the
precise place which gathers in the entirety of individual laments and
distress.

It is in the arena of personal space as performance space that the
powers of the human body are engaged in the management of social
space and its impact on comprehensive space. The citizen is urged to
contribute to the common good through the power of speech and by the
act of movement towards the designated action area. In Joel 2, the willing response of the individual to the call to lament in vv. 15–16 means
that there will be food for all and ensures that enemies will be driven
away from the land. In Joel 3, the gathering in of the people, which leads
to renewal, is mirrored in the scene of the nations' armies being gathered
into one material site (v. 12); here, however, it is the certainty that the
land will be wrested from the control of these nations which is indicated
by the theme of gathering together. The spatial theme at work in both
chapters has the effect of re-balancing the worth of land ownership for
the home community.

In this perspective, material physicality and spiritual modes of
spatiality are interwoven. The focus is a desolate material site and the
manner in which this can best be sustained by the spiritual space of
religious praxis such as cries of distress. When events turn to the better
with the coming of rain, the spiritual attitude of thanksgiving and its
physical expression in other forms of cultic action strengthens the physical order, under-girding society by ensuring a harmony between cosmos
and community. Lament itself functions as a material expression of
emotional fear and spiritual hope and thus enacts social resistance to
hostile conditions within the land occupied by a community. The scene
in Joel 3:12–21 plays out this emphasis on hope and completes the cycle
of ritual action. God declares directly that the nations will be judged and
crushed so that Jerusalem can be rebuilt and its land renewed.

5. *Geopolitics and Geo-piety*

The religious geography of the book of Joel places the stress on the
religious dimension of human affairs. Chapters 1 and 2 assume the
existence of a settled people living on and working agricultural land, as
in Joel 1:11–12 and 2:7–9. The text extends the motif of nurture from
sentient beings to the deity, since God too will go without his due offerings of produce if the land cannot provide food and drink, as indicated in
1:9. The text of Joel 1 sets out a number of scenes in putting across the

message that this is indeed a critical time. These include vines and figs (v. 7), fields (v. 10), the trees (v. 12), seeds (v. 17), pasture and streams (vv. 19–20). This narrative description extends to the farmer's barns (v. 17) and to the temple storehouse (v. 13). It is these individual sites and their state which build up the picture of severity in the reader's mind.

Yet these places are not in fact viewed as independent locations. They are all part of a single reality which is the capacity of a city to feed itself. The text assumes the space of the land to be that of a vast food resource, an idea that turns all the places into icons of one universal space, dealing not with land in general, but with the territory of the city, Jerusalem. From this angle the text concerns itself with political geography, as is more obviously seen in ch. 3. Here the stress falls not on nature, but on human society, as a source of distress. Joel 3:2 implies that it is the fault of the nations that Jerusalem has suffered so badly; one of their crimes is that they took the urban land and divided it up among themselves.

Once again the images of armies and divine intervention are invoked in order to narrate the passing of doom from the home community to the other communities who have engaged with them (3:9–16). It is, however, the space of the land which provides the climax of the scene. Wine, milk and water will flow from the hills and the mountains in this second treatment of the landscape (3:18). Land as sterile and as fertile are the twin spatial markers for the loss and benefit which urban communities incur as sites within both time and space.

It can be argued that the main significance of the space of land as depicted in Joel is in relationship to this urban concern with territory. Such a view engages with the study of political geography which has an interest in this topic of territoriality, under the heading of geopolitics.[30] Geopolitics is, according to Mark Blacksell, engaged with the geography of differentiation, of setting up clear boundaries for ownership of material resources.[31] Using his insight to read Joel makes possible the identification of key geopolitical mapping signs in the prophetic symbolic world. One of these is the dominant image of the Day of the Lord.

30. The topic of political geography is, of course, a vast one, with considerable writing by cultural geographers, sociologists, and political theorists. One recent volume which surveys the contemporary face of political geography from traditional aspects such as state and territory to new profiles such as environmental justice is J. A. Agnew, K. Mitchell, and G. Toal, eds., *A Companion to Political Geography* (Blackwell Companions to Geography 3; Oxford: Blackwell, 2008).

31. M. Blacksell, *Political Geography* (New York: Routledge, 2006), 135. Blacksell's starting point is that geopolitics is a branch of political geography which posits the importance of understanding space as a pre-requisite to understanding the nature of international politics.

This symbol unites time and space. The idea of the day, the suitable time for action, is aligned with the graphic imagery of a great storm in the heavens. The storm is mobile across the spaces of sky and land and draws to itself the essence of war and destruction. It appears in ch. 2 as the ultimate definition of the locust invasion. It is a day of darkness, of black clouds blocking out the light, from which emerges the scene of a vast army on the move (Joel 2:2–10). Such is the powerful energy indicated by this symbol that it causes the earth itself to shake and the planets and stars are obscured and appear to have lost control of their usual functions. This imagery provides the hinge of the textual message in Joel 1–2, just as it does in ch. 3, where vv. 15–16 depict the destructive power of the storm in its impact on both land and sky. Here the Day of the Lord provides the turning point in Jerusalem's fortunes in international politics. This graphic symbol of the Lord as warrior-in-chief of human and insect armies operates both to bring natural events and religious belief into unity and to offer a means of working out the proper borders for human action.

In Joel the land is under the control of the city population while also being outside their authority, since natural forces operate according to the determination of divine design, as indicated in Joel 2:1–5: envisaged as a great storm, this transcendent force is a source of destruction, but also has positive potential, however. For it is the storm which brings the autumn rains which, ch. 2 acknowledges, make the land fertile again. In ch. 3 it is after the deity restores land ownership to the home community that there will be the possibility of enjoying its fruits. This narrative patterning of the function of urban territory via the icon of the "storm" raises issues about the value to be attached to land cultivation; will it be helpful or not to human survival? But the answer to that question is finely tuned between a negative and a positive answer. If land functions here as a comprehensive space its identity is found within the social space of human religious praxis.[32] Territory by itself does not maintain life, only a vibrant spirituality can ensure that land ownership remains productive in the most basic material sense. Since the icon of the storm includes divine agents as well as divine agency it can be regarded as synonymous with that of an "army." It is the imagery of mobility which adds meaning to the static space of "land."

The recent attention given by geographers to space as a matter of "flows" has promoted a less rigid geopolitical viewpoint in which the border line turns into a context for political conversation rather than a

---

32. Cf. ibid., 142.

point of closure. These varied comments lead to the conclusion, as Anssi Paasi states, that a re-valuation of border-as-closure points to the reality that "territories are not frozen frameworks where social life occurs. Rather they are made, given meanings and destroyed in social and individual action."[33] The view that language regarding borders provides a shifting mode of maintaining social identity can validly be applied to the book of Joel to identify the tension in the text between the threat of annihilation and the promise of abundance. If imagery, which operates to set borders, promotes the view that annihilation is a likely reality for both humans and beasts, language, which transgresses those borders, opens up the possibility that even barren land can be renewed. It has been shown above that spatial descriptions of an empty and withered landscape can be used to close down human expectations of survival while imagery of food production flowing down the hills in great abundance expands the likelihood of continued existence.

In each version of this within Joel there is a spatial location which performs the opening-up role. In Joel 1–2 this place is the narrow space of cultic ritual within a temple site. In ch. 3 it is in the valley which becomes a field of battle. In the first version the significant action is that of human ritual performance and in the second it is that of battle-engagement. The first instance deals with action which averts doom, while the second relates to action which leads to doom. The reality of this movement from closure to opening is found in physical acts, but only insofar as these have a symbolic force within the world of the text. They signify the manner in which sacred and secular spaces are intertwined in this prophetic book—as, for instance, with the performance of religious meaning according to set rhythms.[34]

6. *Geo-piety and Power*

Geopolitics opens into the related topic of geo-piety, the assumption that a supreme divine authority governs the universe. The text of Joel as a work of geo-piety can be variously demonstrated, as connected with the essential human frames of life/death. The two profiles of annihilation and survival are visibly in tension in Joel 2, which starts with a negative view of events. By v. 12 this has changed to a sense that there may be possibility for growth: although it is still unclear whether a positive outcome

---

33. A. Paasi, "Territory," in Agnew, Mitchell, and Toal, eds., *A Companion to Political Geography*, 109–23 (110).

34. See Wolff, *Joel and Amos*, 9. Wolff suggests that the whole of the first two chapters of Joel should be read as a lament liturgy.

is viable, since the phrase "who knows whether" in v. 14 is capable of being read either way, the renewed call to proclaim a fast and perform lament implies that so far the community is powerless to change the state of the land. Powerlessness is transformed in v. 18, which notes that Lord "became jealous for his land"[35] and thus insists on growth (v. 21). This imaginative act of reversal may be read in line with David Slater's view that "alternative flows may challenge the geopolitical location of a given society and may encapsulate power to resist or to generate alternative imaginaries."[36] The text can be read as providing abundance as a counter-flow to be reckoned with when the social horizons of continuity are obscured by disaster. This counter-flow offers the reader the opportunity for personal empowerment in that it indicates that individual spiritual effort on behalf of the good of the earth does not go by without achieving its goal, thus not only setting the borders of death, but also allowing for life to transcend them.

The theme of personal empowerment alerts us to the fact that geo-politics is always engaged with the subject of power. John Allen notes that power may be "power over" or "power to."[37] He discusses the politics of "geo-graphing space," that is, "representing it in a way to justify someone's authority over it."[38] The book of Joel is literature which manages the issue of geopolitical power in terms of authority to define land as useful or not. It does so through the attention given to invading armies. The initial reference to the locusts in ch. 1 merges with the depiction of human hordes, in ch. 2, so that the weight of the text is found in the violence used against land and city. Taken as a whole these passages point to an understanding of power as that which is "over." The people lack power over the land in these conditions while a hostile enemy claims complete control over and use of the foliage and trees. The

35. See here J. Barton, *Joel and Obadiah: A Commentary* (OTL; Louisville: Westminster John Knox, 2001), 88. Barton notes that the reference to God's jealousy stresses his intolerance of rivals and his passionate commitment to his people. S. L. Cook, *Prophecy and Apocalypticism: The Post Exilic Social Setting* (Minneapolis: Fortress, 1995), 191, links the idea of God's zealous concern for his people to the Zion language used in the book of Joel.

36. D. Slater, "Geopolitical Themes and Post Modern Thought," in Agnew, Mitchell, and Toal, eds., *A Companion to Political Geography*, 75–92 (84). The interpretation offered here reinforces Slater's view: whatever the concept of geo-politics which is adhered to, it will always deal with issues of actual (dis)empower-ment.

37. J. Allen, "Power," in Agnew, Mitchell, and Toal, eds., *A Companion to Political Geography*, 95–108 (96).

38. Ibid., 102.

second definition of power does, however, occur in Joel, namely, in the aspect of religious performance.

The enactment of lament is viewed as a means of geo-graphing cosmic/comprehensive space and, under the guidance of duly authorized officials, provides the means for re-shaping borders and re-defining land use—a clear instance of a geo-pietistic approach to political geography. Joel 3 indicates that imperial regimes use physical strength to claim a right of power over land and community, but their power may not have the force of cosmic authority; this being the case, the army cannot maintain supremacy. Authority to act powerfully with regard to territory is given from the cosmic to the social level of human existence, a stance endorsed in Zion's favor at the end of Joel. The link between divine sovereignty and human ritual is indissoluble in this approach.

The tension between power as that which defines reality and as that which enables reality brings us back to Wesley Kort's view, that the most helpful approach to the nature of space is that of accommodation— a term which stresses flexibility and the ongoing role of mutual adjust- ment.[39] This construction of spatial meaning balances against the rigidity of ownership and allows for reciprocity of person and place.[40] It also defines place as a gift, something unplanned and surprising which pro- vides a positive experience of place-relations.[41] I would like to suggest that the book of Joel provides an example of this kind of accommodative process in its management of the tension between human expectation and what really happens. Those who commit to land-work can justifiably expect results from the cultivation, but armies, whether locust or human, deprive the concept of expectation of its accompanying adjective, "justi- fied." However, the religious dimension offers both a spiritual tool for understanding this phenomenon and the ability to continue expectation beyond its initial borders. Spirituality which moves into religious praxis bridges the gap between cosmos and social space, between desire and achievement, since it offers a material context for the expression of a more general spiritual energy.

The spatial poetics of Joel operate with a temporal marker, a day of divine activity.[42] According to James Nogalski, the Day of the Lord

39. Kort, "Sacred/Profane," 45.
40. Ibid.
41. Ibid., 46.
42. J. D. Nogalski, "The Days(s) of YHWH in the Book of the Twelve," in *Thematic Threads in the Book of the Twelve* (ed. P. L. Redditt and A. Schart; Berlin: W. de Gruyter, 2003), 192–213 (193). Nogalski reflects on the prevalence of this phrase and its associated concepts in the Book of the Twelve. Joel provides a further

"structures the movement of the book from presumed judgement to the call for repentance to promised restoration and the judgement of the nations."[43] The graphic iconography of the "Day" as simultaneously a heavenly site shapes the message of Joel, with its progression from present to future and beyond. John Barton suggests that the basic level of the book is a natural catastrophe which can be viewed as eschatological if the transformation of the natural order is seen as indicating that nothing can be the same again.[44] This approach allows us to focus on the final form of the book as a narrative space which accommodates history by employing the over-arching visual graphic of the motif of the Day. The rooting of all historical events of hostile action in the intensity of a storm ties a specific event to a timeless icon in such a way that the particular meaning of the one-off event is opened up to broader significance.

The narrative construction of the book of Joel draws a reader's attention to the way in which urban life is governed both by seasonal variations and unexpected occurrences such as invasion by insect pests or by hostile human groups. These events provide the context for a broader reflection on the relationship between a community, its land and a deity. In order to develop this reflection symbolic sites are provided which carry the geo-piety of the book by acting as geo-political symbols. The places of cult and battle thus mediate the value to be attached to land as urban territory; the repeated iconography of the Day of the Lord holds this process together. The portrayal of a storm as co-equal with divine authority creates a textual space which accommodates the physical and spiritual aspects of biblical geography.

Although the subject matter of chs. 1–2 and ch. 3 is different in terms of both threat and means of response, the (re)appearance of the icon of comprehensive space in both parts provides for an underlying unity of construction of thought across the whole book. Overall the text reflects on the significance of land space for a human community which looks out on it from an urban center. The opposing profiles of land as sterile

specific focus for such language within that overall prevalence. Nogalski goes on to argue that this is linked in Joel 2 with the outpouring of the spirit (p. 202).

43. Ibid., 200–201. See also S. J. de Vries, "Futurism in the Pre-exilic Minor Prophets Compared with That of the Post-exilic Minor Prophets," in Redditt and Schart, eds., *Thematic Threads in the Book of the Twelve*, 252–72 (261), and D. J. Simundson, *Joel, Hosea, Amos, Obadiah, Jonah, Micah* (Abingdon Old Testament Commentaries; Nashville: Abingdon, 2005), 119–20.

44. Barton, *Joel and Obadiah*, 27. Barton balances previous theories against each other and his tendency is to provide a commentary which harmonizes what are seen as later additions with an earlier, historical layer.

and as fertile provide book ends to the whole work. Within this frame-work the narrative addresses the causes for these two states by popu-lating the land with symbolic icons of threat, locusts and armies. The material level of existence is refined, in religious terms, by two further spatial icons, the Lord's Day and the enactment of cult. The symbiosis of these latter concepts is what finally defines the value which land can have for the support of human society in that both land and community are subject to divine authority: ritual practices provide the means by which the good relationship between deity, people and land can be restored.

Unfocused Narrative Space in Tobit 1:1–2:14

Ronald van der Bergh

1. *Introduction*

The study of space in narrative has been much neglected in studies on narratology. This unfortunate situation was still lamented as recently as 2009 by Katrin Dennerlein[1]—calling space the stepchild (*Stiefkind*) of narratological studies. The same holds true for biblical studies based on a narratological methodology,[2] even amidst an increase of studies of spatiality in ancient texts.

In narratology, space regularly takes second place to the concept of time.[3] Yet all narratives are set in a spatial world, even if space is not explicitly mentioned.[4] In exactly the same way that narrative actions always happen at a specific time, they are also localized at a specific

---

1. K. Dennerlein, *Narratologie des Raumes* (Narratologia 22; Berlin: W. de Gruyter, 2009), 3. Dennerlein provides a list of narratological introductions, all of which have very little to say about space. This lack of concern is reflected in introductions to biblical narratology, such as S. Bar-Efrat, *Narrative Art in the Bible* (JSOTSup 70; Sheffield: Almond, 1989), esp. 195; Y. Bourquin and D. Marguerat, *How to Read Bible Stories: An Introduction to Narrative Criticism* (London: SCM, 1999)—only treated on pp. 80–82; but see also J. L. Resseguie, *Narrative Criticism of the New Testament: An Introduction* (Grand Rapids: Baker Academic, 2005), 94–105, who grants space somewhat more prominence.

2. Cf. the lack of a spatial investigation in such groundbreaking works as R. A. Culpepper, *Anatomy of the Fourth Gospel: A Study in Literary Design* (Philadelphia: Fortress, 1983); M. W. G. Stibbe, *John as Storyteller: Narrative Criticism and the Fourth Gospel* (Cambridge: Cambridge University Press, 1992).

3. W. A. Kort, *Place and Space in Modern Fiction* (Gainesville: University Press of Florida, 2004), 1 and 10–12; Dennerlein, *Narratologie des Raumes*, 4; M.-L. Ryan, "Space," in *Handbook of Narratology* (ed. P. Hühn et al.; Narratologia 19; Berlin: W. de Gruyter, 2009), 420–33 (420).

4. M. Martínez and M. Scheffel, *Einführung in die Erzähltheorie* (8th repr.; Munich: C. H. Beck, 2009), 123; cf. A. P. Brink, *Vertelkunde: 'n Inleiding tot die Lees van Verhalende Tekste* (Pretoria: Academica, 1987), 107–8; Ryan, *Space*, 420.

place.[5] Consequently, due consideration should be given to both these aspects in a narratological investigation. Fortunately, works such as Dennerlein's *Narratologie des Raumes*[6] and Ryan's contribution to the *Handbook of Narratology*[7] have started rectifying this deficiency in the broader discipline of narratology. The impact of such recent works on the study of biblical literature still needs to be realized. Hitherto, the emphasis of existing studies of biblical space has largely been on explicitly named space, especially toponyms.[8] This contrasts with what has been the concern of narratological studies in general, where especially the symbolic value of space has been highlighted.[9] Clearly, such studies have great value. After all, "narrative space is part of a constructed rhetorical strategy to persuade"[10]—and part of this strategy is certainly the explicit naming of spaces and places of symbolic value. However, implicit references to space also contribute to the text's rhetorical strategy and should not be readily discounted. Biblical narratology has until recently suffered from a lack of methodology to unearth such references and their contribution to a given narrative's meaning;[11] however, this situation is steadily improving.

The present study aims to contribute to the reading of implicit references to space in biblical narrative. It offers a narratological reading

---

5. Dennerlein, *Narratologie des Raumes*, 4; cf. A. Brink, "Die Tyd en Ruimte in Eksodus 2: 'n Studie van die Storie-aspekte in die Narratiewe Teks van Eksodus 2 (Deel 2)," *OTE* 16 (2003): 598–614 (611).

6. Dennerlein, *Narratologie des Raumes*.

7. Ryan, "Space," 420–33.

8. Cf. Brink, "Tyd en Ruimte," 612.

9. Dennerlein, *Narratologie des Raumes*, 46. For an example of such a study on the book of Tobit, see J. Zsengellér, "Topography as Theology: Theological Premises of the Geographical References in the Book of Tobit," in *The Book of Tobit: Text, Tradition, Theology. Papers of the First International Conference on the Deuterocanonical Books, Pápa, Hungary, 20–21 May, 2004* (ed. G. G. Xeravits and J. Zsengellér; Leiden: Brill, 2005), 177–88.

10. W. R. Millar, "A Bakhtinian Reading of Narrative Space and Its Relationship to Social Space," in *Constructions of Space I: Theory, Geography, and Narrative* (ed. J. L. Berquist and C. V. Camp; LHBOTS 481; New York/London: T&T Clark International, 2007), 129–40 (131), basing this statement on work done by Kort (Kort, *Place and Space*). Few scholars would argue that the biblical texts do not share this persuasive aim.

11. See E. Van Eck, *Galilee and Jerusalem in Mark's Story of Jesus: A Narratological and Social Scientific Reading* (HTSSup 7; Pretoria: University of Pretoria, 1995), esp. 137–39. Van Eck's excellent methodological discussion leaves room for a study of this nature, but the rest of his work is mainly concerned with explicitly named space.

of space in the first two chapters of the book of Tobit, with special attention to the importance of what will be termed "unfocused space" below. Due to the limits of this study, not all aspects of unfocused space will be considered, not to mention narrative space as a whole. Rather, the emphasis will be on the concepts of freedom and confinement, on what role these concepts play in the first two chapters of the book of Tobit, and how these concepts are emphasized in the text. References to the symbolic value of cities, the theology of the book, and so on, are of course unavoidable, but these themes will not be pursued further.[12] The value of this mode of reading will be shown in a short comparison of two Greek versions of the tale (G[I] and G[II]). Before turning to the analysis itself, one should add some cursory remarks about theory and method.

2. *Narrative Space, Unfocused Space and the Model-reader*

Narrative space comprises at least three different levels of space: narrator's space, narrating space and narrated space.[13] Narrator's space is that space in which the narrator finds him/herself; narrating space is the world in which the implied reader[14] is located; and narrated space is the world in which the narrative transpires. Although all three levels are of importance, it is especially narrated space which concerns us here.

In narrated space, there should be two distinctions: a general spatiality, such as one could only infer, and a more focused, direct spatiality, when explicit mention is made of space. Chatman calls the latter "discourse-space," further defining it as "the *focus of spatial attention*."[15] Borrowing this concept from Chatman, an appropriate way to indicate this distinction might be to refer to the latter as "focused space" and the former as

---

12. For a summary of the theology of the book, see C. A. Moore, *Tobit: A New Translation with Introduction and Commentary* (AB 40A; New York: Doubleday, 1996), 26–33; B. Ego, "Das Buch Tobit," in *Unterweisung in erzählender Form* (ed. G. S. Oegema; JSHRZ IV/I 2; Gütersloh: Gütersloher Verlagshaus, 2005), 115–50 (137–45). In her article "The Book of Tobit and the Diaspora," in Xeravits and Zsengellér, eds., *The Book of Tobit*, 41–54 (41), Ego advocates a spatial reading of the book, noting especially the important role of the exile as backdrop to the story.

13. G. T. M. Prinsloo, "The Role of Space in the שירי המעלות (Psalms 120–134)," *Bib* 86 (2005): 457–77 (459).

14. The concept of "implied reader" has become all but canonical in narratology.

15. S. Chatman, *Story and Discourse: Narrative Structure in Fiction and Film* (Ithaca, N.Y.: Cornell University Press, 1978), 102. Ryan, *Space*, 423, warns against seeing "discourse-space" as analogous to Chatman's concept of "discourse-time"— that is, the time taken to read the narrative. A more appropriate equivalent, according to Ryan, would be the "spatial extent of the text."

"unfocused space."[16] Instead of being two distinct categories, these concepts form the extremes of a line on which any given spatial attention in a narrative may be plotted. For instance, movement by a character implies some degree of space and spatial attention, but may not be so explicit as to be completely in focus.[17]

Unfocused space encompasses Dennerlein's ideas of indeterminateness (*Unbestimmtheit*) and voids (*Leerstellen*). Whereas indeterminate references to space may still be elaborated upon by, for example, cultural knowledge, voids are simply not reconstructable. Unfocused, indeterminate references to space could also be fleshed out by a healthy mixture of cognitive narratology, which studies "the processes by means of which interpreters make sense of story worlds evoked by narrative representations or artefacts,"[18] and studies of the "experience of space" such as that of Tuan.[19] An obvious problem with the use of such methods is that, in many instances, extraneous material, that is, ideas not contained in the narrative text, may be introduced to the discussion. This is particularly problematic, as narratologists have for a long time stressed the absolute fictionality of the narrative world.[20] However, there is a growing tendency to move away from viewing narratives as being self-contained.[21] Narrative texts are always reliant upon and in dialogue with their respective contexts of origin, whether this conversation is in concurrence or in contrast. Taking this referential quality of a narrative seriously necessitates a concept such as that of Dennerlein's "model-reader" (*Modell-Leser*).[22] Whereas an implied reader is a construct found within the text, the model-reader is situated within the cultural context of the origin of a

16. Another important distinction pointed out by Van Eck, *Galilee and Jerusalem*, 137–39, is between "setting" and "focal space." Van Eck's "setting" carries no meaning, while "focal space" conveys the ideological perspective of the narrative. As such, unfocused space also has the potential for becoming "focal space."

17. Cf. Bar-Efrat, *Narrative Art*, 184–85.

18. D. Herman, "Narrative Ways of Worldmaking," in *Narratology in the Age of Cross-Disciplinary Research* (ed. S. Heinen and R. Sommer; Narratologia 20; Berlin: W. de Gruyter, 2009), 71–87 (85).

19. See, for instance, Y.-F. Tuan, *Space and Place: The Perspective of Experience* (Minneapolis: University of Minnesota Press, 1977), 267. Herman, "Narrative Ways of Worldmaking," 73–74, also highlights the "experience" of space in a narrative.

20. See, for instance, W. Schmid, *Narratology: An Introduction* (trans. A. Starritt; Berlin: W. de Gruyter, 2010), 30.

21. Cf. Dennerlein, *Narratologie des Raumes*, 89; Herman, "Narrative Ways of Worldmaking," 71–72.

22. See Dennerlein, *Narratologie des Raumes*, 8, for a descriptive summary of the concept.

narrative. Biblical scholars, too, have recently pointed out this deficiency in the traditional concept of implied reader.[23] Of course, the use of a model-reader does not grant free license to an interpreter. The "existence" of spatial attributes in a narrative—even if these attributes actually exist or existed in the "real" world—should always be motivated by a reading of the text. In other words, these spatial attributes are only part of narrated space when their existence, stated or implied, is necessary for the understanding of a text.[24] This leaves the fictional aspect of a narrative intact, while taking into account the spatial attributes to which the narrative refers, or which it evokes.[25] The concept of a model-reader is also a prerequisite for reading unfocused space, as it may help the present-day reader to fill in the blanks of indeterminate references to space responsibly. An example of where this concept is helpful may be found below, where the knowledge of the "appropriate" ways of disposing of an executed person's corpse—knowledge gleaned from outside the text—helps highlight the build-up of tension in the narrative.

3. *Introductory Remarks to the Book of Tobit*

The book of Tobit has been described as "one of the finest short stories which have been passed down to us from non-classical antiquity."[26] Probably originating in either Aramaic or Hebrew[27] at around 200 B.C.E.,[28]

---

23. P. M. Venter, "Spatiality in the Second Parable of Enoch," in *Enoch and the Messiah Son of Man: Revisiting the Book of Parables* (ed. G. Boccaccini; Grand Rapids: Eerdmans, 2007), 403–12 (404), to name but one, draws a much more direct line between the text of a narrative and its contemporaneous society. See also the discussion by E. S. Malbon, "Narrative Criticism: How Does the Story Mean?," in *Mark and Method: New Approaches in Biblical Studies* (ed. J. Capel Anderson and S. D. Moore; Minneapolis: Fortress, 2008), 29–57 (33), for a perspective from biblical narratology on a responsible use of a biblical narrative's cultural context.

24. Cf. Dennerlein, *Narratologie des Raumes*, 121: "…nur wenn der Text oder die narrative Kommunikation nahe legen, ihr Vorhandensein anzunehmen, sind sie auch Teil der erzählten Welt."

25. Today, much of the cultural significance as well as the physical characteristics of spatial attributes might be irretrievably lost; cf. Bar-Efrat, *Narrative Art*, 187.

26. R. Bauckham, "Tobit as a Parable for the Exiles of Northern Israel," in *Studies in the Book of Tobit: A Multidisciplinary Approach* (ed. M. Bredin; LSTS 55; New York/London: T&T Clark International, 2006), 140–64 (140).

27. So Moore, *Tobit*, 34; J. A. Fitzmyer, *Tobit* (Commentaries on Early Jewish Literature; Berlin: W. de Gruyter, 2003), 25; Ego, "Das Buch Tobit," 127. For thorough treatments of the question of language, see Moore, *Tobit*, 33–39; Fitzmyer, *Tobit*, 18–28; Ego, "Das Buch Tobit," 120–29. The discovery of Aramaic and

the story was translated at an early stage into Greek, and subsequently into a number of languages, including Latin, Syriac, and Coptic, testifying to its popularity.[29] The Greek comprises the oldest tradition still complete, itself consisting of at least three different recensions. Of these, what has become known as the short recension (G^I) and the long recension (G^{II}) are the most intact.[30] G^I is most probably a revision of G^{II}.[31] These two recensions follow the same general plotline, but differ enough to illustrate the usefulness of the reading of unfocused space for interpreting a narrative, as will be shown in the short comparison below.

Why this specific section of the text? The first two chapters have Tobit, as first-person narrator, tell of his deportation from the land of Israel[32] to Nineveh, his pious struggle with pagan practices and actions (especially in connection with the burial of fellow Israelites),[33] and his eventual blindness as an indirect consequence of this struggle. These two chapters have been described by Zsengellér as the "first journey"

Hebrew fragments of Tobit at Qumran has greatly influenced this debate in favor of a Semitic origin.

28. The date of the book is still somewhat of a point of debate. Because nothing is made of Antiochus IV Epiphanes or the Maccabees, the first few years of the second century B.C.E. is a likely *terminus ad quem*. Opinions vary as to a *terminus a quo*; although considerations have included a date as early as 400 B.C.E., argued by N. Poulssen, *Tobit* (BOT VI/II; Roermond: J. J. Romen, 1968), 8, the broader consensus seems to be the late third century; cf. Moore, *Tobit*, 40–42; Ego, "Das Buch Tobit," 130–31. See also the discussion by M. Rabenau, *Studien zum Buch Tobit* (BZAW 220; Berlin: W. de Gruyter, 1994), 175–90, who identifies different redactional layers in the text and proceeds to date them.

29. For an overview of the different versions and their textual witnesses, see R. Hanhart, *Tobit* (Septuaginta: Vetus Testamentum Graecum auctoritate Academiae Scientiarium Gottingensis VIII/5; Göttingen: Vandenhoeck & Ruprecht, 1983), 11–23.

30. Ibid., 31. Codices Vaticanus and Alexandrinus are the main witnesses for G^I, while G^{II} is contained almost exclusively in Codex Sinaiticus. For a third recension (G^{III}), largely incomplete, see especially S. Weeks, "Some Neglected Texts of Tobit: The Third Greek Version," in Bredin, ed., *Studies in the Book of Tobit*, 12–42. Also see Hanhart, *Tobit*, 7–10, 31–36, for a discussion of the Greek textual witnesses and their coherence.

31. The argument is mainly based on stylistic reasons, with G^I containing far fewer Semitisms; cf. Rabenau, *Studien*, 7; Moore, *Tobit*, 56. Here, too, the Qumran discoveries have all but laid other theories to rest, cf. Fitzmyer, *Tobit*, 3–17.

32. In Tobit, "Israel" refers to both the northern and southern kingdoms; cf. Zsengellér, "Topography as Theology," 181.

33. On the importance of burial practices in Tobit and later rabbinic Judaism, see Moore, *Tobit*, 120.

contained in the book.[34] Tobit 3:2–6 is a prayer by Tobit, while 3:1 may be seen as an introduction to this prayer. Tobit 3:7 introduces not only a third-person narrator, but also a spatial shift (to Ecbatana) and a change of characters (to Sarah and her father's servant-girls). The end of ch. 2 thus seems a viable place to set the limits of this study.[35] As G[II] is the longer version and has a bigger interest in space, it is the appropriate starting point. After the analysis of G[II], differences between it and G[I] will be pointed out in a short comparison.

4. *A Spatial Reading of the "First Journey" in G[II]*

The first spatial marker to be mentioned in Tobit (1:2) is the exile (which plays a prominent role in the greater narrative),[36] and in the same breath, Tobit's hometown (Thisbe). The exact location of this town is not known today, and it is difficult to say whether a model-reader would have perceived the town as fictional or not.[37] What should be said is that the location is very precisely defined in the narrative. The town is south of Kydios, west and above Asser, north of Phogor—thus providing points on three of the four primary horizontal spatial axes. There follows a description of Tobit's character: he walked in the true paths of right-eousness and did many charitable deeds to those who went with him in captivity to the land of Assyria, to Nineveh.[38] The deportation to Assyria

---

34. Zsengellér, "Topography as Theology," 187.

35. In the greater narrative of Tobit, the first two chapters should be read, in conjunction with the following scene concerning Sarah, as laying out the problem, which the hero (Tobias) must solve in the narrative's plot. Nevertheless, Tobit's prayer indicates the end of this first section, just as Sarah's prayer indicates the end of the second section; cf. Fitzmyer, *Tobit*, 47.

36. W. Soll, "Tobit and Folklore Studies, with Emphasis on Propp's Morphology," in *Society of Biblical Literature: 1988 Seminar Papers* (ed. D. J. Lull; SBLSP 27; Atlanta: Scholars Press, 1988), 39–53 (51) even regards the calamities that befall the characters in Tobit as "acute manifestations of the chronic condition of exile"; but see J. J. Collins, "The Judaism of the Book of Tobit," in Xeravits and Zsengellér, eds., *The Book of Tobit*, 23–40 (26), who refers explicitly to Soll, and points out that "[i]t is not so clear…that the misfortunes that befall either Tobit or Sarah are attributable to the situation of the exile in any distinctive way." Ego, "Das Buch Tobit," 147, and Bauckham, "Tobit as a Parable," 140–64, both see Tobit as a type of Israel in exile.

37. On the location, see Fitzmyer, *Tobit*, 96; Zsengellér, "Topography as Theology," 184.

38. Ego, "Das Buch Tobit," 138–41, identifies ἀλήθεια, δικαιοσύνη and ἐλεημο-σύνη as key themes in the greater narrative of Tobit. This also establishes Tobit's piety—another key theme—very early in the narrative. See Poulssen, *Tobit*, 10.

soon turns out to be an anachronous reference, as the reader is once again directed to the land of Israel in v. 4. Tobit's tribe (Nephthali) turned away from Jerusalem and the temple, but he repeatedly (πολλάκις, "many times") goes to Jerusalem in accordance with the law, even "running" to do so. This haste surely reflects Tobit's eagerness to fulfill his religious duties,[39] but the frequency of movement also suggests a considerable degree of freedom[40]—especially when narrated in such close proximity to a reference to the exile.[41] The next few verses describe Tobit's actions in Jerusalem (including some references to space), after which the narration turns again to the exile (v. 10). Tobit is taken captive and transported to Assyria, and (apparently without compulsion) goes to Nineveh.[42] A subsequent spatial reference further attests to a certain degree of freedom: Tobit moves freely from Nineveh to Media under command of King Enemessar.[43] The repetitive nature of the action is portrayed by the imperfect verb (ἐπορευόμην)[44] and implied by v. 15. Tobit's freedom of movement is drastically reduced when Enemessar dies, and the roads to Media "fell away" (ἀπέστησαν). A model-reader would know that Tobit is now prevented from going either too far west (to Israel) or east (to Media). Apart from temporarily fleeing before the wrath of King Sennacherib to an unspecified location (1:19), Tobit finds himself in Nineveh for the rest of the "first journey" narrative. The catalyst for the aforementioned flight is Tobit's habit of burying his fellow Israelites who have been murdered by Sennacherib and "thrown beyond Nineveh's wall" (ἐρριμμένον ὀπίσω τοῦ τείχους Νινευή, v. 17). A model-reader might have been aghast at the idea that Israelites were left unburied, but

39. D. Dimant, "The Book of Tobit and the Qumran Halakhah," in *The Dynamics of Language and Exegesis at Qumran* (ed. D. Devant and R. G. Kratz; FAT II/35; Tübingen: Mohr Siebeck, 2009), 121–43 (127); cf. Moore, *Tobit*, 109.

40. Cf. Tuan, *Space and Place*, 12.

41. A lot may be said about the contrast between Nineveh and Jerusalem. For fuller discussions, see Ego, "The Book of Tobit," 45; J. R. C. Cousland, "Tobit: A Comedy in Error?," *CBQ* 65 (2003): 535–53 (552); and especially Zsengellér, "Topography as Theology," 177–88.

42. The text simply reads: "when I was taken captive, I went to Nineveh" (ὅτε ἠχμαλωτίσθην, ἐπορευόμην εἰς Νινευή).

43. I. Nowell, "The Narrator in the Book of Tobit," in Lull, ed., *Society of Biblical Literature: 1988 Seminar Papers*, 27–38 (35), notes that the repeated mention of Media in the first part of the narrative helps prepare for the action later on. "Enemessar" (Ενεμεσσαρος) is the name used for Shalmaneser (V) throughout the book of Tobit.

44. This occurs with the same effect in 1:3, 6, 7. The aorist is used in v. 15 to indicate inability to perform the action, and in v. 19 for a singular action.

the locale would hardly have been a surprise. Rubbish heaps beyond the wall of a city were often used for the disposal of the bodies of malefactors who had been put to death.[45] After returning to Nineveh, Tobit sits down at Pentecost for a meal and sends his son Tobias to find a poor Israelite to share in the abundance. Tobias returns with the news that an Israelite has been murdered and "thrown in the marketplace" (ἔρριπται ἐν τῇ ἀγορᾷ). While previously the bodies were cast out in an expected location, somewhat out of the public eye,[46] this last body is disposed of in public and in an unexpected location. Although not stated explicitly, the fact that the corpse was "strangled" (ἐστραγγάληται) implies execution.[47] The exact location (αὐτόθι) and public nature (ἐκ τῆς πλατείας, "out of the square") of the disposal are emphasized. The plot has thickened. Tobit has no way of secretly removing the body,[48] but has to brave retrieving it in broad daylight[49] from a public space.[50] Having successfully buried the body, Tobit reaches the relative safety of his own courtyard, and sleeps beside its wall. During the night, the warm excrement of sparrows in the wall above (ἐν τῷ τοιχῷ ἐπάνω μου) drops into his eyes, bringing on white spots. He goes to the doctors to be healed, but his condition worsens until he is completely blind. Ironically, it is not the king's anger because of this final burial that incapacitates Tobit, but rather an indirect chain of events with the main incident occurring in Tobit's very home.[51] This would be surprising to the model-reader, who would have been expecting something more directly related to the public

45. Fitzmyer, *Tobit*, 118. Cf. Moore, *Tobit*, 119–20.
46. The bodies of those executed were presumably still visible to those passing by the rubbish heap, since this would further shame them.
47. Cf. Fitzmyer, *Tobit*, 134. Execution is also implied by mention of the marketplace; cf. P. Deselaers, *Das Buch Tobit: Studien zu seiner Entstehung, Komposition und Theologie* (OBO 43; Göttingen: Vandenhoeck & Ruprecht, 1982), 71.
48. The verb used in 1:18 is κλέπτω, which carries the meaning of stealing or taking something away in secret; cf. Matt 27:64; 28:13.
49. Tobit stores the body in a chamber "until the sun sets" (μέχρι τοῦ τὸν ἥλιον δύειν), which clearly implies that the action on the marketplace is taking place in the daytime.
50. Tobit brings back the corpse to "one of the small houses" (ἕν τῶν οἰκιδίων). This would not have seemed strange, since our model-reader would have known that the corpse would defile the house itself for a period of seven days; cf. Moore, *Tobit*, 128, and Num 19:11–22.
51. The ambivalence of inside/outside situations to portray either safety/danger or danger/safety is noted by M. Bal, *Narratology: Introduction to the Theory of Narrative* (Toronto: University of Toronto Press, 1985), 44. The reversal here helps to stress the irony.

challenge in the marketplace; indeed, it may even have seemed unfair.[52] Moreover, Tobit's experience of space and his freedom of movement have been seriously impeded. Sight is an important aspect of perceiving space,[53] and blindness would have been even more of a restrictive handicap in the ancient world. This is certainly true in the case of Tobit, who effectively ends up a prisoner in (presumably) his own home. Unfocused space helps emphasize his confinement. Tobit's wife receives a goat over and above her normal wage. She has to "go in" (εἰσῆλθεν) to Tobit, clearly implying that he is inside. The sense of hearing also attributes to a sense of space[54]—but in a subdued fashion. In Tobit's case, the use of sound accentuates his loss of the faculty of sight;[55] he becomes aware of the goat only when it bleats, and only after it enters the space in which he finds himself. This creates the impression that Tobit has now become completely sedentary. He is reliant on others: Achicar, before he relocates to Elymais (Tob 2:10), and his wife, who is now the sole bread-winner.[56] Tobit has come from "running" freely and repeatedly from his well-defined home to Jerusalem and back, to a stationary position in a city of exile. With regard to Tobit, the stage has been set for the second journey—that of his son Tobias and the angel-in-disguise, Raphael.[57]

52. Poulssen, *Tobit*, 10, notes the similarities of Tobit to the book of Job, especially with regard to the plight of the righteous ("nood van de rechtvaardige").

53. Tuan, *Space and Place*, 12, 16; Bal, *Narratology*, 94. Tuan, *Space and Place*, 52, also notes that "having the power and enough room in which to act" is an important aspect of experiencing freedom. In Tobit's case, this freedom has been drastically reduced.

54. Tuan, *Space and Place*, 15; Bal, *Narratology*, 94.

55. Cf. Moore, *Tobit*, 134.

56. Cf. Ego, "Das Buch Tobit," 117. It is not stated explicitly that his wife started working only after he was blinded, but this may be assumed. Cousland, "Tobit: A Comedy in Error?," 544, takes the act to be shameful. Cf. R. Egger-Wenzel, "'Denn harte Knechtschaft und Schande ist es, wenn eine Frau ihren Mann ernährt' (Sir 25:22)," in *Der Einzelne und seine Gemeinschaft bei Ben Sira* (ed. R. Egger-Wenzel and I. Krammer; BZAW 270; Berlin: W. de Gruyter, 1998), 23–49, for a nuanced and context-sensitive reading of this interpretation in Sir 25:22.

57. The resolution of Tobit's problems will also be marked by a "skillful control" of the characteristics of narrative space, as indicated by Nowell, *Narrator*, 31, following I. Nowell, "The Book of Tobit: Narrative Technique and Theology" (Ph.D. diss., The Catholic University of America, 1983), 96–97, 165: At Tobias' return, "[t]he perspective of the narrator (and reader) alternates between the view-point of the travellers (11:2–4, 7–8, 10) and of the parents (11:5–6, 9–10)." Thus, step-by-step, the reader is privy to the final bridging of the gap between Tobit (and his wife) and Tobias. Note how, with regard to freedom and confinement, Tobit's wife has to be his eyes and alert him to Tobias' return, and how Tobit stumbles

5. *Differences Between G¹ and G¹¹ with Regard to Narrative Space*

There are quite a number of differences between G¹ and G¹¹, most of which are of stylistic or abbreviatory nature.[58] Some of these differences have indirect consequences for reading narrative space. To name but one example, Tobit's hometown is much less defined in G¹ than in G¹¹, since in G¹ it is simply given as south of Kydios, above Asser—thus providing points on two of the four primary horizontal spatial axes, but vaguely so.[59] Similarly, the contrast between the exile and Tobit's freedom in Tob 1:2–4 is somewhat lessened in G¹, as the concept of "captivity" (αἰχμαλωτεύω / αἰχμαλωσία) is here mentioned only once (in v. 2), as opposed to G¹¹'s two uses of the concept. G¹ says nothing about Tobit "running" to Jerusalem. Consequently, the contrast between captivity and freedom set up at the beginning of G¹¹ is considerably weaker in G¹.[60] In v. 10, the two recensions again subtly differ. Where G¹¹ creates the impression that Tobit went to Nineveh out of free will, G¹ has Tobit explicitly taken there as a captive. G¹¹ therefore assigns more freedom of movement to Tobit at this stage of the narration. Tobit's apparent confinement to Nineveh in G¹ after Enemessar dies is almost identical to G¹¹, except that here the roads "become unstable" (ἠκαταστάτησαν) rather than "fall away" (ἀπέστησαν). This difference only has stylistic impact. Tobit's flight (ἀπέδρασα, "I ran away") in G¹¹ to escape Sennacherib's wrath is much less dramatic in G¹, where he "withdraws" (ἀνεχώρησα). The reference to the disposal of corpses in Tob 1:18 reads almost the same in G¹ as in G¹¹. The second reference, in Tob 2:3, also tells of a corpse thrown in the marketplace (ἔρριπται ἐν τῇ ἀγορᾷ). However, the public nature of the event is not as emphatic as in G¹¹—in G¹, no reference is made of the precise location of the corpse (as in G¹¹—αὐτόθι) or

---

before going out of the door of the courtyard (in G¹¹) or towards the door (G¹). On backgrounding and foregrounding by way of spatial shifts, see D. Herman, *Story Logic: Problems and Possibilities of Narrative* (Frontiers of Narrative; Lincoln: University of Nebraska Press, 2002), 274–77. Herman's work is taken up by Ryan, *Space*, 426.

58. Rabenau, *Studien*, 7.

59. Compare the discussion *supra* of the description in G¹¹.

60. It is worth noting that in G¹, the adverb πλεονάκις ("more often") is used rather than G¹¹'s πολλάκις ("many times"). The intensified form does not contribute much to the effect of movement, which is already present in G¹¹, but certainly underscores Tobit's piety.

its removal "out of the square" (G^{II} reads ἐκ τῆς πλατείας).[61] A final difference between G^{I} and G^{II}, which is important for the present spatial reading, occurs in Tob 2:13. In G^{I}, Tobit's confinement to an inner space is not as clear, as there the goat only "came" (ἦλθεν) to Tobit, whereas G^{II} has "came in" (εἰσῆλθεν). The strong implication that Tobit finds himself *in* a room is not present here.

6. *Conclusion*

The present study sought to investigate only a small portion of the narrative space present in the book of Tobit. The concept of "unfocused space" was introduced to describe the idea of space evoked by implicit references. To understand and make use of this concept of unfocused space, the so-called model-reader was found especially useful, as the "model-reader" may also be informed by, for example, cultural knowledge. This opens the door for biblical narratology to draw on other biblical studies in order better to understand biblical narrative.

A spatial reading which paid close attention to unfocused space in the first two chapters of the book of Tobit revealed a gradual movement from freedom to confinement. This movement is especially accentuated in G^{II}, where an initial contrast between freedom and confinement ("captivity") is set up quite strongly and emphasized throughout the narrative, but it can also be discerned in G^{I}.[62] The difference between the two versions with regard to unfocused narrative space helps to illustrate the impact of paying attention to implicit references to space in a narrative. In the book of Tobit, the use of unfocused space, when read from the perspective of a model-reader, masterfully attributes to the build-up of tension.

---

61. Another difference between G^{I} and G^{II} is G^{II}'s οἴκημα for the temporary storage space of the strangled corpse, where G^{II} uses οἴκιδιον.

62. Moore, *Tobit*, 135, is of the opinion that every aspect of ch. 2 is "more effectively presented in G^{II} than G^{I}." This might not be the case for the whole of G^{II}, but this recension certainly shows more interest in narrative space in the first two chapters of the book than G^{I}. In fact, the only place where G^{I} may be said to show more precision in defining narrative space is in the explicit naming of Rages in Tob 1:14.

FROM URBAN NIGHTMARES TO DREAM CITIES: REVEALING THE APOCALYPTIC CITYSCAPE*

Carla Sulzbach

Biblical and early Jewish writings contain a wide variety of portrayals of cities and city life. Some are plainly descriptive, mentioning walls, gates, towers, residences, streets, public buildings, palaces and temples and function mostly as the backdrop for narrative plot situations. Others paint a more poetic picture of a beloved place of domicile or a picture laced with expressions of awe when confronted with the splendor of the very residence of one's deity. They can also come as loud exclamations of joy or awe and even envy or hatred when the dazzling capital cities of neighboring, sometimes hostile, cultures are discussed.

The two cities on which this essay focuses are Jerusalem and Babylon. This is not a random choice. These two are often juxtaposed in historical, theological and poetic contexts and almost perform a literary dance around each other. The depiction of Babylon especially often borders on the caricatural.[1] Yet beneath this layer, much can be retrieved concerning the actual historical city. The same holds true for Jerusalem. While more often than not, its literary representation is as unreal as that of Babylon, this is, in contrast, not intended as ridicule.

Much of the following urban analyses derive not only from critical spatial theory, but also from the concepts utopia and dystopia.[2] For authors, the choice of using either of the latter two categories depends very much on their perspective. Prophetic texts in particular represent Babylon in the context of an ongoing contest with Jerusalem. Babylon

* An earlier version of this paper was presented at the international SBL meeting in London, July 2011. I wish to thank those who have supplied comments and critically read earlier drafts.
   1. E.g. Isa 13:19; 47; Jer 50:2, 13; 51:58, 64; Dan 4:30; Rev 17:5.
   2. See S. J. Schweitzer, "Utopia and Utopian Literary Theory: Some Preliminary Observations," in *Utopia and Dystopia in Prophetic Literature* (ed. E. Ben Zvi; Helsinki: Finnish Exegetical Society, 2006), 13–26.

becomes a monstrous image of dystopian proportions (not unlike the portrait of Sodom in Gen 19) which will go unmourned when it is finally destroyed. With regard to Jerusalem, both ideas appear. In its utmost utopian poetic heights, it is the golden city which equals, if not surpasses, the very heavens. However, even when it sinks to its lowest depths of depravation, it is painted with the colors of sadness and regret, and above all, hopes for its eventual rebuilding, as witnessed, again, by the biblical prophets and poets.

One of the key principles of critical spatial theory is that space is socially constructed and consequently defined through the ways in which it is acted upon, thought about, and moved in. Thus, the perspectives of societal groups that occupy space determine the nature of that space. Therefore, since diverse groups with differing interests and ideologies may depend on the same space, each distinct perspective yields a different interpretation of that space. This also results in the important idea that a multiplicity of spaces may occupy and define one particular place. The American cultural geographer Edward Soja explains the foundation of this dynamic as follows:

> This process of producing spatiality or "making geographies" begins with the body, with the construction and performance of the self, the human subject, as a distinctively spatial entity involved in a complex relation with our surroundings. On the one hand, our actions and thoughts shape the spaces around us, but at the same time the larger collectively or socially produced spaces and places within which we live also shape our actions and thoughts...[3]

In the thought about space by French philosopher Michel Foucault, utopias constitute "arrangements which have no real space... [U]topias are by their very essence fundamentally unreal."[4] Yet, since much of the actual dynamics that pertain to the realities of the city take place within the human mind, constitute subjective opinions about it, and represent uniquely personal experiences, both the dystopian and utopian aspects will be reflected in the experiences of the individual citizen. Consequently, one person's utopia often is the other person's dystopia. Given that both approaches to space are intimately intertwined with the matter of who is in charge of a particular space, questions of power and marginalization also become a factor.

Spatial theory is informed primarily by the understanding of contemporary spaces, most prominent among which is that of the modern

---

3. E. W. Soja, *Postmetropolis: Critical Studies of Cities and Regions* (Oxford/ Malden, Mass.: Blackwell, 2000), 6.

4. M. Foucault, "Other Spaces: The Principles of Heterotopia," *Lotus International* 48/49 (1986): 9–17 (11–12).

city. However, as spatial thinking transitioned from synchronic modern spaces to literary and ancient spaces, a diachronic dimension was added.[5] Thus, on the synchronic level many viewpoints simultaneously occupy, use, and interpret the same space. At the same time, when looking at the history of a place, a multi-dimensional picture emerges revealing the different occupational strata of that place, each also representing a different point of view with regard to the same space.

These issues will come to play an important role in the description of the role of the city in the apocalyptic worldview. John J. Collins' well-known definition of apocalypticism proposes that an apocalypse is "a genre of revelatory literature with a narrative framework, in which a revelation is mediated by an otherworldly being to a human recipient, disclosing a transcendent reality which is both temporal, insofar as it envisions eschatological salvation, and spatial as it involves another, supernatural world."[6]

Some years later Adela Yarbro Collins suggested an addition to this definition: it is "intended to interpret present, earthly circumstances in light of the supernatural world and of the future, and to influence both the understanding and the behaviour of the audience by means of divine authority."[7]

In reaction to the many responses and new questions, especially regarding the function of the worldview as opposed to its form, Lorenzo DiTommaso now rephrases it as follows:

> Apocalypticism proposes that a transcendent reality, concealed from casual observation yet operative on a grand scale, defines and informs existence beyond human understanding and the normal pale of worldly experience. It reveals a cosmos that is structured by two forces, typically identified with good and evil, which have been in conflict since the dawn of history. It discloses the necessity and imminence of the final resolution of this conflict at the time of the end, and the truth about human destiny.[8]

---

5. C. V. Camp, "Storied Space, or, Ben Sira 'Tells' a Temple," in *"Imagining" Biblical Worlds: Studies in Spatial, Social and Historical Constructs in Honor of James W. Flanagan* (ed. D. M. Gunn and P. M. McNutt; JSOTSup 359; London: Sheffield Academic, 2002), 64–80 (66–69).

6. J. J. Collins, "Towards the Morphology of a Genre," *Semeia* 14 (1979): 1–21 (9).

7. A. Y. Collins, "Introduction: Early Christian Apocalypticism," *Semeia* 36 (1986): 1–11 (7).

8. L. DiTommaso, "The Apocalyptic Other," in *The Other in Second Temple Judaism: Essays in Honor of John J. Collins* (ed. D. C. Harlow et al.; Grand Rapids: Eerdmans, 2011), 221–46 (221).

Many of the aspects that define apocalypticism are reflected in its interpretation of the city.

Before moving on to the function of city within the apocalyptic world-view, though, I first propose a number of categories of cities that can be encountered at every level of society and thought and that will be helpful in understanding the apocalyptic city. These categories are: (1) Cities of the Mind; (2) Real Cities; (3) Literary Cities; (4) Memory Cities; (5) Apocalyptic Cities. While all, except the second, represent some form of literary city they should be distinguished on the level of functionality. Furthermore, the concept of "real city" is slightly deceptive, since it too is subject to interpretation in the minds of its actual inhabitants. For the purposes of this essay, I will therefore limit its basic understanding to the "bare bones" of what constitutes a "real city," that is, its physical outline and its governance that proclaims it to be a city. In any case, however we look at it, through direct observation or through the prism of the per-ception of others, a city is by definition a "socially constructed space." Cities of the Mind imply constructs that are not yet realized, but may be. Specifically, building plans and blueprints come to mind, as well as building instructions. These mental constructs necessarily precede the real city. The next two categories, literary and memory cities, deal with the way that people think about their real cities and/or write about them after moving away, in response to either unrecognizable change, or their cities' demise, and only yearning and memories linger. Lastly, the apoca-lyptic city shares important aspects with numbers 1, 3, and 4, desperately and at all cost wanting to become a real city.

1. *Cities of the Mind*

Mental urban spaces manifest themselves on at least two levels.[9] One is formed by the plans for cities not yet created, but only conceived as an idea. In contrast to the literary city with which it partly overlaps, the city of the mind may suggest a design that could eventually be put into practice, materialize in time and space, providing a kind of preview or proto-image of a city. Under this category fall the blueprints and designs that are found in the biblical text in the form of building instructions for the tabernacle (Exod 25–27; 35–37), the temple and Solomon's royal palace (1 Kgs 5–7) that are communicated through a divine channel, often a dream, to a human recipient, be it a king or other authority figure.

---

9. The term "mental" simply refers to "of the mind." No connection is implied with the discipline of mental space theory, which belongs to the cognitive sciences. The present essay is concerned with results rather than processes.

A similar model is also known from ancient Mesopotamian literature.[10] Although the textual witnesses almost all concern the construction of temples and palaces with little or no interest in the part of the city where the actual inhabitants dwell, a clear connection exists between temple, palace and the rest of the city.

We should note the functioning of the different perspectives that are discussed here. On the level of the real world, the core ideas about designing and constructing a city and/or temple arise from the minds of the royal architects who fulfill commissions originating solely with the ruler. Once this act becomes part of the literary city (no. 3), suddenly it is no longer the king but his deity who becomes the contractor. Moreover, no longer is the architect the artist behind the design, but this too becomes part of the divine commission. Further, whereas in real life the ruler, assisted by the urban planner, determines where a sanctuary is to be built, in the literary reflection the deity instructs the ruler where it should be erected.

The Hebrew Bible offers several building accounts, most of which represent divine initiative.[11] One of the most glorious and detailed biblical examples of a building account for a permanent edifice, even if never realized, is found in the later chapters of Ezekiel (chs. 40–48). There, the priest-prophet is taken on a spectacular tour of a visionary temple city where every last stone and structure is measured by his angelic guide who holds a measuring reed.[12] This vision account was most likely the exemplar for the architectural accounts in the Qumran *Temple Scroll* and *New Jerusalem Text* (4Q232), as well as the book of Revelation.[13]

Another entry into the city of the mind is through the memory space that, in a way, starts to have a life of its own. A new construct is created based on true memories, which at the time that they are experienced and communicated cannot necessarily be turned into reality. Either this is caused by political and societal obstructions, or, because the space is so fantastic and bizarre, it could not be realized under any circumstances.

---

10. See D. M. Sharon, "A Biblical Parallel to a Sumerian Temple Hymn? Ezekiel 40–48 and Gudea," *JANESCU* 24 (1996): 99–109. Also M. J. Boda and J. Novotny, eds., *From the Foundations to the Crenellations: Essays on Temple Building in the Ancient Near East and Hebrew Bible* (Münster: Ugarit Verlag, 2010).

11. There are two exceptions: Gen 4:17, where Cain builds a city at his own volition, and Gen 11, the account of the building of the Tower of Babel.

12. Note that the city specifically contains domestic space for the common people (48:15–22).

13. See L. DiTommaso, *The Dead Sea* New Jerusalem *Text: Contents and Contexts* (TSAJ 110; Tübingen: Mohr Siebeck, 2005), 107–8.

2. Real Cities

There are a number of ways to look at and experience a city. The most obvious is to see it for the material collection of buildings and pathways that turn the space that they occupy into a defined place. The way to undergo it is to enter and become part of the lived space. This means that one may actually call the city "home," "work place," or "social space." One interacts with the various functions of the built environment and in conjunction with this built environment, its inhabitants and/or users create a true lived space. The city becomes a living entity. Needless to say, this description is hardly the final word about what a city entails; rather, it is a beginning. The urban scape only comes to life through the dealings with the people within it. When observing the daily interactions of its inhabitants, we see that the city changes character and color accordingly, depending on whose views and whose interests are fore-grounded.

One particular group of city occupants warrants a separate treatment. These are the resident deity/deities and associated religious experts. A standard city in the ancient Near East as well as in the Greco-Roman period has a major district containing temples and royal palaces. In the ancient Near East, these are usually adjacent, as is the case also with Jerusalem and Babylon. Within the context of a real city, the priestly districts and functions are to be seen from a human perspective. The local deities do not perform autonomous acts, not even those that are ascribed to them. It is all part of a major stage production in which the priests are the main performers, the deity the object of the play, and the residents the audience.[14] However, as will be shown, the deity does get a major and active role to play in all of the other urban models under discussion. Similarly, when a city is conquered and destroyed, the real events show a victorious foreign army and the subsequent destruction of the besieged city is an act of that army, its generals and the ruler of the foreign power. In the descriptions, however, it is no longer the human factor that is responsible for the conflagration, but rather the powers of the resident deity who has retreated and does not want the enemy to gloat too much.[15]

---

14. An example of such a public spectacle is found in the descriptions of the Babylonian New Year festival, during which the cult images of all the gods are led in procession from the temples to the so-called *akitu* house and back. See, e.g., M. van de Mieroop, "Reading Babylon," *AJA* 107 (2003): 257–75 (270–73).

15. Cf. the accounts in 2 Kgs 25:8–12; Jer 39:8; 52:12–15; 2 Chr 36:19; *2 Bar.* 5:3; 6:4–5; 7:1; 80:1–3; Josephus, *War* 6.249–86.

In the texts under discussion, the two outstanding examples of real cities are Jerusalem and Babylon; although within the texts "real" is soon let go in favor of any of the other four categories. In the Hebrew Bible, Babylon gets to fulfill the role of a true metropolis, the capital of a mighty empire, even a "super power," containing qualities that are the source of envy for less prominent cities. It represents everything that even today is lauded in a city; but at the same time, it is criticized for its lewdness, materialism and lack of social policies. Jerusalem is expected to form its ideal counterpart. However, each time when it fails to live up to this expectation, the same devastating epithets are hurled against it as are used to rebuke Babylon.

Since the rise and fall of Jerusalem in biblical and post-biblical texts is often contingent upon that of Babylon, the literary rivalry between these two can be used as a norm for determining how a particular text and city model reflects Jerusalem at any given point in time.[16] This rivalry plays out between real cities in real time, but it is a one-way event. Note that Jerusalem is never an object of longing or envy in the cultural or religious mind of the Babylonians. Only from the standpoint of military conquest is it remotely interesting to Assyrian and Babylonian rulers. Thus, in the real world Jerusalem is besieged, destroyed, rebuilt, and destroyed again. Its population flourishes, is led away, returns, and the cycle continues to a certain extent until it stops for a long time. Babylon, likewise, goes through its real-world vicissitudes.

Meanwhile, the image of Jerusalem created by exilic and post-exilic Israelite writers is not one of the relatively small provincial cities on the periphery of Empire, but increasingly one of the grand capitals of an important monarchy. Their images of Babylon, the "Other" city, show clear traces of hatred, but also envy and perhaps even awe. The biblical authors behind the exilic and Persian-period texts were undoubtedly intimately familiar with the urban sprawl called Babylon. This knowledge became ingrained to such an extent that its afterlife became almost as important as that of Jerusalem. Both images are recycled multiple times and become transformed, almost beyond recognition, during this process. The only other contender in this urban competition is perhaps Nineveh, the glorious capital of the Assyrian Empire. But as this city disappears from history after its destruction by the Babylonians in 612 B.C.E., its literary afterlife in post-biblical texts also fades.[17] Perhaps, it is

---

16. The authors of *2 Baruch* (11:1–2) and *4 Ezra* (3:2, 28, 31) in particular mourn the fact that while Jerusalem is in ruin, Babylon thrives.

17. The description of Nineveh in the book of Jonah can hardly be considered realistic and that in the apocryphal book of Judith even less.

exactly the fate of cities like Nineveh and Babylon that are so telling with regard to the finality of what is here coined the "real city": it gets reduced to rubble, and what remains may be at the most a telling "tell." As the real cityscape disappears, temporarily or permanently, what is left is a displaced population. One option to cope with the loss of home and center for this cohesive group that shares identity, history and fate, is to write about it. This brings us to the literary city.

3. *Literary Cities*

People do not just live in cities. They also write or dream about them. They can remake their existing cities in their own images or create hybrid cities or wholly new ones. They only materialize in written form and from there take on a life of their own.

In the religious context of the ancient Near East, the intricate relationship between deities, the city and the temple often results in the female personification of the city. For the same reason, temple and city can become equated. The literary and mental dislodging of the city from reality begins in the way it is imagined and addressed. In our case, it concerns especially its female personification. A number of progressive stages can be identified in this process. Starting with the mundane fact that the word for city in Hebrew, עִיר, is grammatically feminine, anything said about it is of course stated in the feminine.[18] This notion is easily carried over into a full-blown literary metaphor. In conjunction with the traditional relations between cities and especially male gods, this easily gives rise to understanding cities within an actual feminine context.

The literary version of Jerusalem and Babylon is mainly one of lament, theodicy, or fantasy, but also of limitless glorification. Jerusalem, as well as Babylon, displays an uncanny ability to grow in size in the minds of both authors and admirers. This is not necessarily a result of an apocalyptic take on the city, although in some cases this may be so.[19] One

18. The Akkadian word for "city," *alu*, is masculine; however, feminine use of the word is attested in West Semitic (see *CAD* 1:379–82). The female personification may, in fact, be derived from the fact that the city is seen as a manifestation of the female city goddess or in its relationship vis-à-vis strong male gods.

19. See DiTommaso, "The Apocalyptic Other," 239. It is suggested that the ever-growing gigantic size of temple and city of Jerusalem are connected to "the worldview's radical dualism and the power it accords to the transcendent reality generate hypertropic expectations. End-time punishments and rewards are invariably extreme. Events and objects are equally exaggerated: witness the monumental New Jerusalem of Revelation 20–21." This does not go far enough in explaining the

indication to this effect may be found in the perception of Babylon by Greek admirers.[20] It is in its literary afterlife created by the Greek historians that Babylon acquires its most grandiose descriptions, pertaining to the size of its city walls and gates, as well as with regard to the attractions it was thought to contain.[21] Tom Boiy notes that "[i]f we compare all city descriptions of classical authors, from Herodotus until the writers living during the Roman Empire, with the archaeological remains we see that they do not describe the historical city of Babylon, but a *prototype of an ideal city*... The exaggerated figures fit into the Greek image of the East as a rich and fabulous area."[22]

With regard to Jewish texts that imagine Jerusalem and the temple in the Hellenistic period and beyond, the focus is somewhat different, since we are dealing with authors who describe their own past, even if distant, and have a less than ambivalent relationship with Babylon. Factors such as envy and wanting to "do one over" the other, come into play. In these texts, we see a progressive upsizing of Jerusalem and the temple. For instance, the temple in the Qumran *Temple Scroll* overtakes almost the entire old city of Jerusalem.[23] The *New Jerusalem Text* is consumed by the measurements of the city. Its description (which includes an operative temple) presents a plan that is completely at the service of the temple. In fact, the size of its projected city covers what is now the southern West Bank or Judea,[24] or more interestingly, the Persian-period province of Yehud. A persistent development takes place in which the temple seems to define and subsequently absorb the city. This can be seen especially in the later texts that present the various New Jerusalems. The language referring specifically to temple or city becomes blurred.

occurrences of gigantism of bodies and spaces as it ignores the spatial components of the otherworldly, other-dimensional heavenly realm and its interfacing with earthly sacred spaces.

20.	This did not just apply to Babylon. Other cities, too, captured the imagination of the Greek historians. See C. Halton, "How Big Was Nineveh? Literal Versus Figurative Interpretation of City Size," *BBR* 18, no. 2 (2008): 193–207.

21.	See T. Boiy, *Late Achaemenid and Hellenistic Babylon* (Louvain: Peeters, 2004), 75–78. Further, Van de Mieroop, "Reading Babylon."

22.	Boiy, *Late Achaemenid and Hellenistic Babylon*, 77 (italics mine).

23.	M. Broshi, "The Gigantic Dimensions of the Visionary Temple in the Temple Scroll," *BARev* 13 (1987): 36–37.

24.	M. Broshi, "Visionary Architecture and Town Planning in the Dead Sea Scrolls," in *Time to Prepare the Way in the Wilderness: Papers on the Qumran Scrolls* (ed. D. Dimant and L. H. Schiffman; Leiden: Brill, 1995), 9–22. For a short overview of the contents, see J. C. VanderKam and P. W. Flint, *The Meaning of the Dead Sea Scrolls* (San Francisco: Harper Collins, 2002), 369–75.

Oddly, although the author of Revelation goes to great lengths to claim that the seer saw no temple in the city, its description suggests that the entire structure is in fact a sanctuary. From its very components to the character of its inhabitants, the suggestion seems clear that we are dealing with a replica, or a reflection of the heavenly temple-city.

Not surprisingly, the divine occupies a vital part of the real and the literary city as well as of the authors' mindset. Especially in the poetic and lament texts it is seen that the resident deity (in the Hebrew Bible as well as in cognate literature) provides the city with life, light, and protection; much like a divine generator. However, when the divine abandons the city, it darkens, it becomes lifeless and vulnerable to attack.

4. *Memory Cities*

Like the people that make the city come alive, it too can die. We know of abandoned cities, especially the famous ghost towns of the American West, but also the unfortunate urban scapes that never recovered after devastating catastrophes, be they natural or manmade. Alternatively, they may have changed hands in a violent way and become contested spaces. Either way, for those who lost the city, it becomes a memory city and one of longing. The memories of these cities accompany their displaced citizens. The very important literary genre of city lament also falls under this rubric. The mourning over a city lost to unspeakable violence is usually displayed on a literary level shortly after its demise, describing in graphic detail and most often in poetic stanzas the ruins of the bewailed cityscape together with its many human casualties and their suffering. In the Hebrew Bible, the genre is reflected in the book of Lamentations, the prayers of Ezra and of Daniel, as well as in various Psalms, and in later texts especially in *2 Baruch, 4 Ezra* as well as various rabbinic works.

It is interesting to compare the mourning and praying of Baruch at the site of the ruined temple where he receives aural and visual answers (*2 Bar.* 21–30 and 35–43) with an assurance of an eternal restoration (ch. 32) to that of the visit of R. Akiva and his companions to the ruined Temple Mount (*b. Mak.* 24b) where the sight of a fox exiting the ruins of the Holy of Holies evokes laughter from Akiva. He explains that since the ruin of Jerusalem was foretold by prophetic voice and now had been realized, he was assured that its restoration would also take place since that was foretold by the prophet Zechariah (8:4–5). This latter reference, incidentally, is, in its simplicity, one of the most touching and viable urban descriptions of Jerusalem as a lived space in the entire Hebrew Bible: "Thus says the LORD of hosts: 'Old men and old women shall again sit in the streets of Jerusalem, each one with his staff in his hand because of great age. The streets of the city shall be full of boys and girls playing in its streets'."

When do memory cities cease to be mere recollections of real cities? And what brings them into a different category of new or renewed mental constructs? When distinct memories fade into nostalgia, this is often accompanied by a sweetening of the memories; they become more grandiose. The negative aspects of the remembered object fade into the background. This lays the groundwork for a trajectory on to the apocalyptic city.

5. *Apocalyptic Cities*

The last category deals with those cities of wild fantasy that are derived from all the previous ones. Yet, it consists of only two cities that are engaged in mortal combat in the minds of the framers of the genre apocalypse: Jerusalem and Babylon. The literary rivalry between the two, as seen, was an ancient one and did not begin with the onset of the apocalyptic worldview. Within this genre the rivalry will become full blown and then finally run its course. Even though it seems that only two cities are involved, it is clear that there are many New Jerusalems, with each of the texts highlighting a different facet. They may be utopian, future oriented but not eschatological, or they may be relegated to the eschaton; they may be earthly or heavenly, purely a sacred compound or allow for regular domestic spaces as well. Babylon, as it plays the dark counterpart, will come to stand for all future urban opponents of Jerusalem. Following the destruction of the second temple by the Roman Empire, Babylon becomes a symbol for its hated capital: Rome. Babylon has now become the perennial "Other," standing in for almost any enemy of the Jewish people: a cipher for Not-Jerusalem.[25]At this stage, there is no longer a credible connection with the real, earthly Jerusalem of history or the reality of either a destroyed Jerusalem or the Roman

---

25. This is not only so in its most blatant form in Revelation, where the use of the toponyms Jerusalem and Babylon have little left to do with their historical, material realities on earth, but take on new properties in order to serve a new theology and deal with Rome's persecution of the young Christian churches. However, even Revelation as a text is solidly grounded in its Jewish apocalyptic and biblical precursors and the metaphors are quite thin and ambivalent. In the post-destruction Jewish apocalypses and in early rabbinic materials the "Babylon-is-Rome" metaphor comes about through the collapsing of the two when describing the destruction of the First and Second Temple.

replacement called Aelia Capitolina. Within the uncontested realm of the mind and imagination, the city can become a living entity all by itself. It can seemingly appear from thin air (as in *4 Ezra* 10:27), or come down to earth almost as a missile or a meteorite (as in Rev 3:12; 21:2) or it can be located—temporarily?—in heaven (as in *2 Bar.* 4:2–6).

Since every city, even an imaginary one, is a built environment as well as a lived space, we must ask how the apocalyptic city stands out among the models just mentioned. Probably more than in any other model outlined above, it is liable to represent either a singular utopian or dystopian space, but never a fragmented combination of the two. This may well be a result of the dualistic eschatology embedded in the apocalyptic worldview, in which ultimately "good" will triumph and "evil" be annihilated. Here, Jerusalem gets to represent utopia and Babylon dystopia.

In the passage above, Zechariah describes a future, restored Jerusalem, projected in real time and functioning as a normal city with normal inhabitants. The utopian aspect is provided by the notion that all are happy and all is at peace.[26] However, his vision is a far cry from the stilted and sterile portrayal of the New Jerusalem in Qumran's *New Jerusalem Text*. The measurements of that city display a giant complex with a gridiron street layout filled with identical housing blocks. Moreover, it seems to be specifically a temple city, which makes one wonder about the character of its inhabitants. DiTommaso notes that the preserved parts of the *New Jerusalem Text* lack any mention of urban spaces outside of the temple complex. This in contrast to the *Temple Scroll* (11Q19 xlvii.8, 14, 17), which does mention cities outside of the temple area,[27] and instructs their citizens with regard to the proper way of bringing sacrifice in the temple city. It seems that here the author of the *Temple Scroll* may give a nod to Ezek 48, which describes the eschatological rearrangement of the land with all the twelve tribes restored to their territories and a magnificent temple city at the center.[28] Many

---

26. In Zech 8:3 Jerusalem receives a new name; in Isa 60:14; 62:1, 12 and Ezek 48:35 Jerusalem is exclusively addressed by new names, but in the *New Jerusalem Text* the city is not named at all. In addition, Y. Zakovitch remarks on Zech 8:3 that the fact that only old people and children are mentioned, points to a utopian context, as these represent the vulnerable and dependent members of society; cf. "A Garden of Eden in the Squares of Jerusalem: Zachariah 8:4–6," *Greg* 87 (2006): 301–11.

27. DiTommaso, *The Dead Sea* New Jerusalem *Text*, 153.

28. A. Y. Collins remarks that in contrast to the *Temple Scroll*, Ezekiel makes no mention of other cities. However, that need not be an indication that Ezekiel would only have envisaged the land with one city. He meticulously lays out the rearranged

commentators have noticed that the twelve gates that allow entry into the city and are named for the twelve tribes of Israel may have been inspired by the twelve gates in the enclosure wall of the main temple in Babylon, E-temen-anki.[29] This is the famed ziggurat dedicated to Marduk on which, in turn, Genesis' Tower of Babel is likely modeled.

The apocalyptic city in its literary form undergoes an extreme transformation. No longer is the—female!—personification a mere metaphor, the city actually "plays" a female character. Especially in the prophetic texts and Lamentations the figure of "Daughter" or "Virgin" followed by a geographical name is used when a specific city or region is in the author's mind. Not surprisingly, the two toponyms to which this metaphor is most often applied are Jerusalem and Babylon. It can occur in either positive or negative contexts, but usually in two genres: that of Oracles against the Nations (or Cities) or the Israelite version of the Mesopotamian city lament. In the former, very graphic language is employed regularly in painting the city under reproach as a whore or as a woman being raped (and worse: deserving it!). A radical version is found in Revelation, where Jerusalem and Babylon actually play out opposing female roles—one the Bride of the Divine (ch. 21), the other an urban whore (ch. 17).

The fourth vision of the late-first century pseudepigraphon *4 Ezra* 9:26–10:59 shows the metaphor coming fully alive and then transforming into the actual object of the metaphor: the woman is the city. The seer, who hides behind the identity of the biblical Ezra, is taken to a pristine field. There he has a vision in which a weeping woman who mourns the loss of her son confronts him. At first "Ezra" does not understand that he is not dealing with a real woman and rebukes her on her excessive mourning for her personal loss. While he is in the midst of his reproach, the woman, who is really the personified Bat Tzion, Daughter Zion, transforms into a wondrous cityscape, which is nothing other than the future—or a possible—Jerusalem. Still within his vision, "Ezra" is encouraged to enter the city. Unlike in Ezekiel's vision, the *Temple Scroll*, the *New*

---

tribal territories where the tribes should live. It is hard to imagine that they would not be living in cities and towns; cf. "The Dream of a New Jerusalem at Qumran," in *The Bible and the Dead Sea Scrolls: The Second Princeton Symposium on Judaism and Christian Origins.* Vol. 3, *Qumran and Christian Origins* (ed. J. H. Charlesworth; Waco, Tex.: Baylor University Press, 2006), 235–54 (241).

29. See, e.g., D. I. Block, *The Book of Ezekiel.* Vol. 2, *Chapters 25–48* (Grand Rapids: Eerdmans, 1998), 736–38.

Jerusalem Text and Revelation, there is no mention of measurements of this city and its components. Instead, it is told that what "Ezra" saw was "an established city, and a place of huge foundations" (10:27). The angel explains to "Ezra" that he can only perceive the "vastness of the building, as far as it is possible for your eyes to see it" (10:55). In other words, it is beyond measure. Perhaps, since this entire vista is part of a vision, there is an allusion to the heavenly temple or city, which, as it belongs to the heavenly sphere, would also be beyond the three-dimensional human conception of measurement. For this notion, compare the vision of the heavenly temple in *1 En.* 14.[30] Yet, it seems to me, that in the case of *4 Ezra*, clearly an earthly city is implied, even if a spectacular and future one, which, in the eschatological future may actually take on properties of the heavenly reality. A further unique aspect of this vision is the idea that "Ezra," by entering into the city, will gain knowledge: the city becomes a source that will reveal (apocalyptic) wisdom to the adept, which is meant to calm his fears for the future well-being in the end of days of the people, the land and the city (10:55–59).[31]

Although the apocalyptic city exhibits overlaps with all of the previous models, it does not want to remain a thought; it urgently and desperately wants to manifest itself, break into our mundane material reality. That this need not be a violent transition, unlike the movements and convulsions of the New Jerusalem of Revelation, is illustrated by the vision in *4 Ezra*.

If Revelation's New Jerusalem is a yardstick, we find that the proposed demographics of this city are rather forced and artificial. The population of Ezekiel's visionary Jerusalem is well defined, even somewhat multifaceted, if rather stilted in its description. It has areas of extreme purity, the temple area, and those of more mundane activities, the city itself (square in form) and the adjacent lands (together making up a rectangle) which are designated as profane.[32] The inhabitants of Revelation's New Jerusalem are carefully selected, ascended beings of the utmost purity.[33] They are almost—if not completely—angelomorphic.

30. C. Sulzbach, "When Going on a Heavenly Journey, Travel Light and Dress Appropriately," *JSP* 19, no. 3 (2010): 167–72.

31. See ibid., 174–77, for a response to Michael Stone's "The City in 4 Ezra," *JBL* 126 (2007): 402–7.

32. Ezek 48:15–19. See also Ezek 36:33–38, which is a restoration promise in which God assures the people of renewal for themselves as well as their cities rebuilt in the land by God himself.

33. E.g. the 144,000, 12,000 of each tribe, in Rev 7:1 and 14:1, as well as the references to righteous ones and heavenly beings clad in white garments.

The careful policies of inclusion and exclusion help define the latter as either utopian or dystopian, depending on the eye of the beholder. By necessity, a utopia can only equate a totalitarian society, which tolerates no deviance. This brings up the question of whether the projected occupants of the city in the *New Jerusalem Text* might not be similar in nature to those of Revelation and represent a homogeneous purified population.

The irony is that the luscious city described in Ezek 47–48, and which, no doubt, served as a model for Revelation's New Jerusalem, seems to be a copy of the dazzling city on the water that Babylon was. The authors of the Major and Late Minor Prophets must have been familiar with Babylon's fame, and most likely they even had firsthand knowledge of the city as well as its descriptions. It is important to note, therefore, that the self-appellations of Babylon, as they are found for instance in the various Babylonian creation accounts,[34] are applied in a two-way manner in biblical texts. On the one hand, they are turned on their head and used in an accusatory manner in the Oracles Against the Nations, and, on the other hand, they are appropriated to describe Jerusalem in a similar manner. This occurs to such an extent that even geographical features that are unique to Babylon are redesigned and transposed to Jerusalem. As to the architectural markers, we note specifically the city walls with their multiple gates, eight in all, allowing entry from all sides. For the various visionary Jerusalems this number increases to twelve. Babylon's city gates and walls are named; those for Jerusalem and/or the temple courts are named for the twelve tribes of Israel. Jerusalem receives many names of adulation, as does Babylon. Babylon is a perfect rectangle. Jerusalem is presented as a perfect square, a rectangle, or as a cube. Babylon's walls and sanctuaries are measured in a number of metrological texts.[35] An angelic guide in the presence of a seer measures those of Jerusalem. Babylon is built on the River Euphrates that divides the city in two, with canals feeding off it, connecting it to the major temple complexes. Jerusalem—in real life without a major river[36]—receives a miraculous life-giving river with tree-lined banks, which begins as a small stream from underneath the temple (Ezek 47; Joel 14:8) or from the city itself (Zech 14:8) and then turns into a mighty river that cannot

---

34. See A. R. George, *Babylonian Topographical Texts* (Louvain: Peeters, 1992), 38–41, 237–67.

35. Ibid., 109–42, 414–41.

36. Although there are a few minor water sources, such as the Gihon Spring, which lends its name to one of the four rivers of Paradise (Gen 2:10–14), together with Babylon's river, the Euphrates, and its sister stream, the Tigris.

simply be crossed. It waters the surrounding arid lands (Ezekiel) or splits off into two rivers, reaching the proverbial ends of the earth to the east and the west (Zechariah). This imagery connects the life-giving properties of the river system of Mesopotamia to its cosmic aspect of the primeval waters and then transposes this wholesale onto Jerusalem. With regard to Jerusalem, the imagery has a twofold purpose. On the one hand, it attempts to replicate an Edenic character; on the other hand, it imitates the urban splendor of Mesopotamian capital cities. It can even be suggested that the entire "Garden of Eden" image derives from idealized impressions gained from these magnificent cities. This process of Jerusalem becoming a cosmic center, divinely elected, began already in the biblical traditions. Since Jerusalem already existed as an urban space and could therefore not be made to boast truly divine origins (as could Babylon[37]), the alternative of divine selection was attached to it. This is expressed in the so-called Name theology, where God pronounces that a place is chosen on which he will have his name rest (e.g. Deut 12:11; 14:23; 16:2).

In the works that are the heirs to the exilic and post-exilic biblical texts these images are recycled once more. However, whereas the earlier authors had firsthand knowledge of both cities and must even have been aware of the obvious dissimilarities between the two, the later authors only had the inherited biblical texts to base themselves on, as well as Greek sources such as Herodotus' *Histories*.[38] At the same time, this distance allowed them a great deal of freedom to explore the cities of the mind that they created as they were writing down the interpretations of the urban visions that they experienced. Daniel Merkur[39] has recently argued that meditative exegesis of texts is often the basis for visionary experiences. In other words, the mystic meditates on a text, which may then result in a vision displaying the images suggested by that text. Such a mechanism seems to be clearly at the basis of some post-second temple apocalypses; witness the many clear and obscure references to Jerusalem and Babylon in those texts.

---

37. The sixth tablet of the *Enuma Elish* (Babylonian Creation epic) tells of Babylon's creation by the gods.

38. E.g. Herodotus' account of Babylon in his *Histories*, Book I (see Van de Mieroop, "Reading Babylon," passim).

39. D. Merkur, "Cultivating Visions Through Exegetical Meditations," in *With Letters of Light: Studies in the Dead Sea Scrolls, Early Jewish Apocalypticism, Magic and Mysticism in Honor of Rachel Elior* (ed. D. V. Arbel and A. A. Orlov; Berlin/New York: W. de Gruyter, 2011), 62–91.

Drawing on DiTommaso's recent essay on the more general apocalyptic "Other," we see how Babylon becomes an *urban* apocalyptic
other.[40] At the same time, in a twisted sense of resolution and justice,
Babylon's imagery is consumed by that of Jerusalem. It is odd that for a
worldview that, in conjunction with an overturning of the entire planet,
specifically advocates a violent end to the ultimate urban "Other," be it
the real Babylon or Rome disguised as Babylon, the New Creation would
take the form of a new city. This new city may be called the New
Jerusalem, but it looks an awful lot like Babylon.

6. *Conclusion*

At the extreme high end of the apocalyptic spectrum, John's New
Jerusalem, too, like that of Ezekiel, becomes a New Babylon. In contrast,
Ezekiel's plan for the renewed city, at the low end of the same spectrum,
is grounded and down-to-earth (even if fantastic) and describes an, albeit
peculiar, case of urban planning. Its renewal of creation seems to stop
short at a rearrangement of the geopolitical order of the land of Israel and
the city.

The underlying motivation for the metaphor in Revelation differs
radically from the same image in Jewish apocalyptic writings. In the
latter, the metaphor is used in response to the destruction of the temple,
whereas in Revelation it signals a departure from the need to have a
physical sanctuary. Yet, it applies language that is typical for the standard temple-oriented apocalypses, including many references to the
heavenly sanctuary. As seen above, even the author's claim that there is
no temple in the city is ambiguous, since the text states that in fact the
city's main divine occupants form a temple (21:22). This shift in focus
is quite likely due to the fact that the Jewish apocalypses in no way
separated a continued national existence and individual Jewish identity
as part of a larger Jewish collective—even if dispersed. In fact, their
eschatological hopes still accounted for a restoration at some point in the
future based on greater security and greater proximity to God. For the
audience of Revelation, however, the national Jewish existence had been
dissolved and replaced by a different collective with different membership criteria.[41]

---

40. DiTommaso, "The Apocalyptic Other," 221–26.
41. On the function of the Babylon metaphor in Revelation, see D. Georgi, "Die
Visionen vom himmlischen Jerusalem in Apk 21 und 22," in *Kirche: Festschrift G.
Bornkamm zum 75. Geburtstag* (ed. D. Lührmann and G. Strecker; Tübingen: Mohr
Siebeck, 1980), 353–72.

What is the purpose of the apocalyptic city? On a spatial level, it is a re-creation as well as an extension of its former physical representation. From a temporal perspective, it both precedes and succeeds the material city. The apocalyptic city becomes an urban alpha and omega, a first one and a last one as it now coalesces with its divine source. Further, as a city of the mind, its growth is unencumbered by practical considerations.

New Jerusalem, in its absorbing of Babylon's features and vanquishing its image, makes sure its evil urban twin never rises again for all eternity.

PLACE, SPACE AND IDENTITY IN THE ANCIENT MEDITERRANEAN WORLD: A SPATIAL BIBLIOGRAPHY*

Adams, P., S. Hoelscher, and K. Till, eds. *Textures of Place: Exploring Humanist Geographies*. Minneapolis: University of Minnesota Press, 2001.

Agnew, J. A., K. Mitchell, and G. Toal, eds. *A Companion to Political Geography*. Blackwell Companions to Geography 3. Oxford: Blackwell, 2008.

Albertson, D., and C. King, eds. *Without Nature? A New Condition for Theology*. New York: Fordham University Press, 2010.

Allen, J. "Power." Pages 95–108 in *A Companion to Political Geography*. Edited by J. A. Agnew, K. Mitchell, and G. Toal. Blackwell Companions to Geography 3. Oxford: Blackwell, 2008.

Anderson, B. *Imagined Communities*. London: Verso, 1983.

Appadurai, A. "Disjuncture and Difference in the Global Cultural Economy." *Public Culture* 2 (1990): 1–24.

Bal, M. *De Theorie van Vertellen en Verhalen: Inleiding in de Narratologie*. 4th ed. Muiderberg: Dick Coutinho, 1986. English translation: *Narratology: Introduction to the Theory of Narrative*. Toronto: University of Toronto Press, 1985.

Beal, T., and D. M. Gunn, eds. *Reading Bibles, Writing Bodies: Identity and the Book*. New York: Routledge, 1997.

Beaumont, J., and C. Baker, eds. *Postsecular Cities: Space, Theory and Practice*. London: Continuum, 2011.

Befu, H. "Demonizing the 'Other'." Pages 17–30 in *Demonizing the Other: Antisemitism, Racism and Xenophobia*. Edited by R. Wistrich. Repr., London: Routledge, 1999.

Ben Zvi, E., ed. *Utopia and Dystopia in Prophetic Literature*. Helsinki: Finnish Exegetical Society, 2006.

Benko, G., and U. Strohmayer, eds. *Space and Social Theory: Interpreting Modernity and Postmodernity*. Oxford: Blackwell, 1997.

Bergmann, S. "Theology in Its Spatial Turn: Space, Place and Built Environments Challenging and Changing the Images of God." *Religion Compass* 1, no. 3 (2007): 353–79.

---

   *   This bibliography contains a consolidated list of theoretical spatial studies and applications of spatial theory to ancient texts referred to in this book. We hope that this bibliography will give an indication of work currently being done in the field of spatial studies from different perspectives.

Berlejung, A. "Weltbild/Kosmologie." Pages 65–72 in *Handbuch theologischer Grundbegriffe zum Alten und Neuen Testament*. Edited by A. Berlejung and C. Frevel. Darmstadt: Wissenschaftliche Buchgesellschaft, 2006.

Berquist, J. L. "Critical Spatiality and the Construction of the Ancient World." Pages 14–29 in *"Imagining" Biblical Worlds: Studies in Spatial, Social and Historical Constructs in Honor of James W. Flanagan*. Edited by D. M. Gunn and P. M. McNutt. JSOTSup 359. Sheffield: Sheffield Academic, 2002.

———. "Introduction: Critical Spatiality and the Uses of Theory." Pages 1–12 in *Constructions of Space I: Theory, Geography, and Narrative*. Edited by J. L. Berquist and C. V. Camp. LHBOTS 481. New York/London: T&T Clark International, 2007.

———. "Spaces of Jerusalem." Pages 40–52 in *Constructions of Space II: The Biblical City and Other Imagined Spaces*. Edited by J. L. Berquist and C. V. Camp. LHBOTS 490. New York/London: T&T Clark International, 2008.

Berquist, J. L., and C. V. Camp, eds. *Constructions of Space I: Theory, Geography, and Narrative*. LHBOTS 481. New York/London: T&T Clark International, 2007.

———. *Constructions of Space II: The Biblical City and Other Imagined Spaces*. LHBOTS 490. New York/London: T&T Clark International, 2008.

Bhabha, H. "The Third Space." Pages 207–21 in *Identity: Community, Culture, Difference*. Edited by J. Rutherford. London: Lawrence & Wishart, 1990.

Blacksell, M. *Political Geography*. New York: Routledge, 2006.

Böhler, D. "Das Gottesvolk als Altargemeinschaft: Die Bedeutung des Tempels für die Konstituierung kollektiver Identität nach Esra-Nehemia." Pages 207–30 in *Gottesstadt und Gottesgarten: Zu Geschichte und Theologie des Jerusalemer Tempels*. Edited by O. Keel and E. Zenger. QD 191. Freiburg: Herder, 2002.

Braaten, L. J. "Earth Community in Joel: A Call to Identify with the Rest of Creation." Pages 63–74 in *Exploring Ecological Hermeneutics*. Edited by N. C. Habel and P. Trudinger. SBLSymS 46. Atlanta: Society of Biblical Literature, 2008.

Brinkman, J. *The Perception of Space in the Old Testament: An Exploration of the Methodological Problems of Its Investigation Exemplified by a Study of Exodus 25 to 31*. Kampen: Kok Pharos, 1992.

Bromley, N. "The Spaces of Critical Geography." *Progress in Human Geography* 32, no. 2 (2008): 285–93.

Broshi, M. "The Gigantic Dimensions of the Visionary Temple in the Temple Scroll." *BARev* 13 (1987): 36–37.

———. "Visionary Architecture and Town Planning in the Dead Sea Scrolls." Pages 9–22 in *Time to Prepare the Way in the Wilderness: Papers on the Qumran Scrolls*. Edited by D. Dimant and L. H. Schiffman. Leiden: Brill, 1995.

Bruehler, B. *A Public and Political Christ: The Socio-Spatial Characteristics of Luke 18:35–19:43 and the Gospel as a Whole in Its Ancient Context*. Eugene: Pickwick, 2011.

Buttimer, A. "Home, Reach, and the Sense of Place." Pages 166–87 in *The Human Experience of Space and Place*. Edited by A. Buttimer and D. Seamon. London: Croom Helm, 1980.

Buttimer, A., and D. Seamon, eds. *The Human Experience of Space and Place*. London: Croom Helm, 1980.

Camp, C. V. "Storied Space, or, Ben Sira 'Tells' a Temple." Pages 64–80 in *"Imagining" Biblical Worlds: Studies in Spatial, Social and Historical Constructs in Honor of James W. Flanagan*. Edited by D. M. Gunn and P. M. McNutt. JSOTSup 359. Sheffield: Sheffield Academic, 2002.

Capel Anderson, J., and S. D. Moore, eds. *Mark and Method: New Approaches in Biblical Studies*. Minneapolis: Fortress, 2008.

Chakrabarty, D. *Provincializing Europe: Postcolonial Thought and Historical Difference*. Princeton: Princeton University Press, 2000.

Charlesworth, J. "Background I: Jesus of History and the Topography of the Holy Land." Pages 2213–42 in *Handbook for the Study of the Historical Jesus*. Vol. 3, *The Historical Jesus*. Edited by T. Holmén and S. E. Porter. Leiden: Brill, 2011.

Chatman, S. B. *Story and Discourse: Narrative Structure in Fiction and Film*. London: Cornell University Press, 1978.

Chidester, D. *Savage Systems: Colonialism and Comparative Religion in Southern Africa*. Charlottesville, Va.: University Press of Virginia, 1996.

Clark, M., and M. Sleeman, "Writing the Earth, Righting the Earth: Committed Presuppositions and the Geographical Imagination." Pages 49–60 in *New Words, New Worlds: Reconceptualising Social and Cultural Geography*. Edited by C. Philo. Lampeter: Social and Cultural Geography Study Group, 1991.

Collins, A. Y. "The Dream of a New Jerusalem at Qumran." Pages 231–54 in *The Bible and the Dead Sea Scrolls: The Second Princeton Symposium on Judaism and Christian Origins*. Vol. 3, *Qumran and Christian Origins*. Edited by J. H. Charlesworth. Waco, Tex.: Baylor University Press, 2006.

Cooey, P. M. *Religious Imagination and the Body: A Feminist Analysis*. New York: Oxford University Press, 1994.

Cornell, S. "That's the Story of Our Life." Pages 41–53 in *We Are a People: Narrative and Multiplicity in Constructing Ethnic Identities*. Edited by P. Spickard and W. J. Burroughs. Philadelphia: Temple University Press, 2000.

Cornell, S., and D. Hartmann. *Ethnicity and Race: Making Identities in a Changing World*. 2d ed. Thousand Oaks, Calif.: Pine Forge, 2007.

Corrigan, J. "Spatiality and Religion." Pages 157–72 in *The Spatial Turn: Interdisciplinary Perspectives*. Edited by W. Warf and S. Arias. London: Routledge, 2009.

Darby, D. "Form and Context: An Essay in the History of Narratology." *Poetics Today* 22 (2001): 829–52.

De Jong, I., ed. *Space in Ancient Greek Literature: Studies in Ancient Greek Narrative, Volume Three*. Leiden: Brill, 2012.

Dennerlein, K. *Narratologie des Raumes*. Narratologia 22. Berlin: W. de Gruyter, 2009.

DiTommaso, L. "The Apocalyptic Other." Pages 221–46 in *The Other in Second Temple Judaism: Essays in Honor of John J. Collins*. Edited by D. C. Harlow et al. Grand Rapids: Eerdmans, 2011.

Dittmer, J., and T. Sturm, eds. *Mapping the End Times: American Evangelical Geopolitics and Apocalyptic Visions*. Aldershot: Ashgate, 2010.

Dozeman, T. B. "Biblical Geography and Critical Spatial Studies." Pages 87–108 in *Constructions of Space I: Theory, Geography, and Narrative*. Edited by J. L. Berquist and C. V. Camp. LHBOTS 481. New York/London: T&T Clark International, 2007.

Elden, S. "Politics, Philosophy, Geography: Henri Lefebvre in Recent Anglo-American Scholarship." *Antipode* 10, no. 2 (2001): 809–25.

————. *Understanding Henri Lefebvre: Theory and the Possible*. London: Continuum, 2004.

Eliade, M. *The Sacred and the Profane: The Nature of Religion*. Translated by W. R. Trask. New York: Harcourt, Brace & World, 1959.

Eskenazi, T. C. *In an Age of Prose: A Literary Approach to Ezra–Nehemiah*. SBLMS 36. Atlanta: Scholars Press, 1988.

Flanagan, J. W. "Ancient Perceptions of Space/Perceptions of Ancient Space." *Semeia* 87 (1999): 15–43.

————. "Mapping the Biblical World: Perceptions of Space in Ancient Southwestern Asia." Pages 1–18 in *Mappa Mundi: Mapping Culture, Mapping the World*. Edited by J. Murray. Windsor, Ont.: Humanities Research Group, University of Windsor, 2001.

Fonrobert, C. "The New Spatial Turn in Jewish Studies." *AJSR* 33, no. 1 (2009), 155–64.

Foucault, M. "Of Other Spaces." *Diacritics* 16 (1986): 22–27.

————. "Other Spaces: The Principles of Heterotopia." *Lotus International* 48/49 (1986): 9–17.

Fox, M. V., ed. *Temple in Society*. Winona Lake: Eisenbrauns, 1988.

Geiger, M. "Creating Space Through Imagination and Action: Space and the Body in Deuteronomy 6:4–9." *Constructions of Space IV: Further Developments in Examining Social Space in Ancient Israel*. Edited by M. K. George. LHBOTS 569. New York/London: T&T Clark International, forthcoming.

————. *Gottesräume: Die literarische und theologische Konzeption von Raum im Deuteronomium*. Stuttgart: Kohlhammer, 2010.

————. "Raum." No pages. Cited 14 September 2012. *WiBiLex*. Online: http://www .wibilex.de.

Genette, G. *Narrative Discourse*. Translated by J. E. Levin. Oxford: Basil Blackwell, 1980.

George, M. K., ed. *Constructions of Space IV: Further Developments in Examining Social Space in Ancient Israel*. LHBOTS 569. New York/London: T&T Clark International, forthcoming.

————. *Israel's Tabernacle as Social Space*. SBL Ancient Israel and Its Literature 2. Atlanta: SBL, 2009.

————. "Space and History: Siting Critical Space for Biblical Studies." Pages 15–31 in *Constructions of Space I: Theory, Geography, and Narrative*. Edited by J. L. Berquist and C. V. Camp. LHBOTS 481. New York/London: T&T Clark International, 2007.

Gorringe, T. J. *A Theology of the Built Environment: Justice, Empowerment, Redemption*. Cambridge: Cambridge University Press, 2006.

————. "The Decline of Nature: Natural Theology, Theology of Nature, and the Built Environment." Pages 203–20 in *Without Nature? A New Condition for Theology*. Edited by D. Albertson and C. King. New York: Fordham University Press, 2010.

Green, W. S. "Otherness Within: Toward a Theory of Difference in Rabbinic Judaism." Pages 49–69 in *"To See Ourselves as Others See Us": Christians, Jews, "Others" in Late Antiquity*. Edited by J. Neusner and E. Frerichs. Scholars Press Studies in the Humanities. Chico, Calif.: Scholars Press, 1985.

Gregory, D. et al., eds. *The Dictionary of Human Geography*. 5th ed. Malden, Mass.: Wiley-Blackwell, 2009.

Gunn, D. M., and P. M. McNutt, eds. *"Imagining" Biblical Worlds: Studies in Spatial, Social and Historical Constructs in Honor of James W. Flanagan*. JSOTSup 359. Sheffield: Sheffield Academic, 2002.

Habel, N. C., and P. Trudinger, eds. *Exploring Ecological Hermeneutics*. SBLSymS 46. Atlanta: Society of Biblical Literature, 2008.

Haran, M. "Temple and Community in Ancient Israel." Pages 17–26 in *Temple in Society*. Edited by M. V. Fox. Winona Lake: Eisenbrauns, 1988.

Harley, J. B. "Deconstructing the Map." *Cartographica* 26 (1989): 1–20.

Harlow, D. C. et al., eds. *The Other in Second Temple Judaism: Essays in Honor of John J. Collins*. Grand Rapids: Eerdmans, 2011.

Harvey, D. *Cosmopolitanism and the Geographies of Freedom*. New York: Columbia University Press, 2009.

———. *Justice, Nature and the Geography of Difference*. Oxford: Blackwell, 1996.

———. *The Condition of Postmodernity*. Oxford: Blackwell, 1990.

Häusl, M., ed. *Tochter Zion auf dem Weg zum himmlischen Jerusalem: Rezeptionslinien der „Stadtfrau Jerusalem" von den späten alttestamentlichen Texten bis zu den Werken der Kirchenväter*. Dresdner Beiträge zur Geschlechterforschung in Geschichte, Kultur und Literatur 2. Leipzig: Leipziger Universitätsverlag, 2011.

Hawk, L. D. "The Problem with Pagans." Pages 153–63 in *Reading Bibles, Writing Bodies: Identity and the Book*. Edited by T. Beal and D. M. Gunn. New York: Routledge, 1997.

Heinen, S., and R. Sommer, eds. *Narratology in the Age of Cross-Disciplinary Research*. Narratologia 20. Berlin: W. de Gruyter, 2009.

Henkel, R. "Are Geographers Religiously Unmusical? Positionalities in Geographical Research on Religion." *Erkunde* 65, no. 4 (2011): 389–99.

Herman, D. "Narrative Ways of Worldmaking." Pages 71–87 in *Narratology in the Age of Cross-Disciplinary Research*. Edited by S. Heinen and R. Sommer. Narratologia 20. Berlin: W. de Gruyter, 2009.

———. *Story Logic: Problems and Possibilities of Narrative*. Frontiers of Narrative. Lincoln: University of Nebraska Press, 2002.

Horowitz, W. *Mesopotamian Cosmic Geography*. Mesopotamian Civilizations 8. Winona Lake: Eisenbrauns, 1998.

Houtman, C. *Der Himmel im Alten Testament*. OTS 30. Leiden: Brill, 1993.

Hubbard, P. et al., eds. *Key Thinkers on Space and Place*. London: Sage, 2004.

Hühn, P. et al., eds. *Handbook of Narratology*. Narratologia 19. Berlin: W. de Gruyter, 2009.

Irsigler, H. *Die Identität Israels: Entwicklungen und Kontroversen in alttestamentlicher Zeit*. HBS 56. Freiburg: Herder, 2009.

Iser, W. *The Fictive and the Imaginary: Charting Literary Anthropology*. Baltimore: The Johns Hopkins University Press, 1993.

Janowski, B. "Das biblische Weltbild: Eine methodologische Skizze." Pages 3–26 in *Das biblische Weltbild und seine altorientalischen Kontexte*. Edited by B. Janowski and B. Ego. FAT 32. Tübingen: Mohr Siebeck, 2001.

———. "Die heilige Wohnung des Höchsten: Kosmologische Implikationen der Jerusalemer Tempeltheologie." Pages 24–68 in *Gottesstadt und Gottesgarten: Zu Geschichte und Theologie des Jerusalemer Tempels*. Edited by O. Keel and E. Zenger. QD 191. Freiburg: Herder, 2002.

Janowski, B., and B. Ego, eds. *Das biblische Weltbild und seine altorientalischen Kontexte*. FAT 32. Tübingen: Mohr Siebeck, 2001.

Karrer, C. *Ringen um die Verfassung Judas: Eine Studie zu den theologisch-politischen Vorstellungen im Esra-Nehemia-Buch*. BZAW 308. Berlin: W. de Gruyter, 2001.

Keel, O., and E. Zenger, eds. *Gottesstadt und Gottesgarten: Zu Geschichte und Theologie des Jerusalemer Tempels*. QD 191. Freiburg: Herder, 2002.

Keel, O. *Die Geschichte Jerusalems und die Entstehung des Monotheismus*. OLB 4. 2 vols. Göttingen: Vandenhoeck & Ruprecht, 2007.

———. *Die Welt der altorientalischen Bildsymbolik und das Alte Testament am Beispiel der Psalmen*. Neukirchen–Vluyn: Neukirchener, 1972. English translation: *The Symbolism of the Biblical World: Ancient Near Eastern Iconography and the Book of Psalms*. Translated by T. J. Hallett. Winona Lake: Eisenbrauns, 1997.

Kim, U. "To the Ends of the Earth? Minority Biblical Criticism in Motion." *Reviews in Religion and Theology* 18, no. 1 (2011): 4–12.

Kong, L. "Global Shifts, Theoretical Shifts: Changing Geographies of Religion." *Progress in Human Geography* 34, no. 6 (2010): 755–76.

Kort, W. A. *Place and Space in Modern Fiction*. Gainesville: University Press of Florida, 2004.

———. "Sacred/Profane and an Adequate Theory of Human Place-Relations." Pages 32–50 in *Constructions of Space I: Theory, Geography, and Narrative*. Edited by J. L. Berquist and C. V. Camp. LHBOTS 481. New York/London: T&T Clark International, 2007.

Krüger, A. "Himmel—Erde—Unterwelt: Kosmologische Entwürfe in der poetischen Literatur Israels." Pages 65–83 in *Das biblische Weltbild und seine altorientalischen Kontexte*. Edited by B. Janowski and B. Ego. Tübingen: Mohr Siebeck, 2001.

Lamont, L., and V. Molnár. "The Study of Boundaries in the Social Sciences." *Annual Review of Sociology* 28 (2002): 167–95.

Lawrence, L. *The Word in Place: Reading the New Testament in Contemporary Contexts*. London: SPCK, 2009.

Lefebvre, H. *Introduction to Modernity: Twelve Preludes*. Translated by J. Moore. London: Verso, 1995.

———. *La production de l'espace*. Paris: Éditions Anthropos, 1974. English translation: *The Production of Space*. Translated by D. Nicholson-Smith. Oxford: Blackwell, 1991.

———. *Rhythmanalysis: Space, Time and Everyday Life*. Translated by S. Elden and G. Moore. London: Continuum, 2004.

Levinson, S., and D. Wilkins, eds. *Grammars of Space: Explorations in Cognitive Diversity*. Cambridge: Cambridge University Press, 2006.

Löw, M. *Raumsoziologie*. Frankfurt a.M.: Suhrkamp, 2001.

Madsen, K. D., and T. van Naerssen, "Migration, Identity, and Belonging." *Journal of Borderlands Studies* 18 (2003): 61–75.

Maier, C. M. "Daughter Zion as Gendered Space in the Book of Isaiah." Pages 102–18 in *Constructions of Space II: The Biblical City and Other Imagined Spaces*. Edited by J. L. Berquist and C. V. Camp. LHBOTS 490. New York/London: T&T Clark International, 2008.

————. "Daughter Zion as Queen and the Iconography of the Female City." Pages 147–
    62 in *Images and Prophecy in the Ancient Eastern Mediterranean*. Edited by M.
    Nissinen and C. Carter. FRLANT 233. Göttingen: Vandenhoeck & Ruprecht, 2009.
————. *Daughter Zion, Mother Zion: Gender, Space, and the Sacred in Ancient Israel*.
    Minneapolis: Fortress, 2008.
Malbon, E. S. "Narrative Criticism: How Does the Story Mean?" Pages 29–57 in *Mark
    and Method: New Approaches in Biblical Studies*. Edited by J. Capel Anderson and
    S. D. Moore. Minneapolis: Fortress, 2008.
Matthews, V. H. "Physical Space, Imagined Space, and 'Lived Space' in Ancient Israel."
    BTB 33 (2003): 12–20.
Mayer, R. *Diaspora: Eine kritische Begriffsklärung*. Cultural Studies 14. Bielefeld:
    Transkript, 2005.
McFague, S. "The Body of the World: Our Body, Ourselves." Pages 221–38 in *Without
    Nature? A New Condition for Theology*. Edited by D. Albertson and C. King. New
    York: Fordham University Press, 2010.
McLennan, G. "Postsecular Cities and Radical Critique: A Philosophical Sea Change?"
    Pages 15–30 in *Postsecular Cities: Space, Theory and Practice*. Edited by J.
    Beaumont and C. Baker. London: Continuum, 2011.
McNutt, P. M. "'Fathers of the Empty Spaces' and 'Strangers Forever': Social
    Marginality and the Construction of Space." Pages 30–50 in *"Imagining" Biblical
    Worlds: Studies in Spatial, Social and Historical Constructs in Honor of James W.
    Flanagan*. Edited by D. M. Gunn and P. M. McNutt. JSOTSup 359. Sheffield:
    Sheffield Academic, 2002.
McPhail, K. "Accounting as Space: Accounting and the Geo-politics of Social Space."
    Department of Accounting and Finance, University of Glasgow, Working Paper
    99/4, 1999. Online: http://dspace.gla.ac.uk/bitstream/1905/144/1/99–4%5b1%5d
    .pdf.
————. "A Review of the Emergence of Post-Secular Critical Accounting and a
    Provocation from Radical Orthodoxy." *Critical Perspectives in Accounting* 22
    (2011): 516–28.
McPhail, K. et al. "Accounting and Theology, An Introduction: Initiating a Dialogue
    Between Immediacy and Eternity." *Accounting, Auditing, and Accountability
    Journal* 17, no. 3 (2004): 320–26.
Merrifield, A. *Henri Lefebvre: A Critical Introduction*. New York: Routledge, 2006.
Millar, W. R. "A Bakhtinian Reading of Narrative Space and Its Relationship to Social
    Space." Pages 129–40 in *Constructions of Space I: Theory, Geography, and
    Narrative*. Edited by J. L. Berquist and C. V. Camp. LHBOTS 481. New York/
    London: T&T Clark International, 2007.
Mills, M. M. *Urban Imagination in Biblical Prophecy*. LHBOTS 560. New York/
    London: T&T Clark International, 2012.
————. "Urban Morality and the Great City in the Book of Jonah." *Political Theology*
    11 (2010): 453–65.
Moers, G. *Fingierte Welten in der ägyptischen Literatur des 2. Jahrtausends v. Chr.:
    Grenzüberschreitung, Reisemotiv und Fiktionalität*. Probleme der Ägyptologie 19.
    Leiden: Brill, 2001.
Moxnes, H. "Identity in Jesus' Galilee: From Ethnicity to Locative Intersectionality."
    BibInt 18, nos. 4–5 (2010): 390–416.

Murray, J., ed. *Mappa Mundi: Mapping Culture, Mapping the World*. Windsor, Ont.: Humanities Research Group, University of Windsor, 2001.

Murray, R. *The Cosmic Covenant: Biblical Themes of Justice, Peace and the Integrity of Creation*. London: Sheed & Ward, 1992.

Natter, W., and J. P. Jones III. "Identity, Space, and Other Uncertainties" Pages 141–61 in *Space and Social Theory: Interpreting Modernity and Postmodernity*. Edited by G. Benko and U. Strohmayer. Oxford: Blackwell, 1997.

Nel, P. J. "The Symbolism and Function of Epic Space in Jonah." *JNSL* 25 (1999): 215–24.

Neusner, J., and E. Frerichs, eds. *"To See Ourselves as Others See Us": Christians, Jews, "Others" in Late Antiquity*. Scholars Press Studies in the Humanities. Chico, Calif.: Scholars Press, 1985.

Newman, D. "Borders and Bordering: Towards an Interdisciplinary Dialogue." *European Journal of Social Theory* 9, no. 2 (2006): 171–86.

———. "The Lines That Continue to Separate Us: Borders in Our 'Borderless' World." *Progress in Human Geography* 30 (2006): 143–61.

Nissinen, M., and C. Carter, eds. *Images and Prophecy in the Ancient Eastern Mediterranean*. FRLANT 233. Göttingen: Vandenhoeck & Ruprecht, 2009.

Nünning, A. "Fiktionssignale." Pages 182–83 in *Metzlers Lexikon Literatur- und Kulturtheorie*. Edited by A. Nünning. 3d ed. Stuttgart: Metzler, 2004.

Oakes, P. *Reading Romans in Pompeii*. London: SPCK, 2009.

Paasi, A. "Territory." Pages 109–23 in *A Companion to Political Geography*. Edited by J. A. Agnew, K. Mitchell, and G. Toal. Blackwell Companions to Geography 3. Oxford: Blackwell, 2008.

Philippopoulos-Mihalopoulos, A. "Law's Spatial Turn: Geography, Justice and a Certain Fear of Space." *Law, Culture and the Humanities* 7, no. 2 (2010): 187–202.

Philo, C., ed. *New Words, New Worlds: Reconceptualising Social and Cultural Geography*. Lampeter: Social and Cultural Geography Study Group, 1991.

Prinsloo, G. T. M. "Šeʾôl → Yerûšālayim ← Šāmayim: Spatial Orientation in the Egyptian Hallel (Psalms 113–118)." *OTE* 19 (2006): 739–60.

———. "The Role of Space in the שירי המעלות (Psalms 120–134)." *Bib* 86 (2005): 457–77.

Rautenberg, J. "Stadtfrau Jerusalem und ihre Kinder—zur Bedeutung der Stadt Jerusalem im Gemeinschaftskonzept des Buches Tobit." Pages 51–101 in *Tochter Zion auf dem Weg zum himmlischen Jerusalem: Rezeptionslinien der „Stadtfrau Jerusalem" von den späten alttestamentlichen Texten bis zu den Werken der Kirchenväter*. Edited by M. Häusl. Dresdner Beiträge zur Geschlechterforschung in Geschichte, Kultur und Literatur 2. Leipzig: Leipziger Universitätsverlag, 2011.

Ronen, R. "Space in Fiction." *Poetics Today* 7 (1986): 421–38.

Rothenbusch, R. "Die Auseinandersetzung um die Identität Israels im Esra- und Nehemiabuch." Pages 111–44 in *Die Identität Israels: Entwicklungen und Kontroversen in alttestamentlicher Zeit*. Edited by H. Irsigler. HBS 56. Freiburg: Herder, 2009.

Rowlett, L. "Inclusion, Exclusion and Marginality in the Book of Joshua." *JSOT* 55 (1992): 15–23.

Rutherford, J., ed. *Identity: Community, Culture, Difference*. London: Lawrence & Wishart, 1990.

Ryan, M.-L. "Space." Pages 420–33 in *Handbook of Narratology*. Edited by P. Hühn et al. Narratologia, 19. Berlin: W. de Gruyter, 2009.

Schweitzer, S. J. "Utopia and Utopian Literary Theory: Some Preliminary Observations." Pages 13–26 in *Utopia and Dystopia in Prophetic Literature*. Edited by E. Ben Zvi. Helsinki: Finnish Exegetical Society, 2006.

Scott, J. C. *Weapons of the Weak: Everyday Forms of Peasant Resistance*. New Haven, Conn.: Yale University Press, 1985.

Scott, M. *Delphi and Olympia: The Spatial Politics of Panhellenism in the Archaic and Classical Periods*. Cambridge: Cambridge University Press, 2010.

Shahar, Y. *Josephus Geographicus: The Classical Context of Geography in Josephus*. Tübingen: Mohr Siebeck, 2004.

Shields, R. *Lefebvre, Love and Struggle: Spatial Dialectics*. New York: Routledge, 1999.

Slater, D. "Geopolitical Themes and Post Modern Thought." Pages 75–92 in *A Companion to Political Geography*. Edited by J. A. Agnew, K. Mitchell, and G. Toal. Blackwell Companions to Geography 3. Oxford: Blackwell, 2008.

Sleeman, M. *Geography and the Ascension Narrative in Acts*. Cambridge: Cambridge University Press, 2009.

———. "Mark, The Temple and Space: A Geographer's Response." *BibInt* 15, no. 3 (2007): 338–49.

———. "The Vision of Acts: World Right Way Up." *JSNT* 33, no. 3 (2011): 327–33.

Soja, E. W. "Beyond *Postmetropolis*." *Urban Geography* 32, no. 4 (2011): 451–69.

———. *Postmetropolis: Critical Studies of Cities and Regions*. Malden, Mass.: Blackwell, 2000.

———. *Postmodern Geographies: The Reassertion of Space in Critical Social Theory*. London: Verso, 1989.

———. "Seeing Nature Spatially." Pages 181–202 in *Without Nature? A New Condition for Theology*. Edited by D. Albertson and C. King. New York: Fordham University Press, 2010.

———. "Taking Space Personally." Pages 11–35 in *The Spatial Turn: Interdisciplinary Perspectives*. Edited by W. Warf and S. Arias. London: Routledge, 2009.

———. *Thirdspace: Journeys to Los Angeles and Other Real-and-Imagined Places*. Oxford: Blackwell, 1996.

Söllner, P. *Jerusalem, die hochgebaute Stadt: Eschatologisches und himmlisches Jerusalem im Frühjudentum und im frühen Christentum*. Texte und Arbeiten zum neutestamentlichen Zeitalter 25. Tübingen: Francke, 1998.

Spencer, S. *Race and Ethnicity: Culture, Identity and Representation*. New York: Routledge, 2006.

Sternberg, M. "Ideologie des Erzählens und erzählte Ideologie." Pages 59–80 in *Bibel als Literatur*. Edited by H. P. Schmidt. Paderborn et al.: Fink, 2008.

Sulzbach, C. "When Going on a Heavenly Journey, Travel Light and Dress Appropriately." *JSP* 19, no. 3 (2010): 167–72.

Thompson, L. L. *Introducing Biblical Literature: A More Fantastic Country*. Englewood Cliffs, N.J.: Prentice–Hall, 1978.

Till, K. "Reimagining National Identity." Pages 273–99 in *Textures of Place: Exploring Humanist Geographies*. Edited by P. Adams, S. Hoelscher, and K. Till. Minneapolis: University of Minnesota Press, 2001.

Tuan, Y.-F. *Space and Place: The Perspective of Experience*. 6th printing. Minneapolis: University of Minnesota Press, 2008.

Van Eck, E. *Galilee and Jerusalem in Mark's Story of Jesus: A Narratological and Social Scientific Reading.* HTSSup 7. Pretoria: Promedia, 1995.

Van Houtum, H., and A. Strüver. "Borders, Strangers, Doors and Bridges." *Space & Polity* 6 (2002): 141–46.

Van Houtum, H., and T. van Naerssen. "Bordering, Ordering and Othering." *Tijdschrift voor Economische en Sociale Geografie* 93 (2002): 125–36.

Venter, P. M. "Spatiality in Psalm 29." Pages 235–50 in *Psalms and Liturgy.* Edited by D. J. Human and C. J. Vos. JSOTSup 410. London: T&T Clark International, 2004.

———. "Spatiality in the Second Parable of Enoch." Pages 403–12 in *Enoch and the Messiah Son of Man: Revisiting the Book of Parables.* Edited by G. Boccaccini. Grand Rapids: Eerdmans, 2007.

Warf, W., and S. Arias, eds. *The Spatial Turn: Interdisciplinary Perspectives.* London: Routledge, 2009.

Williams, R. *Keywords: A Vocabulary of Culture and Society.* Rev. ed. London: Fontana, 1983.

Wistrich, R., ed. *Demonizing the Other: Antisemitism, Racism and Xenophobia.* Repr., London: Routledge, 1999.

Wolf, W. "Metafiktion." Pages 447–48 in *Metzlers Lexikon Literatur- und Kulturtheorie.* Edited by A. Nünning. 3d ed. Stuttgart: Metzler, 2004.

Wright, J. L. *Rebuilding Identity: The Nehemiah-Memoir and its Earliest Readers.* BZAW 348. Berlin: W. de Gruyter, 2004.

Wyatt, N. *Space and Time in the Religious Life of the Near East.* Sheffield: Sheffield Academic, 2001.

Yorgason, E., and V. Della Dora. "Geography, Religion, and Emerging Paradigms: Problematizing the Dialogue." *Social & Cultural Geography* 10 (2009): 629–37.

Zoran, G. "Towards a Theory of Space in Narrative." *Poetics Today* 5 (1984): 309–35.

Zsengellér, J. "Topography as Theology: Theological Premises of the Geographical References in the Book of Tobit." Pages 177–88 in *The Book of Tobit: Text, Tradition, Theology. Papers of the First International Conference on the Deutero-canonical Books, Pápa, Hungary, 20–21 May, 2004.* Edited by G. G. Xeravits and J. Zsengellér. Leiden: Brill, 2005.

INDEXES

INDEX OF REFERENCES

INDEX OF AUTHORS

CPSIA information can be obtained at www.ICGtesting.com
Printed in the USA
LVOW07s2355090914

403248LV00004B/58/P